D0072397

STUDIES IN GREEK PHILOSOPHY

VOLUME II: SOCRATES, PLATO,

AND THEIR TRADITION

Gregory Vlastos

STUDIES IN GREEK PHILOSOPHY

GREGORY VLASTOS

VOLUME II: SOCRATES, PLATO, AND THEIR TRADITION

Edited by Daniel W. Graham

B 171 .V538 1995 v.2
Vlastos, Gregory.
Studies in Greek philosophy

PRINCETON UNIVERSITY PRESS

PRINCETON, NEW JERSEY

WITHDRAWN
RITTER LIBRARY
BALDWIN-WALLACE COLLEGE

Copyright © 1995 by Princeton University Press
Published by Princeton University Press, 41 William Street,
Princeton, New Jersey 08540
In the United Kingdom: Princeton University Press, Chichester,
West Sussex

All Rights Reserved

Library of Congress Cataloging-in-Publication Data

Vlastos, Gregory
Studies in Greek philosophy / Gregory Vlastos.
p.   cm.
Includes bibliographical references and indexes.
Contents: v.1. The Presocratics — v.2. Socrates, Plato, and
their tradition.
ISBN 0-691-03311-0
ISBN 0-691-01938-X (pbk.)
1. Philosophy, Ancient.   I. Graham, Daniel W.   II. Title.
B171.V538   1994   180—dc20   94-3112

This book has been composed in Times Roman

Princeton University Press books are printed on acid-free paper and
meet the guidelines for permanence and durability of the Committee
on Production Guidelines for Book Longevity of the Council on
Library Resources

Printed in the United States of America
by Princeton Academic Press

10 9 8 7 6 5 4 3

CONTENTS

ACKNOWLEDGMENTS

THE PAPERS in this volume were previously published as noted below. The editor and the heirs of Gregory Vlastos gratefully acknowledge the permission to reprint granted by the agencies indicated.

1. "The Paradox of Socrates"
   Queen's Quarterly 64 (1957–58): 496–516
   Copyright, the heirs of Gregory Vlastos

2. Platis's *Socrates' Accusers*
   AJP 104 (1983): 201–6
   The Johns Hopkins University Press, Baltimore.

3. Brickhouse and Smith's *Socrates on Trial*
   TLS, No. 4, 524, Dec. 15, 1989, p. 1393
   Times Literary Supplement, London.

4. "Socrates on Political Obedience and Disobedience"
   Yale Review 63 (1974): 517–34
   The Yale Review, Copyright © Yale University, New Haven.

5. "Socrates on *Acrasia*"
   Phoenix 23 (1969): 71–88
   The Classical Association of Canada, Toronto.

6. "Was Polus Refuted?"
   AJP 88 (1967): 454–60
   The Johns Hopkins University Press, Baltimore.

7. "The Theory of Social Justice in the *Polis* in Plato's *Republic*"
   Helen North, ed., *Interpretations of Plato: A Swarthmore Symposium* (Leiden: E. J. Brill, 1977), *Mnemosyne,* Suppl. vol. 50: 1–40
   E. J. Brill, Leiden, The Netherlands.

8. "The Rights of Persons in Plato's Conception of the Foundations of Justice"
   H. Tristram Englehardt, Jr., and Daniel Callahan, eds., *Morals, Science and Society* (Hastings-on-Hudson, N.Y.: The Hastings Center, 1978), pp. 172–201
   Copyright © The Hastings Center, Briarcliff Manor, N.Y.

9. "The Virtuous and the Happy: Irwin's *Plato's Moral Theory*"
   TLS, No. 3, 961, Feb. 24, 1978, pp. 230–31
   Times Literary Supplement, London.

10. "Was Plato a Feminist?"
    TLS, No. 4,485, March 17, 1989, pp. 276, 288–89
    Times Literary Supplement, London.

11. "*Anamnesis* in the *Meno*"
    Dialogue 4 (1965): 143–67
    Dialogue, by the Canadian Philosophical Association, Ottawa.

12a. "The Third Man Argument in the *Parmenides*"
    PR 63 (1954): 319–49
    In the public domain, as certified by the managing editor, *The Philosophical Review,* Cornell University, Ithaca, N.Y.

12b. "Addendum to the Third Man Argument in the *Parmenides*"
    R. E. Allen, ed., *Studies in Plato's Metaphysics* (Routledge & Kegan Paul, 1965), pp. 261–63
    Routledge, London.

12c. "Addenda to the Third Man Argument: A Reply to Professor Sellars"
    PR 64 (1955): 438–48
    In the public domain.

12d. "Postscript to the 'Third Man'"
    PR 65 (1956): 83–94
    In the public domain.

13. "On a Proposed Redefinition of 'Self-Predication' in Plato"
    Phronesis 26 (1981): 76–79
    Van Gorcum, Assen, The Netherlands.

14. "The Role of Observation in Plato's Conception of Astronomy"
    J. P. Anton, ed., *Science and the Sciences in Plato* (Delmar, N.Y.: Caravan Books, 1980), pp. 1–31
    Caravan Books, Delmar, N.Y.

15. "Disorderly Motion in Plato's *Timaeus*"
    CQ 33 (1939): 71–83
    Oxford University Press, Oxford.

16. "Creation in the *Timaeus:* Is It a Fiction?"
    R. E. Allen, ed., *Studies in Plato's Metaphysics* (London: Routledge & Kegan Paul, 1965), pp. 401–19
    Routledge, London.

17. "A Note on the Unmoved Mover"
    PQ 13 (1963): 246–47
    Blackwell Publishers, Oxford.

18. "Minimal Parts in Epicurean Atomism"
    Isis 56 (1965): 121–47
    The University of Chicago Press, Chicago.

19. "Zeno of Sidon as a Critic of Euclid"
    Luitpold Wallach, ed., *The Classical Tradition: Literary and Historical Studies in Honor of Harry Caplan* (Ithaca, N.Y.: Cornell Univ. Press, 1966), pp. 148–59
    Copyright © 1966 by Cornell University. Used by permission of the publisher, Cornell University Press, Ithaca, N.Y.

Essay (1) was reprinted in Gregory Vlastos, ed., *The Philosophy of Socrates* (Doubleday and Co., 1971). Essays (12a), (12d), and (15) were reprinted in R. E. Allen, ed., *Studies in Plato's Metaphysics* (London: Routledge & Kegan Paul, 1965). My thanks to Doubleday and to Routledge for permission to print revisions to the essays made in the reprints.

INTRODUCTION

UNLIKE THE FIRST VOLUME of this collection, which contains all Vlastos' major discussions of Presocratic philosophy, the present volume contains only a fraction of the author's discussions of Socrates and Plato. His *Platonic Studies; Socrates, Ironist and Moral Philosopher;* and *Socratic Studies* comprise much of his major work on these two philosophers. Nevertheless, the present volume fills major gaps in his other collections and shows the wide range of his interest and ability.

"The Paradox of Socrates," originally a lecture for a general audience, provides Vlastos's first extended statement on the Socratic Problem, i.e., the problem of how to reconstruct the views of the historical Socrates from the ancient evidence. We must rely on Plato's Socratic dialogues as the source for Socrates, for only Plato can account for the data. Plato's Socrates—whose conversations Plato fictionally recreates, rather than documenting—has a complex view of how to save Athenian souls. In a discussion that anticipates much of his later interpretation of Socrates, Vlastos sketches salient points of Socrates' method and philosophy and in a famous passage criticizes him for a "failure of love." This essay is still one of the best introductions to the paradox of Socrates.

In his review of E. N. Platis's *Socrates' Accusers,* Vlastos shows his knowledge of and interest in the prosopography of Socrates' accusers. Reviewing Brickhouse and Smith's *Socrates on Trial,* he dissents from the authors on the important role they assign to the *daimonion* in Socrates' thought. In "Socrates on Political Obedience and Disobedience," Vlastos discusses the argument of the *Crito* and attempts to locate Socrates' position between the extremes of passive obedience and political disobedience.

Vlastos reexamines the argument against weakness of will from the *Protagoras* in "Socrates on Acrasia,*" rejecting the account he had given in his introduction to the *Protagoras.* "Was Polus Refuted" discusses the debate between Socrates and Polus in the *Gorgias,* concluding that Socrates' argument is fallacious.

Vlastos makes an important defense of Plato against Karl Popper's criticism, in "The Theory of Social Justice in the *Polis* in Plato's *Republic."* Arguing that there is a legitimate normative and meta-normative theory of justice in the *Republic,* he maintains that justice is based on impartiality, not on inequality as Popper would have it. Although Vlastos defends Plato from charges of subverting the notion of justice, he does not shrink from the consequences, often downplayed by others, that the worker will be as a slave to the intellectual. Plato's theory does indeed fail, but not for want of formal equality: it fails because it rejects substantive equality. In a companion essay, "The Rights of Persons in Plato's Conception of the Foundations of Justice," Vlastos adds to his analysis of justice in the *Republic* the observation that beyond formal equality a further condition is needed to provide a basis for rights: that condition is supplied by the Principle of Functional Reciprocity. But even thus supported, Plato's theory of justice still fails to satisfy minimal conditions established by single-standard moral systems.

In his review of Terence Irwin's *Plato's Moral Theory,* Vlastos accepts Irwin's account of Plato's eudaimonism but criticizes his instrumentalist interpretation of Socratic virtue: virtue is not a mere means to an end. "Was Plato a Feminist?" takes up the problem of Plato's attitude toward women; Vlastos gives a complex answer, maintaining that in some respects Plato favored equal rights for women, in other respects he did not. Behind the apparently different attitudes, Vlastos finds a belief that women could in principle share intellectual excellence with men, although in contemporary Greek societies social and educational disadvantages made equality impossible.

The theory of recollection appears for the first time in Plato's *Meno.* Examining the theory and its data, Vlastos defines recollection as "any enlargment of our knowledge which results from the perception of logical relationships." Plato for the first time marks off non-empirical from empirical knowledge. But he asserts much more than the distinction, for he now comes to hold that sense experience is not a source of genuine knowledge. The new epistemology is introduced along with a doctrine of reincarnation which seems to have inspired the theory of recollection.

Vlastos's 1954 paper, "The Third Man Argument in the *Parmenides,*" is an epoch-making essay (see Introduction to Volume I) that spawned a whole industry of exegesis on the Third Man Argument. The machinery of the Self-Predication[1] assumption and the Non-Identity assumption have become part of the *koinē* of ancient philosophy scholarship. Vlastos's conclusion that Plato's discussion of the argument was a "record of honest perplexity" satisfied no one; scholars quickly attempted to find a Platonic trump card to solve the puzzle or evidence that he modified his later views to avoid the problem. Vlastos responded to early criticisms of his views by Wilfred Sellars and Peter Geach, leading philosophers from opposite sides of the Atlantic, whose attention shows how influential was Vlastos's essay right from the first. A follow-up article, "Plato's 'Third Man' Argument (*Parm*. 132A1–B2): Text and Logic," *PQ* 19 (1969), was reprinted in *Platonic Studies* (see Appendix I of the reprint for a bibliography of recent papers to 1972). But the latter article was more of a restatement and a criticism of alternative views than a new argument, and it is the 1954 paper that constitutes the starting-point of all recent work on the Third Man Argument. Vlastos criticizes an important recent interpretation of

---

[1] Vlastos gives credit for the insight to A. E. Taylor; but the term is Vlastos's.

Self-Predication by Alexander Nehamas in "On a Proposed Redefinition of 'Self-Predication' in Plato."

Plato's views on the study of astronomy expressed in *Republic* VII are the topic of "The Role of Observation in Plato's Conception of Astronomy." Plato's criticism of empirical astronomy have been interpreted, at one extreme, as a rejection of all empirical evidence, and at the other as recommending a temporary moratorium on empirical research until mathematical hypotheses can be developed. Vlastos argues for a middle way: the troublesome phrase "let go the things in the heavens" means to reject sensible phenomena as providing knowledge, but nevertheless use them as data for theoretical astronomy.

It was long the prevailing opinion that Plato's description of the creation of the world was an allegorical representation of an uncreated cosmos. In "Disorderly Motion in Plato's *Timaeus,*" Vlastos's first essay in ancient philosophy, he vigorously criticized this view held by his mentor F. M. Cornford. Vlastos further supported his position some twenty-five years later with the essay, "Creation in the *Timaeus:* Is It a Fiction?" which takes into account arguments of Harold Cherniss.

Although the great bulk of Vlastos's work consisted of research into early Greek philosophy down to Plato, three essays show his knowledge of later Greek philosophy. His short "Note on the Unmoved Mover" criticizes W. D. Ross's claim that Aristotle's Unmoved Mover is an efficient cause. In a detailed and closely argued essay, "Minimal Parts in Epicurean Atomism," Vlastos rejects the interpretations of minimal parts as physically indivisible elements on the one hand, or mathematically indivisible magnitudes on the other; rather, Epicurus holds that the sizes of atoms occur in integral multiples of a minimal size. A sequel, "Zeno of Sidon as a Critic of Euclid," continues his attack on the influential view of the Epicureans as advocates of mathematical atomism. He shows that the Epicurean mathematician Zeno of Sidon cannot be shown to be more than a methodological critic of Euclid.

TEXTUAL CONVENTIONS

E ACH ARTICLE has been reprinted with pagination from the original publication included. In accordance with the scheme of *Platonic Studies*, the original page numbers are enclosed in [brackets], indicating the *end* of a page in the original article. Thus [75] marks the end of page 75 of the original article and the beginning of page 76.

Two asterisks within angle brackets ⟨**⟩ indicate that a cited article has been reprinted in these volumes. Where the asterisks are followed by folios ⟨** x–y⟩, the latter represent a specific reference within the reprinted article.

⟦Double brackets⟧ in the text or notes indicate that material was deleted in the reprint; material in {braces} was added in the reprint; and material in ⟨angle brackets⟩ was added by the editors of these volumes.

ABBREVIATIONS

Note: Alternate forms are given where different abbreviations are used in different articles.

AUTHORS

Aesch.	Aeschylus
Aët.	Aëtius
Alex.	Alexander
Anax.	Anaximander
Andoc.	Andocides
Arist.	Aristotle
Aristoph.	Aristophanes
Athen.	Athenaeus
Cic.	Cicero
Democ.	Democritus
Demosth.	Demosthenes
Diod. Sic./Diod.	Diodorus Siculus
Diog. Laert./DL	Diogenes Laertius
Emp./Emped.	Empedocles
Epic.	Epicurus
Eur.	Euripides
Hdt.	Herodotus
Heracl.	Heraclitus
Hipp.	Hippocrates
Hippol.	Hippolytus
Isoc./Isocr.	Isocrates
Lucret./Lucr.	Lucretius
Lys.	Lysias
Mel.	Melissus
Parm.	Parmenides
Paus.	Pausanius
Pherec.	Pherecydes
Plut.	Plutarch
Polyb.	Polybius
Procl.	Proclus
Sext.	Sextus Empiricus
Simplic.	Simplicius
Soph.	Sophocles
Theophr.	Theophrastus

| Thuc. | Thucydides |
| Xen./Xenoph. | Xenophon |

TITLES

AESCHYLUS

Ag.	Agamemnon
Choe.	Choephoroi
Eum.	Eumenides
PV/P.V.	Prometheus Vinctus
Theb.	Seven against Thebes

ALEXANDER

| Metaph./Met. | In Aristotelis Metaphysica commentaria |

ANDOCIDES

| De myst. | De mysteriis |

ARISTOPHANES

Ach.	Acharnenses
Ran.	Ranae
Thesm.	Thesmophoriazusae

ARISTOTLE

An. post./Post. an.	Posterior analytics
Ath. pol.	Athēnaiōn politeia
De an.	De anima
De gen. anim.	De generatione animalium
De gen. et cor.	De generatione et corruptione
De iuv.	De iuventute
⟨Ps.-⟩ De lineis insec.	De lineis insecabilibus
De mem.	De memoria
De part. anim.	De partibus animalium
De resp.	De respiratione
De soph. el. (Soph. el.)	Sophistici elenchi
E.N.	Nicomachean Ethics
Hist. anim.	Historia animalium
⟨Ps.-⟩ Mech. probl.	Problemata mechanica
Met.	Metaphysics
Meteor.	Meteorologica
Phys.	Physics
Pol.	Politics
Pr. an.	Prior Analytics

⟨Ps.-⟩ *Probl.*   *Problemata*
Rhet.   *Rhetoric*
Top.   *Topics*

CICERO
Acad.   *Academicae Quaestiones*
Acad. prior.   *Academica priora*
De fin.   *De finibus*
ND/De nat. deorum   *De natura deorum*

DEMOSTHENES
Ag. Timarch.   *Against Timarchos*
Ag. Timocr.   *Against Timocrates*
C. Lacrit.   *Against Lacrites*
2 Phil.   *Second Philippic*

DIOGENES LAERTIUS
Vitae Philos.   *De clarorum philosophorum vitis . . .*
     libri decem (etc.)

EPICURUS
Ep. ad Hdt.   *Letter to Herodotus*
Ep. ad Pyth.   *Letter to Pythocles*
K.d.   *Kuriai doxai*

EPIPHANIUS
Adv. haer.   *Adversus haereses*

EURIPIDES
Alc.   *Alcestis*
Bacch.   *Bacchae*
Cycl.   *Cyclops*
El.   *Electra*
Hel.   *Helen*
Hippol.   *Hippolytus*
Or.   *Orestes*
Phoen.   *Phoenissae*
Suppl.   *Supplices*

GALEN
De natur. facult.   *Peri phusikōn dunameōn/De naturalibus*
     facultatibus
Histor. philos.   *Historia philosophica*

HERACLITUS (HOMERICUS)
Quaest. Homer.   *Quaestiones Homericae*

HESIOD
Op.   *Works and Days*
Th./Theog.   *Theogony*

HIPPOCRATES
Art.   *Peri arthrōn embolēs*
Epid.   *Epidēmiai*
De flat.   *Peri phusōn (De flatibus, On Breaths)*
De nat. hom.   *Peri phusios anthrōpou (De natura hominis,
                             On the Nature of Man)*
De nutr.   *De nutrimento*
On Anc. Med.   *Peri archaiēs iētrikēs (On Ancient
                             Medicine)*
On Sacr. Dis.   *Peri hierēs nousou (On the Sacred
                             Disease)*
Peri top. k. anth.   *Peri topōn tōn kata anthrōpon*
Progn.   *Prognostikon*

HIPPOLYTUS
Ref.   *Refutatio omnium haeresium*

HOMER
Il.   *Iliad*
Od.   *Odyssey*

HYPEREIDES
Eux.   *Pro Euxenippo*

IAMBLICHUS
Vita. Pyth./V.P.   *De vita Pythagorica*

ISOCRATES
Adv. soph.   *Adversus sophistas*
Ant.   *Antidosis*
Areop.   *Areopagiticus*
Panath.   *Panathenaicus*

LYCURGUS
Leocr.   *Against Leocrates*
Lyc.   *Lycurgus*

PHILO
De incorr. mundi   *De incorruptibilitate mundi*

PHILOPONUS
Phys.   *In Aristotelis Physica commentaria*

PINDAR

Nem.	*Nemean* odes
Ol.	*Olympian* odes
Pyth.	*Pythian* odes

PLATO

1 Alc.	*Alcibiades I*
Ap.	*Apology*
Charm.	*Charmides*
Crat.	*Cratylus*
Ep.	*Epistulae*
Euth.	*Euthyphro*
Euthd.	*Euthydemus*
Gorg.	*Gorgias*
La.	*Laches*
Menex.	*Menexenus*
Parm.	*Parmenides*
Phaedr./Phdr.	*Phaedrus*
Phil.	*Philebus*
Polit.	*Politicus*
Prot.	*Protagoras*
Rep.	*Republic*
Soph.	*Sophista*
Symp.	*Symposium*
Theaet.	*Theaetetus*
Tim.	*Timaeus*

PLUTARCH

Adv. Colotem (Mor.)	*Adversus Colotem*
De commun. notit. (Mor.)	*De communibus notitiis versus Stoicos*
De E (Mor.)	*De E apud Delphos*
De sera num. (Mor.)	*De sera numinis vindicta*
Lyc.	*Lycurgus*
Mor.	*Moralia*
Sol.	*Solon*
Strom. (Mor.)	*Strōmateis*
Vita Alc.	*Alcibiades*
Vita Isoc.	*Isocrates*
Vita Lys	*Lysander*
Vita Per.	*Pericles*

PORPHYRY

De antr. nymph.	*De antro nympharum*

PROCLUS

Comm. in Crat.	*In Platonis Cratylum commentarii*
Comm. in Eucl.	*In primum Euclidis librum commentarii*
Comm. in Parm.	*In Platonis Parmenidem commentarii*
Comm. in Rep.	*In Platonis Rempublicam commentarii*

ST. AUGUSTINE

Civ. Dei	*De civitate dei*

SENECA

Ep.	*Epistulae*
QN	*Quaestiones naturales*

SEXTUS EMPIRICUS

Adv. math.	*Adversus mathematicos*
Pyrrh. hyp.	*Pyrrhōneoi hypotypōseis*

SIMPLICIUS

Phys.	*In Aristotelis Physica commentaria*

SOPHOCLES

Ant.	*Antigone*
OC	*Oedipous Coloneus*
OT	*Oedipous Tyrannus*

THEOPHRASTUS

De sens.	*De sensu*
Phys. op./Phys. opin.	*Phusikōn doxai/Physicorum opiniones*

XENOPHON

⟨Ps.-⟩ *Ath. const.*	*Athenian Constitution (Athēnaiōn politeia)*
Const. Lac.	*Spartan Constitution*
Mem.	*Memorabilia*
Oec.	*Oeconomicus*

BIBLIOGRAPHIC

Note: Refer to the Bibliography at the end of Volume II for complete documentation of the Vlastos sources.

Allen	R. E. Allen, ed., *Studies in Plato's Metaphysics*. London: Routledge & Kegan Paul, 1965.
Furley and Allen	David J. Furley and R. E. Allen, eds., *Studies in Presocratic Philosophy*. Vol. 1 (1970), Vol. 2 (1975). London: Routledge & Kegan Paul.

Plato I	Vlastos 1971b (*Critical Essays I*)
Plato II	Vlastos 1971c (*Critical Essays II*)
PS	*Platonic Studies* = Vlastos 1973
SIMP	*Socrates, Ironist and Moral Philosopher* = Vlastos 1991
SS	*Socratic Studies* = Vlastos 1994

SCHOLARLY JOURNALS AND REFERENCE WORKS

AGP	*Archiv für Geschichte der Philosophie*
AJA	*American Journal of Archaeology*
AJP	*American Journal of Philology*
AnAW, AnzAW	*Anzeiger der Akademie der Wissenschaften in Wien*
APQ	*American Philosophical Quarterly*
CAH	*Cambridge Ancient History*
CP	*Classical Philology*
CQ	*Classical Quarterly*
CRAI	*Comptes rendus des séances de l'Académie des inscriptions et belles-lettres*
DK	Hermann Diels, *Fragmente der Vorsokratiker,* ed. Walther Kranz, 3 vols. 6th ed., 1951 (or earlier editions as noted). Dublin and Zurich: Weidmann.
Dox. Graeci	Diels, *Doxographi Graeci,* Berlin, 1879
Enc. Brit.	*Encyclopaedia Britannica*
GöttNachr.	*Nachrichten von der Königlichen Gesellschaft der Wissenschaften zu Göttingen/ der Akademie der Wissenschaften zu Göttingen*
IG	*Inscriptiones Graecae,* ed. Prussian Academy of Sciences, Berlin, 1873–.
JHI	*Journal of the History of Ideas*
JHP	*Journal of the History of Philosophy*
JHS	*Journal of Hellenic Studies*
LSJ	H. G. Liddell and R. Scott, *A Greek-English Lexicon,* rev. by H. S. Jones and R. McKenzie. New (9th) ed., 1940. Oxford: Clarendon Press.
OED	*Oxford English Dictionary,* ed. J. A. Simpson and E. S. Weiner. 2nd ed. 1989. New York: Oxford.
PAA	*Proceedings of the American Academy of Arts and Sciences*

PAS	*Proceedings of the Aristotelian Society*
Phil. Woch.	*Philologische Wochenschrift*
Philol.	*Philologus: Zeitschrift für klassische Philologie*
PQ	*Philosophical Quarterly*
PR	*Philosophical Review*
Proc. Arist. Society	*Proceedings of the Aristotelian Society*
RE	*Paulys Realencyclopädie der classischen Altertumswissenschaft*, rev. by G. Wissowa et al. Stuttgart, 1893–1978.
REG	*Revue des études grecques*
Rev. phil.	*Revue de philologie, de littérature et d'histoire anciennes*
Rhein. Mus.	*Rheinisches Museum für Philologie*
RM	*Review of Metaphysics*
SPAW	*Sitzungsberichte der preussischen Akademie der Wissenschaften*
TAPA	*Transactions and Proceedings of the American Philological Association*
TLS	*The Times Literary Supplement*

Miscellaneous

ad fin.	at the end
ad init.	at the beginning
ad loc.	at the place
apud	cited by/quoted in
ca.	circa (approximately)
et sq.	and the following
pace	with due respect to
Pap.	Papyrus
per contra	on the contrary
per impossible	though impossible
q.v.	which see
s.c.	namely
sub fin.	before the end
s.v.	under the word

PART ONE

SOCRATES

1

THE PARADOX OF SOCRATES

[**M**OST OF THE RESULTS of scholarly work are not communica-
ble to the public or even to scholars in other fields. They are
reportable, certainly; but that is not the same thing, else why
should these reports prove so boring? In this I see nothing to be ashamed of;
university presidents and foundation potentates have no cause to scold us over
it. In spite of glib talk of the community of scholarship on ceremonial occasions, the world of scholarship is of its very nature separatist, if not downright
sectarian. Here the people who do the work, instead of the hiring or the paying or the talking, go out singly or in small groups, scattering widely, to do
different jobs with different tools in different locales. To appreciate the value
of what these search-parties turn up, one should know their language, which is
not a carelessly concocted jargon, but an idiom ingeniously devised to say
things which can be said in no other way; one should also be acquainted with
their methods of collecting facts, assessing evidence, and testing generaliza-
tions. How can the outsider, who has not learned the vocabulary or the syntax
or the discipline of a given field of investigation, be expected to get the point
of findings in that field? And is it [496] surprising if, missing their point, he
should think them pointless—bizarre, or picayune, or merely dull?

Are we then to give up the idea of a community of scholars? As a humanities association, you have the faith that such a community can exist, and I did
not accept the honor of your invitation to come to tell you that yours is a *credo
quia impossibile*. But perhaps you might allow me to tell you that your faith
(and mine) is a *credo quia difficile*. Scholarship of itself does not breed
community—only communities. To bring together companies of specialists
into a grouping that is not a conglomerate but a community, something more
than scholarship is needed. What is that? I should be willing to call it *humanism*, if you would go along with my homespun definition of a humanist as "a
scholar who makes a strenuous effort to be human." There are various ways of
being *in*human, and all of them are offenses against community. Some of
these are graver than others, as are cruelty and pride as over against, say, mere
grumpy eccentricity. The scholar's form of inhumanity is probably the least

An address to a meeting of the Humanities Association of Canada at Ottawa on June 13, 1957.
From *Queen's Quarterly* 64 (1957–58):496–516. Reprinted in Gregory Vlastos, ed., *The Philosophy of Socrates* (Garden City, N.Y.: Doubleday, 1971), pp. 1–21. Minor changes have been
made in punctuation and spelling. Copyright, the heirs of Gregory Vlastos. Material from reprint
used by permission of Doubleday and Co.

objectionable of all, generally harmless, even benignant, for the by-products of his work are sure to bless his kind in one way or another in the end. But it is inhumanity nonetheless, a withdrawal from the common language and the common values of humanity.

Historically, the humanist has been the learned man aware of the perils of this alienation of learning from humanity. In the confident period of the Renaissance, the first generations of humanists looked to scholarship itself to heal the breach. They thought that to be a humanist it is enough to be a scholar. To revive their hope today would be to indulge in an illusion. Today it is a well-known fact that one can be a good scholar, an excellent one, without a peer in one's field, yet not be a humanist at all. To be a humanist nowadays calls for a special effort: first, to find the relevance of our individual work to our common humanity; secondly, to state our findings in common speech—by which, of course, I don't mean folksy talk, but (for those of us who speak English) just the Queen's English, unassisted by a suitcase full of technical glossaries. For most of us this is costly and hazardous work: costly, for it takes time which the scholar in us grudges to anything but scholarly work; hazardous, because it compels [497] us to say things we have not weighed as carefully as the scholarly conscience would require, so that, while saying them, we are never wholly free from the suspicion that we may not mean all we say, if only because we don't know precisely what we mean. Here are two good reasons for refraining from the performance on which I am about to launch. Yet in spite of cost and hazard, this work is worth attempting from time to time, for unless some of us are willing to do it I fail to see how the community of scholarship can be anything but a phrase, and humanism anything but a memory.

It was some such thought as this—not just vanity, nor just the pleasure of a reunion with my Canadian friends, though I plead guilty to both—that made me accept your invitation. And the same thought fixed the choice of the topic. For Socrates is one of those rare figures that have the power to interest scholars in several fields—the philologist, the philosopher, the historian, the critic of culture, the student of religion; and not only scholars, but all sorts and conditions of men. As a person and as a thinker, he has, I believe, the truly human importance that entitles him to your attention for the duration of this address.]]

The Socrates [[I have in mind]] {of this book} is the Platonic Socrates, or, to be more precise, the Socrates of Plato's early dialogues. That this figure is a faithful imaginative recreation of the historical Socrates is the conclusion of some very reputable scholars, though not of all. It is [[also]] the conclusion [[I have reached myself after working on the problems at first hand]] {I would be prepared to defend myself}. [[To report on this work in any detail would be out of keeping with the purpose of this address. But you are certainly entitled to some assurance that my Socrates is not Platonic fiction but historic fact. This I can give you in a few plain words:]] {To try to do this in detail would be out of place in this Introduction. All I can do here is to indicate the main consideration which has led me to this conclusion.}

There is one, and only one, serious alternative to Plato's Socrates, and that is Xenophon's. The two are irreconcilable at certain points, and these are crucial:

Xenophon's is a Socrates without irony and without paradox. Take away irony and paradox from Plato's Socrates and there is nothing left. [498]

Xenophon's Socrates is so persuasive that, "whenever he argued," Xenophon declares, "he gained a greater measure of assent from his hearers than any man I have ever known" (*Memorabilia* 4.6.16). Plato's Socrates is not persuasive at all. He wins every argument, but never manages to win over an opponent. He has to fight every inch of the way for any assent he gets, and gets it, so to speak, at the point of a dagger. Xenophon's Socrates discourses on theology and theodicy, argues for the existence of a divine mind that has created man and ordered the world for his benefit. Plato's refuses to argue over anything other than man and human affairs.

Plato's Socrates maintains that it is never right to repay evil with evil. He says this in studied defiance of the contrary view, axiomatic in Greek morality from Hesiod down, and fixes here the boundary-line between those who can agree with him on fundamentals and those who can't. Xenophon's Socrates has never heard of the boundary-line. He stands on the wrong side, the popular side, parrots the common opinion that the good man will "excel in rendering benefits to his friends and injuries to his enemies" (*Mem.* 2.6.35).

What does this prove? If Plato and Xenophon cannot both be right, why must Plato be right? That his Socrates is incomparably the more interesting of the two figures, in fact the only Socrates worth talking about, proves nothing. We cannot build history on wish fulfillment. Fortunately there is another consideration that proves a great deal. It is that Plato accounts, while Xenophon does not, for facts affirmed by both and also attested by others. For example, that Critias and Alcibiades had been companions of Socrates; or again, that Socrates was indicted and condemned on the charge of not believing in the gods of the state and of corrupting its youth. Xenophon's portrait will not square with either of these. Not with the first, for his Socrates could not have attracted men like Critias and Alcibiades, haughty aristocrats both of them, and as brilliant intellectually as they were morally unprincipled. Xenophon's Socrates, [499] pious reciter of moral commonplaces, would have elicited nothing but a sneer from Critias and a yawn from Alcibiades, while Plato's Socrates is just the man who could have got under their skin. As for the second, Plato, and he alone, gives us a Socrates who could have plausibly been indicted for subversion of faith and morals. Xenophon's account of Socrates, apologetic from beginning to end, refutes itself: had the facts been as he tells them, the indictment would not have been made in the first place.

⟦So I trust you may be reconciled to the thought of parting company with Xenophon for the rest of this address and may even concur with me that the best thing we can do with this very proper Athenian is to make an honorary Victorian out of him and commend him to the attentions of some bright young man who would like to continue the unapostolic succession to Lytton Strachey. But that still leaves us with the question:⟧ How far can we then trust Plato? From the fact that he was right on some things, it does not follow, certainly, that he was right in all his information on Socrates, or even on all its essential points. But we do have a check.[1] Plato's *Apology* has for its *mise en scène* an all-too-public occasion. The jury alone numbered 501 Athenians. And since the town was so gregarious and Socrates {a notorious} ⟦its⟧ public character ⟦number one⟧, there would have been many more in the audience. So when Plato was writing the *Apology,* he knew that hundreds of those who might read the speech he puts into the mouth of Socrates had heard the historic original. And since his purpose in writing it was to clear his master's name and to indict his judges, it would have been most inept to make Socrates talk out of character. How could Plato be saying to his fellow citizens, "This is the man you murdered. Look at him. Listen to him,"[2] and point to a figment of his own imagining? This is my chief reason for accepting the *Apology* as a reliable recreation of the thought and character of the man Plato knew so well. ⟦You will notice that⟧ here, as before, I speak of *recreation,* not reportage. The *Apology* was probably written several years after the event, half a dozen years or more. This, and Plato's genius, assures us that it was not journalism, but art. Though the emotion with which [500] Plato had listened when life and death hung on his master's words must have branded those words into his mind, still that emotion recollected in tranquility, those remembrances recast in the imagination, would make a new speech out of the old materials, so that those who read it would recognize instantly the man they had known without having to scan their own memory and ask, "Did he open with that remark? Did he really use that example?" or any such question. This is all I claim for the veracity of the *Apology.* And if this is conceded, the problem of our sources is solved in principle. For we may then use the *Apology* as a touchstone of the like veracity of the thought and character of Socrates depicted in Plato's other early dialogues. And when we do that, what do we find?

We find a man who is all paradox. Other philosophers talked *about* paradox. Socrates did not. The paradox in Socrates is Socrates. But unlike later

---

[1] {In a fuller discussion I would have added other checks, notably Aristotle's testimony.}

[2] Here and throughout {this introduction}, I use single quotation marks to indicate an *imaginary* quotation, reserving regular quotation marks for citations from the texts.

paradoxes—Scandinavian, German, and latterly even Gallic—this Hellenic paradox is not meant to defeat, but to incite, the human reason. At least a part of it can be made quite lucid, and this is what I shall attempt in the main part of this [address] {essay}. For this purpose I must put before you the roles whose apparently incongruous junction produces paradox:

In the *Apology* (29d–e) Socrates gives this account of his lifework:

> So long as I breathe and have the strength to do it, I will not cease philosophizing, exhorting you, indicting whichever of you I happen to meet, telling him in my customary way:
>
> > Esteemed friend, citizen of Athens, the greatest city in the world, so outstanding in both intelligence and power, aren't you ashamed to care so much to make all the money you can, and to advance your reputation and prestige— while for truth and wisdom and the improvement of your soul you have no care or worry?

This is the Socrates Heinrich Maier had in mind when he spoke of "the Socratic gospel."[3] If "gospel" makes us think of the Christian gospel, the evocation is not inappropriate at this point. Socrates could [501] have taken over verbatim the great questions of our gospels, "What shall it profit a man, if he gain the whole world, and lose his own soul?"

The only gloss I need add here is a caution that [you] {one} should not be misled by the otherworldly associations with which the word *soul* is loaded in our own tradition and which were nearly as heavy in the Greek. If there is anything new in the way Socrates uses the word *soul,* it is that he quietly narrows down its meaning to something whose supernatural origin or destiny, if any, is indeterminate, and whose physical or metaphysical structure, if any, is also indeterminate, so that both theological and antitheological, mystical and naturalistic, doctrines of the soul become inconsequential. His is a gospel without dogma, You may hold any one of a great variety of beliefs about the soul, or none of them, without either gaining or losing any essential part of what Socrates wants you to think about and care for when he urges you to "care for your soul." In particular you don't have to believe in the immortality of the soul. Socrates himself does believe in it,[4] but for this faith he has no argument. In the *Apology* he muses on how pleasant it would be *if* it were true, the soul carrying along to Hades all its intellectual equipment, so it could carry on Socratic arguments with no more fear of interruption. Such a life, he says, would make him "unspeakably happy." But he does not say this is a good reason for believing in it, or that there is some other good reason. He says nothing to exclude the alternative he mentions: total extinction of con-

---

[3] *Sokrates* (Tübingen, 1913), 99. 296ff. [All things considered, this book is the best single study ever made of Socrates.]

[4] {The question is left open in the Apology. But see *Crito* 54bc.}

sciousness; death could mean just this, and if it did, there would be nothing in
it to frighten a good man or dissuade him from the "care of the soul." The soul
is as worth caring for if it were to last just twenty-four more hours as if it were
to outlast eternity. If you have just one more day to live and can expect nothing but a blank after that, Socrates feels that you would still have all the reason
you need for improving your soul; you have yourself to live with that one day,
so why live with a worse self, if you could live with a better one instead?

How then is the soul improved? Morally, by right action; intellectually, by
right thinking; the two being strictly complementary, so that you can't have
one without the other and, if you do have either you will be sure to have the
other. This, of course, is his famous doctrine that "virtue is knowledge,"
which means two things: [502]

First, that there can be no virtue without knowledge. This is what gives
such intensity to Socrates' arguments, such urgency to his quests for definition. He makes you feel that the failure to sustain a thesis or find a definition is
not just an intellectual defeat, but a moral disaster. At the end of the *Euthyphro,* that gentleman is as good as told that his failure to make good his
confident claim to know "exactly" (5a, 15d) what piety is means not just that
he is intellectually hard up, but that he is morally bankrupt. I am stating what
Socrates believes, in as extreme a form as Plato allows us to see it. One of the
many things for which we may be grateful to Plato is that, as Boswell said of
his own treatment of Johnson, he "did not make a cat out of his tiger." Unlike
Xenophon's cat, Plato's tiger stands for the savage doctrine that if you cannot
pass the stiff Socratic tests for knowledge you cannot be a good man.

No less extreme is the mate to this doctrine: that if you do have this kind of
knowledge, you cannot fail to *be* good and *act* as a good man should, in the
face of any emotional stress or strain. The things which break the resolution of
others, which seduce or panic men to act in an unguarded moment contrary to
their best insights—"rage, pleasure, pain, love, fear" (*Prot.* 352b)—any one
of them, or all of them in combination, will have no power over the man who
has Socratic knowledge. He will walk through life invulnerable, sheathed in
knowledge as in a magic armor, which no blow from the external world can
crack or even dent. No saint has ever claimed more for the power of faith over
the passions than does Socrates for the power of knowledge.

So here is one side of Socrates. He has an evangel to proclaim, a great truth
to teach: Our soul is the only thing in us worth saving, and there is only one
way to save it: to acquire knowledge.

⟦Well,⟧ what would you expect of such a man? To propagate his message, to
disseminate the knowledge which is itself the elixir of life. Is this what he
does? How *could* he, if, as he says repeatedly in the dialogues, he does not
have that knowledge? Plato makes him say this not only in the informality of
private conversations but also in [503] that most formal speech of all, the

Apology. If he is wiser than others, Socrates there declares (21d), it is only because he does not *think* he has the knowledge which others think they have but haven't.[5]

Could this be true? If it were, then on his own teaching he too would be one of the damned. But [if there ever was a] {no} man [who] {ever} breathed greater assurance that his feet were planted firmly on the path of right [, this is surely Socrates]. He never voices a doubt of the moral rightness of any of his acts or decisions, never betrays a sense of sin. He goes to his death confident that "no evil thing can happen to a good man" (*Ap.* 41d)—that "good man" is himself. Can this be the same man who believes that no one can be good without knowledge, and that he has no knowledge?

But there is more to the paradox. It is not merely that Socrates *says* things—as in his disclaimer of moral knowledge—which contradict the role of a preacher and teacher of the care of the soul, but that he *acts* in ways which do not seem to fit this role. Socrates' characteristic activity is the *elenchus,* literally,"the refutation." You say *A,* and he shows you that *A* implies *B,* and *B* implies *C,* and then he asks, "But didn't you say *D* before? And doesn't *C* contradict *D?*" And there he leaves you with your shipwrecked argument, without so much as telling you what part of it, if any, might yet be salvaged. His tactics seem unfriendly from the start. Instead of trying to pilot you around the rocks, he picks one under water a long way ahead where you would never suspect it and then makes sure you get all the wind you need to run full-sail into it and smash your keep upon it.

This sort of thing happens so often in Plato's Socratic dialogues and is so perplexing that one can't help wondering whether the historical Socrates could have been really like that. I have had to ask myself more than once whether this pitiless critic, this heartless intellectual, this man who throws away his chances to preach a gospel so he may push an argument instead, is not, after all, only a Platonic projection and tells us more about the youthful Plato than about the aged Socrates. As often as this doubt has reared its head in my mind, I have chopped it down by just going back to the *Apology.* Here, where Socrates' evangelistic mission is stated so emphatically, it is most distinctly implied that his customary conduct did not fit the [504] evangelist's role. I am thinking, of course, of that story[6] about the supposed oracle of Delphi that no one was wiser than Socrates; this supposedly started Socrates on his search for someone wiser than himself, trying everyone who had the reputation for wisdom: first the statesmen, then the poets, then, scraping the bottom of the barrel, even the artisans, only to find that the wisdom of all these people, from top to bottom, was worse than zero, a minus quantity. What to make of this whole story is itself a puzzle for the scholar, and I will

---

[5] {And see especially *Gorg.* 506a, 508e–509a.}
[6] {*Ap.* 20e–21a.}

not try to crack it here. But whatever the Pythian priestess may or may not have said in the first place, and whatever Socrates may or may not have thought about whatever she did say, the one thing which is certain is this: the story frames a portrait of Socrates whose day-in, day-out role was known to his fellow-citizens as that of a destructive critic, whose behaviour looked from the outside like that of a man who saw nothing in his interlocutors but balloons of pretended knowledge and was bent on nothing else but to puncture them. So the *Apology* confirms the conduct which presents our paradox. It tells of a Socrates who says the care of the soul is the most important thing in the world, and that his mission in life is to get others to see this. And yet it also as good as says that if you were going down the Agora and saw a crowd around Socrates, you could take three to one bets that Socrates would not be saying anything about the improvement of the soul, nor acting as though he cared a straw for the improvement of his interlocutor's soul, but would be simply arguing with him, forcing him into one corner after another, until it became plain to all the bystanders, if not the man himself, that his initial claim to know this or that proposition was ridiculously false.

Here then is our paradox. [[Are we ready for the answer? Perhaps you are, but I am not, for there is]] {But there is no use looking for the answer until we have taken into account} still another side to Socrates [[I must bring up, and I will, if you can bear the suspense. It is]] {:} the role of the *searcher*. "Don't think," he says to the great sophist, Protagoras, "that I have any other interest in arguing with you but that of clearing up my own problems as they arise" (*Prot.* 348c). Or again, when that nasty intellectual, Critias, accuses him of just trying to refute him instead of advancing the argument, Socrates replies: [505]

> And what if I am? How can you think that I have any other interest in refuting you, but what I should have in *searching myself,* fearing lest I might fool myself, thinking I know something, when I don't know? (*Charm.* 166c–d)

Moments of self-revelation like these are rare in the dialogues. Socrates is not a character out of Chekhov introspecting moodily on the public stage. He is a man whose face is a mask, whose every word is deliberate, and who seems calculated to conceal more than to reveal. One gets so used to this artful exterior that one is left unprepared for moments like these and is apt to discount them as irony. I speak for myself. This is the way I used to take them. And so long as I did, I could find no way through the paradox of which I have been speaking. But then it occurred to me that in the statements I have just [[read]] {cited}, Socrates means to be taken at his word, and in this one too:

> Critias, you act as though I professed to know the answers to the questions I ask you, and could give them to you if I wished. It isn't so. I inquire with you . . . because I don't myself have knowledge. (*Char.* 165d)

Can he really mean this? He can, if in such passages he is using "knowledge" in a sense in which the claim to know something implies the conviction that any further investigation of its truth would be useless. This is the sense in which the word "knowledge" is used in formal contexts by earlier philosophers, and nothing gives us a better sense of the dogmatic certainty implied by their use of it than the fact that one of them, Parmenides, presented his doctrine in the guise of a divine revelation. In doing this Parmenides did not mean in the least that the truth of his philosophy must be taken on faith. He presented his system as a purely rational deductive argument which made no appeal to anything except the understanding. What he meant rather is that the conclusions of this argument have the same certainty as that which the devotees of mystic cults would attach to the poems of Orpheus or of some other divinely inspired lore. This, I suggest, is the conception of wisdom and knowledge Socrates has in mind in those contexts where he disclaims it. When he renounces "knowledge," he is telling us that the question of the truth of anything *he* believes can always be sensibly reopened; that any conviction he has stands ready to be reexamined in the company of any [506] sincere person who will raise the question and join him in the investigation.

Consider his great proposition that it is never right to harm the enemy. Would you not think that if there is anything Socrates feels *he knows,* this is it; else how could he have taken his stand on it, declaring that for those who believe it and those who do not "there can be no common mind, but they can only despise each other when they confront each other's counsels" (*Crito* 49d)? But even this he is prepared to reexamine. He continues to Crito:

> So consider very carefully whether you too are on my side and share my conviction, so we can start from this: that neither doing nor returning wrong nor defending oneself against evil by returning the evil is ever right? Or do you dissent and part company with me here? For myself this is what I have long believed and still do. But if you think differently, go ahead, explain, show me. (49d–e)

You would think this hardly the time and place to reopen this issue, but Socrates is quite willing. And I suggest that he is always willing; that he goes into every discussion in just this frame of mind. Previous reflection has led him to many conclusions, and he does not put them out of his mind when jumping into a new argument. There they all are, and not in vague or jumbled up form, but in a clear map, on which he constantly relies to figure out, many moves in advance, the direction in which he would like to press an argument. But clear as they are, they are not finally decided; everyone of them is open to review in the present argument, where the very same kind of process which led to the original conclusion *could* unsettle what an earlier argument may have settled prematurely, on incomplete survey of relevant premises or by faulty deductions. Nor is it only a matter of reexamining previously reached conclusions; it is no less a matter of hoping for new insights which may crop up right in this next argument and give the answer to some hitherto unanswered problem. And if this is the case, Socrates is not just the fighter he appears to be on the surface, intent on vindicating predetermined results by winning just one more victory in an ordeal by combat. He is the investigator, testing his own ideas in the course of testing those of his interlocutor, watching the argument with genuine curiosity to see whether it will really come out where it should if the results of previous arguments [507] were sound, and scanning the landscape as he goes along, looking for some new feature he failed to notice before.

Does this show a way out of our paradox? I think it does. It puts in a new light the roles that seemed so hard to reconcile before. Socrates the *preacher* turns out to be a man who wants others to find out his gospel {so far} as possible by themselves and for themselves. Socrates the *teacher* now appears as the man who has not just certain conclusions to impart to others but a *method of investigation*—the method by which he reached these results in the first place, and which is even more important than the results, for it is the means of testing, revising, and going beyond them. Socrates the *critic* is much more than a mere critic, for he exhibits his method by putting it to work; even if not a single positive result were to come out of it in this or that argument, the method itself would have been demonstrated, and those who saw how it works could put it to work for themselves to reach more positive conclusions. Even Socrates the *professed* agnostic becomes more intelligible. His 'I don't know' is a conscientious objection to the notion that the conclusions of any discussion are secure against further testing by further discussion. Seen in this way, Socrates no longer seems a bundle of incompatible roles precariously tied together by irony. He seems one man, unified in his diverse activities by the fact that in all of them he remains the searcher, always pursuing his own search and seeking fellow-seekers.

May I now give you a particular illustration, for I would not like to leave this solution hanging in generality. I take the *Euthyphro,* though almost any one of Plato's early dialogues would do. On your first reading of this dialogue, you come to the end with a sense of disappointment that after all this winding and unwinding of argument no positive result seems to be reached, and Socrates is ready, as he says, "to begin all over again" with the original question, "What is piety?" As you watch Euthyphro hurry off, this is what you feel like telling Socrates: 'I don't believe you really care for that man's soul, for if you did, how could you have let him go with his head stuffed with his superstitions? You know that the pollution he fears has nothing to do with the only piety you think worth talking about, the kind that [508] will improve what *you* call the soul. Why then not tell him this, and show him the difference between religion and magic?'

But if you go back and reread the dialogue more carefully, you can figure out Socrates' reply:

That is what I did try to show him. But I wanted him to find it out for himself. For this purpose it would have been no use telling him his notion of piety was all wrong, which would not even have been true. It was *not* all wrong, but a jumble of right and wrong beliefs, and my job was to help him see that he could not hold both sets at once. If he could see this, he would become his own critic, his own teacher, even his own preacher, for if this man could see the implications of some things he already believes; I would not have to preach to him that he should care for his soul as it should be cared for. He would be doing his own preaching to himself.

Socrates might then add that though he failed in this objective, the fault was not entirely his own. For sheer sluggishness of intellect it would be hard to beat this complacent fanatic whom Plato ironically calls *Euthyphro,* "Straight-thinker." How straight he thinks on matters of religion, we may judge by his response when Socrates shows him that, on his view, religion is a business-relationship between men and gods, a barter of divine favors for human offerings. Faced with this consequence, our Mr. Straight-thinker sees nothing positively wrong with it: "Yes, you may call it (piety) a commercial art, if you like" (14e). Yet even with such unpromising material on his hands, Socrates tries hard and makes good headway, coming at one point within a stone's throw of success: He gets Euthyphro to admit that piety cannot be defined as "that which is pleasing to the gods," i.e., as obedience to any demand the gods might happen to make on men; the demand must itself be *just,* and piety must consist of discharging services we *owe* the gods. Socrates then pushes Euthyphro to say what sort of services these might be. Why do the gods *need* our services, he presses; what is that "wonderful work" (13e) the gods can only achieve through our own cooperating efforts? I suppose it was too much to expect Euthyphro to see the answer once Socrates has led him so far, and say to himself, in line with Socrates' reasoning, with all of which he agrees:

> Since the gods are great and powerful [509] past all imagining, they surely don't need our services to improve *their* estate; and since they are also good and benevolent, they do desire what is best for us—and what can this be, but the improvement of souls? Isn't this then the object of piety, this the discharge of the highest obligation we owe the gods?

Socrates evidently thought this was *not* too much to hope, that Euthyphro would have seen for himself on the strength of the Socratic prodding. When Euthyphro went hopelessly off the track in a wordy tangent, Socrates remarked (14b–c):

> Certainly, Euthyphro, you could have answered my main question in far fewer words, if you bad wished. . . . Just now when you were on the very edge of telling me what I want to know, you turned aside.

Clearly Socrates has *not* been playing a cat-and-mouse game with Euthyphro in this dialogue, putting questions to him only to pounce on the answers and claw them to pieces. He has been doing his best to lead Euthyphro to the point where he could see for himself the right answer. What he positively refuses to do is to *tell* Euthyphro this answer, and this, not because he does not think Euthyphro's soul worth the saving, but because he believes there is only one way to save it and that Euthyphro himself must do the job by finding one right way, so that he too becomes a searcher. Whether or not you think Socrates was right in this, I trust you will agree with me that he was at least consistent.

But *was* Socrates right? [A scholar could ignore that question in good conscience. A humanist cannot. He could, of course, turn the question back to you, as Socrates would. But it is pretty late for me to start playing Socrates now, and it would hardly be consistent with so un-Socratic a performance as an unbroken monologue to a speechless multitude. Anyhow, to follow Socrates at this crucial point would be to imply that I *do* think him right after all. And the fact is that] on some fundamental points I think him wrong.

I do not think the Socratic way is the only way to save a man's soul. What Socrates called "knowledge" he thought both necessary and sufficient for moral goodness. I think it neither. Not necessary, for the bravest men I ever met would surely have flunked the [510] Socratic examination on courage. Why this should be so would take long to unravel, and I have no confidence I could do it successfully. But I don't need to for the point at issue. For this I need only stick to the fact: that a man can have great courage yet make a fool of himself when he opens his mouth to explain what it is that he has. I am not saying that it would not be a fine thing if he could talk better and know more. I am not depreciating Socratic knowledge. I am only saying it is not necessary for what Socrates did think it necessary. And I would also say that it is not sufficient. For this I need no better example than that famous saying of his, in the *Apology* (29a–b), that the fear of death is the pretence of wisdom. "Why do we fear death? Because we think we know it is a great evil. But do we *know* this? No. We don't know anything about death. For all we know to the contrary, it might be a great good." So argues Socrates and implies confidently that if you saw all this, your fear of death would vanish. Knowledge—in this case, knowledge of your ignorance of what death is and what, if anything, comes after it—would dissipate your fear. You couldn't fear death or anything else unless you knew it to be evil. But why couldn't you? "Because it would be absurd," Socrates would say. But could it not be absurd and exist just the same? Aunt Rosie is afraid of mice, but she knows quite well that a mouse can do her no great harm. She knows she runs a far graver risk to life and limb when she drives her car down Main Street, but she is not a bit afraid of that, while she is terrified of mice. This is absurd, but it happens; and her knowing it is absurd does not prevent it from happening either but only adds shame and guilt to fear. This is not evidence of a high order; it is just a *fact* that does not square with Socrates' theory.

But Socratic knowledge has all too little interest in facts. That is the main trouble with it. Socrates' model for knowledge was what we would call deductive knowledge nowadays. The knowledge he sought, and with such marked success, is that which consists in arranging whatever information one has in a luminous, perspicuous pattern, so one can see at a glance where run the bright lines of implication and where the dark ones of contradiction. But of the other way of knowing, the empirical way. Socrates had little understanding [511], and he paid for his ignorance by conceit of knowledge, failing to understand the limitations of his knowledge of fact generally, and of the fact of knowledge in particular. Had he so much as felt the need of investigating knowledge itself as a fact in human nature, to determine just exactly what, as a matter of fact, happens to a man when he has or hasn't knowledge, Socrates might have come to see that even his own dauntless courage in the face of death he owed not to knowledge but to something else, more akin to religious faith.

But to explain Socrates' failure merely in this way would be itself to concede more to Socrates' theory than the facts allow, for it would be to explain it as only a failure of knowledge. I will put all my cards on the table and say that behind this lay a failure of love. In saying this, I am not taking overseriously the prickly exterior and the pugilist's postures. I have already argued that he does care for the souls of fellows. But the care is limited and conditional. If men's souls are to be saved, they must be saved his way. And when he sees they cannot he, he watches them go down the road to perdition with regret but without anguish. Jesus wept for Jerusalem. Socrates warns Athens, scolds, exhorts it, condemns it. But he has no tears for it. One wonders if Plato, who raged against Athens, did not love it more in his rage and hate than ever did Socrates in his sad and good-tempered rebukes. One feels there is a last zone of frigidity in the soul of the great erotic; had he loved his fellows more, he could hardly have laid on them the burdens of his "despotic logic,"[7] impossible to be borne.

Having said all this ⟦as I felt I had to, confronting Socrates as man to man⟧, let me now add that grave as these complaints are, they do not undermine his greatness. Let me ⟦tell you in the last part of this address⟧ {try to say} why in spite of this or a longer bill of particulars which might be drawn against him, he is still great.

Let me start where I just left off: his character. To be different in some way or other from everyone else, one need not be a great man; one need only be a

---

man. But to find in this difference the material for a personal creation where-
with to enrich the common life of humanity [512]—this is a difficult achievement for anyone and was exceptionally so for Socrates, for his initial endowment was so discouraging: physical ugliness. This he had to live with among a
people who adored beauty. Socrates solved the problem classical antiquity
would have judged insoluble. In the world of the fine arts—plastic, graphic,
auditory—classical antiquity just took it for granted that if the product is to be
fine the materials must be beautiful to begin with. Socrates proved this was
not so in the medium of personal life. He showed how there at least art could
fashion beauty out of ugliness. He did this by stylizing his deformity, making
an abstract mask out of it, and so detaching himself from ⟨it⟩ that, while he
could never put it off, he could always laugh at it as from a great distance with
his mind. And as a good artist does not drop a theme once he gets hold of it,
but puts it to new and surprising uses, so Socrates with this theme of ugliness
as a comic mask. He made his words common and vulgar, like his face. He
said he could not make fine speeches or even understand the fine ones others
made. His memory, he said, was short, he could only take things in a sentence
or two at a time; nor could his wits move fast, so everything must be explained
to him in painfully slow, dragging steps. His manners, too, he said, were
poor; he must be forgiven if he could not be as polite in argument as other
men. With this cumulative renunciation of ornaments of culture and graces of
mind, he built his character. Its surface traits, uncouth, ludicrous to the casual
eye, were so severely functional, so perfectly adapted to the work he had to
do, that men with the keenest eye for beauty, men like Alcibiades and Plato,
found more of it in Socrates than in anyone they had every known. The test of
art is, Will it last? And for this kind of art, Will it last in adversity? Socrates'
art passed this test. The self behind the mask was never shown up as just
another mask. He was the same before his judges as he had been in the marketplace. When he took the poison from the hands of the executioner, there
was "no change of colour or expression on his face" (*Phaedo* 117b).

Second, Socrates was great as a reformer of morality: not a social reformer,
but a reformer of the conscience which in the very long run has power to make
or break social institutions. A poet like [513] Aristophanes sensed this, without really understanding it; so did Callicles in the *Gorgias* (481c), when he
asked Socrates:

> If you're serious, and what you say is really true, won't human life have to be
> turned completely upside down?

I trust that even some of the incidental illustrations I have used before in this
address will document the truth of this rhetorical question. Think of the answer to "What is piety?" Socrates is fishing for in the *Euthyphro*. How could
Athenian piety remain the same, or how could ours for that matter, if Socrates
is right on this, if man's obligation to the gods is one he would have to his own
self, even if there were no gods: to improve his own soul? Again, how many

practices or sentiments in Socrates' world or ours would remain intact if his conviction that it is never right to return evil for evil were taken seriously as really true?

There is also another change Socrates wrought in the texture of the moral conscience, one which is scarcely mentioned in the books about him. I cannot hope to remedy this deficiency here. But I can least remind you that Greek morality still remained to a surprising extent a class-morality. The conviction that high-grade moral virtue was possible only for a man who was wellborn or, at least, moderately well-off, ran wide and deep. The disinheritance of a majority of the urban population—not only the slaves, but the freeborn manual workers—from the life of virtue is a reasoned belief in Aristotle. Even that radical remolder of the social fabric, Plato, did not reject the dogma; he only sublimated it. Socrates did reject it. He expunged it from the universe of moral discourse, when he made the improvement of the soul as mandatory, and as possible, for the manual workers as for the gentleman of leisure, when he redefined all the virtues, and virtue itself, in such a way as to make of them not class attributes but human qualities.

But even this is not his greatest contribution. If the solution of the paradox of Socrates I put before you in this address is correct, then certainly Socrates himself would have attached far more importance to his method of moral inquiry than to any of its results. If we could get past the palaver of his mock-humility and make him say in simple honesty what he thought was his greatest achievement, he [514] would certainly have put that method far above anything else. I trust I need not argue all over again this point which is as crucial to my estimate of Socrates' greatness as it was to the resolution of the paradox ⟦I have put before you. Let me only remind you⟧ {I can only point out} that if what I am now contending were not true, that paradox would not have been there. Had he valued the results of his method above the method itself, he would have been just a preacher and teacher of moral truths, not also the professed agnostic, the tireless critic, examiner and reexaminer of himself and of others; in other words, he would not have been the Socrates of the Platonic dialogues and of this ⟦address⟧ {book}.

Why rank that method among the great achievements of humanity? Because it makes moral inquiry a common human enterprise, open to every man. Its practice calls for no adherence to a philosophical system, or mastery of a specialized technique, or acquisition of a technical vocabulary. It calls for common sense and common speech. And this is as it should be, for how man should live is every man's business, and the role of the specialist and the expert should be only to offer guidance and ⟦advice⟧ {criticism}, to inform {and clarify} the judgment of the layman, leaving the final decision up to him. But while the Socratic method makes moral inquiry open to everyone, it makes it easy for no one. It calls not only for the highest degree of mental alertness of which anyone is capable, but also for moral qualities of a high order: sincerity, humility, courage. Socrates expects you to say what you really believe about the way *man* should live; which implies, among other things, about the way *you* should live. His method will not work if the opinion you give him is just *an* opinion; it must be *your* opinion: the one you stand ready to live by, so that if that opinion should be refuted, your own life or a part of it will be indicted or discredited, shown up to be a muddle, premised on a confusion or a contradiction. To get into the argument when you realize that this is the price you have to pay for it—that in the course of it your ego may experience the unpleasant sensation of a bloody nose—takes courage. To search for moral truth that may prove your own life wrong takes humility that is not afraid of humiliation. These are the qualities Socrates himself brings to the argument, and it is not entirely clear that he realizes how [515] essential they are to protect it against the possibility that its dialectic, however rigorous, would merely grind out, as it could with impeccable logic, wild conclusions from irresponsible premises.

But is there not still a residual risk, you may ask, in making the Socratic method the arbiter of moral truth, inviting thereby every man to take, on its terms, a place in the supreme court which judges questions of morality? Certainly there is a risk, and a grave one. For though the method has some built-in protection against moral irresponsibility—the one I have just mentioned—it offers no guarantee whatever that it will always lead to truth. On this Socrates himself, if the foregoing interpretation of his agnosticism was correct, is absolutely clear. His "I don't know" honestly means "I could be mistaken in results reached by this method." And if Socrates could be mistaken, how much more so Tom, Dick, and Harry. Why then open it to them? Socrates' answer is clear: Because each of them is a man, and "the unexamined life is not worth living by man" (*Ap.* 38a). I could not go so far as he did at this point. I believe that many kinds of life are worth living by man. But I do believe that the best of all is the one in which every man does his own examining. I have dissented earlier from Socrates' assumption that his is the only way by which any man's soul can be saved. But I can still give wholehearted assent to Socrates' vision of man as a mature, responsible being, claiming to the fullest extent his freedom to make his own choice between right and wrong, not only in action, but in judgment. I do not see how man can reach the full stature of his manhood unless he claims the right to make his own personal judgments on morality; and if he is to claim this right, he must accept the implied chance of misjudgment as a calculated risk. This is the price he must pay for being free. I am using now, you notice, very un-Socratic language, and I will compound the offense by adding that this Socratic vision of human freedom, of which the Socratic method is an expression, could not be appropriately described as knowledge, and that the best name for it is faith. That the man who had this faith to a supreme degree should have mistaken it for knowledge, is yet another part of the paradox of Socrates⟦—but one which I cannot attempt to unravel this evening⟧.

2

PLATIS'S *SOCRATES' ACCUSERS*

P LATIS EXAMINES virtually every scrap of ancient testimony bearing
on the identity and character of the three accusers and on the motives
of the prosecution. He canvasses the whole gamut of scholarly opinion
on all aspects of the subject, illustrates it by copious quotations, and appraises
it critically. This is the most [201] thorough treatment of the topic yet produced in any language, and the conclusions it reaches are in every case entitled to respect. I shall review them briefly.

To start with Meletus. An influential view, vigorously championed by John
Burnet (*Plato's Euthyphro, Apology, and Crito* [Oxford 1924] *ad Euth*. 2b9),
still favored by W.K.C. Guthrie (*History of Greek Philosophy,* vol. 3 [Cam-
bridge 1969], 381), identifies him with the Meletus who is named by Andocides as one of the prosecutors at *his* trial for impiety (*De myst.* 94). On the
further assumption that the latter was *also* identical with the author of ps.-
Lysias 6 (*Against Andocides*)—that "monument of religious fanaticism"
Burnet rightly calls it (*loc. cit.*)—this produces an attractive hypothesis, af-
fording all by itself, Burnet argued, "an intelligible motive for the prosecution" (ibid.). However, the hypothesis is doubly insecure: neither of its assumed
identities is attested by ancient authority. And Platis adduces a variety of
circumstances which make it unlikely that the prosecutor of either Andocides
or Socrates could have been that fledgling poet, "young and unknown" (Plato,
Euth. 2b8) at the time of those trials. Standing on the same description of
Meletus in the *Euthyphro*—our clearest and firmest clue to his identity—
Platis also rebuts another well-sponsored misidentification (traceable back, as
he shows, to Greco-Roman times), the one with the tragic poet and scoliogra-
pher by that name (cf. Aristophanes, *Frogs* 1302; frs. 149, 150, 435 Koch).
Since this man is satirized in Aristophanes' *Georgoi,* produced not later than
422 B.C., he could hardly have been described as "young and unknown" in
399. I need not go into the other misidentifications Platis rebuts in his careful
review of the evidence. He leaves us with no choice but to agree that Meletus,
though formally the mover of the *graphē,* was a person of no account, used as
a mere tool by Anytus whom, as is well known, Plato regards as in all but
name the effective accuser (*Ap.* 31a5 taken with 18b3). *Pace* Burnet, Meletus

Review of ᾽E. N. Πλατής, Οἱ κατήγοροι τοῦ Σωκράτη. Φιλολογική μελέτη. (E. N.
Platis, *The Accusers of Socrates: A Philological Study.*) Athens, 1980. Printed privately. From
AJP 104 (1983): 201–6. Used by permission.

would not need to be (though, for all we know, he may have been) a hyper-fanatic to have served as a front man for Anytus.

In Lycon's case the interesting question is whether he could have been the character by that name in Xenophon's *Symposium*, chaperoning at that banquet his beautiful young son, Autolycus, current inamorato of the host, the super-rich, bland, and dissolute Callias. A variety of scholars—among them the most recent editor of Xenophon's *Symposium* (Francois Ollier, *Xenophon: Banquet, Apologie de Socrate* [Paris 1961], 28)—had argued that Xenophon could not have given a future accuser of Socrates the role assigned to Lycon here, that of a father, solicitous for the morals of his son in the delicate social circumstances of that occasion, grateful to Socrates for his praise of *sōphrōn erōs* (his parting words are, "By Hera, Socrates, you seem to be *kalos kagathos*" [9.1]). Platis argues persuasively on the other side: Xenophon's apologetic interests would have been well served by a dramatic fiction where Socrates, so far from "corrupting" young men, incites them to *kalokagathia*. The picture which emerges from Platis' discussion of assorted references to Lycon in the comic poets is that of a pretty political boss who makes his way in the world as the complaisant husband of the beautiful and brilliant Rhodia and as the client and political handyman of rich Athenians—a "spineless" individual, whose personal feeling for Socrates, whatever it may have been at the time of the trial, would not likely stand in the way of rendering his current patron whatever services might be demanded of him. [202]

Now for Anytus. Powerful and honored leader in the newly restored democracy (Plato, *Meno* 90b; Andocides, 1.150), admired for his scrupulous adherence to the provisions of the amnesty at grave personal loss (Isocrates 8.33), he has had a good press: Heinrich Maier (*Sokrates* [Tübingen 1913], 472), "ein ehrlicher patriotischer Mann"; Bury-Meiggs (J. B. Bury, *History of Greece,* 3rd ed., rev. by Russell Meiggs [London 1951], 580), "the honest democratic politician." Platis agrees ("honest—this is beyond doubt," [200]) —too easily, it seems to me, in view of what he does with two reports which reflect unfavorably on Anytus' personal character:

(1) Aristotle's *Ath. Pol.* (27.5) reports that Anytus had once bribed wholesale a heliastic court (the first occurrence of *dekazein to dikastērion,* according to Aristotle) to win acquittal on a charge of treason—an unfair one, no doubt: the squadron under his command had been prevented by a storm from coming to the relief of Pylos. The veracity of this report (though supported by both Diodorus and Plutarch) has been rejected (most recently by J. Humbert, *Socrate et les petits Socratiques* [Paris 1967], 47n. 1) by scholars who follow Wilamowitz (*Aristoleles und Athen* [Berlin 1893], vol. 1, 128) in holding that Aristotle had been deceived by a malicious fabrication of the Socratics. Under Platis's critical scrutiny, this suspicion proves groundless. Should he not then concede that accolades to Anytus' character need to be taken down a peg or two, if at one time in his life he had not scrupled to save his skin by subverting judicial process?

(2) Platis makes a convincing case for taking our Anytus to be the *sitophulax* by that name in Lysias 22.8–9, holding office in 388–87. The defendant in that trial is a metic wheat-retailer, accused of buying from the importers more than the legally permissible maximum of 50 *phormai,* who claims that he had done so "at the bidding of the magistrates." The other *sitophulakes* deny the charge. Anytus, called to the stand, is handled with kid gloves by the prosecution, which is not surprising, considering the great power he had exercised in the state not so long before. He is not required to answer the plain question, "Did you, or did you not, bid this man *buy* more than fifty *phormai?*" and is let off with the plea that "he had not ordered [the wheat-retailers] to buy *and hold in store* [more than 50 *phormai*] but had only counseled them not to buy against each other [i.e., not to engage in competitive bidding]" (ibid. 9). Whatever may be the truth of this matter (Platis adopts a plausible conjecture by Wilamowitz as to what really happened), what remains beyond doubt, as Platis observes (184), is this: Anytus gave some instruction or other to the retailers—small fry, people with no political clout—which put them in breach of the law and exposed them to a capital charge, while leaving him judicially invulnerable. Added to the preceding, far graver, blot on Anytus' record, it leaves one still more skeptical of the image of the "honorable man" built up for Anytus in the scholarly literature.

What personal motives might he have had for prosecuting Socrates? We hear of none in Plato's *Apology.* (The "many resentments" aroused in those subjected to elenctic examination by Socrates [22e6–23a2] and by youthful imitators of him [23c2–d2] could hardly qualify: even extreme exasperation at such harassment could not have led one of its victims to indict Socrates for an offense punishable by death.) But Xenophon appends the following tale to his *Apology of Socrates:* After the trial, Socrates, looking at Anytus, declares: "He [203] killed me because I had said that a man accorded the highest offices by the city should not have educated his son among hides [i.e., in the tannery business]," and prophesies that "for lack of a worthy supervisor" the lad would come to a bad end—and, true enough, the boy becomes a drunkard (30–31). What shall we think of this story? If true, it offers us on a silver platter Socrates' personal estimate of *the* motive for the indictment ("he killed me because . . . "). I submit that we should be very suspicious of it on several grounds (see K. von Fritz, "Zur Frage der Echtheit der xenophontische *Apologie des Sokrates,*" *Rhein. Mus.* 80 [1931], 36–69 at 44–49) and especially on one to which little attention seems to have been paid: the lack of any recounting of it by later authors hostile to Anytus: eager to blacken his name, they would have been strongly inclined to regurgitate it, if they had had any confidence in its truth. Particularly significant, it seems to me, is its cold-shouldering by Libanius, given his own (rather absurd) conviction that the reason for Anytus's hostility to Socrates was the latter's habit of referring to tanners, which Anytus mistook for disparaging allusions to the source of his own wealth (*Apology of Socrates* 26, 28–29). If Libanius had given any credence at all to Xenophon's tale, he would have had ample reason to advert to it: it would have cast a glaring light on Anytus' villainy, making Socrates the scapegoat for his own self-reproach at the sorry education he was giving his son. The same would be true of two much earlier authors, both of whom wrote Apologies for Socrates—Lysias, not long after Socrates' death, and Demetrius of Phalerum, late in the fourth century. Though both are lost, it is a reasonable guess that neither of them repeated that story; for had they done so, it is hard to believe that others would have failed to follow their example. That the tale has left no trace in the whole of the tradition that has survived to us is tantamount to antiquity's vote of nonconfidence in it.

Platis appears to think he can extract a sliver of evidence in support of that lurid tale in Xenophon—"a clear hint of its truth" (p. 195)—from Anytus' encounter with Socrates in Plato's *Meno* (89e ff.). In that passage Socrates argues that if political virtue were teachable, Themistocles and other famous Athenians would have succeeded in passing on theirs to their sons. This angers Anytus and he responds with a veiled threat: those who slander others may be made to suffer for it, "especially in this town, as you yourself may come to know" (94e–95a). I submit that this exchange, viewed in context, though entirely consistent with the truth of Xenophon's story, gives no evidential support to it—not the slightest. Certainly, if Anytus had had a son stuck away in the family tannery, it would have touched a raw nerve to be reminded that the sons of illustrious predecessors of his had been learning music, riding, and wrestling (93d1–5, 94b2c5) at the same age. But the text does not say or imply that this is what provoked him. Nothing is said by Socrates in Plato's text to suggest that Anytus had done worse for his son than they had done for theirs. Socrates makes no such comparison at all. It would not have been to the point for what is being debated: Anytus shares the common belief (he implies as much at 92e3–6) that any Athenian who is *kalos kagathos* can teach virtue to others; and Socrates cites outstanding cases of reputed *kalokagathia* where this is manifestly false. Anytus' annoyance is sufficiently motivated in the text by the collision of incontrovertible fact with a dogmatist's fancies. It does not need to be explained by going outside the text to postulate a father's sense of guilt for putting his son into trade instead of sports and music. [204]

I trust I have not made too much of the tale in Xenophon, a minor item in Platis' account of Anytus on which he puts no weight when he comes to construct his positive view of Anytus' reasons for contriving the prosecution. Platis sees these reasons as strongly public-spirited: he acted to protect Athens' traditional values from the corrosive acids of that rationalist criticism of moral ideas which found in Socrates its most energetic agent. In support of this judgment, Platis makes excellent use of the same Platonic text: the encounter of Socrates with Anytus in the *Meno*. He focuses on the latter's outburst at Socrates' mention of sophists as professed teachers of virtue—"may no such madness seize anyone close to me, relative or friend, citizen or alien, to make him go to such men to be ruined by them. . . ." (91c)—a remark whose vehemence is unsurpassed by any of the nasty things said about sophists elsewhere in our sources and which is, in any case, rude in the extreme, for it is made in the presence of Meno, Anytus' own *xenos,* professed pupil of Gorgias, and is followed up crescendo, moments later, by a tirade against the "madness" of "parents and guardians who let their wards suffer such damage" and "of the cities which let those people get in and don't drive them out—be it an alien or a citizen who tries to do that sort of thing" (92b). Anytus is depicted here as being only a step away from the decision to institute the suit against Socrates: when a powerful leader inveighs at the "madness" of a city that suffers such pests in its midst, he is all but saying that Socrates should be flushed out of Athens. For who would doubt that in Anytus' eyes Socrates himself is a sophist? That is how he lived in the tradition, as is clear from Aeschines' well-known remark, half a century later ("Athenians, you put to death Socrates the sophist because he had educated Critias" [1.173]), and it could hardly have been otherwise in his own lifetime. As Grote remarks (*History of Greece* [vol. 8, Everyman ed., London 1906] 315): "It is certain that if in the middle of the Peloponnesian war, any Athenian had been asked, 'Who are the principal Sophists in your city?' he would have named Socrates among the first." In the *Apology* we see Plato making Socrates impute directly to Anytus the identical sentiment Anytus is made to express about Socrates in the *Meno:*

> He [Anytus] said [in his prosecutory address to the court] that either this suit should not have come to court [i.e., that Socrates should have preferred self-exile to standing trial: Burnet's reasonable interpretation of the remark *ad loc.*] or, once it did, it is imperative that you should put me to death for, if I were acquitted, your sons, practicing what Socrates teaches, would be thoroughly corrupted. (*Ap.* 29c1–5)

Thus we are told twice over—both in the *Meno* and the *Apology*—that what Anytus takes to be Socrates' deleterious effect ("corruption," *Meno* 91e4, *Ap.* 29c5) on the minds of those affected by his teaching is *the* motive, the only one worthy of mention in Anytus' prosecution of Socrates. In arguing for the same thing, Platis has the full support of our most perceptive and trustworthy witness.

Did Anytus think of that "corruption" in political, no less than moral, terms? In particular, did he think of it as subversive of loyalty to the democracy? The view that Socrates was in fact an ideologist of the extreme right, a crypto-oligarch, dies hard. It was resuscitated recently in a book which appeared too late to reach Platis' bibliography: *Class Ideology and Ancient Political Theory* (Oxford 1978) by Ellen M. Wood and Neal Wood. An even less critical version [205] of that view had previously appeared in Greece: John Kordatos, *History of Ancient Greek Philosophy* (in Greek), 2nd ed., Athens

1972. Platis argues strongly against this position. Having labored in the same cause (cf. my review of the book by Wood and Wood in *Phoenix* [34 (1980), 347ff.]), I can appreciate all the better the force of a new argument Platis brings to the case by citing the stand of Lysias, whose political orientation is not in doubt: it is manifest in the lavish aid he furnished from his own purse to the embattled exiles at Phyle (c.f. Paul Cloché, *La Restauration démocratique à Athènes en 403* [Paris 1915], 164, 467) and in sentiments voiced in the fragment of the speech (*Oratio* 34 in Lamb's edition of Lysias [London 1930]) he wrote for an upper-class Athenian speaking in opposition to Phormisius' motion which, if passed, would have disenfranchised five thousand landless Athenians. Certainly, we must agree with Platis that if Lysias had thought Socrates an enemy of the restored democracy, he could not have entered the lists on Socrates' behalf by producing for him an *Apology,* probably in rebuttal of Polycrates' *Accusation of Socrates,* whose attack on Socrates had been strongly political. But I think that Platis overstates his case when he argues not only that Socrates was no partisan of oligarchy, but that he could not have been so perceived by a responsible leader of the restored democracy. Why couldn't he? Was Anytus in a position to know what Socrates was saying in his personal contacts? Could we blame him if he believed the worst? We know how harshly Socrates judged the democracy in public criticisms of it: we have a perfect specimen of them in the Platonic *Apology:*

> If I had entered politics long ago I would have perished long ago. . . . There is no man who will preserve his life for long in Athens or anywhere else if he genuinely sets himself against the multitude to prevent the perpetration of much injustice and illegality in the city. (31d)

If in a public speech Socrates could imply that political life in Athens was such a jungle of iniquity and lawlessness that an Athenian undertaking to fight for just causes in his own city would be virtually signing his own death warrant, why should not Anytus see in Socrates a disaffection that was so extreme that it would not stop short of subversion?

I regret that in the space at my disposal I cannot proceed to develop this and related points or to review much else well worthy of comment in Platis's book. In closing, let me say that despite the criticisms I have offered I consider this work an admirable book. I have learned more from it than from anything I have ever read on its topic. And may I add that it is written in elegant demotic Greek. Those who can read it will enjoy it on this count, no less than for its learning and for its strongly argued—at times impassioned, but never intemperate—historical judgments. Though its author does not hold a university post, the quality of learning he displays in this book would do credit to a university.

3

BRICKHOUSE AND SMITH'S *SOCRATES ON TRIAL*

P LATO'S *APOLOGY OF SOCRATES* is one of the acknowledged classics of world literature. Protesting unfamiliarity with the ways and
language of the law courts, Socrates proceeds to make a speech which
is a triumph of artless art, a dazzling achievement of seemingly unstudied
forensic rhetoric. But what relation does it bear to the discourse heard by the
Athenian court which found Socrates guilty of impiety and sentenced him to
death in 399 B.C.? If he did speak in his own defence—even this has been
doubted—does Plato's *Apology* aim at "historicity"? No one would seriously
think of it as Plato's effort at word-perfect recall of the speech he had heard
Socrates make. But though certainly composed in Plato's own style and diction, could it not have been, like the speeches of Thucydides (an obvious
parallel), an account which "comes as close as possible to the general sense of
what was truly said" (Thucydides, 1.22.1)? The contrary view—that what we
get from Plato is outright invention unconstrained by historical veracity—has
found favor with a redoubtable minority of Platonists. Should we follow them
against the more widely held view supported in this book?

For well-researched, sober, unprimped-up answers to this and many other
questions which pop into our head as we read Plato's masterpiece, we could
hardly do better than begin with Thomas C. Brickhouse and Nicholas D.
Smith's well-documented essay on it, *Socrates on Trial*. Readers who have
been swept off their feet by the late I. F. Stone's bestseller on the same topic,
The Trial of Socrates (see *TLS*, October 7–13, 1988; "Letters," November 4–
10) will find here facts from which an honest effort to get at the truth should
start. Here in highly accessible form is detailed comment on the Platonic
Apology with copious references to other primary evidence on the case, and
also, what is no less essential in a domain where expert assessment of the facts
is scarcely less important than are the facts themselves, on the spectrum of
diverse conclusions which equally learned authorities have drawn from the
same data. The authors' mastery of the scholarly literature is impressive.
Their bibliography lists well over seven hundred items (books or articles) and
it is not for show. Judging from those of their references which I have read
myself, they have indeed digested the incredibly complex data on which they
report. Only at one's peril could one fail to take cognizance of their results.

But painstaking though their research has been, it suffers from a serious

Review of Thomas C. Brickhouse and Nicholas D. Smith, *Socrates on Trial* (Oxford: Clarendon Press), 1989. From *TLS* No 4,524, Dec. 15, 1989, p. 1393. Used by permission.

gap. They have made no systematic effort in this book to assess the relative reliability of its two principal sources and explain the rationale of preferring one to the other when the two clash. They make no sustained investigation of the array of conflicts in the figure of Socrates purveyed by Plato ("Socrates^P," I shall be calling him, for short), on the one hand, and by Xenophon ("Socrates^x"), on the other. Let me list just four of these, the ones with the most direct bearing on the argument of this book.

[1] Socrates^P deviates radically from traditional religious belief. He holds that, contrary to what "the many say," the gods can only cause good; of their own nature they are *incapable of causing evil* (Plato, *Rep.* 379 b–c). Socrates^x believes with "the many" that the gods have power to do both good *and evil* (Xenophon, *Mem.* 1.4.16).

[2] For Socrates^x observance of the customary cult is at the center of pious conduct: "the pious man is rightly defined as he who knows the customary usages [of prayer and sacrifice] concerning the gods" (*Mem.* 4.6.4). When this definition of "piety" is put up to Socrates^P (Plato, *Euth.* 14c), he tears it to shreds. The essence of piety he locates within its rationally determinable ethical content.

[3] Socrates^P professes to have no moral knowledge, hence to be unable to teach virtue. Socrates^x does not make this profession. He has a superabundance of moral knowledge and teaches it volubly.

[4] Socrates^P is an unflinching rationalist. Though his gods are, like the gods of Socrates^x, the supernaturals of common belief who communicate with men through divinations, prophetic dreams, and so forth, yet unlike Socrates^x, he never looks to such things for an extrarational source of knowledge.

Do our authors keep track of these differences? They do not. At [3], though their Socrates is in fact, as he should be, Socrates^P, they ignore the contrary picture in Xenophon where Socrates' paradoxical profession of ignorance is systematically suppressed. Neither do they investigate the difference at [4]. Worst of all, they ignore the differences at [1] and [2] which leave Socrates^x bound to conventional religious belief and practice, while Socrates^P is one of the great religious radicals of history—not a "flaming" one, for his assaults on establishment dogmas are never incendiary: they are confined to solvents of orthodoxy as gentle as irony (he leaves his opponents guessing at what he means) and elenctic argument (he refutes them only by showing that in disagreeing with him they are in disagreement with themselves). How does this gap in the research affect the book's argument?

As explained in the blurb, "the authors argue, contrary to virtually every modern interpretation of the *Apology,* that Plato offers a straightforward, scrupulously truthful, sincere defence against the charges he [Socrates] faces." On the face of it, this is a far more attractive thesis than is Xenophon's (*Mem.* 4.8.6–10; *Ap.* 1–9) that Socrates aimed to provoke condemnation, looking to death by hemlock (a de luxe form of execution) as a welcome deliverance from the ills of old age. Though Xenophon is certain of Socrates' innocence—as much so as is Plato—it never seems to occur to him that if Socrates had really connived in his own conviction he would have been a willing accomplice in a terrible miscarriage of justice. So, in preferring Plato's testimony on this point, our authors are on strong ground: Plato's should be preferred, if only because his, and only his, is consistent with the rocklike integrity of Socrates' character attested in both Xenophon and Plato.

But before we get to worrying whether or not Socrates' defence was sincere, what we would like is some sort of answer to a prior question: how did he ever come to such a fix? If he was in fact one of the most pious men in Athens (on this both Xenophon and Plato agree), how could his enemies have thought that an indictment of him for *impiety* could be made to stick? Once the second of the four differences between Socrates[x] and Socrates[P] above is noticed, a good clue to the answer is at hand: if Socrates had espoused and practiced the cult-oriented piety Xenophon ascribes to him, the prosecution's chance of getting a lot-selected court (packed by traditionalists, as it was bound to be) to vote for a conviction on this charge wouldn't have had a prayer. What lot-selected Athenian court would have convicted of *impiety* someone who had been "most visible of men" in cult-service to the gods (*Mem.* 1.2.64)? Accordingly, to rebut the charge of "not believing in the gods of the State," the first thing Socrates[x] does is to assure the court that he had often been seen "sacrificing in the common festivals and on the public altars" (*Ap.* 11; *Mem.* 1.1.1). Socrates[P], on the other hand, makes no allusion to whatever sacrificing he may have done. What he gives the court instead is something traditionally minded Athenians would have found baffling as *evidence of piety:* his dedicated philosophizing on the streets of Athens.

Socrates[P] does not even tell the court that *he believes* in the city's gods. The god whose missionary he says he has been in Athens he leaves anonymous throughout his speech—never calling him by his proper name, Apollo, nor by any of his cult-names (Phoebus, Pythius, and the like). Claiming that he has been "the god's" gift to the city (*Ap.* 30e), that this god is the city's god, Socrates[P] never *says.* Well, does Socrates believe in the city's gods? The point is moot. His gods, like the city's, are true supernaturals—mysterious beings in a world apart, endowed with powers to invade at will our own and cause in it changes unaccountable by natural causes. But unlike the city's gods, Socrates[P]'s gods never lie, rob, rape, kill innocent people. His gods are *incapable* of doing any of these things. Socratic dialectic has stripped them of their most dreaded attribute: power to destroy anyone who incurs their ire.

So what is Socrates to do? Is he in a position to offer the court what our authors believe he does—"a straightforward, scrupulously truthful, sincere defence" against the charge of not believing in the city's gods? To do so he would have had to clean out the Augean stables of the Olympian pantheon, explaining to his judges the difference between his gods and theirs in words they could understand. Imagine a free-thinking radical Christian preacher, unorthodox but devout, defending the bona fides of his gospel before a Church court packed with Bible-belt fundamentalists. Socrates' plight is as bad or rather worse, for unlike our Christian who would happily regale his court with a verbal marathon on liberation theology, Socrates is hamstrung by his conviction that lecturing is impotent to impart truth: he rejects it on principle. To show his judges why true gods could never be the cause of evil he would have had to go at them one at a time, engaging them in elenctic argument to disabuse them of their conceit of wisdom and help them to find their own way to previously unknown, unimagined truth. Since this option is denied him, what else could he do in all sincerity but what Plato has him do: affirm positively his loyalty to "the god" and let his judges make of it what they will?

But I have yet to come to the gravest of the difficulties we all have to face in our effort to make sense of Socrates: what to do with his famed *daimonion*—that inner voice which has been coming to him since childhood? Socrates[x], revelling in this gift, works it as Socrates' private oracle, rivaling the public ones in giving him foreknowledge of future events for the benefit of friends and himself. Our authors rightly disdain to credit Socrates with such occult prognostications. They do, however, concede that through his *daimonion* Socrates has "direct and certain access" to "some moral truths." They are not unaware of the pitfalls of allowing him two distinct, independent paths of knowledge-seeking—one of them human, rational, argumentative, hence unavoidably fallible in its results; the other divine, suprarational, emanating from the infinite wisdom of God, yielding the finality and certainty to which the conclusions of elenctic argument could never aspire. So they try to restrict to the utmost whatever knowledge of the latter sort they will allow Socrates to get through the *daimonion*. They insist that what Socrates could get by this means is "next to nothing . . . virtually worthless in the pursuit of truth Socrates seeks philosophically." But how could it be "next to nothing" if by this means Socrates could count on getting, as they claim he does, access to some moral truths straight from God—truths which are "logically independent of whatever beliefs he may have about the nature of virtue?" And how could it be "virtually worthless" in Socrates' pursuit of philosophical truth if, as they maintain, his confidence in the validity of his whole method of philosophical investigation is derived from the *daimonion* ("the god would not sanction a deceitful instrument")? Surely, something has gone wrong.

They would not have got themselves into this muddle if they had taken account of the fourth of the differences between Socrates[p] and Socrates[x], noted above. Only the former makes rational argument the court of last appeal in the search for truth: "not now for the first time but always I have been the sort of man who is persuaded by nothing except the proposition which seems best to me when I *reason about it*" (Plato, *Crito* 46b). Though our authors have minded Plato's dialogues for information on disputed points, this text they must have missed: they never quote it or refer to it in any way. Conversely they fail to trace out the implications of that crucially important word by which Socrates refers to his monitions from "the god": the *daimonion*.

As grammarians have noticed, that word (literally, *the divine*) is "elliptically substantial"—an adjective flanked by a semantic hole where a substantive must be understood. What is that substantive? The "divine" *what*? Plato's text leaves no doubt as to the answer: "the divine *sign*" (*sēmeion*). Socrates refers to it as "his customary sign" (*Ap.* 40c) or even as just "the sign" (*Ap.* 41d). So his *daimonion* is his susceptibility to certain peculiar subjective states he takes to be signs from the god. These signs are not self-interpreting. They call for interpretation which is left entirely for Socrates to supply, allowing him to use his reason to his heart's content in the process. So what "the voice" tells him can never constitute a "divine revelation" in the proper sense of this term ("disclosure of *knowledge* to man by divine or supernatural agency" *OED*).

That those peculiar subjective states in Socrates' head are caused by divine or supernatural agency he never doubts. But that they constitute *knowledge* he never says—certainly not when he refers to the most important of the ones into which he reads the "command" of his god "to philosophize, examining himself and others" (*Ap.* 28e). Contrary to what our authors maintain, knowledge from this source Socrates does not claim. He doesn't say he *knows* that the god has commanded him to philosophize, but that he "believed and assumed" that he was so commanded, in other words, that this was the meaning of the signs (the "voice," prophetic dreams, etc.) from which he inferred that this is how he should spend his life in the service of the god. The correctness of this interpretation would not be "logically independent of whatever beliefs he has about the nature of virtue." It would be entirely dependent on the structure of the beliefs on which he based that interpretation and on the reasoning which convinces him that the god's goodwill for the Athenians would be well served by a Socrates who dedicated his life to philosophizing on the streets of Athens.

Nothing in Socrates has been more perplexing to posterity than his *daimonion*. It was this side of him that provoked Voltaire to say in a bitchy aside that Socrates was "un peu fou ou un peu fripon." A less sturdy rationality could easily have been destabilized by Socrates' susceptibility to those strange mental states he called "his *daimonion*." It was a remarkable achievement to domesticate that unpredictable little beast, keeping it as a source of personal reassurance, but never allowing it to trump rational argument as a source of knowledge. How this could have been missed by our conscientious and well-informed authors, I shall not try to explain. But let me insist: despite errors of judgment, like those I have pointed out, they have written a good book. If their scholarship had been less exact, if their claims had been vaguer and less scrupulously documented, their mistakes would have been harder to nail down.

4

SOCRATES ON POLITICAL OBEDIENCE

AND DISOBEDIENCE

IN THE *CRITO* (51b–c) Socrates proclaims the duty of political obedience in terms which are, to all appearance, unqualified:

> In war, in court of law, *everywhere,* one must do as one's state and fatherland command, unless one can persuade her that the command is contrary to the nature of justice.

In the *Apology* (29c–30c) he seems to imply a no less unqualified right of political disobedience:

> If you were to say to me, "Socrates, this time we will not listen to Anytus, we will let you off, but on this condition: you must no longer engage in this search of yours and philosophize: if you are caught doing so you will die," if you were to let me off on this condition, I would say to you: "Athenians, I am fond of you, I love you. But I will obey the god rather than you. As long as I have breath and strength, I will not stop philosophizing."

> Whether you listen to Anytus or not, whether you let me off or not, I will go on doing as I have been doing, even if I were to die many times.

No man has ever prized self-consistency more than did Socrates. He tells Callicles in the *Gorgias* (428b–c):

> As for myself, I would rather that my lyre were out of tune, or a choir I was training, and that the greater part of mankind should dissent from me and contradict me, than that I should be out of tune within my own single self.

Can it be that in the matter of political obedience Socrates was out of tune with himself?

One would have thought this question would hit between the eyes every critical reader of the dialogues. How strange then to see it persistently ignored. For example: We read in G. R. Morrow's [517] *Plato's Cretan City* (Princeton, 1962)—the most massive contribution of the past decade to Plato's political theory—that

From *The Yale Review* 63 (1974):517–34. Used by permission. Minor changes have been made in punctuation.

there is no hint in any of the dialogues that Plato recognizes the right of civil disobedience. A citizen may try to persuade the laws that they are wrong, as Socrates put it in the *Crito* (52A), but he may not disobey.

What then of the passage I have just cited from the *Apology?* Does Socrates say there that if "the Athenians"—the sovereign arbiter of law in Athens—were to command him to stop philosophizing he would try to persuade them that the command is wrong but that, if persuasion failed, he would obey? Does he not say unequivocally that if he were so commanded, he would disobey? Morrow does not tell us what we are to make of this. There is no allusion to our passage in the *Apology* in his copiously documented book.

This way of taking the statement in the *Crito* as Socrates' first and last word on political obedience in total oblivion of what appears to contradict it flatly in the *Apology,* is fairly typical not only in our own time but in the past as well. Here is an example from the eighteenth century. It is from David Hume's essay "Of the Original Contract" (1748):

> The only passage I meet with in antiquity, where the obligation of obedience to government is ascribed to a promise, is in Plato's *Crito,* where Socrates refuses to escape from prison, because he had tacitly promised to obey the laws. Thus he builds a Tory consequence of passive obedience on a Whig foundation of the original contract.

Hume must have read the *Apology.* Could he have really thought its Socrates an advocate of "passive obedience?" Hume does not say. He gives no hint of having ever faced the question.

On those comparatively rare occasions on which scholars have faced the question, the encounter has not produced a convincingly reasoned resolution of the problem. If space allowed, I would review the most promising efforts and try to explain just why, in my opinion, they don't quite crack the puzzle. But I need all my space for the solution I want to offer here. I shall argue that there is no inconsistency between Socrates' stand in the two dialogues, because the reasoning by which he justifies [518] obedience in the *Crito* will itself show that a man with those reasons for obeying the law in the circumstances of the *Crito* would have as good reasons for disobeying it in the very different circumstances which he conjures up in the *Apology.*

His reasons for obedience are introduced as follows in the *Crito* (49e–50a):

> SOCRATES: If one has made with someone an agreement which is just, ought he to keep it? Or may he shuffle out of it?
> CRITO: He ought to keep it.
> SOCRATES: Then consider: If we were to go out of here without the state's consent, would we be injuring those whom we ought least of all to injure, or not? And would we be keeping our just agreements, or not?

Here are two distinct questions, and we would expect Socrates to take up each in turn, explaining exactly what the question is, what reasons for saying "yes" to it, and with what implications and complications. So doubtless Socrates would have acted if he had continued to speak *in propria persona*. But in a curious act of self-abnegation—an act without parallel in the Platonic corpus—he yields the floor to a majestic surrogate, the personified "Laws and Community" of Athens, and they go on to deliver so un-Socratic a speech that George Grote called it "a discourse of venerated commonplace." There is no dialectic here: no definition of terms, no facing up to obscurities and perplexities, no consideration of counterexamples. Time and again we see the diction running to hyperbole and the thought blown about by gusts of feeling. I for one cannot but regret this feature of the *Crito,* and when Paul Shorey assures us that the dialogue is a "masterpiece of art," I would retort that Plato would have served us better by leaving this kind of art to the rhetoricians and sticking to his own Socratic last. But neither would I doubt that, for all its high-flown oratory, the harangue of the Laws is meant to develop a line of reasoning which in a different dramatic setting would have been laid out in the familiar Socratic style. Let me then try to reconstruct this, taking out of the impassioned homiletics just what will go over into cool argumentative prose.

First, the contention that if Socrates were to break jail he [519] would be "injuring those whom we ought least of all to injure." This is (in part) how it is argued in the exalted language of the laws:

> And since we brought you into the world, and gave you nurture and culture, can you deny that you are our child and our servant, you and your forbears before you? This being the case, would you think of putting yourself on a level with us in the matter of justice, so that it would be just for you to retaliate for whatever we do to you?

> Are you so clever that you cannot see that your fatherland is entitled to even greater honor and respect than are your father and your mother and all your ancestors—that she is more sacred and more highly esteemed by gods and by men of understanding—and that when she is angry with you, you should be more forbearing and gentle than towards your own father: you should do whatever she bids, unless you can persuade her to excuse you; if she orders you to suffer in silence stripes or imprisonment, if she sends you into battle to be wounded or die, you should obey.

> In war, in court of law, everywhere, one must do as one's state and fatherland command, unless one can persuade her that the command is contrary to the nature of justice. (50e2–7; 51a7–b6; b8–c1)

And here is all I can salvage from this extraordinary passage: Those who in times past have rendered us enormous benefits have put us under an obligation of gratitude which entitles them to special forbearance on our part. The greatness of our debt to them will warrant our bearing many risks and sacrifices to spare them injury. For the same reason, in dealing with them, we would forego certain forms of self-defense which might result in harming them. Thus, if one's father were to speak brutally to one or to strike one in a fit of anger, one would not be justified in resorting to harsh words or counterblows, as one might against a stranger. Socrates' native state, being his greatest earthly benefactor, much greater than his parents, has an even stronger claim on him of the same sort. So, even if on occasion, as in the present instance, it would subject him to an injustice, he must submit, he must not hit back, he must refrain from any action that would cause it serious harm.

That such an argument has force I would not dispute. But [502] how far will it take us? The crucial question, deliberately left unanswered in the more guarded language I have used, is, What are the limits within which a beneficiary owes grateful compliance to his benefactor? In the looser rhetoric of the text, it sounds as though there were *no* limits. Could Socrates have really meant this? He could not, surely, in the case from which he reasons by analogy, where the benefactor is the parent: My father, let us say, did well by me in all the ways a father should, gave me affection, a good home, the best of schooling, and a fine start in my profession. But then one day, at age thirty, I find out that he has been leading a double life, half of it as a pillar of suburbia, the other half in Cosa Nostra, where he now finds himself in trouble and calls on me for help—the kind of help I could only give him by getting into the underworld myself. Would anyone seriously impute to Socrates the notion that filial gratitude now obligates me to become a part-time gangster? How then could we credit Socrates with the notion that gratitude to the fatherland would clamp on one the moral obligation to act immorally at its behest? Let me construct an example from an episode within Socrates' own lifetime.

In the fourth year of the Peloponnesian War, Mytilene, one of the states in the Athenian League, revolted to join Sparta. The populace of the island, recruited into the army by the ruling oligarchs to fight off the force Athens had sent against the rebels, turned against their rulers and made them surrender the island to the Athenian general on terms to be decided in Athens by the Assembly. When that body met to debate the terms, Cleon, the reigning demagogue, moved a proposal whose ferocity was without precedent in recorded Hellenic history: that all the adult males of Mytilene should be executed, and all the women and children sold into slavery. The motion carried. If implemented, it would have been the nearest thing to genocide that Greece had ever known. And the barbarity of the measure was aggravated by its indiscriminateness: it treated the people of Mytilene as though they had shared their rulers' offense against Athens, while everyone knew that the people, having no voice in the oligarchic government, could not be [521] held morally responsible for their government's action in the first place and that moreover they had opposed and frustrated its action when arms were put into their hands.

Now let us imagine Socrates receiving a lawful order to cooperate in some

RITTER LIBRARY
BALDWIN-WALLACE COLLEGE

way with the execution of that motion, e.g., required to convey it to the captain of a warship in the Peiraeus who is to sail at once for Mytilene and see to it that the decision is carried out there by the Athenian force. Would Socrates really say that because of the great benefits he has received from Athens in times past he is now morally obligated to be a party to this infamy? Would he not rather reckon his very gratitude to Athens a positive reason for declining? In the *Apology* (34b–35d) he explains why he does not grovel, plead for mercy, and bring his wife and sons to weep and wail on his behalf, by saying that such conduct is dishonorable—it would distract the judges from their proper job, which is not to yield to sentiment but to give sober judgment— and if he stooped to it, he would be *disgracing Athens*. By the same token, in my example, his love for Athens, his solicitude for her good name, would interdict obedience. By defying the order, or by derailing its execution, he would have helped reduce the moral blot on Athens. He would have shown the world his fatherland bred also men of a different stripe from Cleon, men who would rather die themselves than be accomplices in such a crime.

I trust I have already given grounds for thinking that the "everywhere" in the citation could not be meant in the unqualified way in which it occurs there: if it did, it would belie the import of the supporting argument. Gratitude could not be a reason for yielding everywhere to the demands of a beneficent fatherland; in given circumstances it would itself be a reason for resisting her demands.

Now for Socrates' other reason for law-obedience: he must obey the law because he made a compact or agreement to obey it. Just by residing in Athens after he had attained majority and had become acquainted with her laws in comparison with those of other states, he had put himself on record as agreeing to obey and is now honor-bound to keep the agreement. [522]

His reasoning here is even more elliptical than before. He ignores the question that would have been flung in his face had this been a dialogue instead of a harangue: "What business have you to say that you made an agreement or compact when you never *said* anything to anybody to this effect, made no oath, signed no deposition, and all you can point to is that you acted in a certain way?" This is a reasonable question, indeed an unavoidable one, for without a clear answer to it the rest of the argument would be a blur: we literally would not know what it is all about, since it is so strongly premised on the notion of a tacit or nonverbal contract. Let me then answer on Socrates' behalf.

If there were actions that generate obligations *equivalent* to those resulting from agreements or compacts, then we could call them "tacit (or, nonverbal) agreements" to call attention to this property of theirs. Are there such actions? Yes, many. Here is a very simple one. I pick it to bring home the generality of the notion; so my taking it not from Socrates' world, but from ours, should not be held against it.

Think of what happens when we take our place in a line of persons waiting their turn. Just by queuing up behind them, and then moving along with them as the queue moves on, we are understood to be agreeing to follow the rules that govern this practice. We incur the same obligations as we would have if, on arrival, we had said out loud, "I know the rules of the queue and I promise to stick to them." If we had said that to each of the people who were already there and kept repeating it to everyone who joined the queue thereafter, our obligation to obey those rules would have been no greater; no further obligations would have been generated by tacking on that rigmarole.

One of the things which this example shows is that tacit agreement can generate obligations of unquestionable validity even in circumstances where it is highly questionable that we had a free choice in taking the relevant action. Suppose I have just missed my plane to San Francisco and must exchange my ticket to catch the next flight out. I go to the only desk where this [523] may be done at the airport and find five others ahead of me. Do I have a "free choice" on whether or not to join the queue? In the plain and natural sense of that term, I don't: I have no viable alternative; there is, literally, no other way of making the next flight to San Francisco. To assure me that I do have alternatives after all, you would have to fall back on the fact, if it is a fact, that I do not have to take the next flight to San Francisco or, perhaps, that I do not have to get there at all—that is to say, you would have to argue that I do have a free choice in respect of the ends to which queuing up here and now is the indispensable means. But once those ends have been set by sufficiently weighty considerations—say, that I am a highly skilled brain surgeon, the only one available for the required operation—I have no choice but to join the queue. If I happened to be a bizarre sort of anarchist, who thinks the queue is a mechanical, depersonalizing practice, or has other conscientious or aesthetic objections to it, I would just have to lump them and queue up with the other robots. Would that annul or even diminish the self-obliging consequences of my act? No.

Thus, suppose that as I near the desk an elderly couple of my acquaintance turns up, headed for the same desk, looking very frail and worried. Seeing what a hardship it would be for them to start at the end of that slow-moving line, am I free to bring them into the line, just ahead of me? I am not. If there were only one of them, say just the wife, I would be free to give up my own place to her, turning over to her all the waiting time I have earned myself. What I am not free to do is to take from the people behind me without their consent time which they have earned under the same rules and hand over the package to my elderly friends. That would be cheating. That my getting into that line had been a forced choice for me in the first place would make no difference: it would not give me now the right to bend the rules in my friends' favor.

But, of course, this is not the end of the matter. Suppose that as my friends approach I see that one of them is gravely ailing and in imminent danger of collapse. That *would* make a difference. I would then feel free to bring them into the line and [524] stay at their side to see them through their business at the desk. I would feel not only free, but morally bound, to do this, and would have no hesitation in saying so in response to dirty looks from the hatchet-faced lady just behind me. Why so? Well, why are the rules of the queue themselves obligatory in the first place? Because of the moral character of this practice—that of an *ad hoc* mutual benefit association, an austerely equitable one, exacting equal sacrifices from everyone who enters it to produce by means of just those individual sacrifices common benefits distributed on equal terms to their producers. But the sacrifices are minuscule and the benefits too are modest enough. And it is consonant with our sense of justice that a person who is in clear and present danger of great and irreparable harm is entitled to special treatment. This is what happens here. My obligation to observe the rules of the queue is overridden by another obligation which I judge to stand higher under the norms of justice—the very norms which give the rules of the queue their morally obligatory character in the first place.

In elucidating Socrates' notion of a tacit agreement by using this example, I introduced a modification that is needed to free that notion from a plausible but false and quite gratuitous assumption that accompanies it in the text. The Laws tell Socrates that he is duty-bound to obey them because he has had all along the option of staying in Athens or moving out, so that his staying was a free choice on his part, expressing his preference for the law and government of Athens to those of states to which he could have moved. That he had hardly set foot beyond Attica except on military service, that he had reared his family in Athens—such things are taken as conclusive evidence that the Athenian legal order was more to his own liking than that of any other state. To quote:

> So strongly did you prefer us and agree to be governed in accordance with us that, among other things, you bred children here—so much to your liking did you find the city. . . . You did not prefer to us either Sparta or Crete, which you used to say are well-governed, nor any other Greek or barbarian city: you got out of Athens no more than did the lame, the blind, and the maimed. (52c–53a) [525]

What is this but the now familiar "love us or leave us" line? And is its sophistry less transparent here than in its present-day applications? Suppose that, born and reared in state X, I go on living in that state, though well acquainted also with the laws of states Y, Z, and W. Does that show that I prefer the laws of X to those of Y, Z, and W? Might I not have a thousand other reasons for staying put?

Think of Socrates' own case. In Athens he had by birth full civic rights—a privilege he would not have had anywhere else in the world, and could not have expected to get, for ancient states had no regular provision for naturalization. Among these rights which Athens guaranteed to him was free speech:

there was probably more of this in Athens than anywhere in the world and, in any case, vastly more of it than in a place like Sparta or Crete, which were notoriously intolerant, xenophobic, and logophobic. In Athens Socrates had a better chance to meet in argument the leading lights of Greece—both foreigners, like Gorgias, Protagoras, Prodicus, Hippias, and natives, like Critias, Sophocles, Aristophanes. Are these not reasons enough for staying in Athens to bring up his family there—not to speak of others, including the obvious one that had he moved to a foreign state he would have robbed his children of that most precious birthright: civic status. Why then assume that since he had not emigrated, he must have preferred—and "strongly preferred" —the Athenian legal order to every other in his world? And as for saying that he could have emigrated had he chosen to do so, there *is* a sense in which this would be true—it would have been physically possible, and also politically: he *could* have had his exit visa. But in just that same sense the brain surgeon in my example could have abstained from joining the queue—he could have opted out of that operation in San Francisco on which his patient's life depends. This sacrifice of competing values, which could be sternly prohibitive in so many cases, is forgotten in the discourse of the laws when they insinuate that Socrates had been living in Athens with a kind of political menu in his hands which listed the legal orders of contemporary states and offered him his pick for the asking. [526]

So this part of the argument should be cut out, and I have suggested how very simple would be the needed surgery. All would be well if Socrates would agree on the following definition for his notion of a nonverbal agreement:

A given action constitutes such an agreement if, and only if, it generates obligations equivalent to those which would have been incurred by a verbal agreement.

This frees the notion from the assumption that the obligations are generated because the action is chosen from among viable alternatives to each of which it is preferred. This assumption is in any case unnecessary, since Socrates says quite enough to give us to understand that he has another ground of obligation, at bottom the same as for the queue of my example: the action is self-obligating because by means of it the agent draws upon a pool of benefits which is secured by the cooperation of the beneficiaries and is distributed justly among them. To say that this is what Socrates has in view is not, of course, to say that he has spelled it out—this, all too obviously, he has not— but that he has an intuitive sense of it whose explication, had he been able to achieve it, would have involved my formula or something like it. In the text we see him refer to different parts of it, without quite managing to pull them together into a tight pattern. He refers for one thing, as we saw above, to the enormous benefits he derived from having been reared and having lived within the Athenian legal order. Moreover, he implies that this legal order is just. For he refers explicitly to the substantive justice of the content of the nonverbal agreement he has made with the Laws. He does so in the statement I quoted earlier which begins, "If we have made with someone agreements which are just," and ends, "would we be keeping our just agreements, or not?" To say this is to imply that agreements generate moral obligation only if, and because, they are in accord with justice. So he must think of the Athenian legal order which he is bound to obey in virtue of the "just" agreement he had made, as itself a just legal order. That he so thinks of it is also apparent when he represents the Laws as saying: [527]

> We have distributed to you and to all other citizens all of the fair things it was in our power to bestow. (51c)

Athenian law, as Socrates thinks of it, is not oppressive but beneficent, and not in a niggardly way but to the limit of its ability; and its beneficence is impartial: the "fair things" it bestows are not for a privileged minority but for "all the citizens," for the whole of the civic body.

Here then is how Socrates' reasoning would have looked if it had been made fully coherent, with the obvious gaps filled in, and the implicit appeal to the idea of fairness worked bodily into the argument: The legal order of Athens is an association which produces for all of its citizens great benefits of individual security, welfare, and culture. Law-obedience is the form in which every citizen pays his dues to the collective enterprise. By exercising the rights of citizenship in a state like Athens, he gives his fellows to understand that he agrees to carry his individual share of the aggregate burden, undertakes in all fairness to do his part, as he expects them to do theirs. To disobey the law is to default on this undertaking; that is why it would be like breaking a promise: it would be welshing on a commitment which is not the less real for being tacit.

If we explicate the Socratic rationale of law-obedience in some such way as this, we can see how it would work at a point where it gets out of line with that miniature I used as a model of an obligation-fraught action. In the queue of my example, we have a single set of rules of uniformly sterling moral quality. In the Athenian state, we have a medley of rules of varying moral quality: some of them would measure up to our highest ideals of justice, while others, at the opposite end of the spectrum, would strike us as savagely unjust. Moreover, in this state, as in any other, we must reckon with legally authoritative actions by officials and official bodies whose justice is similarly variable: perfectly just upon occasion, approximately just much of the time, at times flagrantly unjust—what could be more unjust than the decision of the court that sentenced Socrates to death? This being the case, how shall we construe our obligation [528] vis-à-vis the state? Shall we answer, as did Thoreau in his famous essay, "The only obligation I have a right to assume is to do at any time what I think right?" This would be obviously correct if our state were a celestial society whose legal order could be counted on to be invariably just.

In this dream of a state, we could say what Thoreau did, since we would be assured in advance that we would never be required to do anything except what we think right and would only think right what is right. But the conditions which would make Thoreau's dictum tautologously true would also make it politically irrelevant: under conditions such as these, what need would there be of what we call a "state," i.e., of an association whose first premise is that a reliable public order has to be guaranteed by coercion when persuasion fails?

The Socratic rationale of political obligation, as I have reconstructed it, is built to the specifications of human, not angelic, nature. Its morality is not a fantasy. When Socrates thinks of the injustice of the court's verdict as a possible reason for absconding, he has the Laws reply:

> Was that our agreement? Or was it that you would abide by the verdicts of the adjudications of the state? (50c)

And why should the latter have been the agreement? Because only so would there have been any chance of operating on a fair and equitable basis that mutually beneficent civic partnership of which the judicial process is a vital part. That when disputes arise on whether the law has, or has not, been broken in a given case, these should be adjudicated by due process and that parties to the dispute should be bound by the outcome of that process—this is the very heart of a legal order. In accepting the benefits of that system, we are "agreeing" to this feature of the system along with the rest of it, knowing in advance that there are bound to be unjust, no less than just, judicial decisions and that there can be no antecedent guarantee that when we ourselves are up for trial the decision will be just. How can we help "agreeing" to all this, if we are going to "agree" to the existence of a legal order? Or are we going to say that we do [529] "agree" to it, but only so long as the unjust decision never hits us? Would that be fair? Would it not be claiming a privileged exemption from one of the unavoidable risks of the cooperative partnership, a risk everyone must carry if the scheme is to work?

"But if that is the right way to understand agreement as a ground of political obligation in the Socratic theory," you may now ask, "would it not confirm Hume's reading of the *Crito?* Would not the theory turn out to have a 'Tory consequence of passive obedience'?" It would not. What the theory tells me is that I am under the obligation to obey the system as a whole and that this extends to every one of its laws and lawful commands, be they just or unjust. This obligation I also have on the ground of gratitude, which I discussed above. But this ubiquitous obligation does not expunge others which are distinct from it and on occasion might go contrary to it, so that I could only discharge one or more of these by disobeying the law. To be sure, Socrates does not say so in the *Crito.* Had he done so, his position in this dialogue would not have been so persistently misunderstood as a "doctrine of absolute submission" to the state. But elsewhere, in the first book of the *Republic*, commonly recognized as one of the early, Socratic, dialogues, we can see that he is well aware of possible collisions between duties.

The example there (331c) is well known: If I have promised a friend to return to him on demand a lethal weapon and, when he comes to claim it, I see that he is deranged, I ought not to do as I have promised. Why not? Has the obligation to keep promises now lapsed? Of course not. This is always there—but only as *an* obligation, one among many. Another obligation under the rules of justice is to refrain from doing anything in one's power which would cause directly catastrophic damage to a friend or, for that matter, as Socrates explains in the same dialogue (334b–335e), to any man, friend or foe. When these two obligations collide, the former must give way. What causes them to collide? Circumstances. In ordinary circumstances there is no conflict between the obligation to keep promises to one's friends and that of acting with due concern for their welfare [530]. But there are contingencies— rare, but not impossible—in which they do conflict. When this happens, we are not only free to break our promise to our friend, we ought to do so: it is our moral duty. If we were to return that weapon when it is clear that this would cause his death, his blood would be on our hands, and the fact that his blood was spilled by the keeping of a promise would not wash them clean.

In restating the reasoning behind Socrates' example in the *Republic*, I imported the modern distinction between what one has an obligation to do and what, on balance, one ought to do. This has no precise counterpart in Plato's vocabulary or, for that matter, in that of any Greek moralist of the classical period. But the substantive distinction is very much within Socrates' line of vision as is clear from his example, and we need only apply it to his rationale of political obligation in the *Crito* to see how it squares with his declaration of dutiful disobedience in the *Apology*. There is no inconsistency because the circumstances are so different. Just think how very different they are:

The disobedient action contemplated in the *Crito* would not have been open defiance of the law, but fraudulent evasion of it, involving lying and the corruption of public servants. Hence it could not have counted as what we have come to call, after Thoreau and Gandhi, "civil disobedience," for this occurs only when a member of a rule-governed society chooses to break its rules publicly in order to protest an injustice. Since protest is of its essence, such an action is in itself a statement—"symbolic speech," as constitutional lawyers have come to call it in this country. Hence, if the action is to qualify as civil disobedience, the meaning of its statement must be clear and its sincerity must be convincing. Those who witness it or hear of it must not be left in doubt on these two points. Just from the action itself, they must be able to see what the agent is saying by means of it and that he means what he is saying. Both conditions are met perfectly by the disobedience to which Socrates commits himself in the *Apology*. People who saw him holding forth as usual in the marketplace in open violation of a court order or law that had just made this conduct punishable by death would not [531] be left in any doubt of what it was that Socrates was signaling across to them by means of it or of the authenticity of the signal. Not so in the *Crito*. If the news were to get out that Socrates had broken jail and skipped over the border to Boiotia, is it at all likely that the action would be read as a protest against the injustice of his condemnation? The possibility is so remote, it is not even mentioned in the *Crito* when the pros and cons of the escape are debated: escape is read there only as saving Socrates from execution. It is only under this description of the action that the contemporary reader is called upon to assess its morality. It is taken for granted that what it would exemplify would be subverting a just law to save one's skin, not breaking an unjust law to protest injustice. Once the action is seen in that light, how could a man like Socrates have countenanced it for a moment? If a man who had made throughout his life such extraordinary professions of virtue were now to lie and bribe his way out of a judicial penalty, hundreds of others would feel licensed to do the same, especially among the youth that idolized Socrates. What damage that would have done to Athens, whose libertarian institutions could only work if they elicited a large measure of spontaneous, uncoerced, law-obedience. Moreover, what appeal would the skin-saving operation be expected to have for a man who had shown so little eagerness to prolong his life at the time of his trial? He had then publicly scorned exile as an alternative to the death penalty. If he were to escape now, he would be taking by dishonorable means what he could have had then honorably for the asking. His legs would now give the lie to his words. The indifference to death he had professed would be shown up as a sham, a theatrical pose, and he would reach his foreign destination a dishonored, discredited, man.

Consider, conversely, what he would have to do if he were to obey the command in the *Apology:* give up his philosophic quest. He tells his judges how he thinks of this. It is a service to the state which represents the greatest benefaction he or any man has ever rendered it (30a). Moreover, it is his "service to the god," (23c, 30a), his obedience to "the god's command" [532] (28e). What he means by his service to Athens is clear enough: "the unexamined life is not worth living by man" (38a); so his dialectic, which teased and mocked and bullied and bludgeoned his interlocutors into self-examination, opened up to them the possibility of a life worth living by man. What he means by his service to "the god" is far less clear, concealed by multiple skins of irony which it would take another essay to peel off. But this much is clear, as everyone would agree: it represents to him a duty which stands to any merely human duty as does the majesty of the gods to the pettiness and brittleness of man. How then could his duty to obey the state require him to give up the vocation which is his duty to "the god" *and* to the state *and,* not least, to himself? He had discharged this duty throughout the greater part

of his adult life and found such happiness in it that now at age seventy, looking back on it, he sees death as a gain if it enables him to go on plying his craft
in Hades: to argue there with men like Odysseus, he tells his judges, would
make him "inconceivably happy" (41c). He reminds his judges that he had
proved in battle his willingness to risk his life in obedience to lawful command (28d–e). But to obey *this* command, he would have to give up something he had prized more than life, and which the state should have valued
more than obedience: his moral identity. The character Socrates had created
for himself—the person he had come to *be* for his own and all subsequent
generations—would have been shattered had he now chosen to muzzle himself at the behest of the state; by prolonging his physical existence on those
terms he would have committed moral self-destruction. Of what use would
such a wreck of a man be to Athens? What fidelity to any lesser duty could be
expected from a man who had betrayed what he believed to be his highest
duty?

But if all this is true, you may object, why does not Socrates say so in the
Crito? Why does he leave us with that inflexible universal "on the battlefield,
in court of law, *everywhere,* one must do as one's state and fatherland command?" Why does he not qualify? If it is the word, "everywhere," that is
troubling you, your objection is verbal, and I can meet it by reminding [533]
you that the logic of his position does indeed leave him with the obligation to
obey state authority *everywhere,* but without expunging other obligations because of which there would be times and places when he ought not to obey.
But your objection may be a different one. What you may want to know is
this: if Socrates does recognize the relevance of that distinction, why does he
not use it here? Why does he not apply it to the obligation to obey the law in
the *Crito* as he applied it to the obligation to return to deposit in the *Republic?*
The answer lies in a pedestrian fact, whose very obviousness is apt to keep it
from our view when we peer into the bottom of the well, looking for some
profounder truth. If we look, as we should, not to the incidental sentence in
which the word "everywhere" occurs, for this may be only part of the inflated
rhetoric of the passage—it will be plain that this argument does not address
itself to the general question, "Should every citizen of any state in any circumstances whatever obey the law?" but to the sharply particularized question,
"Should this citizen of this state in these circumstances obey the law?" What I
have tried to show is that one who had Socrates' reasons for a "yes" to this
concrete question would have compelling reasons for a "no" to the abstractly
general one.

5

SOCRATES ON *ACRASIA*

I DEALT with this topic briefly twelve years ago in an introduction to the
Protagoras,[1] designed for the use of beginners in philosophy. The medium tempted me to simplifications which I have since had occasion to
regret. But I have no great confidence that if I had then dealt with the topic in a
more leisurely and thorough way I would have managed to avoid the blem-
ishes of that earlier treatment. For I would not have had the benefit of the
discussions that were to follow. More was to be contributed on this topic by
English-speaking scholars in the following nine years than had appeared in the
preceding forty.[2] From criticisms of my own views and from new ideas that
have appeared in this literature, I have learned more than I could possibly
acknowledge in detail.[3] Though they have not altered my basic interpretation
of the Socratic position, they have led me to understand it more clearly and at
a deeper level. With this help I have made a fresh study of the main text in
which the Socratic thesis is advanced and defended: *Protagoras* 352a–358d,
whose results I now wish to present.

I. THE SOCRATIC THESIS

It is announced as follows in the opening paragraph of our passage: "If a man
knows good and evil, nothing will overpower him so that he will act otherwise
than as knowledge commands" (352c). There are three things here which call
for clarification. I shall speak of these briefly, and then go on to another matter

From *Phoenix* 23 (1969):71–88. Reprinted by permission. Minor changes to spelling and
punctuation have been made. It is a pleasure to offer this paper to my esteemed friend, George
Grube, whose own interpretation of the argument in *Prot.* 351b ff. has both clarified my understanding of it and stimulated me to keep working on it over the years. For bibliographical references here and hereafter, see the works listed at the end of the article under the author's name.

[1] Listed in the bibliography below.

[2] The main contributions by English-speaking scholars in the preceding period are in the papers
by Grube, Hackforth, Stocks, and in the books by Grube, Shorey, and Taylor; since 1956 in the
papers by Allen, Bambrough, Gallop, Gulley, Santas, and Sullivan, and the books by Crombie
and Walsh.

[3] My greatest debt is to the two papers by Professor G. Santas and to correspondence with him.
I must also acknowledge my great debt to Professor David Gallop, not only for his excellent
critique of my previous views in his published paper but also for detailed comments on an earlier
draft of the present paper which have helped me to make some useful revisions.

which also calls for consideration, before proceeding in the next Section to analyse the arguments Socrates puts up in defence of his thesis: [71]

(1) The only actions the thesis has in view are those the agent "wants" to do[4] or "chooses"[5] to do or does "intentionally."[6]

(2) From a statement that comes later, after the argument is completed, it might look as though the thesis is meant to cover also actions which go contrary to what we *believe* to be evil (or less good than others open to us at the time), even if we do not *know* them to be such:

> . . . No one will do something if he knows (*eidōs*) or believes (*oiomenos*) that a better one is open to him. . . . Then no one intentionally goes after evil, or what he believes to be evil; it is not in human nature, it seems, to go after what one thinks to be evil instead of good. (358b, c)

But the original statement above and all of its subsequent restatements throughout the debate speak only of the power of *knowledge*—not of belief as well. Knowledge, says Socrates, is a "powerful, lordly, and commanding thing," not to be "dragged about like a slave" by pleasure, pain, and passion (352b, c). No one would seriously suggest that Socrates would have wished to say the same thing about belief ungrounded in knowledge. In all of the early dialogues, moral virtue is construed in terms of knowledge.[7] Socrates' only interest in true opinion ungrounded in knowledge is polemical: he brings it up only when attacking its master-manipulator, the sophist.[8] So the citation from 358b,c could scarcely have been meant to suggest that in the absence of knowledge true opinion would do as well for the purposes of Socrates' thesis. What it probably means is that we cannot act contrary to what we believe *when we do have knowledge*.[9] If it did mean more than this, we would [72]

---

[4] *ethelō*, 355b2, 358d2.

[5] *haireomai*, 358d3.

[6] *hekōn*, 358c7.

[7] Compare the Socratic definition of courage as *knowledge* (*sophia* in *Prot.* 360d, *epistēmē* in *La.* 194e–195a) of what is and is not to be feared with the Platonic as "the power and unfailing conservation of true and lawful *belief* about things which are and are not to be feared" (*Rep.* 430b; cf. 429c). And note Aristotle's stress on the role of knowledge in the Socratic doctrine of acrasia (*E.N.* 1145b21–27, 31–34 and 1147b14–17) and of moral virtue (*E.N.* 1144b28–30). (For the meaning of *acrasia*, see n. 16 below.)

[8] *Gorg.* 454d. I should explain that I consider the second part of the *Meno* (80b5ff.) to be an exposition of Platonic, i.e., not Socratic, doctrine. That right opinion is as good a "lord" (*hēgemōn*—cf. *hēgemonikon*, *Prot.* 352b4) of action as is knowledge (97a, b) is a break with Socratic doctrine (fully as much as is the theory that knowledge is recollection); it is used (96e–97c) to refute the Socratic thesis that "virtue is knowledge" which had been adopted provisionally (as a "hypothesis") at 89a–c.

[9] No such thing, of course, is said in the text. But it can be reasonably inferred from the fact that in the above citation from 358b,c Socrates is not advancing a new thesis but merely summing up what he thinks (with the consent of the company) has been proved in the foregoing argument (352a–357e). Gulley, who takes a different view (92: he understands Socrates to mean that either

not know what weight to attach to the claim; we would have to treat it as dogma unsupported by argument, since all Socrates attempts to prove in the argument he has just concluded is that we cannot act contrary to our *knowledge* of good.

(3) A terminological point: "good" and "evil," and their comparative and superlative forms, are used in the debate to express both first-order and second-order valuations, without any alternative expressions or any auxiliary linguistic devices to mark off the difference. When Socrates says that the man who knows "good" will never be "overpowered" so as to choose "evil" instead, he is speaking of the goodness or badness of courses of action, particularized in concrete situations as viable alternatives between which the agent has to choose.[10] These are good or bad *on the whole* or *all things considered,* since they are generally (invariably, in the examples in this passage) mixed bags of "goods" and "evils" of another sort: they are complexes of components to which first-order value assignments have already been made. Saying that an action is *good or bad* is a second-order value-judgment which is, in principle, a computation:[11] we are supposed to (*a*) itemize the goods we would gain and the evils we would suffer both now and in the future by choosing a given action, (*b*) assign numbers to the values in each of the two

---

knowledge or belief will do), does not explain how he squares it with the fact that there is no argument for a power-of-belief thesis in our passage (or, for that matter, anywhere else in the early dialogues). Perhaps he thinks (though he does not say so) that a parallel argument for a power-of-belief thesis could be extrapolated from the one for the power-of-knowledge thesis in our passage. This would ignore the fatal disanalogy between belief and knowledge which is implied by what is said in 356d–357a, where "the power of appearance" is contrasted with that of the "measuring art" (356d4ff.) or "knowledge" (357a1): the latter "saves our life" (356d3; e2; e8–357a1) because it delivers us from the "wanderings," the "ups and downs," the reversals (356d4–6) of mind to which we are prey so long as we have nothing but the former to guide us and bring us serene stability (356e1–2) instead. To have belief without knowledge would be to live in "the power of appearance" and hence to lack that stability of conviction so essential for moral self-control: If at a given moment one believed that X is better than Y, one would be able to withstand Y (which could be a very juicy morsel indeed) only if one were able to hang on to that belief for dear life; if that belief was not grounded in knowledge then, according to Socrates, it would not have the requisite stability and could shift, at the very next moment, to the contrary belief that Y is better than X after all, in which case one could have the juicy morsel with an easy conscience. (Compare the way Plato tackles this problem in *Rep.* 412e–413c and 429c–430b, when he had become convinced that for most people virtue could not be a matter of knowledge, but only of right belief (cf. preceding note), so that, in their case, self-control would depend on the firmness of *extra-cognitive* supports of tenacity of belief—a problem which never bothered Socrates, since for him virtue was always assured of a rock-like base in knowledge.)

[10] This would be a sufficient reason for his use of the articulate neuter plural, *t'agatha kai ta kaka* here (352c5) and frequently thereafter in the course of the debate, since he is thinking throughout of the particular goods and evils the agent has to weigh in reaching a considered choice.

[11] It is supposed to be comparable to operations we perform in determining the magnitude of the spatial dimensions and weights of physical objects (356a8–b3; c8–d3).

categories, and (c) pronounce the action "good" or "evil" depending on which of the two aggregates is the larger.[12] [73]

Now for a substantive point which is only implicit in the discussions but is crucial for my interpretation of the passage: Socrates puts no restrictions on what we are to count as good and evil in our first-order valuations. His only explicit requirement is that we are to aggregate them rationally and thereby "measure" the value of the actions between which we choose. He does assume, of course, that our first-order valuations will not be perverse or mad; it is not likely that he would recognize as "knowledge" of good and evil the result of a computation which included among the first-level items a sadist's glee at another's pain or a maniac's preference for the destruction of the universe to the scratching of his finger. But once one has allowed for such tacit exclusions, what surprises one in this passage is the high degree of moral permissiveness Socrates seems to display, his willingness to waive on this occasion his usual insistence that the goods of the soul be given the highest of priorities and ranked far ahead of physical pleasure, comfort, health, or safety.[13] Of this moral gradient there is not a word, not even a hint, in this discussion. In the examples the higher goods are systematically ignored. Only the following are mentioned as actions known to be good: taking physical exercise, dieting, and submitting to medication and surgery; living within one's income; accepting military service.[14] Now why should Socrates pitch his examples so low in this debate? The most likely explanation is that he wants to meet his adversaries on their own level of first-order preference-rankings. These people are the general mass, "the multitude." He cannot count on them to have discovered, as he has, the superiority of the things of the spirit. But things like [74] health, financial solvency, and imperial patrio-

---

[12] The Socratic procedure in this passage invites comparison with the Bayesian model of deliberation in present-day decision theory (see, e.g., Jeffrey, ch. 1) in spite of glaring differences: Socrates' description of the measurement of pleasures and pains by analogy with that of physical lengths and weights (356a8ff.) shows that he has no inkling of the difference between a "ratio scale" and an "interval scale" of measurement (for a lucid explanation, see Rapoport 24–28), the former of which could have no valid application to the ordering of pleasures and pains; more generally, Socrates talks in a way which suggests that he is unaware of the difficulties in the way of measurement of subjective items like pleasures and pains—difficulties which modern decision theory seeks to surmount by resorting to the notion of subjective probability to give meaning to the assignment of cardinal values to goods and evils (see Jeffrey, ch. 3; Rapoport 30ff.). Socrates' conception of his model of deliberation is unsophisticated, and the model itself is archaic, taking no account of risk as such in contradistinction to utility or desirability and thus being unable to do justice to decisions under conditions of risk. In spite of these and other differences, the affinity of the two models is unmistakable; both make the fundamental assumption that in principle first-order valuations can be represented by numbers and second-order ones by the end-results of algebraic additions.

[13] As, e.g., in the *Apology,* the *Crito,* and the *Gorgias,* and even in the *Protagoras* itself in the latter part of the protreptic dialogue with young Hippocrates (313a–314b).

[14] 353c–354b.

tism[15] he can be sure will fall within the ambit of their own sincere first-person evaluations. And he is content to work with these throughout this debate.

Indeed, to say he is "content" to do this would be to understate the point. He is eager to do it, and for a good reason: Most cases of acrasia[16] occur when the agent is only half-convinced of the goodness of an action, accepting the conventional judgment of it with an undertone of doubt tinged with resentment, suspecting it will be others, not himself, whom it will really benefit.[17] Socrates, on the other hand, is absolutely sure that all morality, from its lowest to its highest ranges, represents the dictates of enlightened self-interest.[18] For this he would have been quite prepared to argue—on this as on any other occasion.[19] But had he done so here, he would have sidetracked the debate. How then, in default of such an argument, could he have hoped to block off counter-examples which he himself would consider spurious—cases in which our supposed knowledge of the good we betray has no grounding in our own unconstrained, sincerely felt, convictions about good and evil? Only by resorting to some manoeuvre that would keep the argument on terrain which represents common ground between himself and his present adversaries. To execute this manoeuvre, he needs some sort of theoretical cover. He finds this in the hedonistic premise he foists on the "multitude" in this discussion. [75]

This, I submit, is the most promising solution to that long-standing puzzle: the fact that Socrates should have based his whole argument on the premise that "good" is logically convertible with "pleasant," and "evil" with "pain-

---

[15] καὶ πόλεων σωτηρίαι καὶ ἄλλων ἀρχαί, 354b4—a realistic, if unpleasant, characterization of the average Athenian's motivation when shouldering civic obligations as burdensome as hoplite service. Pericles is even more explicit in Thucydides: the common weal on which the Athenian citizen's personal safety and welfare depends (2.60.2–4) involves the maintenance of *turannis arché* over other states (2.63.2; the very same point rubbed in by Cleon for a different purpose, 3.37.2).

[16] I use *acrasia* and *acratic* as the English words they have now become for all practical purposes in recent philosophical discussions, anglicizing the spelling accordingly. None of the terms by which the Greek word has been translated into English are exact equivalents: "incontinence" has sexual connotations which are singularly inappropriate in notable instances of acrasia (e.g., Achilles' failure to control his anger, or a soldier's bolting in the face of danger). "Weakness of will" or "moral weakness" are somewhat better, but neither "will" nor "moral" answers to anything strictly connoted by *akrasia*.

[17] What is called *allotrion agathon* by Thrasymachus in *Rep.* 343c.

[18] For Socrates not only morality, but even love or friendship, has a self-interested motivation: cf. the doctrine that *philia* is for the sake of utility in the *Lysis* (210c, d; 215d; 218e–219a) with Aristotle, *E.N.* 1156a 10–12, "those who love each other for the sake of utility do not love each other for themselves, but because of some benefit they get from one another" and his definition of *philos*, "one who wishes and does good [to his *philos*] . . . for the sake of his *philos*, or one who wishes for the existence and life of his *philos* for that person's sake," 1166a3–5 (cf. 1156b9–10 and 1168b2–3; also *Rhet.* 1361b36–37 and 1380b35–1381a1).

[19] As, e.g., in the arguments against Polus and Callicles in the *Gorgias*.

ful." That this is meant to express out-and-out hedonism there is no good reason to doubt;[20] we know that Plato used it for this very purpose in the *Philebus;*[21] and while this is a much later dialogue, neither is there evidence that Plato's use of these terms had changed in the interim.[22] Just how then does this premise find its way into the debate? To get the clearest possible answer to this question, it is essential, I think, to straighten out the logical relations of three distinct propositions which are involved in the discussion: the first is the logical convertibility of "pleasure" with "good" and of "pain" with "evil"; let us call this assertion "*H*" for the hedonistic position which it epitomizes. Now *H* is logically equivalent to the conjunction of

(*A*) All pleasure is good and all pain is evil

with

(*B*) All good is pleasure and all evil is pain.

A and *B,* taken singly, express radically different views: *A* tells us that pleasure is good, but not that it is the *only* good; the latter is precisely what is expressed by *B.* Similarly in the case of pain: it is *B,* not *A,* which says that pain is the *only* evil. Clearly, then, one could assert *A* while denying *B;* in that case one would be taking up a very mild and moderate position to which the overwhelming majority of philosophical moralists, ancient and modern, would subscribe. Only if one went so far beyond *A* as to assert *B* would one be committing oneself to hedonism.

That Socrates himself would hold *A* is only to be expected. And since *B* is uncongenial to his whole moral outlook[23] and since he says nothing in the course of the debate which directly commits him to *B,* his position must be "*A* but not *B.*" As for the "multitude," it looks at the start as though they would not even concede *A:* they are said [76] to call "some pleasant things evil, and some painful things good" (351c4). But when the argument gets under way, Socrates has little trouble in showing that they balk at *A* because of an elementary misunderstanding: they have been calling actions "pleasant" and "painful" only if they are *immediately* such; once it is explained to them that the

---

[20] At this point I am rejecting the view I adopted in 1956 (xli) that the convertibility of the two sets of predicates is only meant to assert "(a) that pleasure is *a* good (not the only one), (b) that whatever is best will in fact be the most pleasant."

[21] 60a, where it is associated with the view that pleasure is the *orthos skopos* for all living creatures, the one at which "all ought to aim"—a formula which comes very close to that used in the *Protagoras* in the argument with the "multitude" (354b7–c1; d8–e1).

[22] In 1956 I had assumed that there had been such a change (without suggesting that there was textual evidence of it), in order to explain the problem with which one is left if one does grant that Socrates' argument for his thesis in our passage is predicated on a hedonistic premise (I had called attention to the gravity of his problem, xl, n. 50). I now see an alternative solution to the problem (see the penultimate paragraph of the next section) which can dispense with that assumption.

[23] Cf. xl–xli of my Introduction (1956).

pleasure and pain which present actions yield in the future must also be taken into account, they agree at once that those actions which are pleasure-enhancing (or pain-reducing) both now and hereafter are good, and those which are pain-enhancing (or pleasure-reducing) in the same way are evil (353c9–354b7); so they have no reason for disagreeing with *A*. And the line of questioning Socrates employs to push them as far as *A* actually pushes them much farther: he extracts from them the admission that, in judging a given course of action good or evil, they look to *nothing but* its yield of pleasure and pain:

> Is it not evident to you . . . that these [courses of action] are evil *for no other reason* (*di' ouden allo*) than that they eventuate in pains and deprive you of other pleasures? . . . And those [other courses of action], are they good [in your judgment] because their outcome is pleasure and the cessation or prevention of pain—or because of something else? Or can you say that you call them "good" *with an eye to any aim other than pleasure and pain?* It is my opinion that they would say: "We don't."[24]

And to say this would be, of course, to agree to *B*. [77]

---

[24] 353e–354a1; 354b–c2. The same point is hammered in twice over again in the rest of the paragraph and gets even greater prominence near the start of the next paragraph (354e8–355a5). As has been often pointed out, in these passages Socrates makes it exceedingly clear to the "multitude" that they, and they alone, are bearing the burden of this assumption; he gives them repeatedly the chance to dump it, if they have second thoughts about it. Sullivan rightly insists on the significance of this point. But he fails to see that *only* here is the "multitude" shown to be committed to *B*. He does not realize that the formula that "pleasures *qua* pleasures are good and pains *qua* pains are bad" (his excellent paraphrase of 351c4–6) is only a statement of *A* and is not equivalent to *H;* he calls the formula a "formal" commitment to hedonism (21; and cf. 23, where Sullivan cites 351c as stating that "good = pleasure *simpliciter*"). Surely this is false: "pleasure *qua* pleasure is good" is perfectly consistent with, say, "knowledge *qua* knowledge is good" or, for that matter, with there being umpteen other things as well, *F, G,* etc., such that *F qua F* is good, *G qua G* is good, and so forth. I suspect that Sullivan failed to clarify in his own mind the distinction between propositions *A, B,* and *H,* and to interrogate our text accordingly; had he done so, he would have surely read 351c4–6 and 351e1–3 quite differently. However, there *is* something in the passage which may have misled Sullivan and other excellent commentators who have also read these two texts in the same way (Taylor, 258; Hackforth, 41; Grube (1933), 205). This is the fact that at the end of this paragraph Protagoras talks as if Socrates' statement in 351e1–3 *were* equivalent to the *identification* of "pleasant" and "good" (351e3–7, where τὸ αὐτὸ . . . ἡδύ τε καὶ ἀγαθόν is obviously meant to formulate the proposition under debate). But that *Protagoras* should say this in no way commits Socrates; all it reveals is the confusion of Protagoras' immediate state of mind (he has been taking quite a beating in the debate and is badly rattled by this time), for a moment earlier (d1–2) he had given an *entirely different* statement of the disputed proposition—ὡς τὰ ἡδέα τε ἀγαθά ἐστιν ἅπαντα καὶ τὰ ἀνιαρὰ κακά—a letter-perfect formulation of *A,* which only in a daze could any serious philosopher confuse with the *identification* of "pleasant" with "good," least of all the Protagoras of this dialogue who, a few lines earlier (350d–351a), had made a special point of the nonconvertibility of the "All *S* is *P*" type of proposition. There is no indication in the text that Socrates agrees with Protagoras' last remark: ignoring it, he proceeds to give a new, positive, turn to the debate, with a fresh start at 352a1, after which Protagoras is virtually cashiered as an active contributor to the discussion.

We can now see how the two parties stand in the debate *vis-à-vis* the hedonistic premise, *H*. The "multitude" is stuck with it, since they are shown to admit both *A* and *B*. But not Socrates: he does not join them in conceding that actions are to be reckoned good or evil only with a view to pleasure/pain. But if he does reject *B*, why does he not say so? Because this would open up another big issue, sidetracking him from his immediate goal, which is to make good to the "multitude" his great claim about the "power of knowledge." To avoid this diversion, he contents himself with vindicating his claim *within a limited area:* that zone of moral choice in which he too would admit that one can make sound judgments even if one takes nothing but pleasure and pain (immediate and eventual) into account. There are cases, thousands of them, in which not only those low characters, those people of the multitude, but even the most upright of men (Socrates himself, for instance) could reach correct assessments of the goodness or badness of actions without resorting to any standard other than that of pleasure and pain. In these cases the convertibility of "good" with "pleasant" and of "evil" with "pain" need not be challenged; it may be taken as simply expressing a normal principle of low-grade moral choice. If Socrates' thesis about the power of knowledge is true, it should work in these cases. And if it does work here, it will not follow that it will work only here. We shall see in the next section that Socrates' argument for the "power of knowledge" is so constructed that one part of it—a logically self-contained part—is not logically tied to the hedonistic premise.

II. SOCRATES' ARGUMENT FOR HIS THESIS

Professor Santas (1966, pp. 5–7, 12–13) has given an excellent account of the strategy of Socrates' argument against the "multitude": he does not undertake to prove to them directly that a counter-example to his thesis could not occur but rather that if, *per impossibile,* it did occur, their own explanation of the supposed occurrence would turn out, on investigation, to be "ludicrous" (*geloion*); and by "ludicrous" in this connection he could only mean that it would be either self-contradictory, or else at variance with truths so obvious and so firmly established that [78] no one in his senses would want to gainsay them. Socrates undertakes to press this indictment against that explanation of acrasia which he takes to be by far the most common of all: that men who know the better will do the worse because they are "overcome" or "defeated" by desire for pleasures.[25] Let us call this proposition "*M*" (for the "multitude" who are supposed to hold it) and formulate it more exactly, retaining Socrates' own

---

[25] ὑπὸ τῶν ἡδονῶν ἡττᾶσθαι, 352e–353a, which I take to be an ellipsis for "being defeated [by desire] for pleasures." This is the only way in which pleasure could be thought to "defeat" or "overcome" an intentional agent.

expression, "defeated by pleasures," for acrasia, which is supposed to occur because the gent's desire for certain pleasures proves stronger than his desire to do X, knowing this to be better than an alternative, Y, which is also open to him in that situation:

(*M*) Knowing that X is better than Y, one chooses Y because one is defeated by *pleasures*.

Socrates moves against *M* by exploiting (355b–c7) the convertibility of "good" and "pleasure," to which the "multitude" have agreed.[26] Substituting "goods" for "pleasures," he transforms *M* into

(*Mg*) Knowing that X is better than Y, one chooses Y because one is defeated by *goods*.

This move, Socrates feels, pushes his adversaries out of a highly plausible, self-confident position into one which is so shaky on the face of it, that he immediately pronounces it "ludicrous" (355c8–d3).[27] But just why? What is there "ludicrous" about *Mg?* The answer comes in the following stretch of dialogue (355d1–e3), where the prosecutor is that "insolent fellow," Socrates' rude-spoken *alter ego,* called in here as in the *Hippias Major* (286c ff.) to rub the opponent's nose into the [79] dirt, while Socrates with the supposed concurrence of Protagoras (hence the "we") does the answering for the multitude:

How ludicrous is the thing you are saying—that

(*1*) [=*Mg*] a man, knowing that certain things are bad and that he ought not to do them, does them, defeated by goods.

(*2*) "Are the goods then, in your estimation,"[28] he will ask, "unworthy or

---

[26] As I explained above (penultimate paragraph of Section I) what the "multitude" have been made to agree to is *H,* the conjunction of *A* and *B,* and this is doubtless all Socrates means when he sums up their view as asserting (*i*) "that the good is nothing but pleasure and evil nothing but pain" (355a1–2), which he understands to entail (*ii*) that "good" and "pleasant" are "names" for the same thing, and that so too are "evil" and "painful" (355b5–c1 and 5–6). Now (*ii*), taken at face value, amounts to saying that the relation of the two terms in each pair is *identity.* But Socrates surely means no such thing; the primitiveness of his logical vocabulary, as recorded (or simulated?) by Plato, could be responsible for the overstatement here (as also earlier in the dialogue, 329d1; 349b1–6, where "wisdom, temperance, courage, justice, and piety" are all said to be names "of one thing," while it is perfectly clear from the accompanying argument that all that is meant is *that any two of them are logically convertible.* Cf. my Introduction [1956], liv, end of n. 10). Both (*i*) and (*ii*) must be understood as asserting no more than the reciprocal implication, or convertibility, of the two predicates. So must the expression used by Protagoras in 351e5–6.

[27] A development anticipated already at 355a.

[28] I take the sense of *en humin* to be the one mentioned (but rejected) by Adam *ad. loc.,* "before your tribunal," comparing *Gorg.* 464d5, *en paisi diagōnizesthai.* Guthrie translates the sentence, "Am I to suppose that *the good in you* is or is not a match for the evil?" The phrase I have italicized is similarly rendered in the Apelt translation as revised by A. Mauernsberger and

worthy to overcome the evils?"[29] Clearly, we shall have to say that they are not worthy; otherwise the man who, we said, had been defeated would not have erred.

(3) "How then," he will ask, "could goods be unworthy of evils, or evils of goods? How else than when these [i.e., the goods] are greater and those [the evils] are smaller? Or when these are more numerous, and those less numerous?" We shall have to agree.

(4) "So it is clear," he will say, "that this is what you mean by 'being defeated': taking greater evils in exchange for[30] fewer goods."

The language is loose and clumsy by modern standards, but not intolerably so, and there can be no doubt of what Socrates means at each step of the reasoning. The question is whether a man will choose to do or to refrain from doing a bad action, Y. The hypothesis, *1*,[31] is that the man chooses to do Y, knowing it to be an "error"[32] (a bad [80] choice, the choice of the bad alternative). From just that it is inferred in *2* that the goods in Y are not worth ("are not worthy to overcome") its evils: for if they had been, the choice of Y would not have been the "error" which, by hypothesis, it is. *3* goes on to lay down the general principle that the goods in a given option are worth its evils if, and only if, when both are aggregated the aggregate goods exceed the aggregate

---

A. Capelle: "Dann ist also *das Gute in euch nicht* wurdig, das Schlechte zu besiegen?" If the reference were to a struggle between good and evil in the agent's soul, the pronoun would have been in the third person singular: the agent is spoken of consistently in the singular throughout the argument. Moreover, the notion of a "struggle in the soul" (which has so often been read into this sentence) is quite irrelevant to the specific question which is being asked here. All the questioner wants to know is how the "multitude" (*not* the acratic man) would estimate the comparative value of the goods and evils in the alternative options: do *they* think that the evils exceed the goods (and in that sense are "worthy to overcome": see next note), or the reverse? Cf. Gallop 123n. 6, who gives further reasons against the Guthrie rendering but apparently clings to the notion that the people to whom the question is being put are somehow merged with the acratic man whose soul is "the seat of conflict" between good and evil.

[29] For the meaning of "worthy to overcome," see Gallop 124.

[30] For the meaning of *anti*, see Stocks 102–4: "*anti* is used of compensation. The noun in the genitive which follows it is the *compensating good*." He compares *Lysis* 208e, *Phaed.* 255e.

[31] Which is formally equivalent to *Mg*. To see this, we need only rewrite *Mg* as, "Knowing that Y is worse than X, one chooses Y because one is defeated by goods." The difference of this from *1* is clearly only a matter of wording.

[32] The use of *exēmartanen* in 355d6 connects the formulation of the thesis about acrasia with which Socrates works in this whole passage with the crisper formula *oudeis hekōn hamartanei*, often ascribed to Socrates in the scholarly literature, though Socrates himself never puts his own thesis in just that form in the Platonic dialogues (for an approximation to it, see *Gorg.* 509e5–7), possibly because this formulation gives no scope for the recognition of knowledge (as distinct from true belief or opinion) and because *hekōn* is not free from ambiguity: it may carry the narrower sense of "willingly, not reluctantly" (as, e.g., at *Prot.* 345e ff., especially at 346b7–8, οὐχ ἑκὼν, ἀλλ' ἀναγκαζόμενος) rather than the broader sense of *intentionally*.

evils. Hence, the conclusion in *4*: the hypothesis, *1*, is discredited, having been shown to entail (via *2* and *3*) that the man chose Y, whose aggregate goods did *not* exceed its aggregate evils, thus knowingly preferring the lesser good represented by Y to the greater good represented by his other option, X.

Just how then does this argument show that *1* is "ludicrous"? When one first comes across this proposition in the text, one gets a strong impression that Socrates considers it a kind of self-contradiction. This is how it struck me when I wrote the Introduction in 1956,[33] and I do not think that I have been the only one to take it in this way.[34] A closer study has convinced me that this interpretation simply will not fit the text. To get anything like a self-contradiction out of *1*, we would have to understand it to mean

> (*1a*) Knowing that Y is the worse option, the agent chooses it because of his desire for *good* (i.e., for good as such).

This would indeed be a patently self-refuting account of acrasia. For if a man's choice *were* actuated by his desire for good, it would be the choice of the better option, i.e., the very choice which the "defeated" man did *not* make. Hence the proposed *explanans*—desire for good—would belie the *explanandum*—the fact that the worse option was chosen. But to get *1a*, we have had to make an inconspicuous, but by no means negligible, departure from the text: in *1* the text speaks of the man being defeated not by "good," but by "good*s*."[35] And it does so for good reason. The plural is mandatory, since Socrates' only warrant [81] for pinning *1* on his adversaries is its derivability from their own professed view *via* allowable substitutions. But this is the form in which their adherence to *M* had been expressed in the text a few lines earlier (355a6–b3):

> You say that it happens often that a man, knowing that evils are evils, nevertheless does them, though it is possible for him not to do them, because he is beguiled and seduced *by pleasures*. And again you say that a man, knowing the goods, does not want to do them *because of the pleasures of the moment*, by which he is defeated.

The only correct substitutions for the italicized phrases would be "by goods" and "because of the goods of the moment," respectively. If so, the man's defeat would be explained not by his desire for good as such, but by his desire

---

[33] Though I only expounded this interpretation (xxxixff.) in glossing the *second* Argument (355e4ff.), which operates with the converse substitution of "more pleasurable" for "better." It is only on this assumption—that Socrates thought that *M* would be transformed into a self-contradictory statement by one or the other of the substitutions—that I maintained that Socrates offers a deductive proof for his thesis that knowledge is (i.e., is a sufficient condition of) virtue.

[34] So apparently Walsh, 54.

[35] Translating faithfully the plural of the text 355d3. It is true that the singular *tou agathou* had been used just before (c7); but this was only to refer collectively to the various particular goods which, it is being alleged, would "defeat" the victims of acrasia. Cf. note 10 above.

for those particular goods which he can have here and now if, and only if, he opts for Y. Amending *la* to implement this important difference, we get

> (*1b*) Knowing that Y is the worse option, the agent chooses it because of his desire for *its goods*.

And now we lose the self-contradiction in *1a*. We got self-contradiction there because only the choice of a good action could be presumed to be explicable by a man's desire for good. In *1b* this fails us: it is *not* true that the only choice one could hope to explain by a man's desire for a particular good or set of goods is the choice of a good action. There are many cases where a desire for a particular good—this sweet, this fortune, this woman—can only be satisfied *via* bad action, i.e., by actions which do offer us a seductive, head-turning good but are nevertheless *bad on the whole*. So while there is contradiction in "I choose this action, knowing it to be bad on the whole, *because I want good*," there is no contradiction in "I choose it, knowing it to be bad on the whole, *because I want this particular good* (which I can get only by choosing this action)." If Socrates had thought there was self-contradiction in the latter, despite appearances to the contrary, he would have had to argue for it; but the fact is that there is nothing in the text that could count as an argument for self-contradiction in *1b*.

Once this line of interpretation has been closed off, we are left with just one way of understanding how the argument from *1* to *4* was supposed to demonstrate the "ludicrousness" of *1*: Socrates must have thought the conclusion so incredible in itself as to discredit any proposition which entails it—hence to discredit *1*, which entails *4* via *2* and *3*. And that this must be the correct interpretation is confirmed by the very design of the argument. A man who, having made a charge, produces a sequence of propositions to prove it[36] would stop when, and only when, he has reached the proposition which he thinks clinches [82] the indictment.[37] Just what is there, then, in *4* that could be thought to do this? Nothing but the fact that here the *refutand* has been shown to entail that the man would choose the smaller good, knowing it to be the smaller. This is what Socrates takes to be so rank an impossibility that to confront his adversaries with this consequence of their thesis is to leave them speechless, utterly crushed.[38]

---

[36] This is clearly the force of the *ara* in e2.

[37] Though the argument against *M* continues (*M* is refuted all over again *via* the converse substitution of "more pleasurable" for "better," to be discussed shortly), *there is not one word of further argument for Mg* after 355e3. The praise of the "measuring art" which follows (356c4ff.) the refutation of *M via* the second substitution contains no additional argument against *M*. All it does is to point up *the consequences* of its refutation *via* the two substitutions: since (as has now been demonstrated) one who *knows* that X is better than Y cannot choose Y in lieu of X, we must look, for the "salvation of life," (356d, e) to the appropriate knowledge, i.e., to the "measuring art."

[38] Professor Gallop, who saw (118–19) that the interpretation of the charge of "ludicrousness" I had given in my 1956 Introduction was wrong, went on to argue that the refutation of *M* is not

But why so? What makes Socrates so sure that no one could knowingly choose the smaller of two goods offered him? He does not say. But there are two propositions from which this would follow, given *3* above:

(*S1*) If one knows that X is better[39] than Y, one will want X more than Y.[40]

(*S2*) If one wants X more than Y, one will choose X rather than Y.[41] [83]

(Here, as in *M* and *Mg* above, X and Y stand for exclusive alternatives between which the agent must choose at the given moment.) That Socrates takes *S2* pretty much for granted is clear from the fact that he repeatedly speaks of "wanting" (*ethelein*) a given option to express the very notion of choosing it—as, for instance, in the last period of the citation from 355a, b above, where "does not want to do them" is clearly an ellipsis for "does not want [and does not choose] to do them."[42] As for *S1*, this would follow from two fundamental Socratic tenets:

(*S3*) All men desire welfare.[43]

(*S4*) Anything else they desire only as a means to welfare.

---

meant to be complete until a much later point in the text (357d–e), because only then, Gallop claimed, Socrates convicts the exponent of *M* of self-contradiction and by the following reasoning: "The proposition under attack says that a man may know evil things . . . yet do them . . . , because he is overcome by pleasure. But if 'being overcome by pleasure' means 'being ignorant,' the proposition will be self-contradictory. For it will amount to saying that one could know a course of action to be evil yet take it needlessly, because one did *not* know it to be evil. The absurdity will consist in ascribing to the agent both knowledge and ignorance of the same thing" (119). In my opinion, this interpretation could not be right for a number of reasons (cf. Santas [1966], 12n. 14), of which the following (not in Santas) strikes me as the most conclusive. To be guilty of the alleged self-contradiction, Socrates' adversaries would have had to hold both *M* and the view that acrasia is due to ignorance; but the latter is Socrates' view, not theirs. To be sure, beaten into a pulp by Socrates' dialectic, they are left no option but to concede it in the end (cf. especially 357d1–3: "if you were now to laugh at us [*sc.* for our view that 'defeat by pleasure' is only ignorance], you would be laughing at yourselves"; that is to say: at this point you have been forced by the argument to acknowledge the very view you had been ridiculing a moment earlier). But this concession is extracted from them only *after* they had been compelled to give up *M* (they had no comeback at 355e3, nor yet at 356c3). So in their battered and chastened state, no less than in their previous arrogantly wrongheaded one, they would not sustain the charge: to be convicted of self-contradiction, a man has to maintain a thesis and its contrary *at the same time*.

[39] Here and in the sequel, "better" means "better for the agent"; cf. n. 18 above.

[40] A more complete statement would be, If *at a given moment* one knows, etc., one will want, etc., *at that moment*. The same addition should be made in the interest of completeness in *S2*.

[41] At this point I owe a great debt to an unpublished paper by my colleague, Donald Davidson. The formulation of the two premises follows closely two of his own which he discusses without reference to Socrates but which struck me at once, when I came across them, as going to the heart of the Socratic assumptions about intentional action whose corollary is the denial of acrasia.

[42] And cf. n. 4 above.

[43] *Eu prattein,* "to fare well," or "to do well," used interchangeably with *eudaimonein,* "to be happy" (cf., e.g., the substitution of *eudaimones einai* in *Euthd.* 282a in the restatement of a doctrine previously expressed by the use of *eu prattein* in 278e).

S3 Socrates states in the most explicit and emphatic way:

> Do not all men want to fare well? Or is this not one of these things which I feared a moment ago it would be ludicrous to question? For surely it is silly to ask such a question. For which man does not want to fare well? (*Euthd.* 278e)

Though "faring well" or being happy are never formally explicated, so much is clear: for Socrates, as for Plato and Aristotle after him, these terms denote the state in which good is possessed and enjoyed. So when Socrates declares that "everything men do, they do for the sake of good" (*Gorg.* 468b) and that "good we desire; what is neither good nor evil, and what is evil, we do not desire" (ibid. 468c), he is implying that, except for welfare itself and the goods which make it up, we desire things only as a means to welfare, i.e., *S4*. Given *S3* and *S4*, *S1* would follow: If a man knew that X is better than Y, he would know that he can get more good through X than through Y. So, given *S3*, he would want X, since it would secure him the increment of good and welfare which he would forfeit by choosing Y and, given *S4*, he would not want Y, for the converse reason.[44] And since the better of two actions could only be the one which secures to the agent the greater aggregate good (*3* in the above argument for *Mg*), the impossibility of choosing the lesser aggregate good in preference to the greater would follow. It [84] would be a consequence of *S2*, *S3*, and *S4*, all of which Socrates would take to be axiomatic truths.[45]

Having thus demolished *Mg* to his satisfaction, Socrates proceeds (355e3–356c3) to refute *M* all over again by exploiting the converse substitutability of "pleasant" for "good" (and hence of "more pleasurable" for "better"):

> (*Mp*) Knowing that X is more pleasurable than Y, one will choose X when one is defeated by *pleasures*.

To show that this is false, Socrates finds it sufficient to point out that if it were true the alleged "defeat" would entail choosing Y, while knowing that it is the more painful[46] of the two options, for the sake of the pleasures it offers, though "it is clear" (356a–d) that these are not worth ("not worthy to overcome") its pains. Why is this "clear"? Because the multitude had agreed[47] that

---

[44] The same implication in *Meno* 77c–78a: No one could desire evils, knowing that they are evils, i.e., that they would "harm him" or "make him wretched and unfortunate."

[45] Needless to say, the impossibility of choosing an option which one knows to be less good than another has enormous plausibility taken all by itself. This explains why Socrates does not deduce it on this occasion from other beliefs of his which do entail it.

[46] Literally, "knowing that it is painful" (*gignōskōn hoti aniara estin*, 355e7). Throughout the whole discussion, the wording pays little attention to the fact that all that counts in the choice between X and Y is their comparative, not their absolute, goodness or badness, pleasurableness or painfulness. The thought, of course, is unaffected by this blemish.

[47] Cf. n. 24 above.

pleasure is the only good, pain the only evil,[48] and it is now added that a given set of pleasures are worth a given set of pains if and only if the aggregate magnitude of the pleasures exceeds that of the pains. This being the case, it is implied that to choose Y, knowing it to be on balance the smaller pleasure-package, would be to knowingly prefer the smaller good to the greater, which is taken, as before, to be a patent impossibility, whose entailment by *Mp* refutes *Mp*. If his adversaries had not seen the impossibility of that consequence, Socrates would stand ready to derive it from the principle of psychological hedonism to which they had agreed at an earlier stage of the debate.[49]

The great difference between this argument against *Mp* and the preceding one against *Mg* is that here the refutation of *M* requires the premise that pleasure is the only good:[50] only this would warrant the [85] substitution of "more pleasurable" for "better." That Socrates should make this the high point of his refutation of *M* in this debate against "the multitude" is understandable. As we saw at the end of Section I above, Socrates has good reason to think that the defence of his thesis about acrasia will be specially effective against his present adversaries if offered them under a hedonistic umbrella. But what if he were addressing a different kind of adversary who would have cogent and clearheaded reasons for rejecting hedonism and would, therefore, scorn the Socratic thesis about acrasia if he thought it a logical dependency of the equation of the good and the pleasant? Would none of Socrates' arguments in our passage be usable against such an opponent? Has Socrates so tied his refutation of *M* to the hedonistic construction of good that if the latter were denied the refutation of *M* would fail? This is what I believed when I wrote my Introduction in 1956 and what many others have believed, from Hackforth in 1928 to Santas in his latest paper [1966].[51] It has now become clear to me that this is false.

---

[48] I.e., to proposition *B* (cf. the last three paragraphs in Section I above).

[49] I agree with Santas (1966, p. 10n. 12) that 354c3–5 should be construed as psychological hedonism, adding, however, that the formulation is vague and hasty, suggesting that Socrates had little interest in working out this doctrine. The passages cited by Sullivan, 19, as expressions of psychological hedonism are at best indirect evidence for this doctrine.

[50] I.e., proposition *B*, or *H* (which entails *B*).

[51] But Santas registers an important advance in pointing out that Socrates' argument in our passage "can be 'freed' from its hedonistic premises, in the sense that some other plausible Platonic [he means: Socratic] non-question-begging premises can be found which can be successfully substituted for the hedonistic premises," 20–21. I have taken the next step, which is to show (as I proceed to do in the text above) that one of the two arguments in the text, the one against *Mg*, is *already* free from dependence on hedonistic premises. The same thing would have been evident to Santas if he had not *imported* hedonistic premises into his analysis of the argument against *Mg*, reading all references to good and evil as references to pleasure and pain. Naturally, a hedonist would so read them. But in that case the equations "good" = "pleasant," "evil" = "painful," would be an extra premise supplied by the hedonist himself. There is nothing to this effect—in fact, not a word about pleasure or pain—in the text of the argument, nor yet in

For suppose I were to say to Socrates, "I despise hedonism, but I subscribe to M. Refute me, if you can"! Would he have any trouble in getting from our passage[52] all the ammunition he would need to blast me as effectively as he did the "multitude" in the text? Denied now the use of H (that "good" and "pleasant" are convertible) as a lemma for deriving Mg from M, would he not see that *he does not need H* for this purpose, since A (that all pleasure is good) would serve him just as well? For this master-dialectician it would have been child's play to see that if he got me to grant him A, I could not then fail to concede Mg, since "all pleasure is good" entails that "defeated by pleasures" entails "defeated by goods" and hence warrants the substitution of [86] "goods" for "pleasures" in M, which transforms it into Mg. Having thus forced me to Mg, he could proceed beyond it exactly as in the text. Everything in the present argument would tell as strongly against me as it would against a hedonist; for no support from H is needed, or offered, for *2* or *3* above, from which *4* follows directly. The same would be true in the case of the tacit premises ($S1$, $S2$, $S3$, $S4$), which Socrates would have invoked, if pressed, to justify at *4* the impossibility of anyone's knowingly preferring the lesser to the greater good: none of these depend at all on the convertibility of "good" and "pleasant" or on any other hedonistic premise. Thus the refutation of M by means of the refutation of Mg is a self-contained argument which would be as valid against non-hedonists as against hedonists, provided only the former granted that pleasure was *a* good, which was the general view among contemporary philosophers, rejected only by that fierce eccentric, Antisthenes.

One further observation, recording a by-product of the foregoing inquiry, which might nonetheless well be the most interesting of its findings: It concerns the import of $S2$, $S3$, $S4$,[53] the foundational tacit premises of the refutation of Mg. Each of them is plausible in the extreme, and their joint power is so great that Socrates could have relied on them alone to make a still more formidable assault on M than he achieves in either of the explicit arguments he deploys against it in our passage. For if those tacit premises were all true, one would not need to resort to a round-about attack on the doctrine of acrasia,[54] arguing that if it did occur the defeat-by-pleasure explanation of its occurrence would not work, and that a supplementary defeat-by-passion explanation would not work either.[55] Armed with those tacit premises, one could launch a

---

its tacit premises, if these are supplied, as they should be, from the known Socratic doctrine, to whose clarification Santas himself had made a distinct contribution in his 1964 paper.

[52] Including the false start, 351b3ff., where Socrates asks Protagoras if he will agree to proposition A (cf. n. 24 above).

[53] And $S1$, which is entailed by $S3$ and $S4$.

[54] Cf. the first paragraph of the present Section, for the indirection of the attack on acrasia in our passage.

[55] The defeat-by-passion explanation was mentioned alongside of the defeat-by-pleasure/pain in 352b, alluded to again in 352e1–2, and then dropped all through the subsequent argument which is solely directed against the defeat-by-pleasure/pain explanation. But at the end of that

perfectly direct attack, showing by the simplest of arguments that the occurrence of acrasia would then be an outright impossibility: Given *S1* (consequence of *S3* and *S4*), if we *know* that X is better than Y, we are going to *desire* X more than Y; and given *S2*, if we *desire* X more than Y, we are going to *choose* X in lieu of Y. How then could it ever happen that we should choose Y in lieu of X? The strength of the [87] Socratic thesis shows up to best advantage in those axioms of his which so connect desire with knowledge of good, on the one hand, and with choice, on the other, that the impossibility of choosing the option known to be the worse appears to follow inexorably.[56]

BIBLIOGRAPHY

Adam, J., and A. M. Adam, *Platonis Protagoras* (Cambridge 1893).
Allen, R. E., "The Socratic Paradox," *JHI* 21 (1960), 256–65.
Apelt, O., *Platons Dialog Protagoras*, 3rd ed., ed. A. Mauernsberger and Annemarie Capelle (Hamburg, 1956).
Bambrough, R., "The Socratic Paradox," *PQ* 10 (1960), 229ff.
Bluck, R. S., *Plato's Meno* (Cambridge 1961).
Crombie, I. M., *An Examination of Plato's Doctrines,* Vol. 1 (London 1962), 289ff.
Gallop, D., "The Socratic Paradox in the *Protagoras,*" *Phronesis* 9 (1964), 117ff.
Grube, G., "The Structural Unity of the *Protagoras,*" *CQ* 27 (1933), 203–7 at 205–6.
————, *Plato's Thought* (London 1935), 59–62.
Gulley, N., "The Interpretation of 'No One Does Wrong Willingly' in Plato's Dialogues," *Phronesis* 10 (1965), 82–96.
Guthrie, W. K. C., *Plato's Protagoras and Meno* (Penguin Classics: London 1956).
Hackforth, R., "Hedonism in Plato's *Protagoras,*" *CQ* 22 (1928), 39ff.
Jeffrey, R., *The Logic of Decision* (New York 1965).
Rapoport, A., *Two-Person Game Theory* (Ann Arbor, Mich. 1966), Ch. 2.
Santas, G., "The Socratic Paradoxes," *PR* 73 (1964), 147ff; "Plato's *Protagoras* and Explanations of Weakness," ibid. 75 (1966), 3ff.
Shorey, P., *What Plato Said* (Chicago 1933), 129–32.
Stocks, J. L., "The Arguments of Plato, *Prot.* 351b–356c," *CQ* 7 (1913), 100ff.
Sullivan, J. P., "The Hedonism in Plato's *Protagoras,*" *Phronesis* 6 (1961), 9ff.
Taylor, A. E., *Plato, The Man and his Work,* 3rd ed. (London 1929).
Vlastos, G., *Introduction to Plato's* Protagoras (Library of Liberal Arts; New York 1956), at xxxviii–xlv.
Walsh, J. J., *Aristotle's Conception of Moral Weakness* (New York 1963), 22–27 *et passim.*

---

argument, Socrates talks as though he has *also* demolished the defeat-by-passion explanation as well (357c4). He is evidently assuming that his explicit argument implicitly does this further job as well. How so? For a beautifully clear, fully satisfying answer, see Santas (1966), 20–22.

[56] An earlier draft of this paper, circulated among colleagues and students, had elicited (in addition to the detailed critique by Professor Gallop: cf. n. 3 above) a number of helpful criticisms—more of them than I could have tried to acknowledge by name. The revision and expansion of the paper was done at the Center for Advanced Study in the Behavioral Sciences at Stanford, where I was privileged to hold a Fellowship during a part of 1968.

6

WAS POLUS REFUTED?

POLUS THINKS that if one had to choose between *adikein* and *adikeisthai*—between wronging another and suffering wrong oneself—the former would be the better option. But he admits that it would be the "uglier" (*aischion*) (*Gorg.*, 474c). This admission (to which I shall refer as "*T*" hereafter), writes Professor E. R. Dodds, "proves fatal to his case, as Callicles will point out at 482d."[1] Is this a correct diagnosis of Polus' defeat? "Because of just this concession," says Callicles (*loc. cit.*), "he was tripped up in the argument and his mouth was stopped." Is this really true? So all modern commentators seem to have thought: I have not seen one word to the contrary in the literature.[2] I believe that this opinion is mistaken. It is not Polus' profession of *T* that proves fatal to his case, but his failure to keep his wits about him in the ensuing argument. [454] Had he brought a clearer head to this encounter, he could have stuck to *T* and passed unharmed through the elenchus, accepting its first three premises pretty much as they stand in the text, conceding the next two with reasonable qualifications, and rejecting its conclusion with logic entirely on his side. A brief review of the argument will, I trust, bear out this claim.

Here is a fairly literal translation of the essential lines in 474d3–475b1:

> SOCRATES. In the case of all beautiful things—such as bodies, colors, figures, sounds, practices—don't you call them "beautiful" with an eye to something?
>
> *1* For example, beautiful bodies to begin with: don't you call them "beautiful" either on account of their usefulness for some particular purpose or because of a certain pleasure, if they delight their beholder in beholding them (ἢ κατὰ ἡδονήν τινα, ἐὰν ἐν τῷ θεωρεῖσθαι χαίρειν ποιῇ τοὺς θεωροῦντας;)?
>
> *2* So (*houtō*) too in the case of all such other things as shapes and colors? Don't you call them "beautiful" either because of a certain pleasure (*dia hēdonēn tina*) or because of their usefulness or both? . . .

From *AJP*, 88 (1967): 484–60. Used by permission.

[1] *Plato: Gorgias* (Oxford, 1959), p. 249. I should like to take this opportunity to express my great debt to this book. I have found it the most valuable commentary on a Platonic dialogue to appear in English since F. M. Cornford's *Plato's Cosmology* (1937).

[2] While it is frequently stated or implied that Socrates here "established," "proved," etc. his own doctrine that to suffer wrong is better than to do it. For typical views, see, e.g., A. E. Taylor, *Plato, the Man and His Work* (4th ed., London, 1937), p. 114; P. Shorey, *What Plato Said* (Chicago, 1933), p. 140; J. Moreau, *La Construction de l'idéalisme platonicien* (Paris, 1939), p. 72; P. Friedländer, *Plato, the Dialogues: First Period* (Eng. transl., New York, 1964), p. 257.

3 And likewise (*hōsautōs*) in the case of sounds and everything else which pertains to music? . . .

4 And further in the case of laws and practices: does not their beauty fall within the scope of usefulness or pleasure or of both? . . .

5 And is not the beauty of things we learn (*to tōn mathēmatōn kallos*) the same? . . .

C So when one of two beautiful things is the more beautiful, it must be so by surpassing the other in one or the other or both of these two respects: pleasurableness, usefulness, or both. . . . And when one of two ugly things is the uglier, it must be so by surpassing the other in painfulness or in evil.[3] . . . [455]

There is no suggestion here that the conclusion (*C*) represents one of Polus' standing convictions. Socrates does not say or hint that he had found any such doctrine in Polus' book. Nor does he claim that *C* follows from anything Polus had said so far in this discussion. He mounts the above epagoge to win Polus' acceptance of *C* on the spot. Polus is therefore free to admit or reject it on its own merits or those of the argument by which Socrates purports to prove it. Let us examine the premises of this argument from Polus' point of view:

Premises *1, 2,* and *3* would cause him no trouble whatever, provided that a certain qualification, made expressly in premise *1,* is understood—as it should be from the wording of the text—to carry over into premises *2* and *3* as well. Bodies are said in premise *1* to be beautiful if (and only if) they are useful for their respective purpose or if they give *the viewer* a certain pleasure *in viewing them.* I have italicized the vital qualification which must also be understood to apply to the beauty of shapes and colors in premise *2* and then again (*mutatis mutandis*) to sounds and other elements of music in premise *3.* A close reading of the text should convince anyone that this is indeed what is meant. It is only for stylistic reasons that the phrase κατὰ ἡδονήν τινα, ἐὰν ἐν τῷ θεωρεῖσθαι χαίρειν ποιῇ τοὺς θεωροῦντας, is not repeated in premise *2* nor reproduced in a suitable variant in premise *3:* because the pace is very quick and Socrates clips his sentences, reducing verbal baggage to the absolute minimum. A second look at premise *2* will show that when he says καὶ τἆλλα πάντα οὕτω, he does expect the sense of the omitted phrase to be supplied from premise *1,* thereby specifying as before the import of the qualifying pronoun in *dia hēdonēn tina:* that "certain" pleasure is evidently, once

---

[3] There is no sculduggery in the substitution of "evil" for "harmfulness" at this point, nor was there any when Polus was made to substitute "good" for "usefulness" a little earlier (475a3) in lines I omitted from the citation. "Good"/"evil" can be used with this sense, and anyhow the outcome is unaffected by the substitution. Socrates would have got the same result by adding just one more step in his final assault on Polus: operating with the disjunction "more painful or more harmful" as the definiens of "uglier," Socrates, having secured the admission that wrongdoing is the more painful, could have proceeded to argue that, if it is uglier, *it must be more harmful* and, therefore, more evil. That extra step would have given Polus no chance to squirm out of the conclusion. On his view, no less than that of Socrates, what is harmful is indeed evil.

again, that which the viewer derives in viewing the objects. The same thing, with a verb for hearing substituted for *theōreisthai*, is meant to be understood in premise *3* to fill out the meaning of *hōsautōs:* the indicated parallelism would fail unless the pleasure to be had from beautiful sounds, melodies, etc. were felt by their hearer when he hears them.

Suppose now that, instead of going on to pile up more premises in the epagoge, Socrates were to draw his conclusion from *1, 2,* [456] and *3*. To cover in just the same way moral, political, and intellectual, along with sensible, instances of beauty, he would have needed only some such formula as this: the beautiful is that which is useful or else *that which delights those who see or hear or contemplate it.*[4] Call this definition *"D"* for convenient reference. Polus could have accepted this with perfect security: the admission would have been as harmless to his case as that of the Socratic premises from which *D* is drawn. Nor could Socrates himself object to it, since it remains scrupulously faithful to his first three premises.[5] The difference from *C* is nonetheless considerable: instead of "pleasure" without qualification in *C,* we have in *D* pleasure arising in sensuous apprehension or mental representation of an act or object. This would make all the difference to the outcome of the elenchus. The questioning that breaks Polus in the text begins as follows:

> SOCRATES. First of all then let us consider if to do wrong is more painful than to be wronged, and who are the ones who suffer the greater pain: those who do wrong, or those who suffer it? (475b8–c3)

If he is to admit this line of questioning, Polus might as well give up at once. For when the question is so put, it answers itself: if one man wrongs another with impunity,[6] the victim naturally will feel the greater pain. And if *C* has been admitted as the operative definition of "beautiful" and "ugly," Polus would not object to the cast of Socrates' question. *C* would indeed empower one to settle which of the two happenings is the uglier by inquiring which of the two is the more painful, putting no strings on the further question, 'More painful *for whom?*'[7] [457] thus making it entirely legitimate for Socrates to slant it the way he does in the citation, asking if it is more painful "for those

---

[4] Good Greek for the italicized phrase would be ὃ χαίρειν ποιεῖ τοὺς ὁρῶντας ἢ ἀκούοντας ἢ θεωροῦντας.

[5] As should be clear even from the suggested phrasing of *D* in the preceding note: the verb *theōrō,* used in its primary sense of "seeing" in premise *1,* can also carry (and often does, not only in Plato and Aristotle, but also in the orators and Epicurus: examples in LSJ, *s.v.*) the extended sense of "mental viewing," "contemplating," and I have put it to this use in the above formula for *D.*

[6] That the wrongdoing which is in view here is entirely successful and meets with no punishment or rebuff is the presupposition of the whole discussion.

[7] I use first-instance single quotes for imaginary quotations, reserving first-instance double quotes for verbatim citations from the translated text.

who do wrong or [for] those who suffer it?" If, on the other hand, *D* had been the agreed-upon definition, the question Socrates would have had to ask would be, 'Which is the more painful to see or hear or contemplate?' hence 'Which is the more painful *for those who observe or contemplate* the two events?'[8] To that question the answer is, at best, indeterminate. Polus might have argued with some plausibility that most of us would find the former more painful than the latter and, on that ground, that it is "uglier," just as he had maintained at the start: except in rare, abnormally softhearted souls he might have urged, resentment is more easily aroused than pity, more strongly felt and more disturbing to the one who feels it; hence most people would be more pained at the sight or thought of prospering villainy than that of suffering innocence. Whether or not he would be right on this last point is of no consequence in itself. This much at least is clear, and this is all that matters: if Polus had had the sense to opt for *D* instead of *C* a moment earlier, a line of argument would have been open to him which would have sufficed to save him from the abject capitulation to which he is forced by Socrates in the text.

What then of premises *4* and *5?* It is here that the qualification expressed in premise *1* is, to all appearance, dropped.[9] The [458] question now becomes simply whether or not "usefulness or pleasure" is what accounts for the beauty of the items introduced in this lap of the argument: laws, practices, *mathē-mata.* Had Polus been on the *qui vive,* he would have sensed the shift which this entailed and pulled his adversary up short over it, insisting that in the case of these more abstract objects, no less than that of bodies, colors, shapes, and sounds, the pleasure to the actual or ideal beholder is what accounts for beauty. This would have been a reasonable stand for him to take, and had he

---

[8] These would, of course, include the principals themselves, aggressor and victim, as well as their respective partisans. But what is being asked here is, in effect, "How would *anyone* react?" and the response of those who are personally involved would count only so far as it reflects this *general* point of view. Though nothing, of course, is said to this effect, some such assumption is required already in premises *1, 2,* and *3,* else "*x* pleases the beholder or the hearer" would lose all plausibility as a sufficient condition of "*x* is beautiful." Pleasure deriving from ego-involvement would be clearly irrelevant. If the sight of an armchair pleases me simply because it reminds me of grandpa (a sweet old man who left me a fortune) or the sound of a bell only because it portends my dinner, I would scarcely be tempted to think them beautiful on that account.

[9] Taylor unaccountably fails to notice this very obvious fact. He misrepresents Socrates as arguing that "the same thing ['serviceable or immediately agreeable in contemplation or both'] holds good when we speak of 'fine' or 'noble' usages and callings in life, or of the 'beauty' of a science. We mean that the usage or business or science in question either is highly beneficial or 'creates in the disinterested spectator a pleasing sentiment of approbation' or both . . . " (*loc. cit.* in note 2 above). The anachronistic reference to a "disinterested" spectator would have been misleading even in a paraphrase of premises *1, 2,* and *3.* It is perverse when read into premises *4* and *5* where nothing is said or implied about a spectator at all. On this reading of the five premises, one would have at least expected Taylor to notice that *C* does *not* follow from them. But he continues in all innocence, "It follows that by calling anything 'ugly' or 'base,' we must mean that it is either disserviceable, or painful, or both."

taken it he would have stymied Socrates, who would have had to look for some other way to discredit the view, as common now as it was then, which admits the "ugliness" of doing wrong but prefers it all the same to suffering wrong.

Did Plato, when wrote the *Gorgias,* realize how hollow was the victory Socrates won in this debate? I do not think so. The mood of this dialogue is solemn, even tragic. Its hero is in dead earnest. He would have scorned an *ad hominem* triumph. Plato makes him sum up the outcome as a vindication of the truth—"So I spoke the truth that neither I nor you nor any other man would prefer to do wrong than to suffer it" (475e)—with Polus himself now forced to "witness" this truth and "vote" for it (476a). It would have been a mockery of Socrates to put such words into his mouth if Plato had not thought them warranted by the facts. So Plato himself misjudged the facts which he depicted. He thought Socrates' dialectic had refuted Polus' doctrine, when all it had done was to refute the man. Since, as should now be clear, a true estimate of the outcome depends entirely on seeing the implications of the difference between C and D—between "pleasant" and "pleasant to the beholder"—Plato could not have seen, or seen clearly, how the mere shift from the latter to the former would suffice to vitiate [459] a definition of beauty. He had come within sight of this when he wrote the *Hippias Major.* There he noted how absurd it would be to say that an action was beautiful merely because it was pleasant, citing eating, drinking, and sexual intercourse as examples, remarking about the latter that "all would contend with us that, while it is most pleasant, if we are to do it, we should not do it in anyone's sight, for it is ugliest to view (ὡς αἴσχιστον ὂν ὁρᾶσθαι)" (299a5–6). He could have been led toward the essential point from just this example if he had analyzed the difference as that between what pleases the agent on one hand, the spectator on the other. But he did not. He analyzed it in terms of the difference between what pleases when perceived through sight and hearing (298a)[10] and what gives pleasure to other parts of our sensorium. He evidently failed to see that if the pleasurableness of an act is to be made the basis of its beauty then, in addition to other criteria which it must satisfy, it must involve the kind of pleasure that is felt by one who apprehends or represents it to himself, sensuously or imaginatively. For only this kind of pleasure is capable of that "disinterestedness" which, as Kant[11] and others have argued, is the true hallmark of aesthetic pleasure.

---

[10] Though without implying that this gets to the bottom of the problem. The discussion is aporematic. For Plato only form (in his sense of the term) is beautiful; he thinks sight and hearing important only because he thinks of them as the media through which sensuous instantiation of form is perceived.

[11] *Critique of Judgment,* I (1), "Analytic of the Beautiful."

PART TWO

PLATO

A. ETHICS, SOCIAL AND POLITICAL THEORY

7

THE THEORY OF SOCIAL JUSTICE IN THE *POLIS* IN PLATO'S *REPUBLIC*

A FEW YEARS AGO an international committee of classical scholars decided that 1974 was to be the 2,400th anniversary of Plato's birth.[1] The computations which led them to this result are no concern of mine: I have no desire to look this gift horse in the mouth. I accept it "without prejudice," as the lawyers say, welcoming it as a ceremonial date which offers a once-in-a-lifetime challenge to take stock of Plato's achievement in its entirety and reassess each of his many-sided contributions to Western thought. With this in view, I put this question to myself: "What is that aspect of Plato's thought which has suffered the most in my lifetime through misunderstanding or neglect?" To this my answer has been, unhesitatingly, "his theory of social justice." If other students of Plato disagree, as they well may, I shall not anticipate their objections and try to bring them around to my view: this would require a critical review of what has been written on this topic in the last half-century—an undertaking which would call for a major monograph all by itself. All I can do here is to remind them that once the storm unleashed by the chapter on this topic in Sir Karl Popper's *The Open Society and Its Enemies* had blown [1] over—a decade after the publication of his book (1945)[2]—no study in depth of Plato's theory of social justice has appeared in English,[3]

From Helen North, ed., *Interpretations of Plato* (Leiden: E. J. Brill, 1977) (*Mnemosyne,* Suppl. Vol. 50), pp. 1–40. Used by permission.

[1] This paper was to have been my contribution to a symposium celebrating the 2,400th anniversary of Plato's birth at an international congress of classical scholars in Madrid in August 1974. When I withdrew (for political reasons) from that congress, I was able to avail myself of another chance to participate at an academic celebration of that anniversary at Swarthmore College in November 1974. The first draft of this paper was written for the latter occasion. It has been subsequently revised and much documentation has been added—in fact, considerably more than could be accommodated within the present volume. A more complete version of this paper will appear in a book I expect to publish shortly, dealing with various aspects of Plato's theory of social justice. (Note: This aim was not fulfilled—ed.) I wish to express thanks for criticisms or suggestions from various scholars who have read or heard earlier drafts, including Professors R. E. Allen, Harold Cherniss, Daniel Devereux, Andreas Graeser, G. F. Hourani, David Gauthier, Warner Morse, Martin Ostwald, Michael Rohr, Christopher Rowe, Laszlo Versenyi, and A. D. Woozley.

[2] See Appendix A. My references to the book (all of them by author's name only) will be to the reprint of the (revised and enlarged) fourth edition in the Harper Torchbook series (New York, 1962).

[3] In marked contrast to the plethora of work on and around what Plato calls "the justice of a

though in the past two decades journal articles and books on Plato have been pouring out in greater volume than ever before. So there should be room for a new assessment of what is after all by common consent the first full-blown philosophical theory of justice in the Western world.

Since the space at my disposal is limited, the theory I shall discuss here is exclusively the one in the *Republic*.[4] This is where Plato expounds first and in the fullest terms his novel conception of social justice. On that topic he has virtually nothing further to say until he comes to write the *Laws*. To that last work of his we have to look for his second thoughts on social justice. But these would have no great interest for us if we had not known those first ones which he now tacitly amends. Of this fearless self-correction I shall have a word to say at the end. For the rest I shall [2] be glad to keep within the covers of the composition which is by general consent the greatest product of his genius.[5]

I

But first I must try to establish that there is such a thing as a theory of *justice* in that dialogue whose formal theme is *dikaiosunē*. As is well known,[6] this

---

private man," much of it triggered by a paper by David Sachs, "A Fallacy in Plato's *Republic*," *PR* 73 (1964), 141–59: this essay was followed by series of papers during the next decade, all of them concerned primarily (some of them exclusively) with psychic, in contrast to political, justice. The thinness of the literature on Plato's theory of social justice in the fifties and sixties may be verified by a glance at the bibliographical listings in the section on the *Republic* in H. Cherniss, *Lustrum* 4 (1960), 153ff. (more titles, but not much more substance, in the section on "Politics and Society" in the sequel, *Lustrum* 5 [1960], 470ff.). The sixties marked the appearance of R. C. Cross and A. D. Woozley, *Plato's Republic: A Philosophical Commentary* (London, 1964); Donald Kagan, *The Great Dialogue: History of Political Thought from Homer to Polybius* (New York, 1965); and Sheldon Wolin, *Politics and Vision* (Boston, 1960, 28–68): there are noteworthy remarks on Plato's theory of social justice in each of these, but none of the three deal with the topic in sufficient depth and detail.

[4] And in the *Republic* itself, I shall discuss only the norm encapsulated in the "doing one's own" definiens (433a–b), which involves the just relations of persons and classes within the *polis* and *to* the *polis*: the quoted catch-phrase is introduced (433a8) as a contraction for a fuller definiens (433a4–6), where what comes to be called "one's own" in the catch-phrase is clearly and unambiguously a function "which concerns the *polis*" (ἕν . . . τῶν περὶ τὴν πόλιν). Let me emphasize that this norm is not meant to determine

    (a) what a *polis* owes to other *poleis*, or
    (b) what individual members of a *polis* owe to individual members of other *poleis*, or
    (c) what persons who are not members of a *polis* owe to anyone else.

[5] It should go without saying that, even so, all I shall attempt to offer will be the elements of the theory—its bare essentials. What I present here may be supplemented to some small extent by earlier remarks on Plato's social and political theory in my *Platonic Studies* (Princeton, 1973) in the following passages: 11–19, 32, 117–26; 146–53; 192–203; 210–17. (To this work I shall refer hereafter by the abbreviation *PS*.)

[6] Though seldom expressly recognized. Even Paul Shorey, usually so sensitive to the value of

word is no true equivalent of our "justice." Why should we then assume that what ours denotes is what Plato's theory is all about?[7] To this day the question has gone unanswered. It has yet to be made clear why it is that when we impute to Plato a theory of justice in the *Republic* on the strength of what he says there about *dikaiosunē* we are not being the victims of a fossilized mistranslation. Let me then try to prove what heretofore has been so frequently assumed without proof. To this purely semantic argument I shall devote the first few pages of this paper.

Aristotle, with his good ear for ambiguity, is the first to notice the one in *dikaiosunē*. He resolves it in the opening paragraphs of Book 5 of the *Nicomachean Ethics*.[8] *Dikaiosunē* is used, he says, both as a generic term—for "complete" (i.e., comprehensive) social virtue[9]—yet also as the name of *a* social virtue—for "a [3] particular *dikaiosunē* (*en merei*, or *kata meros*, *dikaiosunē*, 1130b16–17 and 30),[10] whose semantic identity he pins down in two ways: first, by associating it with "equality,"[11] defining it as "proportional"[12] or "geometrical"[13] equality; second, by contrasting it with *pleonexia*.[14] In the *Rhetoric* he takes a different tack. To the ambiguity in *dikaiosunē* he does not here allude at all. And the terms he now uses to define the word are quite different: "the virtue because of which each has his own (*ta*

Greek words, does not discuss the problem either in his translation (listed in the bibliographical "Additional Note" at the conclusion of the notes, below) or in his analysis of the *Republic* in *What Plato Said* (Chicago, 1933), 208ff. But there are honorable exceptions. Thus R. C. Cross and A. D. Woozley (*Plato's "Republic," a Philosophical Commentary* [London, 1964; hereafter I shall refer to this book by its authors' names only]) say in their Preface that "'justice' is a thoroughly unsuitable word to use as a translation of the Greek word"; they resign themselves to it because "there is now so little hope of changing the usage."

[7] *Pace* demurrers, scholars who have been writing on the *Republic* give every impression of making this assumption. In my essay "The Argument in the *Republic* that 'Justice Pays,' *JP* 65 (1968), 665–754 (reprinted in corrected and expanded form in *PS*, 111ff.) I sidestepped the problem, saying I would use *justice* and *just* "merely as counters."

[8] Having adverted to the ambiguity earlier in the *N.E.* (1108b7–8, περὶ δὲ δικαιοσύνης, ἐπεὶ οὐχ ἁπλῶς λέγεται . . .), and still earlier, in the *Topics* (106b29, εἰ γὰρ τὸ δικαίως πολλαχῶς λέγεται . . .).

[9] ἀρετὴ . . . τελεία, ἀλλ' οὐχ ἁπλῶς ἀλλὰ πρὸς ἕτερον, 1129b26–27; οὐ μέρος ἀρετῆς, ἀλλ' ὅλη ἀρετή, 1130a9. The second of these two descriptions is the one to which he alludes most frequently in the sequel (1130a23, b7, 12, 18, 19, 25): it is the all-inclusiveness of *dikaiosunē* as social virtue (and of *adikia* as social vice) that distinguishes this first use of the word; so *teleia* in the first description must have the sense of "complete" rather than "perfect."

[10] A "part" of (social) virtue (*meros aretēs*, 1130a9).

[11] *To ison*, 1129a34 and 1130b9, τὸ δίκαιον ἴσον, ὅπερ καὶ ἄνευ λόγου δοκεῖ πᾶσιν, 1131a13–14. Cf. below, n. 62.

[12] τὸ μὲν οὖν δίκαιον τοῦτο, τὸ ἀνάλογον, 1131b16, the latter being a contraction (cf. τοῦ ἴσου τοῦ κατ' ἀναλογίαν, 1134a5–6).

[13] καλοῦσι δὲ τὴν τοιαύτην ἀναλογίαν γεωμετρικὴν οἱ μαθηματικοί, 1131b12–13.

[14] This contrast is his major clue to the discrimination of the narrower use of *dikaiosunē* from the wider one: he does the job by picking out the narrower use of *adikia* which is covered by *pleonexia* (1130a17ff.: cf. *PS*, 116).

hautōn . . . echousin) and in conformity with the law." He follows this up with a matching definiens of *adikia* as "(the vice) because of which each has what is another's (*ta allotria [echousin]*) and not in conformity with the law" (1366b9–11). Which sense of *dikaiosunē* and its antonym is being defined here? The wider or the narrower one?

Consider the phrases *ta hautou echein, ta allotria echein*. By suitable use of possessive or reflexive pronouns the Greeks could refer to property-rights. By means of them they could make the fundamental juristic distinction for which they, unlike the Romans, had no special terms:[15] the one between possession and ownership—between the fact of having something in one's own use and control and the *right* to so use and control it. By the use of these phrases, that distinction could be made not only in the domain of property-rights, but far beyond it. Consider the following from Demosthenes:[16] Having remarked that Philip would be stupid if he thought the Athenians had meant to cede to him Amphipolis just because [4] they had passed a decree that he was to "have" (i.e., keep) what he "had" (i.e., held),[17] Demosthenes proceeds:

> For it is also possible to have what is another's (ἔστι γὰρ ἔχειν τἀλλότρια)—not all who have something have what is their own (οὐχ ἅπαντες οἱ ἔχοντες τὰ αὐτῶν ἔχουσι).[18]

Since what is under dispute is not Philip's ownership of some real estate but his sovereignty over a Greek city, it is clear that Demosthenes is taking the phrases *ta hautou/ta allotria echein* as unrestricted to property-rights, hence easily applicable in this case to political rights as well. This leaves no reasonable doubt that when those same phrases turn up in Aristotle's definitions of *dikaiosunē* and *adikia* in the *Rhetoric*, in a context where they are perfectly general, totally unattached to any specific right of any sort, their reference must be so inclusive as to cover all possible rights;[19] so "the virtue because of

---

[15] Classical Greek contains no technical counterparts to the terms by which this distinction (between *possessio* [from *possedere*, literally "to sit upon"], on one hand, and *dominium* or *proprietas*, on the other) is upheld in Roman law. *Ktaomai* can be used to mean either "to possess" or "to own" (examples of both uses in LSJ).

[16] 7 (*On Halonnesus*), 26.

[17] ἔχειν αὐτὸν ἃ εἶχεν. The intent of the decree was that existing sovereignties should be preserved (Philip was to *own* what he had previously *owned*), hence that the Athenian title to Amphipolis ("recognized by all Greeks and by the King of Persia," ibid., 29) should remain inviolate. Philip's "stupid sophism" (τὸ σοφὸν αὐτοῦ ἠλίθιον, *loc. cit.*) gave normative force to the first occurrence, factual to the second: he is to *own* what he now holds (having annexed it by force).

[18] I.e., not all who possess something have a good title to its ownership.

[19] The parallel use of *suum* in Roman jurisprudence is instructive. Comparing the two definitions of *iustitia* quoted from Ulpian at the start of the *Digest of the Institutes of Justinian* (both of them takeoffs from a Greek original, the definiens of *dikaiosunē* which Plato ascribes to Simonides of Ceos in *Rep.* I, 332a, τὰ ὀφειλόμενα ἑκάστῳ ἀποδιδόναι),

which each has his own" must be the one which secures to each of those affected by its exercise the unimpaired possession and enjoyment of his rights. This being the case, there could be no doubt as to which of those two senses of *dikaiosunē* which had been sorted out in the *Ethics* Aristotle is now defining in the *Rhetoric:* When the definiens refers to a virtue whose exercise has that result, what else but "justice" could the definiendum be? I for one, know of no better way of defining "justice" than as the [5] disposition to govern one's conduct by respect for the rights of those whom that conduct affects.[20]

Let us then come to Plato with those two uses of *dikaiosunē* tracked down by Aristotle: first as a generic term for which the biblical word *righteousness* would be our nearest equivalent, and then as a species of that genus which we know to be the very one we call "justice."[21] Was Plato using *dikaiosunē* in the first of these two senses, or in the second, or in some third sense, when he defined it in Book 4 (433a–b) as "doing one's own," using here this popular catch-phrase for the first time[22] as philosopher's shorthand for the much longer expression which precedes it in the text:

each single person's pursuing that single practice in[23] the *polis* which his own nature is best fitted to pursue. (433a5–6)[24] [6]

---

(1) *iustitia (est) suum cuique tribuere,*

(2) *iustitia est constans et perpetua voluntas ius suum cuique tribuere,*

we can see that Ulpian, whose native tongue, unlike Aristotle's, does furnish him in *ius* with a special term for our "right" (the sense in which we speak of "a right to . . ." is conserved perfectly in expressions like *ius testandi, ius connubii,* and so forth), feels free to use *suum* in (1) as a mere contraction for what is expressed more fully by *ius suum* in (2), thus relying on "one's own" to have fully as general and abstract a signification as "one's own *right.*"

[20] I have encountered nothing better since submitting many years ago (in "Justice and Equality" in *Social Justice,* ed. R. Brandt [Englewood Cliffs, N.J., 1962], 53) the following definition: "An action is *just* if, and only if, it is prescribed exclusively by regard for the rights of all whom it affects substantially." (Hereafter I shall refer to this essay by title only).

[21] The dictionaries blur this vital distinction by allowing "righteous" or "upright" as a normal use of "just," along with that of "equitable" or "impartial" (so *The Shorter Oxford English Dictionary* and *Webster's New Collegiate Dictionary*), ignoring the fact that this would be true enough of earlier usage (e.g., in the King James' Version of the Bible) but that the use of "just" to mean "righteous" is now so rare as to be virtually an archaism. For sensitive comment on the idiomatic use of "justice," see H.L.A. Hart, *The Concept of Law* (Oxford, 1961), 153ff.

[22] Plato had not so used it in any earlier passage—not even in the *Republic*. The same words occur in 370a4 (ἀλλ' αὐτὸν δι' αὐτὸν τὰ αὑτοῦ πράττει) but there they carry only the ordinary, commonplace, sense of "doing one's own work," and the clause I have cited is being used to designate the unspecialized, jack-of-all-trades, activity (the very opposite of Platonic *dikaiosunē!*) to which one would be forced if one lacked the privilege of living in a functionally articulated economic society which allows each person to specialize in the one kind of work he can do best, *this* being the primitive "adumbration" of *dikaiosunē* (ἀρχήν τε καὶ τύπον τινα τῆς δικαιο-σύνης, 443c1–2) at the lowest, purely economic, form of human association.

If this is the definiens, what is the definiendum being used to mean—
"righteousness," or "justice," or something else?

That it is not "righteousness" I take to be a sure inference from the first of
the three arguments by which Plato supports his definition: the non-identity of
dikaiosunē with wisdom or with courage or with *sōphrosunē*—all three
of them treated in this context as forms of social, no less than personal,
excellence[25]—is a premise of that argument. Plato argues (433b7–e1, and cf.
also 427e–428a) that what is denoted by "doing one's own" is of such vast
importance for the excellence of a *polis* that it must have one of the great
generally recognized social virtues as its name, and that this name can only be
dikaiosunē, for each of the others has been otherwise accounted for. The
validity of this inference has been often attacked and the truth of its premises
has been denied, particularly with respect to the alleged non-identity of
dikaiosunē with *sōphrosunē* which, it has been claimed, are as good as synonyms in Plato's idiolect.[26] I would defend Plato on this last count[27] though
not on the first.[28] But neither attack nor defense would be [7] even remotely

[23] I settle reluctantly for this weakening of the force of the preposition in *tōn peri tēn polin*
(with precedents in Lindsay, Shorey, Cornford), having failed to hit on a closer rendering without
indulging in such over-translation as Robin's, "parmi les fonctions qui interessent l'Etat." (For a
listing of the translations to which I refer here and elsewhere in this paper, see the Additional Note
at the end.)

[24] Cf. the fuller expansion of the "doing one's own" phrase I gave in *PS* (119) with its supporting texts:

engaging in that form of social conduct which constitutes the greatest possible contribution
which nature has fitted one to make to the happiness and excellence of one's *polis*.

[25] Plato could hardly have been more emphatic on this point: he defines, each of them first as a
social virtue in the *polis* (427e–432a) and then much later (442b11–d1), as a personal virtue (an
excellence of soul).

[26] C. W. Larson, "The Platonic Synonyms, *Dikaiosunē* and *Sōphrosunē*," *AJP* 72 (1951), 395–
414.

[27] The criticism is misconceived insofar as it rests on the assumption that if Plato thinks of
those two names as necessarily co-extensive (as he, of course, does) he *must* be using them as
synonyms. Cf. "equilateral triangle" and "equiangular triangle": the phrases are necessarily co-
extensive, but who would wish to say that they are synonymous? Cf. *PS*, 232n. 27 *sub fin.*

[28] Plato would be justified in assuming, as he does in this argument, that

(a) the word *dikaiosunē* names a social virtue whose importance to the (moral) excellence of
a *polis* is second to none, and
(b) this virtue is not identical with any of the three he has so far identified.

If he had then drawn his conclusion by merely *assuming* that

(c) this virtue is identical with the one denoted by his proposed definiens for *dikaiosunē*,

he would have been guilty of an obvious *petitio principii*. But the fact is that he *argues* for (c);
it must be true, he claims, because

(d) the virtue denoted by his proposed definiens is the one which makes it possible for a
polis to come to have, and to retain, each of those other three virtues.

relevant to the only point I need to make here, namely that Plato is at least as sure of the non-identity of *dikaiosunē* with each of his other great social virtues as of the correctness of his proposed definiens. If he were not, he would not have given us this argument.

May we then without further ado proceed by simple elimination, to infer that since he is not using *dikaiosunē* to mean "righteousness" in this passage, he must be using it to mean "justice"? That would be too easy. For it is no secret that Plato's use of language can be boldly—even perplexingly—revisionary.[29] So how can we be sure that his redefinition of *dikaiosunē* is not being offered in that vein? Clearly we cannot without further evidence. Do we have such evidence? I want to argue that we do.

First of all, we can assure ourselves that when at the start of Book 2 Glaucon poses the great question, "Is *dikaiosunē* profitable?" he is using the word to mean not "righteousness" in general, but "justice" in particular. Of this we have twofold evidence:

(a) His language anticipates both of the devices Aristotle is to use in the *Nicomachean Ethics* to isolate the narrow use of *dikaiosunē* from the generic one: Glaucon pairs no less closely *dikaiosunē* with equality and *adikia* with *pleonexia;* he uses "respect for equality" (*tēn tou isou timēn*) as a simple variant for "respect for justice" (359c6), and *pleonexia* as equivalent to *adikia* (359c5).

(b) Glaucon's conception of *dikaiosunē* and *adikia* conforms perfectly to the Aristotelian definitions of these terms in the *Rhetoric;* he uses "to abstain from what is another's" (*apechesthai tōn allotriōn*, 360b6) and "to keep hands off what is another's" (*mē haptesthai* [*tôn allotriōn*], 360b6; and cf. 360d4) as equivalents of *adikein.*

Second, we can assure ourselves that this use of *dikaiosunē,* so prominent in Glaucon's speech in Book 2, has not faded out by the time Plato has reached the "doing one's own" definiens in Book 4. The evidence for this comes in the second of the three [8] arguments (433e3–434a1) in support of that definiens: Holding that

(1) judges (in the ideal *polis*)[30] instantiate *dikaiosunē*

If (d) were true, it would be a very respectable reason for the truth of (c). Plato assumes that (d) is intuitively true: his Socrates need only state it in that rotund nine-line period (433c4–d5) to elicit Glaucon's unhesitating concurrence. Unhappily, it will not strike others in the same way. Perhaps Plato thinks it will by the time they have read the rest of the *Republic* and have had the chance to see for themselves how much can be expected from the instantiation of "doing one's own" in his ideal *polis.* In that case he is forecasting our eventual agreement; but a forecast is not an argument, so the *petitio* is still being incurred.

[29] Cf. my remarks in *PS,* 115–17 on the extraordinary redefinition of "individual" *dikaiosunē* as "psychic harmony" in 443c9ff.

[30] That this is what is meant is clear from the imperative (*prostaxeis dikasein*): "you" (i.e., the legislation we are now proposing for the ideal *polis*) would so order.

because

(2) it is their aim[31] to ensure that neither litigant "shall have what is another's or be deprived of his own" (μήτ' ἔχωσι τἀλλότρια μήτε τῶν αὑτῶν στέρωνται),

it follows, Plato claims, that

(3) "the doing and the having of what is one's own (ἡ τοῦ . . . ἑαυτοῦ ἕξις τε καὶ πρᾶξις)" is *dikaiosunē*.[32]

This claim enables us to see how "doing one's own" ties up with "having one's own" in Plato's thinking: He is assuming[33] that where *A* is "doing his own" with reference to *B* and *C*, *A* is acting with the intention that *B* shall have *B*'s own and *C* shall have *C*'s own and neither of them shall have what is another's, and that it is because *A*'s action is governed by this intention that his conduct toward *B* and *C* instantiates *dikaiosunē*. And Plato is counting on this hookup between the "doing one's own" by *A* and the "having [9] one's own" by *B* and by *C* to establish the correctness of the "doing one's own" definiens of *dikaiosunē*.

Clearly, then, this definiens dovetails into the one produced by Aristotle in the *Rhetoric*. In both cases the *dikaia praxis* would be the one governed by the intention[34] that each of those affected by it shall "have what is his own" and neither of them shall "have what is another's." Therefore having satisfied ourselves above that in the Aristotelian definition the definiendum is used to mean not "righteousness" but "justice," we may be equally satisfied that it is

---

[31] *Ephiemenoi*, 434e6. Aristotle is content to define "justice" in the *Rhetoric* in terms of the (normal) result of the exercise of the virtue, making no specific reference to the intention which governs its exercise. But, of course, there is no difference of doctrine between Plato and Aristotle on this point: neither does Plato bring in explicitly the idea of intentionality into his "doing one's own" definiens, while, conversely, that idea represents one of the most fundamental elements in Aristotle's concept of moral virtue, including, of course, the virtue of justice: καὶ ἡ μὲν δικαιοσύνη ἐστὶ καθ' ἣν ὁ δίκαιος λέγεται πρακτικὸς κατὰ προαίρεσιν τοῦ δικαίου, 1134a1–2.

[32] While recasting, not just abbreviating, Plato's argument, I am keeping responsibly within the intentions of its layout in Plato's text. (1) is implicit: (if the "rulers" who are to be commissioned to judge law suits in the Platonic *polis* (433e6–7) did not instantiate *dikaiosunē*, the inference at (3) in 433e12–434a1 would be a wild *non sequitur*. So (1) may be supplied. And it must be tied to (2) by a "because" (which is not in the text) for the same reason: were it joined only by "and," the conclusion in (3) would not follow: the fact that the aim of the judges is the one mentioned in (2) would not advance the claim made in (a part of) (3) that the achievement of this aim is *dikaiosunē* unless the judges' instantiation of *dikaiosunē* itself followed from (2). I offer a similar analysis of the passage in *PS*, 120–21.

[33] And so confidently that he does not put in so much as a word to justify the assumption, though it would be as plain to him as it is to us that if this assumption were not true (3) would not follow from (1) and (2), neither of which mentions "doing one's own."

[34] Cf. n. 31 above.

used in the same way in the Platonic. Viewed by Aristotle from the standpoint of those affected by its exercise, "justice" is defined as conduct which results in their "having their own." Viewed by Plato from the standpoint of the agent exercising it, it is defined as that "doing his own" which will have just that result. Now we can understand not only *that,* but *why,* that peculiar catchphrase could be seriously meant as a definiens of justice, and this in spite of the fact that it only mentions "doing," instead of "having" one's own, i.e., refers directly only to duties, not to rights: the duty it has in view is *the duty of justice*—that unique, general, second-order duty we are to discharge *in* each of our many particular first-order duties by so governing our conduct as to respect the rights of all whom our conduct affects.

If this argument is correct, Plato's use of the term *dikaiosunē* in the *Republic* can be explained as follows: Deprived of a special term for "justice," he is content to take a word which had this as *one* of its two senses in the language and to use it as though "justice" was simply what it meant, quietly ignoring its broader use to mean "righteousness."[35] If Plato had anticipated Aristotle's insight into the ambiguity in *dikaiosunē,* we might have had a defense of its use to mean "justice" in the *Republic.* But there is nothing in Plato's text, here or anywhere in the corpus, to show that he had noticed the two uses.[36] That being the case, he had all [10] the less reason to be self-conscious about his using *dikaiosunē* to mean "justice." This was the only use Socrates had in view in Plato's earlier dialogues when he placed *dikaiosunē* on a par with *sōphrosunē, andreia, sophia,* and *hosiotēs* as one of the five "parts" of virtue.[37] This would be the use that would naturally come into the *Republic* through its Socratic portico, Book 1;[38] and nothing happens thereafter to force Plato to reflect on its alternate generic use to mean "righteousness" and elicit from him a formal argument to justify his continued adherence to its narrower use. So we have good reason to concur with the traditional view that *dikaiosunē* in the *Republic* is properly translated "justice" and may now pro-

[35] Which is what Aristotle too was content to do in the *Rhetoric.* Though acutely aware in other contexts of the ambiguity in *dikaiosunē* (cf. n. 8 above), he acts here as though this is *the* sense of the term and proceeds to offer a definition which fits just that sense, blandly ignoring the other which he has recognized so fully in the opening chapters of Book 5 of the *N.E.*

[36] For this reason my argument that *dikaiosunē* is being used to mean "justice" in the crucial passage (443–44) which puts forward and defends the "doing one's own" definiens would not be invalidated *if* it could be shown that upon occasion Plato slips into the broader use of *dikaiosunē* in the *Republic:* in the absence of a formal disambiguation of the term, a certain amount of wobbling in its application would not be too surprising. I say, "*If* this could be shown." It has not yet been shown, to my knowledge.

[37] *Meno* 78d–79c; *Prot.* 329c ff. And cf. *PS,* 225n. 8, and 267.

[38] Where the species-use of *dikaiosunē* is clear (a) from Polemarchus' offering the "giving to everyone his due" definiens of the word (331e), which Socrates treats as relevant, though inadequate, and (b) from Socrates' taking *pleonektein* to be its contrary (349b ff.), which we know from Aristotle (cf. pp. 71–72 above) to be an acceptable differentia of the species-use of *dikaiosunē.*

ceed with a clear conscience to investigate the theory of justice which Plato encapsulates in the definition he gives in Book 4.

II

What is the point of the theory? Why should Plato, why should anyone, produce a theory of justice? For one or both of the two possible purposes which I shall call, following current idiom, "meta-normative" and "normative" respectively. The latter the philosopher shares with the practical moralist, the critic of politics, the social reformer. The aim here is to determine what social, economic, and political rights people ought to have in consequence of the moral rights they do have. The meta-normative purpose is uniquely the philosopher's and the metaphysician's. It seeks to understand that peculiar dimension of our being which makes justice integral to our humanity—so much so that the creature we call "man" would not be fully human if he did not have rights and duties, and therewith a concern for justice. Plato's theory has both of these purposes. I shall start with the first, giving it the lion's share of the discussion. Only toward the end will I reach the second.

Let me then go directly to the central intuition which forms the normative core of Plato's theory. This is the justice of reciprocity [11] in the pursuit of happiness and excellence:[39] it would be just for us to give of our best to benefit others who would be willing to give of their best to benefit us. A rudimentary implementation of this norm Plato had found already in that curiously abstract form of social intercourse depicted in Book 2 (369a ff.), calling it there a "*polis*," though well aware that it is only an economic society.[40] Men's goal here is nothing higher than material well-being, and at its lowest level—the fulfillment of the bare necessities of life, food, clothing, shelter, and the like.[41] Yet even so it exhibits a pattern of conduct which Plato hails as

[39] Here and hereafter (as also earlier, in the expansion of the "doing one's own" definiens in n. 24) I feel free to write "happiness and excellence" in contexts where Plato would be content to speak of *eudaimonia* without explicit reference to *aretē* because for him "true" or "real" happiness *entails* excellence. But in translations or paraphrases, I shall write only "happiness" for *eudaimonia* in the Platonic text.

[40] He can do this by taking advantage of the ambiguity in *polis*, which can be used to mean either "city" or "state" (and other things besides: see LSJ *s.v.*), making things difficult for his translators: thus Shorey starts by translating "city" at 368e3–5, shifts to "state" at 369a1–5 and b5, then to "city or state" at c4, finally settling down at c9 to "city" for the rest of the passage. That Plato means no more than "city" in this whole passage is suggested by his saying that "*polis*" is "a name" for "this settlement" (*tautēi tēi sunoikiāi*, 369c4), and it is made certain by the fact that his account of it abstracts rigorously from all political institutions (no mention of government, laws, courts, army, and the like).

[41] The ones which must be satisfied if man is "to exist and to live" (τοῦ εἶναι τε καὶ τοῦ ζῆν ἕνεκα, 369d1–2); the means of their satisfaction are "the necessaries" (*t'anankaia*, 373a5).

"the original principle" of justice[42] because through what goes on here— division of labor and exchange of goods and services on the open market—all the participants benefit reciprocally. Each of them maximizes his efficiency by concentrating all his energies on a single line of work (typically a "craft" [*technē*] and is thus enabled to give his fellows the best service they could expect from a person of his particular endowment and acquired skills, reaping the benefits of the like service from his associates. But all this happens without planned foresight of the common good and hence with no possibility of extending the area of mutually beneficent give-and-take into the higher reaches of well-being.[43] For that very reason all that can be [12] reached here is that low-grade communal achievement which Glaucon calls, a little too scornfully, "a city of pigs" (372d).

Over against this Plato sets another city where centrally planned pursuit of the common good governs the life of all, laying down for each a comprehensive pattern of conduct tailored to his native aptitudes, offering him whatever facilities he needs, first of all, to learn how to give his best to his fellows and then to give them that best, the same being done for everyone in the polis, so that all may be both burden-bearers and benefit-reapers, each according to his individual capacity for work and for enjoyment. This would be Plato's vision of the just *polis*. The definition of *dikaiosunē* I quoted a moment ago, "each single person's pursuing that single practice in the *polis* which his own nature best fits him to pursue"—the expansion of the "doing one's own" catchphrase—becomes the formulaic crystallization of this vision, once it is understood that this "single service in the *polis*," though vocationally based, is not meant to be restricted to on-the-job activity but to extend over the whole of one's conduct in the *polis*, private no less than public.[44] So understood, the

---

[42] ἀρχήν τε καὶ τύπον τινὰ τῆς δικαιοσύνης, 443c1.

[43] All we get at this lowest level, as Plato sees it, is a common good which, of itself, constitutes neither happiness nor excellence (he uses neither of these two words in his description of it) but which provides nonetheless an indispensable component of happiness and which, moreover, requires excellence of material craftsmanship: cf. the use of *kallion* in 370b4 and c3 in the justification of the division of labor and of *kalos* for the same purpose in 374a6–c2 and in the back reference to it in 394e3–4, εἷς ἕκαστος ἓν μὲν ἂν ἐπιτήδευμα καλῶς ἐπιτηδεύοι, πολλὰ δ' οὔ.

[44] It is of the essence of Plato's conception of the pursuit of the good life that all persons should "have in life a single goal (σκοπὸν . . . ἐν τῷ βίῳ ἕνα) with a view to which they must do *everything* they do (οὗ στοχαζομένους δεῖ ἅπαντα πράττειν ἃ ἂν πράττωσιν) both in private and in public" (519c2–4). Those who do not have such an all-controlling purpose are *apaideutoi* (519b7–8)—and there is no more damning epithet in Plato's vocabulary. Without *paideia* any virtue is a fake virtue, as is stated explicitly in the case of courage in 430b6–10: even if you do have all the right beliefs concerning what is, and is not, to be feared, but lack the proper *paideia*, your virtue will be "brutish and slavish . . . and should be called anything but 'courage.'" (On this passage and the closely related one in the *Phaedo* (68d–69a), see *PS*, 137 and nn.) It follows that if you *are* "doing your own," what you do is being dictated by a purpose which commands all your energies and controls all your activities, down to the last detail. For my earlier argument for

definition tells us that it is our supreme duty—the one that determines all others—to so conduct ourselves that each and all of our activities will contribute maximally to that happiness and excellence of our *polis;* and that if, and only if, we so conduct ourselves we shall be acting with due regard for the rights of all within the *polis.*

What then is the *polis?* I do not mean, What is its juridical [13] status? That would be another story—but, What is its status in Plato's moral ontology? If his definition of "justice" is to keep faith with his central intuition, the *polis* whose happiness and excellence is the end of all just conduct within its frontiers can be nothing but the people themselves who are its members—all of them in all of their institutionalized interrelations.[45] I contend that this is all the *polis* is for Plato. I must argue for this claim, for it has often been denied. Grote denied it flatly over a century ago in his monumental book on Plato. Let me quote him:

> Plato announces explicitly the purpose of all his arrangements: to obtain happiness for the whole city: by which he means, not happiness for the greatest number of individuals, but for the abstract unity called the City, supposed to be capable of happiness or misery, apart from the individuals, many or few, composing it.[46]

A similar thesis has been strongly affirmed in our time by Sir Karl Popper[47] in his *Open Society and Its Enemies.*[48] Assuring us (169) that

> Plato says frequently that what he is aiming at is neither the happiness of individuals nor that of any particular class in the state, but only the happiness of the whole,[49]

[14]

---

this thesis, adducing a number of other texts (the appositeness of 519c2–4 had then escaped my notice), see *PS,* 122 and 124–25 with nn.

[45] I say "all" of those interrelations, because for Plato the *polis* is coextensive with all the associations of its members, be they economic, familial, educational, recreational, cultural, or religious, no less than that unique association for which the term "political" would be ordinarily reserved, i.e., the one which in a given territorial area (a) exercises supreme control over the use of physical coercion and (b) maintains a legal order.

[46] *Plato and the Other Companions of Socrates* (London, 1888), vol. 4, 139 (The first, three-volume edition had appeared in 1865).

[47] Also, somewhat less strongly by Cross and Woozley: they claim that for Plato "the state is itself an individual" (76), a "super-individual" (132), but that this is only an *implication* of Plato's explicit doctrines, never "clearly recognized" (132) by Plato, and not a consistently sustained implication (78, 132). My criticism of this interpretation will be directed exclusively to the full-strength form in which it is expounded by Grote and Popper.

[48] Cf n. 2 above, and Appendix A.

[49] Taking the cited statement at face value, and ignoring for the moment the fact that "the whole" is meant to be a stand-in for a disputed entity (the "super-individual"), the statement would be quite innocuous, except in one special case—the crucial one—where "the happiness of individuals" is that of *all* the individuals who compose the whole. In any other case (including, not least of all, the one most likely to come to mind, where "the happiness of individuals" is construed in terms of the Benthamite formula used by Grote in the statement cited from him above, "happiness for the greatest number," and "greatest" could stand for some number short of

Popper calls this "whole" a "super-individual,"[50] to indicate that it is distinct from any and all of the individuals who compose it and superior to each and all of them in value.[51]

Now I am not going to suggest that this view is a whole-cloth fabrication. A great thinker who is also a great stylist must be held co-responsible for the deeper misunderstandings of his text. Certainly there are passages which spin cloth for Grote and Popper.[52] To go through them and ponder their precise import would call for another paper. Fortunately there is no need to do this here. The falsehood of the imputation can be established without having to go so far afield. Let me focus on the very passage to which Grote refers in the lines I quoted from him, *sc.* to that long paragraph near the very start of Book 4 where Plato speaks of "creating the happy *polis*" (τὴν εὐδαίμονα πλάττο-μεν πόλιν, 420c3). What he means by this phrase becomes clearer in his repeated references to the happiness of "the whole *polis*," which contrast it invariably with the happiness of a particular group within the *polis*—never with that of *all the people* in the *polis*.[53] What we are told in the [15] above quotation from Popper Plato "says frequently," he never says even once for

---

the full totality), what Popper says would be entirely correct. What is surprising is that it should pass muster for the crucial case even in the eyes of so lucid a thinker and careful reader of Plato's text as Richard Robinson. (Cf. the first of the two quotations from him under (2) in the Appendix A below.)

[50] P. 76; also "a kind of super-organism" (79).

[51] The second of these allegations is easily documented, though only by filling out the ellipses which Popper (usually an exact writer) allows himself freely in this case: "the individual is lower than the state" (79); "the state . . . must be placed higher than the individual" (76). In the case of the former, I cannot recall any passage in which the "super-individual" is explicitly contrasted with *all* of the people who compose it (though often enough with unquantified "individuals") but the contrast is unambiguously implied by the choice of the term "super-individual," on the safe assumption that this could hardly be meant to be rhetorical bombast devoid of exact philosophical import, as it would be if it were simply meant to name the totality of individuals in their multiple interrelations.

[52] Many of them are reviewed and their alleged support of the ascription of the "super-individual" view to Plato is rebutted in Jerry Neu's paper, "Plato's Analogy of State and Individual," *Philosophy* 46 (1971), 238–54. Particularly valuable is his terse identification (245 and nn., especially n. 21) of the misunderstanding of Platonic ontology ("misplaced degrees-of-reality theory") incurred in Popper's allegation (79–80) that for Plato the state has greater "reality" than its citizens and is itself "the perfect individual" of which the individual citizen is "a kind of imperfect copy"—mistakes which R. B. Levinson's critique (pp. 518ff. of the work cited in n. 97 below) had failed to spot.

[53] *Hen ti ethnos* vs. *holē hē polis*, 420b6–7; *oligous . . . tinas* vs. *holēn*, c3–4; making the members of some particular trade *makarious* vs. contriving that *holē hē polis eudaimonēi* e1–7; *pleistē eudaimonia* for the guardians *or* for the whole *polis*, 421b5–7; *hen ti genos* vs. *en holēi tēi polei* 519 e2–3. The Cross-Woozley handling of these passages is unobjectionable. Here is their excellent gloss on the first of them:

The aim is to provide the conditions of happiness, not for one class (*ethnos*), but for the city as a whole. Whether or not this entails the concept of a city as an entity over and above the individuals who comprise it (and the analogy of the statue in 420c–d perhaps suggests that it

the crucial case where "the happiness of individuals" is that of *all* the individuals in the state: in none of them does Plato draw that contrast at all. To be sure, there is a passage—just one in the entire Platonic corpus, to my knowledge—where Plato does, in effect, compare the happiness of the whole *polis* with that of all the people who compose it; and it is instructive to test the Grote-Popper hypothesis against it: Plato is here considering what would happen if all the subgroups in the *polis* could be given their heart's desire of self-indulgent happiness in childish disregard of the consequences for the performance of their duties and therewith for the happiness of everyone else:

> Don't require us to give the guardians the sort of happiness that would make them anything but guardians. For in the same way we could dress up the farmers in gorgeous robes and deck them out with gold, and tell them to work the land at their pleasure; and we could have the potters too recline in banquet-couches, left to right, boozing and feasting, with their potter's wheel at their side to potter with when they are so disposed; and all the others too we could make happy in the same fashion, so that indeed the whole city might be happy (ἵνα δὴ ὅλη ἡ πόλις εὐδαιμονῇ). 420d5–e7 (translation adapted from Shorey's)

Here the happiness of the whole *polis* is not treated as something distinct from the happiness of the citizens; it is collapsed with theirs. The fact that the hypothesis is counterfactual—it would turn the *polis* into an amusement-park, a "country-fair" (*hōsper en panēgurei,* 421b2), and the result would be disastrous *un*happiness—in no way affects the point at issue, which is that *if* all the people in the *polis* could be made happy in this crazy way, then the whole *polis* would *be* happy.

But there is another passage which provides stronger evidence for my case, for it distinctly implies, as this one perhaps does not, the very contrary of what Plato has been supposed to have said "frequently." When the philosophers are sentenced to a fifteen-year [16] exile from their intellectual paradise to do a stint of service in the Cave, this is how Socrates explains the rationale of the verdict (519e1–520a2):

> You have forgotten, my friend, that it is not the law's concern to secure superior happiness for a single class in the state, but to contrive this[54] in the whole *polis,*[55]

---

does not), at least it entails the idea of a man being prepared to subordinate his own interests to those of others. (97)

[54] I.e., superlative well-being. Here I disagree with Shorey's gloss on 519e3: he says that the reference of "this" is "happiness, not of course exceptional happiness." When he wrote that "of course," Shorey must have forgotten that in his translation of 420b6–7 he had resolved the same ambiguity of reference in the opposite way (writing "the greatest possible happiness of the city as a whole" for ὅτι μάλιστα ὅλη ἡ πόλις [διαφερόντως εὐδαίμων ἔσται]). It would make as good sense to say that the whole *polis* is "exceptionally" happy as to say this of a particular class within it, so long as the referents of the comparison are appropriately different (other cities, in one case; other classes within the same city, in the other).

[55] *En holēi tēi polei.* The force of the preposition is lost in some translations of the phrase

harmonizing the citizens by persuasion and compulsion, making them impart to *one another* the benefit which each of them can bring to the community (ποιῶν μετα-διδόναι ἀλλήλοις τῆς ὠφελίας ἣν ἂν ἕκαστοι τὸ κοινὸν δυνατοὶ ὦσιν ὠφελεῖν).

What is described in the second dependent clause of the citation as "contriving this [superior happiness] in the whole *polis*" is redescribed in the terminal clause as the citizens' "imparting *to one another* the benefit which each can bring to the community." Thus for them to "impart benefit to the community" (*to koinon ōphelein*) *is* to "impart benefit to one another"; they, and they alone, are the beneficiary; the well-being of the *polis* is theirs.[56] How Grote, splendid Hellenist and exceedingly close student of the *Republic* that he was, could have missed the import of this passage, must remain a mystery. How Popper missed it, though also mysterious, becomes a little less so when we notice that when he quotes this passage the crucial words "to one another" drop out of his translation.[57] When put back where they should be—and where [17] they are in all of the other translations I have consulted,[58] with the single exception of Cornford's,[59] on which Popper's seems modeled[60]—they leave no reasonable grounds for doubt on the point at issue. They show di-

---

(Cornford: "of the commonwealth as a whole"; Bloom: "for the whole city"). The phrase is faithfully rendered, as above, in Lindsay, Shorey, Robin.

[56] That is why he feels free to speak of this, indifferently, as

    (a) happiness "in" the polis (*en tēi polei,* 519e3), or
    (b) happiness "for" it (εἰ πλείστη εὐδαιμονία ἐκείνη ἐγγίγνεται, (421b6–7), or
    (c) happiness "of" the *polis* (τὴν εὐδαιμονίαν . . . τοῦ τε ἀνδρὸς καὶ τῆς πόλεως, 566d5).

Since it is the happiness of the persons who compose the city, it may be described either literally, as in (a), i.e., as something that happens *within* it, or a little more freely in (b) and in (c) as happiness "for" or "of" the city.

[57] This is how he translates (80) 519e5–520a1: "It makes them all share in whatever benefit each of them can contribute to the community." In this rendering Plato's statement would not be inconsistent with Popper's interpretation: it would not forbid his taking "the community" (*to koinon*) here to mean the "super-individual," understanding Plato to be saying that each of the citizens is to bring his contributions to the "super-individual" and receive in turn *some* share in the riches pouring into *it*.

[58] Schleiermacher-Kurz, Lindsay, Shorey, Robin, Bloom. Also Jowett (but in the revised [4th, 1953] edition, Jowett's "one another" was changed to "others"—why?).

[59] Which reads, *"making them share whatever benefits each class can contribute* to the common good." (I have italicized the words which recur in Popper's translation, cited in n. 57 above). This translation is even less exact than Popper's: *hekastoi,* whose reference is clearly to *tous politas* in the preceding line, becomes "each class": and "the common good" for *to koinon* is unnecessarily free.

[60] The recurrence in Popper's ⟨translation⟩ of the words I have italicized in my quotation of Cornford's in the preceding note makes this a virtual certainty. But the vital blemish—the omission of "with one another" after "share" in each of the two translations—cannot be explained by supposing that Popper was following Cornford's blindly: he corrected inexactness in Cornford at two other points in this sentence.

rectly that contribution to the happiness of one's *polis* means for Plato contribution to the happiness of everyone within the network of interrelations which bind the life of everyone in the *polis* to the life of everyone else.

So my interpretation of the "doing one's own" *definiens* of "justice" keeps well in line with what I called the "central intuition" in Plato's theory. The duty of justice it defines is fulfilled in doing one's best to contribute to the happiness and excellence of everyone in the *polis,* and to that alone.

If we did fulfil this duty, could we ourselves count on equal treatment? The question would leap to the mind of Plato's reader then, no less than it does now, indeed then more than now, for the linguistic bond of justice with equality was even closer for the Greeks than it is for us: *to ison, isotēs,* would be the very words to which they would turn for a natural, unstrained, one-word variant for *to dikaion, dikaiosunē.*[61] This is what leads Aristotle to declare that "justice *is* equality, as all men think even apart from argument." [18][62] And this is certainly how Plato himself understands the common view: both Socrates and Callicles in the *Gorgias,*[63] and then again Glaucon at the start of Book 2 of the *Republic,*[64] take it for granted that for the public at large "justice" and "equality"—*to dikaion* and *to ison*—can be used interchangeably. What then is Plato's answer to my question? At first sight there seems to be none: no word for "equality" gets into the text of Books 4 and 5 where he propounds, defends, and applies his definition of "justice," nor yet in any later book in this extensive dialogue, except in 8, in his brush with democracy, where he handles the word brusquely in noncommittal reportage,[65] or wry epigram,[66] or poison-dipped gibes,[67] without a moment's pause to pick it up

---

[61] For such uses of *isos,* see the examples in LSJ, *s.v.* ἴσος (sense B, I, 2) and in *PS,* 184, n. 78 *sub fin.* An earlier example not cited by either is Theognis 543–44:

χρή με παρὰ στάθμην καὶ γνώμονα τήνδε δικάσαι,
Κύρνε, δίκην, ἴσόν τ' ἀμφοτέροισιν δόμεν.

[62] Cited in n. 11 above. The sense would be the same if we translated *aneu logou* "apart from theory."

[63] First Callicles (483c5 and 484a1), then Socrates (488e–489a) use *to ison echein* to express the opposite of *adikein* (= *pleon echein*). This is one of the very few points on which the adversaries agree without argument.

[64] See the reference to 359c6 on p. 75 above.

[65] Democracy is said to come about "when the poor, winning out, kill some of the other party, expel others, and *give an equal share (ex . . . isou metadōsi) of the constitution and the offices to the rest, making most of the appointments to office by lot*" (557a)—the italicized clauses are a neutral, noncontroversial description of a democratic regime, which would be as acceptable to democrats as to their adversaries: *ex isou metadidonai* (or *metechein) tēs politeias* would be a standard way of referring to the uniquely democratic allocation of civic rights; see, e.g., the references given in *PS,* nn. to 193–94, and cf. 174n.41.

[66] 558c5–6.

[67] 562d–e (where *homoious, homoion* are being used as variants for *isous, ison*: cf. *exisousthai,* 563a1); 563b7–9. There is cheap exaggeration in these two passages, and the last plays

and probe its meaning. Does this betray evasiveness or uncertainty in his attitude to equality? By no means. Plato knows his own mind well and manages to speak it forcefully in spite of a defective vocabulary, though the message would have been clearer with the right words than it is now without them. The one he needed most urgently at this point is Greek for "impartiality": for this there is only *isotēs,* and to recognize this use of *isotēs* you would have to distinguish *formal* from *substantive* equality,[68] *equal regard for* [19] *rights* from *regard for equal rights*[69]—a distinction that had yet to be made and was never made in the classical period: it is still missing in Aristotle when he links up *to dikaion* with *to ison* in the *Nicomachean Ethics.*[70] I want to argue that nevertheless there is no wobbling or confusion in Plato's attitude to impartiality; his moral commitment to it is firm and fiercely uncompromising.

We see this in the treatment he prescribes for that class to which he was most strongly tempted to be partial: his own. Every secular aristocracy known to man has used its power to corner for itself privileged wealth, sex, and leisure. Plato's aristocracy is to have absolute control of the coercive appa-

---

to the male chauvinist gallery in a way which is surprising to say the least after Plato's bold words on the emancipation of women in Book 5. Popper is perfectly right in speaking of these passages as "abusive attack on democracy," "cheap cracks," 254.

[68] To say this is not to imply that if you had not drawn that distinction (or an equivalent one) you could not have used *isos, isotēs* to mean "impartial," "impartiality." To follow a rule of language, one does not have to know the rule, still less to know that one is following it in a particular case: cf. *PS,* 241n. 53. Thus Plato found it natural to speak of an *impartial* judge as an "equal" one (*Laws* 957c, τὸν μέλλοντα δικαστὴν ἴσον γενέσθαι . . .) though he had never *recognized* in his writings that *isos* can be used to mean just that.

[69] The first corresponds to formal justice, which is a second-order component of justice, consisting in respect for the second-order right to have all of one's substantive rights respected. (Cf. my "Justice and Equality" ([above, n. 20], 55.) The difference between formal and substantive equality becomes clearer if one reflects on the fact that, within wide limits, they are independent variables. Thus formal equality comports with extreme variations in substantive equality: if A is a slave and B a citizen, then, so far as legal justice is concerned, formal equality will be satisfied if and only if each of the vast inequalities in their legal rights is strictly enforced. Conversely, substantive equality does not entail formal equality. Thus the substantive right which persons of all colors have to "the equal protection of the laws" under the constitution of the United States may be nullified by a racist law-enforcement officer who thumbs his nose at formal equality. Plato's stand on equality, as I shall be arguing, could be lucidly described as full commitment to formal equality, unaccompanied by any commitment to substantive equality, though without going to the other extreme: no commitment to substantive *in*equality either.

[70] The best he can do toward locating the idea of impartiality on his conceptual map is to note that what he calls "commutative" justice is not "geometrical" but "arithmetical" equality (*N.E.* 1131b32ff.). This is not nearly good enough, since as he (and others) use "arithmetical" equality it is in the first instance a concept of *substantive* equality, referring primarily to those equal rights of citizenship which are characteristic of the democratic constitution. What he needs (and fails) to locate is that particular species of "arithmetical" equality which could be shared by both proponents and opponents of democratic equality.

ratus of the state[71] and is, therefore, able to grab and keep as much of each of these three [20] kinds of goodies as it wants.[72] But Plato decrees that the rulers are to have not more, but less, of each than will their subjects. Private property will be denied the Guardians absolutely.[73] Like Lenin's first soviet, they are to subsist on workingmen's wages.[74] Private family will be also denied them; during long stretches of their adult lives—thirty-five for men, twenty for women—they must endure the misery of celibacy relieved at infrequent intervals[75] by the bleak gratifications of reproductive service to the state.[76] And for fifteen years they must also renounce what Plato thinks they would covet most of all[77]—the chance to do full-time intellectual work. Historians tell us that no ruling class has ever surrendered of its own accord functionless privilege it had power to keep. When Plato insists that his philosophers submit to these massive renunciations simply because those privileges would be socially unfunctional and counterfunctional,[78] he declares unmistakably his commitment to impartiality: his actions speak more loudly than would words. [21]

And he does more: he discloses at the same time the principle of the allocation of substantive rights entailed by his conception of justice—a principle

[71] Though this is, of course, built into the political structure of the *Republic* (the military, the only arms-bearing group, in the *polis,* are under the sole control of the philosophers), one is apt to forget it, because references to internal repression or compulsion are so rare: 415e1–2 is the clearest; and Professor Michael Rohr has pointed out to me the implied use of force in 465a8–9.

[72] Plato calls this to our attention. He has Adeimantus ask how Socrates could justify the denial of property to the guardians when "the *polis* really belongs to them." Socrates recalls this later on (466a): "Do you remember that someone reproached us earlier for not making the guardians happy, who with power to have all the property of the citizens (οἷς ἐξὸν πάντα ἔχειν τὰ τῶν πολιτῶν) were to have no property (οὐδὲν ἔχοιεν)?"

[73] 416d–420a.

[74] παρὰ τῶν ἄλλων τροφὴν λαμβάνοντας, μισθὸν τῆς φυλακῆς, 464c1–2.

[75] Just when these are to come is not stated. They may all fall within the duration of an annual festival, as Cornford conjectures (*Plato's Republic,* 159 n. 2). The essential constraint is that the number of the occasions on which intercourse is permitted will be just sufficient to impregnate all the women who are due to bear children during a given year.

[76] It may be objected that Plato, a homosexual (cf. *PS,* 25n. 74), would not consider this deprivation particularly burdensome. The objection has no force: the proposals have in view a constituency within which the desire for heterosexual intimacy is widely distributed at the usual pitch of intensity. Otherwise, the prospect of more frequent stud-service (460b) and of milder sexual liberties with partners of both sexes (466c1–3) would not be the incentives to martial valor which they are obviously meant to be. (On the difference between 460b and 466c1–3 conflated by Popper [150–51] as by others, see *PS,* 22n. 65).

[77] Judging from the earnestness of his apologia for the justice of the infliction of this hardship on the philosophers (519d–521b).

[78] Obviously so in the case of the third (on the implied assumption that the job of government would not be done as well if relegated to a nonphilosophical bureaucracy), and certainly so in the case of the first two as well (on the explicit assumption that private property and private family would be morally corrupting: cf. n. 85 below).

which otherwise we would not have known, for he never spells it out, and we could not have squeezed it out of his central intuition of reciprocity in the pursuit of happiness. For all this says is that everyone will behave justly if, and only if, he so conducts himself as to maximize his individual contribution to the common happiness; and that if he so behaves, he may be assured that he too will have *a* share in the collective product of the like contributions of others. How big will be *his* share relatively to that of others, it does not say. Plato never tackles this question in the *Republic*. And if we had had to guess our way to his answer without further directions from him, we would have been likely to guess wrong: the plausible, indeed the only reasonable, inference would have been that his rule of distributive justice is contained in the doctrine of "proportional" equality[79] with which Plato flirted both before and in the *Republic* and was eventually to marry in the *Laws*. He alludes to it in the *Gorgias* under the caption of "geometrical" equality.[80] He makes momentary use of it in Book 8 of the *Republic*, leaning on it there for the effect of the quip about democracy "distributing a sort of equality to equals and unequals alike" (558c).[81] And he praises it to the skies in the *Laws*, declaring there that "to distribute more to the greater (merit), less to the lesser"[82] would be "always precisely what constitutes political justice"[83] and natural, divinely ordained, [22] justice to boot. But when he comes to work out the allocation of rights in the central books of the *Republic*, he cold-shoulders it[84] not even a remote

---

[79] Popular among fourth-century conservatives: Isocrates, *Nicocles* 15 (cited in n. 89 below), and *Areopagiticus* 21–22 (who speaks of it as *kat' axian timān hekaston*); Aristotle, *N.E.* 1131a30ff. (cf. n. 12 above), and *Pol.* 1280a9ff. and 1301a26ff.

[80] 508a6–7, where "geometrical equality" is identified with *dikaiosunē* in opposition to the *pleonexia* advocated by Callicles. For comment see E. R. Dodds, *Plato, Gorgias* (Oxford, 1959), 339–40; and *PS*, 195n.119.

[81] Cf. my comment on this in *PS*, 194.

[82] 757c1–6, τῷ γὰρ μείζονι πλείω, τῷ δ' ἐλάττονι σμικρότερα νέμει . . . , τὸ πρέπον ἑκατέροις ἀπονέμει κατὰ λόγον.

[83] 757c6–7, ἔστι γὰρ δήπου καὶ τὸ πολιτικὸν ἡμῖν ἀεὶ τοῦτ' αὐτὸ τὸ δίκαιον. The significance of the *kai*, lost in some translations—but preserved in A. E. Taylor's (otherwise uncomfortably inflated) rendering, "this sheer justice is always also the statesmanlike policy"—I take to be: this "proportional" (*kata logon*, 757b5–6) allocation, which is sanctioned by both God (*Dios krisis*, b7) and nature (πρὸς τὴν αὐτῶν φύσιν ἑκατέρῳ, c3), is not only ideally best ("the truest and best," b6), but *also* practicable (for the second-best state envisaged in the *Laws*) and thus the statesmanlike allocation (*politikon*, c6). Plato's enthusiasm for "proportional" equality here makes him overstate its validity. No sooner has he said that this *is* political justice than he has to backtrack and admit (757d6ff.) that the other "equality," the mechanical or arithmetical one (757b4–5), must also be allowed a place, regrettably so, "for it breaks off from the correct justice when it occurs" (παρὰ δίκην τὴν ὀρθήν ἐστι παρατεθραυμένον, 757e2).

[84] The significance of this fact seems to have gone unnoticed in the scholarly literature, where he is regularly cited as upholding the principle of "proportional" equality in the *Republic* on the strength of 558c: Barker, *Greek Political Theory* (4th ed. New York, 1951), 139n.2; K. Bringmann, *Studien zu den politischen Ideen des Isokrates* (*Hypomnemata*, No. 14, 1965), 86;

allusion to proportional equality there, and for good reason: it would have implied that the Guardians, who do the most for the *polis,* have a right to all of its largest rewards, while, as we have seen, Plato repeatedly mandates not bigger and juicier Plums for the biggest contributors, but smaller and drier ones, hygienic prunes instead of hedonic plums.[85]

If Plato had undertaken to make "proportional" equality the central, instead of a merely tangential, principle of distributive justice in the *Republic,* he would have discovered how limited are its uses for this purpose. It works, so far as it does work, only for *socially distributable* compensations. It cannot regulate the greatest by far of the rewards vouchsafed to the philosophers— the one which comes to them through their very love of "Justice itself," in their mystical communion with the Form,[86] and in the effect this has on their own soul: the incarnation of the eternal harmony in the tissues of their psyche.[87] The question of anyone's distributing [23] this to anyone does not arise: it is that reward of virtue which is virtue itself. As to distributable rewards, honor is the one that can, and will, be shared out to the philosophers in quantities worthy of their matchless contribution; they will be billionaires of honor in the Platonic state.[88] But in respect of other kinds of socially distributable goods, Platonic justice would flout "proportional" equality. It would outrage Isocrates[89] and co. by giving less of some of the major means of

---

R. Maurer, *Platons "Staat" und die Demokratie* (Berlin, 1970), 75ff. My own comment on 558c in *PS,* 194 (in the essay, *"Isonomia Politikē,"* originally published in 1964) also misses this point.

[85] Considerations of political hygiene decide the economic and sexual deprivations inflicted on the Guardians: if they were allowed private property, they would become "hateful masters, instead of allies, to the other citizens" (417a–b); and if allowed the personal bonds engendered by private family (and also, presumably, extramarital sexual attachments), the total emotional identification with the *polis* would be fractured (462a–e). Popper's dictum that for Plato "morality is nothing but political hygiene" (107: see my comment, *PS,* 14–15) is false only because of its wild overstatement; there is indeed a large dose of political hygiene in the morality of the *Republic.*

[86] See *PS,* 52–53 and 54–56. And cf. n. 109 below.

[87] 500c2–d1:

Viewing and contemplating that which is ordered and forever invariant . . . (will not the philosopher) imitate it and, so far as possible, assimilate itself to it? Or do you think it would be possible not to imitate that with which one holds loving converse? . . . So the philosopher, consorting with the divine and the harmonious, will himself become divine and harmonious so far as this is possible for man.

[88] Quasi-divine honors will be accorded to them:

And the state should establish public memorials and sacrifices for them, as to divinities if the Pythian oracle approves or, if not, as to divine and godlike men. (540b7–c2 in Shorey's translation)

[89] Isocrates' account of the principle of proportional equality:

make the largest distribution to the best, the next largest to the next best, and in the same proportion to the third, fourth, and so on. (*Nicocles* 15)

happiness to those who give the *polis* more. That is why I have been suggesting that to reach the general principle of rights-allocation in the *Republic* we should follow him in forgetting all about "proportional" equality. His unstated, but firmly followed, rule is that each has a right to those, and only those, socially distributable benefits which will maximize his contribution, regardless of the ratio which the value of services rendered bears to that of benefits received. This model of just distribution would not require us to make output to individuals proportionate to the value of their input. Quite the contrary: it would constrain us to curtail rights when leaner rations are more likely to yield better service.

Given this model, and the collateral assumptions which Plato makes about what is best done by whom, the allocation of rights which produces the social structure of the rationally ordered *polis* of Plato's vision becomes completely lucid: both its political inequalities, which are catastrophic, and its socioeconomic equalities, which are substantial, become intelligible without any need to refer to "proportional" equality at all. The right to participate in the functions of government—in any such function whatsoever, be it executive, deliberative, legislative, judicial, electoral, or administrative—is denied absolutely to the populace; it is handed over *in toto* to a tiny minority of intellectuals[90] simply and solely because this function, like every social function, belongs of right [24] to those who can do it best, and Plato is persuaded that the philosophers would do it best and better without than with participation by the governed. The question of making government the exclusive prerogative of the philosophers as a reward for their preeminent virtue does not arise; if it did, the answer would be in reverse: because they are so virtuous, they can be expected to make bigger sacrifices in personal happiness for the common good, the biggest of them being the very exercise of the right to govern, which Plato thinks a painful bore. And to the question of allowing them greater liberty as a reward for virtue, the answer would be the same: in respect of personal liberty they are not to be better off, but worse off, than the producers. If a philosopher were to voice a forbidden thought[91] or sport a deviant haircut, he would be censured more severely than would others lower down the social scale who do not have to carry so heavy a burden of exemplary virtue. Similarly in the economic area, the design of rights is strictly functional and

---

[90] *Tōi smikrotatōi ethnei*—so small that there would be "many more" coppersmiths than Guardians in the *polis* (428d11–e7).

[91] Popper is surely right in rejecting the claim that Plato believed in free speech for the upper classes (270): free speech would be meaningless unless it included the liberty to advocate unorthodox views (not merely to voice them noncommittally in argument) and to do so in public forums (not merely *in camera*). But Popper goes too far in maintaining (ibid.) that Plato would not even permit the philosophers free discussion among themselves. For this there is no positive evidence whatever and it would take evidence of the most unambiguous kind to convince us that Plato would deny to his philosophers the lifeblood of philosophical inquiry which courses through his own dialogues.

yields, on one hand, the radical equality of monastic poverty for the philosophers and, on the other, a sharp reduction of inequality in the distribution of
wealth among its producers: neither opulence nor indigence will be allowed
them because either deviation from the norm of modest sufficiency would be
detrimental to good craftsmanship.[92] [25]

III

So we would be misdescribing Plato's view if we were to say with Popper that
for Plato "justice meant inequality."[93] Plato never said anything to imply this.
What he would have said if required to put his view into that kind of language
is that justice could mean either equality or inequality, depending on which of
the two would be most conducive to "doing one's own." The greatest interest
of his theory for the student of the spectrum of variations in philosophical
concepts of justice is that here, if anywhere in Western thought, we have the
chance to see what the link of justice with equality would look like if it were
reduced to the equal right to functional reciprocity, on one hand,[94] and to
formal equality, on the other. We would miss our chance if we construed Plato
as a root-and-branch adversary of equality, for we would then be, in effect,
denying him any concept of justice at all: without formal equality at the very
least, justice would be as much of a contradiction as would triangularity without angularity. And though formal equality is, tautologously, a formal principle, adherence to it is no formality. The moral dimension of the principle is
impartiality, and I have been at pains to underline the sincerity of Plato's

---

[92] 421c–e. To realize how drastic would be the curtailment of inequalities in income in the
Platonic *polis* in contrast to the status quo, one should remember that Plato envisages an economy
of self-employed farmers and craftsmen (working, presumably, with individually owned slaves),
while the economic inequalities of contemporary Athens were due mainly to the existence of an
entrepreneurial class and, even more, to a class of absentee landowners and rentiers living on
inherited wealth, like Callias, reputed to be the richest man in Athens; we may form some idea of
his income from the fact that Nikias, who was not particularly famous for his wealth, was still
rich enough to own a thousand slaves he hired out at an obol a day to a concessionaire at the silver
mines at Laureion (*Xenophon, Poroi* 4, 14; the same passage mentions two other Athenian gentlemen who hired out respectively six hundred and three hundred slaves to mine operators).

[93] "Why did Plato claim, in the *Republic*, that justice meant inequality if, in general usage, it
meant equality?" (92).

[94] The rule of distributive justice mentioned on p. 89 above—"that each has a right to those,
and only those, socially distributable benefits which will maximize his contribution"—defines an
equal right, entailing equal treatment for all members of the *polis* in that their function is their
sole title to the benefits distributed within the *polis*. Hence all are assured that all contributions of
equal value will be equally rewarded, and that their individual reward, be it equal or unequal to
that of others, will be fixed on the scale which is most likely to elicit from each maximal contribution to the happiness and excellence of the *polis*—that is to say (as I have argued on pp. 80–84
above), the happiness and excellence of every member of the *polis*, including their own.

commitment to this exacting and costly virtue. Only when we have realized that to this extent Plato is at one with us—he has concern, burning concern, for justice, not for some artifact of his own invention which he chooses to name "justice"—can we measure the distance which separates his justice from ours because of the difference in our respective convictions on the relation of justice to substantive equality. [26]

That distance is greatest for those committed to the liberal view of justice. Here let me speak for myself: Plato's principle of the justice of reciprocity in the pursuit of happiness and excellence I would, of course, accept. But all rights generated by that principle I would subordinate to those generated by the principle of equal human dignity. And these are strictly equal: inhering in man's humanity,[95] not in his excellence or productivity, they are untouched by variations in excellence or productivity. Not that I would be less concerned for high achievement than was Plato, but that my very concern for this derives from my concern for humanity. When I ask: "What is excellence for? What is science for, and art, and every other value-creating form of human endeavor?" I can only answer, "For the sake of human beings—those now living and those yet unborn—whose lives may be made thereby more secure and more free, may be ennobled and enriched." In this capacity—as, in Kant's phrase, ends-in-themselves[96] and, therefore, as the ends for which all the gains of civilization are, in the last analysis, mere means—human individuals are all absolutely equal and are so recognized in the precepts of morality[97] and in democratic law. The allocation of differential rights must, therefore, start from a base of substantive equality, taking that as the rock-bottom foundation of all other rights. Plato's scheme has no such base. Its substantive differentials are bottomless. He therefore [27] accepts as entirely just inequalities entailing personal subjection so extreme as to be unparalleled in Greek experi-

---

[95] In Locke's phrase, "they belong to men as men, and not as members of society" (*Two Treatises on Civil Government*, 2, 14). He says this of (the right to) "truth and keeping of faith"; but he would certainly affirm it of all those rights which he deems "inalienable" and "imprescriptible."

[96] See Appendix B.

[97] This fundamental point is insufficiently stressed—seldom even mentioned—in discussions of human equality (in the moral, not the biological, import of this notion). It is particularly relevant to a critique of Plato, who not only fails to recognize that our common moral precepts define constraints on conduct which are equally binding on all (as they must, to be equally protective of all) but, in effect, denies this presupposition in his discussion of the "noble lie": the obligation to speak the truth does not rest equally on all; it holds for private citizens addressing rulers, but not reciprocally (389b, 414ff.): the fact that the asymmetry is rationalized (lying is permitted only for the good of those lied to, and only the rulers have knowledge of the good) does not mitigate the inequality but, on the contrary, enforces it. Popper's charge that "Plato established for his philosopher kings the duty and privilege of using lies and deceit for the benefit of the city" (328) is exactly correct. Levinson's reply (*In Defense of Plato* [Cambridge, Mass., 1953], 435) concedes the charge of "lying propaganda"; the defense he offers—that there is "some truth" in the Platonic "noble lie"—is beside the point.

ence, except in slavery; and Plato does not hesitate to depict it as idealized slavery.

He does so late in Book 9 (590c2–d6) in one of the least noticed passages in the *Republic*,[98] though it is surely one of the most revealing:

> Why do you think the condition of the manual laborer is despised?[99] Is it for any reason other than this: when one has by nature a feeble portion of the best part [of the soul] (i.e., reason), he cannot rule the brood of beasts within him, but can only serve them and learn to flatter them? . . .

> Therefore, that he too may be ruled in like manner as the best man, we say that he ought to be the slave[100] of that best man who has the [28] divine thing in him—not that we think the slave should be so ruled to his own hurt, as Thrasymachus thought about the governed, but because it is best for everyone to be ruled by the divine and rational thing—preferably his own and in him, or else imposed on him from the

---

[98] 590c2–591a3. I have referred to this passage in my "Slavery in Plato's Thought" (*PS*, 151 and n. 17, where I comment on the earlier use of this passage by B. Bosanquet) and then again in my essay "The Individual as Object of Love in Plato" (*PS*, p. 13 and n. 34) and, more briefly, in other essays. It is cited to good effect by J. Neu on p. 248 of his paper (above, n. 52); and there are valuable notes on the passage in Shorey's translation. I can recall no reference to it in many of the discussions of Platonic justice to which it would be highly germane—Popper ⟨above, n. 2⟩, Barker ⟨above, n. 84⟩, Murphy (*Interpretation of Plato's "Republic"* [Oxford, 1951]), Cross and Woozley ⟨above, n. 3⟩—but cannot check for lack of an *index locorum* in any of these books except Popper's, which does *not* list it in its index. There is no reference to it in G. R. Morrow, *Plato's Cretan City* (Princeton, 1960). None in L. G. Versenyi, "Plato and his Liberal Opponents," *Philosophy* 46 (1971), 222–37, who reproduces its main ideas *in propria persona* ("The freedom of the natural slave, the man so devoid of a knowledge of what is good for him that he is incapable of ruling himself for his own good, is not good for the slave. For his own good, he should be ruled, absolutely, by someone who knows" [232]).

[99] "Reproach" in Lindsay's and Shorey's translations of *oneidos* is surely wrong: it would convey the implication that manual labor is *morally* discreditable, which, of course, is not what Plato means here and is not necessarily contained in the proper connotation of *oneidos* (to be sure, this is normally used to mean "reproach, censure"; but it can also be used more loosely to cover unfavorable response [elicited by nonmoral, as well as by moral, properties]). Cornford's rendering of *oneidos pherei* "discredited as debasing," gets the sense right, but only by overtranslating. With *oneidos pherei* here about "banausic" occupations, cf. *epirrētoi . . . eisi* in Xenophon, *Oec.* 4, 2–3, where the reason offered is that these employments make bodies "more womanish" and *thereby* make the souls "feebler" (a common sentiment: for Plato's version of it, see 495d–e, with Adam's and Shorey's notes *ad loc.*), while Plato's point here is that the intellectual deficiency in the "slave's" congenital endowment (his "nature": *phusei echei* 590c3, to be compared with *phusis* in 433a6) is the basic (and unavoidable) cause of his moral debility.

[100] *Doulos*, "servant" in Jowett, "subject" in Cornford (followed by H.D.P. Lee) in their translations of this passage, are surely too weak for *doulos* here. That "chattel slave" is *not* meant here is no objection: neither is "slave" in English confined to this more restricted sense which is the *primary* one of *doulos* and the *exclusive* one of *andrapodon*. With the use of *doulos* here, cf. that of *douleia* in 563d6, κἂν ὁτιοῦν δουλείας τις προσφέρηται: here too the word is not meant in its literal sense of chattel slavery, but to make Plato's point the word should still be rendered "slavery" (as it is by Lindsay, as is also *doulos* in the present passage).

outside, so that so far as possible we may all be alike and friends, governed by the same thing.

Here in microcosm is Plato's vision of just relations between two persons whose luck in the natural lottery has been grossly unequal. The one with low congenital endowment of intelligence ought to be, and for his own good, so stripped of any right to self-determination that Plato (who is not squeamish— he is not Benjamin Jowett) does not hold back from using *doulos* to describe that role, though well aware that the word is one of the ugliest in the language: few carry stronger charges of scorn and terror. Plato uses it nonetheless, confident that he can upgrade it, purge it of this ugliness by marrying it to one of the most attractive: *philos*. Plato's message is that the *doulos* can be *philos*. The punch line is "so that so far as possible, we may all be alike and friends, governed by the same thing"; but the punch is weakened in English because "friend" is not as strong as *philos*. [101] Plato is not speaking of two people who just happen to be on good, friendly terms, exchanging pleasantries at the street corner, and the like. That in itself would be remarkable enough, considering that one of them is said to be the other's "slave." We might have expected that such a surrender of one's freedom to another human being would leave one bitterly resentful, nursing a scarcely concealed hostility for the man who stands over one's head with the right to dictate one's every action. But when Plato speaks of the manual worker as the intellectual's *philos*, it is love, not mere friendship, that he means—love according to Plato's [29] understanding, [102] sustained by solidarity in the pursuit of happiness and excellence, since each gives indispensable support to the other's quest: If they did not have each other, both would fail: the philosopher, for he would then have to divert precious time and energy to meaningless drudgery; the manual worker too would fail, and more disastrously, for without direction from above his life would be bestial: he would be ruled "by the brood of beasts within him." [103] So only by pooling their disparate resources, fixed ineluctably for

---

[101] Thus, consider Apollo's statement about Admetus in Euripides' *Alcestis* (15), πάντας δ᾽ ἐλέγξας καὶ διεξελθὼν φίλους. How ludicrous it would be to take this to be saying that Admetus made the round of his *friends*, asking each in turn if one of them would die for him. No one in his senses could address such a question to persons other than those to whom one is bound by the deepest ties of love. Needless to say, *philos* is not always used in so strong a sense. But its normal use is stronger enough than that of *friend* to make *philous* exactly right in the above statement, where "friends" would be hopelessly wrong (unless qualified directly or by the context). And cf. *PS,* 4.

[102] See *PS,* 13ff.

[103] It should be emphasized that Plato predicates his *apologia* for this type of symbiotic relation solely on the conviction that it is genuine *philia* and does *not* also argue for it on the ground that (a higher sort of) *freedom* would also be realized in it. When Versenyi produces such an argument on Plato's behalf (*loc. cit.* in n. 98 above), he fails to make it clear to the reader (perhaps does not realize it himself) that it is totally foreign to Plato's own thought. Plato would

each by nature, can either of them have the chance to find the best life for himself and make the best that can be made of himself. If the worker has even a glimmering of this truth, how could he resent the deprivation of rights which casts him in the role of slave to "the best man"? How could you fail to respond with love to one who stands by you to share with you day by day his "divine" gift of reason?

Plato is making here two remarkable assumptions: on one hand, the natural depravity of nonintellectual man; on the other, the [30] intellectual man's capacity for incorruptible virtue. The manual worker, congenitally weak in reason, if granted the right to make autonomous moral choices for himself, would make predictably bad ones, and if he had the power to indulge them, his life would be, like the tyrant's in Book 9, a seething mass of sensuality, cupidity, and vanity. For such a man, hope of salvation lies only in living under another's moral tutelage. The intellectual, on the other hand, Plato credits with such marvelous perfectibility that having other human beings completely in his power could not corrupt him. His check over the "brood of beasts" within *him* would be so secure that he would never yield to the temptation to treat his "slave" as anything but a friend.

How was it that Plato found both of these assumptions reasonable? The answer lies in that deeper, meta-normative, stratum of his thought, the metaphysical subsoil of his moral philosophy, his two-world doctrine of reality. This is, of course, well-known; no one could miss it; the central books of the *Republic* are given over to it. But not all of its links with the moral and political doctrine that preceded are on the surface, though they are not far below it either. The one that strikes me as the most significant is this: Plato's bifurcation of reality produces a bifurcation of humanity.[104] It breaks up the

---

certainly agree with Versenyi that "freedom . . . is good only to the extent that it is accompanied by knowledge" and that "this is the freedom Plato's state is designed to provide." But Plato would *not* have said that "this (Platonic) state, *far from denying freedom,* liberates man better than any rival polity, be it as 'liberal' as it may" (my emphasis). On the contrary, Plato would recognize that his state *does* deny freedom to most of its citizens (for their own good, of course) and that there is to be far less freedom in his state than in contemporary Athens, which in his view (557b–558b; 562b–564a) is swimming (and drowning) in freedom. That is the whole point of his speaking of the manual worker's relation to the philosopher in our passage as "slavery." When Plato runs up the flag of "freedom," side by side with *philia* and "wisdom," as he does (only) in the *Laws* (693b, 701d; cf. Appendix C below), it is not because he has found his way to a sublimated concept of freedom (such as St. Paul was to epitomize in the phrase "whose service is perfect freedom"), but because he has *given up* the paradigm of *douleia* of producer to philosopher he had championed with full conviction in the *Republic,* has turned away from political absolutism, and is now arguing for a "mixed constitution," a mean between "monarchy" and "democracy" (697c, 699e, 756e), still presenting *douleia* and freedom as opposites (694a). The *douleia* to which he now gives unqualified approval is *slavery to the laws*—not to a man, no matter how enlightened (700a; and cf. the new conception of state officials as "servants of the laws" (*hupēretas tois nomois,* 715c–d]).

[104] For an analogous (and no less devastating) division of humanity within Aristotle's very

human family into two different breeds of men. One, by far the largest, is doomed to live outside the real world of truth and value; it will never know the eternal Forms of Justice, Beauty, Goodness and the rest. The moral judgments of such persons, and not only their judgments—the valuations that govern the longings, anxieties, and terrors of their lives—are either secondhand, consisting of what they have been *told* is just and good and beautiful, or else, when firsthand, are hedonic calculations within the sense-bound world of their experience:[105] their soul, stuck [31] inside an animal, knows only animal pleasures—the ones to pacify the greedy tastebuds, the itchy epidermis, of the polymorphous brute. People in this predicament can make no proper estimates of happiness.[106] Their pains are real enough, but most of what they know of joy is only relief from pain, illusion of pleasure, a grey mistaken for white against the black.[107] This is how Plato pictures their lot:

> Bent over their tables, they batten like cattle with stooping heads and eyes glued to the ground; so they guzzle and copulate, and in their insatiable greed they kick

---

different metaphysical framework, see J. M. Rist, "Aristotle: The Value of Man and the Origin of Morality," *Canadian Journal of Philosophy* 4 (1974), 1–21.

[105] If one of Plato's cave-dwellers were to venture beyond the moral standards he has been taught by his betters and try to figure out for himself the rights and wrongs of conduct, he would be lost. All he would reach by his own efforts would be the pseudo-morality Plato described in the *Phaedo* as a calculus of hedonic utilities ("exchanging pleasures for pleasures, pains for pains, fears for fears, like coins, the smaller for the bigger, the bigger for the smaller" [69A]), producing the fake virtue of persons who are "temperate because of intemperance" and "brave because of cowardice" (68d–69a): cf. *PS*, 137n.79.

[106] The far-reaching political implications of the doctrine of false pleasure in the *Republic* have seldom been noticed. The doctrine seals the disqualification of non-philosophers to make judgments concerning the general happiness; they are not even fit judges of *their own* happiness.

[107] 584e7–585a5:

> And would it surprise you if those who have had no experience of the real thing make many unsound judgments, and when it comes to pleasure and pain and the in-between state, they are so conditioned that when moving into pain their impressions are correct—they really are in pain—but, when moving from pain to the in-between state, though they do have a strong impression of getting fulfillment and pleasure, they are fooled; like men who compare grey only with black, having had no experience of white, they are only comparing pain with the lack of it, having had no experience of pleasure?

Plato is not suggesting that the illusion he is describing can occur only in the case he mentions, i.e., when relief from pain is mistaken for pleasure. In his earlier description (583c ff.) the phenomenon is perfectly symmetrical: hedonic illusion may occur when loss of pleasure is felt as pain (583e1–2; 584a4–8) as in the converse case. His point in the passage I have cited is best understood if one recalls his doctrine that, with trivial exceptions (e.g., that of odors in 584b), the "real" pleasures are intellectual, hence out of the range of the mass-man's experience. He is the man Plato is talking about in the citation: he knows the black of the hedonic scale (physical pain is as real for him as for the philosopher) but not its upper ranges of dazzling white (spiritual bliss is a closed book to him), so he mistakes for pleasure his moments of relief from pain. This is the pervasive delusion of his life, endemic to his condition, and Plato is content to disregard the opposite error because he thinks its incidence would be negligible in this case.

and butt one another to death with horns and hooves of steel, because they can never satisfy with these unreal things the part of themselves which is itself unreal and is incapable of lasting satisfaction.[108]

Now think of the other breed. When the philosopher breaks out of the shadow-world of the Cave into the light-filled, sun-drenched world of Form, what he achieves is not only intellectual illumination but, simultaneously, in one and the same experience, moral regeneration [32].[109] To see the Form of Justice out there in all its beauty, irradiated by the Good, is not only to recognize in it the truth behind all of his previous gropings after it, but to be seized with a love for it which fills him with passionate longing to make it the ordering principle of his own life and of the life of his *polis*. This is the mystical element at the core of Plato's metaphysics. I call it "mystical" because no fully rational explanation can be given of the implosion set off in the philosopher's soul by the vision of Form which makes a new man out of him. The varieties of mysticism are legion. It can be wholly this-worldly, as in Zen. In Plato it is radically otherworldly—as much so as in Augustine or Paul. Through Plato we get a glimpse of what Christian otherworldliness would have been like if it had not been informed by *agapē* and its ethics had not been humanized by the man-centeredness of its Jewish God. A moment ago, speaking for humanistic ethics, I said that when I ask, "What is excellence for?" I can only reply, "For humanity." Plato would protest that my question is senseless: excellence, he would say, eternally complete in the world of Form, is not for anything or anyone: it simply *is,* and its imperative to us is only the imperious love its being evokes in any soul capable of knowing it. He would turn my question around: "What is humanity for?" he would ask. And his reply would not be so unlike the one in the Westminster Confession. Substitute "Form" for "God" and it would be the same: The chief end of man is to glorify Form and enjoy it for ever. If you are a Platonic philosopher, you have found the meaning of your life, your true vocation, in faithful service to the Forms of

---

[108] 586a–b, translation mainly after Cornford.

[109] Cf. the citation from 500c2–d1 in n. 87 above, and cf. the representation of vision of Form in the *Symposium* (212a) as a procreative union which issues in the birth of "real virtue, not images of it," and in the corresponding passage in the *Republic* about the philosopher's "real union with reality" (490b5), from which "a sound and just disposition, accompanied by *sōphrosunē* (490c) is bound to follow. Cf. also the earlier description of the philosopher's "unremitting passion for any knowledge that will reveal to him that reality which is eternal and immune to the vagaries of generation and decay" (485b1–3), a passion which absorbs most of the psychic energy that in other men usually goes into concupiscence (485d6–12: the "hydraulic" metaphor), so that he becomes "temperate and free from the love of money" (485e3) and could not be "a bad partner (*dussumbolos*) or unjust" (486b7). I have touched all too briefly on this aspect of Platonic mysticism in *PS,* 52, and regret that I did not pursue it elsewhere in that book, failing to do so in section VI.2.ii of the essay on "Justice and Happiness in the *Republic*" where it is particularly relevant.

Justice, Beauty, Goodness, and the rest. You are [33] possessed by a transcendent love beside which earthly passions pale. You have discovered bliss which turns the prizes of this world into trash.[110]

I started off in this paper with a semantic investigation and find myself now in the thick of mystical metaphysics. Let me state more clearly than I have yet done the rationale of the itinerary. The gravest charge brought against Plato within my lifetime has been the imputation of bad faith: knowing that justice meant equality, Plato made it mean inequality "to make propaganda for his totalitarian state." The quotation is from page 92 of Sir Karl Popper's *Open Society and Its Enemies.*[111] Though my object in this paper has not been to defend Plato's theory—as is abundantly clear by now, I consider it indefensible—but only to understand it, I could scarcely have achieved my end without facing up to the charge that the theory had been, to begin with, a well-intentioned[112] lie. Accordingly I dealt at some length with the claim that Plato severs all of the ancient ties of justice with equality. Made plausible in the extreme by the fact that there is not a word about equality in Plato's formulation of the theory, I argued that [34] it is nonetheless false, for if we look beyond the verbal texture of the theory to its normative force, we will find that it is firmly committed to that formal equality which is the backbone of justice and that it dictates a measure of substantive equality in one area of the life of the *polis,* the economic. At that point I had to ask myself how Plato could still be led to wipe out every vestige of human, as distinct from functional, rights, thereby stripping his fellow-townsmen not only of those rights that answered to the greatest achievement of their corporate life—

---

[110] "Trash" or "nonsense" (*phluaria*) Plato uses repeatedly to underscore the triviality of the sensible and the sensual in contrast to the ideal and intellectual: *Phaedo* 69c, the body "fills us with loves and appetites and fears and all sorts of phantoms and trash"; *Republic* 515d, the philosopher, once out of the Cave, will come to understand that all he saw there was "trash"; *Symposium* 211e, the Idea of Beauty, seen at the height of the ascent, is "beauty unalloyed, pure, unmixed, not full of human flesh and color and a lot of other mortal trash." And Plato has many other images for the trashiness of physical things and satisfactions: they are "images," "phantoms," "shadows": they are "small" (in the *Theaetetus* [173e], he adds "and nothings" *smikra kai ouden*). It may be asked: If we were to take Plato at his word on this point, should we not have to infer that the philosopher's renunciations of material sources of happiness would cost him nothing? The answer is that so they would, if he were a discarnate soul; in his present state of incarnation, he is bound to desire intensely the creature-comforts of property and sex and to feel the cost of their deprivation.

[111] "Why did Plato claim, in the *Republic,* that justice meant inequality if, in general usage, it meant equality? To me the only likely reply seems to be that he wanted to make propaganda for his totalitarian state by persuading the people that it was the 'just' state. . . . But his attack on equalitarianism was not an honest attack" (92–93).

[112] Popper has never questioned the good intentions of Plato's totalitarianism: "I believe in the sincerity of Plato's totalitarianism . . . his ideal was not the maximum exploitation of the working classes by the upper class; it was the stability of the whole" (108).

participatory democracy—but even of their individual right to moral autonomy, all this unflinchingly in the cause of impartial justice. The shock of the encounter with a moral vision so alien to one's own, so hostile to one's deepest convictions, may shake its credibility, and the temptation to think it dishonest may then be overwhelming. That is the point at which I had to turn to its background assumptions, first in moral psychology and ultimately in metaphysics. These are the ones I have laid out in the terminal part of this paper. Had I shared them, I would not have found Plato's view of justice incredible. I might have found it compelling.

In matters of intellectual honesty, proof of the pudding comes after the eating, sometimes a long time after. Suppose that in your middle years you give the world a theory that is so brilliantly original, so stamped with your individuality, that now for you and others your ego and the theory are inextricably tangled up. Decades later it begins to dawn on you that something about that theory is not quite right—confused or false. What will you do then? Will you suppress the doubt? Or will you look as hard at the new evidence which threatens your theory as you once did at the old which shored it up? If my reading of the *Parmenides* as "record of honest perplexity" is correct,[113] that is what Plato did when doubts assailed him about his greatest creation, the Theory of Forms. And just this, surely, is what he did still later to his theory of justice. In this case I think there is no "if" about it.[114] No serious [35] reader of the *Laws* could reasonably doubt that Plato wrote into it, without the slightest hedging, propositions which contradict the very tenets I have presented in this paper as indispensable supports of his meta-normative theory of justice.[115] He now declares flatly that no mortal nature can bear without corruption the strain of autocratic power (713c; cf. 691c and 875a–d); his former faith—that one who surrenders his power of self-determination to a philosophic master will never have cause to rue it—has now collapsed.[116]

---

[113] "The Third Man Argument in the *Parmenides*," *PR* 62 (1954), 319–49 (reprinted in Allen, 231–64 (**2.166ff.) Section D, "The Record of Honest Perplexity."

[114] As there decidedly is in the case of the import of the *Parmenides*, where my interpretation, though shared by a number of scholars, is strongly contested by others: some have seen the *Parmenides* as an outright admission by Plato that his theory is logically bankrupt and has to be abandoned, while others, at the other extreme, have seen there nothing more than a didactic exercise in which Plato warns his public against plausible misinterpretations of his theory.

[115] See Appendix C below.

[116] In a review article which appeared in 1957c (reprinted in *PS,* 204ff. at 212–16), I discussed this drastic modification in Plato's system of political beliefs, arguing there that the change must have occurred after the composition of the *Politicus,* and conjecturing that it must have come after the third journey to Syracuse, which dashed for good whatever hopes he had still cherished that under suitable instruction Dionysius the Younger might yet become a philosopher king.

And Plato now declares with equal conviction that "slaves and masters can never be friends" (757a); the faith that the *doulos* can be *philos* has also collapsed.[117]

Seeing this we could guess that the allocation of rights which had left the great majority of the civic body politically disfranchised is now far from anything Plato's sense of justice would approve. We do not need to guess. We see Plato rehabilitating in the *Laws* many of those democratic rights he had wiped out in the *Republic*. Though he does not discuss the earlier theory, does not allude to it [36] in any way, we can be certain he has abandoned it.[118] I do not know of any other case where the creator of a major philosophical theory moved out of it so coolly when he found himself unable to give continuing adherence to its supporting assumptions.[119]

---

[117] The sentence I have quoted is no mere *obiter dictum*. It articulates a doctrine which Plato expresses with fervor, if not with full consistency, in the *Laws*. He introduces it in Book 3, where he announces the new-found trinity of political norms: "the *polis* should be free, intelligent, and in amity with itself ἐλευθέραν τε . . . καὶ ἔμφρονα καὶ ἑαυτῇ φίλην, 693b; (cf. 701d and n. 103 above). He proceeds to explain the bond he now sees between *philia* and freedom: "Monarchy" and "democracy" (representing, respectively, extremes of "slavery" and "freedom" (694a) are the political archetypes ("mother"-forms); constitutions "must of necessity partake of both, if there is to be freedom and *philia* along with wisdom" (693d–e). He reinforces this with a pseudo-historical moralistic homily in which the Persians flourish under an idealized Cyrus because under him "they maintained the due mean (*to metrion*) between slavery and freedom. . . . For when rulers gave subjects a share of freedom (*eleutherias* . . . *metadidontes*) and advanced them towards equality (*epi to ison agontes*) the soldiers were more *philoi* with their officers," etc.; "consequently at that time they made progress in every way because of freedom, *philia*, and shared intelligence" (694a–b).

[118] In the *Laws* we see neither hide nor hair of the "doing one's own" definiens of *dikaiosunē*. What then, exactly, is the theory of social justice that Plato has settled for in the *Laws*? The answer is not clear. Earlier (n. 83) I referred to his (apparently) total endorsement of "proportional equality": to call this *alēthestatēn kai aristēn isotēta* (757b6), to say that it is *Dios krisis* (b7) and that *to prepon . . . aponemei* (c5–6) and, finally, that *to politikon* ("true policy") lies in following out "precisely *this* justice" (*tout' auto to dikaion* c6–7) is, on the face of it, to recognize proportional equality as the very essence of justice. However, immediately after saying this, Plato proceeds to concede that the "arithmetical equality" of the lot ("the equality of measure and weight and number" [757b6–7]), which is "virtually opposite (to proportional equality) in its practical import" (757b2–3), must also be employed, though only as a matter of practical necessity (*anankaion*, 757d5: *anankē*, e3)—without it civic discord would ensue (757d7–e1)—and used "as little as possible" (*hoti malista ep' oligois*, 758a1). Whatever may be the upshot of this curious compromise between "the two equalities" (a big dose of one of them, with a dash of the other), it should be evident that the end result is a far cry from the theory of distributive justice in the *Republic*, since that theory (i) is by no means committed to "proportional equality," as I have argued in Section II, and (ii) does not need to be compromised by its opposite for the sake of avoiding civic discord, for it is conceived as being itself the very means of fostering civic *philia* (as I have argued in Section III).

[119] See Appendix C below.

APPENDIX A

In view of the repeated criticisms I have been making in this paper of *The Open Society and Its Enemies,* I beg to explain two things:

(1) My strictures are offered in a spirit of high respect for its author's stature as a philosopher, and also for his courageous counter-affirmation of great liberal principles whose denial by Plato has been all too often soft-pedaled—at times even justified—by scholars. In its *confessio fidei,* I find *The Open Society and Its Enemies* entirely admirable. My disagreements with its treatment of Plato are solely over questions of scholarly interpretation which are matters of legitimate and indeed unavoidable argument: when one's conclusions are at variance with those of an influential author, to shirk controversy would scarcely betoken esteem for him or for his subject.

(2) My criticisms would have been unnecessary if in the course of the three decades that have elapsed since its publication its gravest misunderstandings of Plato's theory of justice had either been corrected (even in part) by Popper himself or else had been nailed down by his numerous critics. Neither of these things has happened. In the "Addenda" to the 1962 edition of his book, Popper says he "changed [his] mind on Plato's physical cosmology between the first and second editions" of the book, but not on Plato's moral and political philosophy (335). Nor have the errors in the [37] latter area been fully identified and rebutted by other scholars. Even the best of the original reviews known to me—Richard Robinson's "Dr. Popper's Defense of Democracy," *PR* 60 (1951), 487–507—conceded too much. Thus Robinson appears to agree with Popper that Plato "aimed at the good of a superbeing, 'the city as a whole,' rather than at the goods [*sic*] of all the citizens" (493). And when protesting the claim that Plato's silence on equality as a basic ingredient of justice was dishonestly manipulative, Robinson tacitly concedes it, affirming only (what Popper never denied: see n. 112 above) that it was well-intentioned ("If Plato deliberately kept quiet about the equalitarian view of justice, he did so with good intentions towards men. . . . " [500]). The most comprehensive critique, R. B. Levinson, *In Defense of Plato* ⟨above, n. 97⟩, a work of earnest and industrious scholarship, succeeds in throwing much light on disputed passages and repeatedly supplies a useful corrective to one-sided claims in Popper, but fails as a defense of Plato because it misses the very substantial measure of truth in some of Popper's charges (beginning with the charge of "totalitarianism") while, conversely, it appears to concede a claim of Popper's—that "only the members of the ruling class are educated" (267n.13)—which should most certainly have been challenged, for it is a mainstay of the brutal ("human cattle") view of the lower classes Popper ascribes to Plato; and there is not a particle of direct evidence for it (see the best Popper can do for it: 227n.33, and 267n.13), while there is a strong (in

my opinion, conclusive) case against it (for the lines along which it may be made, see *PS*, 137, and my rebuttal of Guthrie's sponsorship of the same view in Vol. 4 of his *History of Greek Philosophy* [Cambridge, 1975] in my review of the book in *TLS* for Dec. 12, 1975, 1474–75).

APPENDIX B
(for note 96)

The concept of a human being as "an end in himself," introduced by Kant, needs to be freed from a grave defect in his formulation of it, as I have pointed out briefly in "Justice and Equality" (cited above, n. 20, 48–49). I referred to that discussion of Kant's phrase in *PS*, 10n. 24 (the reference is indispensable for my use of the phrase in my essay on "The Individual as an Object of Love in Plato"), and I hope to expand that discussion in a sequel to the present essay. For the present the following may suffice: I accept without reservation Kant's basic distinction between *things,* whose value is *conditional* (it depends on their being valued by someone, p. 57 of the Rosenkranz-and-Shubert edition of the *Grundlegung der Metaphysik der Sitten*) and *replaceable* (whatever has this kind of value "can be replaced by something else which is equivalent," ibid., 65) and which we may use as mere means to our own ends, and, on the other hand, *persons,* whose value (or "dignity," *Würde*) being *unconditional* and *irreplaceable,* we may never so use. When he proceeds to identify implicitly the latter sort of value with *moral merit* (see the quotation in n. 40 of "Justice and Equality," ⟨above, n. 20⟩), I dissent. This is surely an error, and its consequences would be disastrous: the identification would entail that a person's moral achievement is the only thing which endows him with unconditional and irreplaceable value and interdicts use of him by others as mere means to their ends. Were this true, a person's value would not be unconditional, for *it would be forfeited in case of moral failure,* and this is surely false: moral failure may call for censure and punishment, but these are themselves predicated on the assumption that a [38] delinquent remains a person and retains the special value which attaches to persons in contradistinction to things, as Kant himself would be the first to recognize. Once the Kantian conception has been purged of this error, we are left with the notion of a person who as an end-in-himself has value for himself, valuing his own existence and all other persons and things from his own unique subjective point of view and does not need to be valued by anyone else in order to have that kind of value ("the value of the valuer," as I speak of it in "Justice and Equality," *loc. cit.*). In respect of this kind of value, which all men share with one another and with no other creature in the physical universe, all men are of equal value.

APPENDIX C
(for notes 115 and 119)

Paul Shorey, fervent apostle of the "unity of Plato's thought," pushed it so far as to maintain that even the *Laws* marked no substantial change in Plato's doctrines ("Plato's *Laws* and the Unity of Plato's Thought," *CP* 9 (1914), 345–69). It is instructive to see what happens when he seeks to maintain his thesis in the face of those two drastic changes to which I have referred in the text above and in the three preceding notes:

(1) The statement that "slaves and masters can never be friends" (757a1), which contradicts so flatly the doctrine of *Republic* 590c–d, is simply ignored. So are the thrice-repeated assertions (693b3–4, 693d8–e1, 701d7–9) enunciating the new trinity of political goals, where *philia* and *eleutheria* appear side by side (n. 117 above). I have ransacked the text of Shorey's paper and the many scores of references in its notes without finding a single reference (or even a single allusion) to any of those four passages in the *Laws*. (It should go without saying that the omissions are not due to ignorance— Shorey's knowledge of the Platonic corpus is matchless—nor yet due to the wish to divert the reader's mind from unsettling evidence. We are faced here with the sad spectacle of a very great scholar so blinkered by his preconceptions that he fails to notice all too familiar texts which contradict his theory.)

(2) The passages I cited in the text above in which Plato now records his conviction that autocratic government will corrupt the autocrat are duly recognized in Shorey's paper: he includes references to 691c and 713c and to a part of 875a–d within a string of references in n. 8 to p. 355 in support of the (perfectly correct) statement that in the *Laws* Plato (a) invokes the notion "of a converted autocrat to bring about the revolution and inaugurate reform" but (b) recognizes the impracticability of "benevolent autocracy as a continuing form of government" (355). In the note Shorey calls attention to the fact that *with respect to (a)* there is scarcely any difference in doctrine between the *Laws,* on one hand, and the *Republic* and *Politicus,* on the other. But he blandly ignores the fact that *there is a vast difference with respect to (b)*: what is the rule of the philosophers in the *Republic* and of the philosopher-scientist in the *Politicus,* if not "benevolent autocracy as a continuing form of government"? Plato, though well aware of the precariousness of such a form of government, does not say in either of these two dialogues that it is incapable of durable instantiation; in particular, he does not say in either of them, as he does thrice over in the *Laws,* that it is impracticable because the uncorrupted tenure of dictatorial power is beyond human capacity. Later (358) Shorey remarks (I intersperse reference-marks in the quotation) that "the paradoxical communism of the *Republic* is (i) [39] mainly designed to impose disinterestedness on the guardians, and (ii) thus in a measure anticipates the objection of the *Laws* and *Politicus* that human nature cannot endure unlimited

power." Shorey is, of course, correct in the case of (i). But in the case of (ii) he ignores the vital difference that in the *Republic* Plato lays down institutional arrangements which he believes *can* enable the human nature of his philosophers to bear unlimited power without corruption, but undertakes no such thing in the *Laws,* for the very good reason that he has now come to believe that this weakness in human nature is incurable. (For Shorey's assimilation of the position of the *Politicus* to that of the *Laws* in the preceding quotation, cf n. 116 above.)

ADDITIONAL NOTE

The principal translations of the *Republic* to which I have referred (by name of author only) in this paper are as follows:

Bloom, A. (New York, 1968).
Cornford, F. M. (New York, 1945).
Jowett, B., 3rd ed. (Oxford, 1892); 4th ed., revised by D. J. Allan and H. E. Dale (Oxford, 1953).
Lindsay, A. D. (London, 1906).
Robin, L. (Paris, 1950).
Schleiermacher, Fr., revised by Kurz, D. (Darmstadt, 1971).
Shorey, P. (London, 1930).

8

THE RIGHTS OF PERSONS IN PLATO'S CONCEPTION
OF THE FOUNDATIONS OF JUSTICE

IN BOOKS 2 TO 7 of the *Republic* (hereafter "*R.*") Plato undertakes to do something never previously attempted in the history of the West: to determine on purely rational grounds all of the rights which all of the members of a particular society ought to have. The society he has in view is a Greek polis. He does not question the restrictions on its membership—the exclusion from it of all the persons in its territory except those whose title to civic status is hereditary.[1] So he ignores two large classes of persons whose presence in his native city had been for generations indispensable to its economic existence: resident aliens and slaves.[2] Of neither group is it stated that it is to exist in the ideal state of the *R.* To resident aliens there is no reference. To slaves there is just one—but it is not so unambiguous as to put beyond controversy the question of whether or not this institution is being retained when so much else is being discarded in the remaking of the polis.[3] I have myself participated in this controversy, arguing for the affirmative.[4] In this chapter I shall follow Plato's example and ignore aliens and slaves in discussing his theory.

From H. Tristram Englehardt, Jr., and Daniel Callahan, eds., *Morals, Science and Society* (Hastings-on-Hudson, N.Y.: The Hastings Center, 1978), pp. 172–201. Used by permission. Minor changes have been made in punctuation. This paper is a companion piece to my earlier essay, "The Theory of Social Justice in the Polis in Plato's *Republic*" (to which I shall refer hereafter by the abbreviation *SJR*), in a symposium entitled *Interpretations of Plato*, ed. Helen North, as a supplementary volume to the Dutch classical journal *Mnemosyne*, 1977, pp. 1–40 ⟨**2.69ff⟩. For certain aspects of Plato's theory—particularly the foundations of the social theory in Plato's moral psychology and metaphysics, which I have not attempted to develop in the present paper, I must refer the reader to *SJR*, sec. 3, pp. 26–34 ⟨**2.90–97⟩.

[1] In this respect Plato's theory of justice rests on a "historical" base in the technical sense of this term introduced by Robert Nozick, *Anarchy, State and Utopia* (New York: Basic Books, 1974), pp. 152ff.: a historical contingency (in this case, the accident of civic birth) is to determine who are to have the rights defined by Plato's theory.

[2] For slavery as an integral component of the economy of classical Greece, see especially M. I. Finley, "Was Greek Civilization Based on Slave Labor?" *Historia* 7 (1959): 145–64.

[3] *R.*, 433d. Other references to slavery are even more problematic. For my discussion of all the passages which have any bearing whatever on the question, see my paper "Does Slavery Exist in Plato's *R.*?" *CP* 63 (1986):291ff., reprinted in my *Platonic Studies* (hereafter "PS") (Princeton: Princeton University Press, 1973), pp. 140ff. The best argument to the contrary is in R. E. Levinson, *In Defense of Plato* (Cambridge, Mass.: Harvard University Press, 1953), pp. 167–73.

[4] Cf. the preceding note.

But I can hardly do so without at least calling attention, in passing, to one of the implications of Plato's willingness to blanket in silence the very existence of two groups of human beings whose lives were [172] intertwined with his throughout his life. From just this fact, we can infer that the idea of *human* (or "natural") rights—rights which, in Locke's phrase, "belong to men as men and not as members of society"[5]—is lacking in Plato's conception of morality. It is so alien to its basic assumptions that he does not even allude to it—to say nothing of undertaking to argue against it, explaining why he finds it inconsistent with his concept of justice.

How does Plato propose to ascertain the rights of those who are to be the members of his polis? By a purely a priori method: Socrates undertakes to discover the nature of justice by constructing a "perfectly good" (427e) polis. To be perfectly good, it will have to be, among other things, perfectly just. So if we don't know what justice is, we can find out by inspecting the finished construction. The structure of rights and duties exhibited in this perfectly just society will tell us what is the just allocation of rights and duties in a polis.

Is this procedure epistemically viable? If we don't know what justice is to begin with, how can we tell what to put into our construction to get a perfectly just polis out of it at the end? To discover justice by this method, would we not have to know the very thing we are looking for—before we found it? Plato would not be unprepared for this question. He must know that his proposal will look paradoxical. Earlier, in the *Meno,* he had confronted what he calls there the "eristic argument":

> It is humanly impossible to go looking either for what one knows or for what one does not know. One would not go looking, surely, for what one does know—there would be no need of that, if one already knows it—nor yet for what one does not know—for then one would not know what to look for. (80e)

Plato's answer to this paradox is his doctrine that "learning is recollecting"—that all discovery is a matter of reawakening in the soul knowledge it once possessed in a primordial past and can now recover, if it will only make the right use of what is still left in it of that initial deposit (81a–d). This, he implies, is what happens in the interrogation of the slave boy (82a–85b). The question put at the start, "What is the side of a square whose area is twice that of a given square?" baffles the boy. But his [173] mind is not a blank. Though he has never learned geometry, he has some understanding of what "square" means, can recognize squares, can tell some of their properties, and can reason his way to other properties they are bound to have if they already have the ones which make them recognizably square. Let him proceed in step-by-step

---

[5] John Locke, *Second Treatise of Civil Government,* chap. 2, para. 14. These are rights which Locke takes to exist in "the state of nature" and cannot be overridden by the positive laws of any society at any time in any place.

inference from those simple truths which are already in his mind in the form of scattered true beliefs, and he will wind up sooner or later discovering the answer to the initial question.

Though Plato does not allude in the *R.* to the doctrine of recollection and makes no comment on the epistemic side of the inquiry in Books 2 to 5, there is no reason to doubt that the answer to the objection would be the same. At the start of the inquiry, we don't know what we shall come to know at the end; but this does not preclude our having sundry true beliefs about just dealings between man and man—beliefs that Socrates can bring in by bits and pieces, as the inquiry proceeds, and weave into a coherent pattern which will exhibit the social structure of the perfectly just polis. These beliefs are not announced as principles of justice. They are introduced as principles of rational action whose intuitive appeal is meant to be so high that none of the interlocutors will wish to challenge them—as they in fact do not, taking them to be the plain common sense of social conduct with which everyone would agree. But there is no doubt that they are meant to be valid principles of justice, else how could Socrates have expected them to serve him as stepping stones to the final result: insight into the nature of justice?

The construction starts with a settlement that Socrates chooses to call a polis (369c4, etc.) though it is only a simple form of economic association. Falling in with this fiction, I shall call this primitive make-believe polis "protopolis." Its people had to choose between two options: on one hand, self-sufficiency, every man working only for himself, relying on his own labor to meet all of his needs; on the other, interdependence, every man working for himself *and* for each of his neighbors, by specializing in the production of one of the commodities which both he and they need, and exchanging the product against those produced by others, each of whose labor has been similarly specialized. In choosing the second option, the people of protopolis could be [174] viewed as forming a mutual benefit association: by dividing the labor and exchanging its product, everyone's efficiency is enhanced, the common standard of living is raised, so everyone's work benefits everyone, including himself. That Plato so views this pattern of economic life is reasonably clear from his description of it: He speaks of the participants as cooperators, not competitors—as "partners and helpers" (369c), each of whom "places his own work at the disposal of all in common" (369e, in Lindsay's translation).[6]

Plato can view this process in this way because he does not see the shift from the first to the second option as a shift from production for use to production for the market and therewith to production for profit. For Plato both options involve production for use: for one's own needs only, in the first; for the needs of all, in the second. His description gives no place to production

[6] Or, more literally, as "each making his own work common to all." (For the translations I shall be using, see the list in n. 49 below.)

for an abstract, impersonal market, where sellers compete for buyers, their competition providing a pricing mechanism for their products, and pitting producers against one another in a contest which punishes the less efficient by driving them out and rewards the more efficient by offering them a bigger share of the market, thereby allowing them to enlarge the scale of their operations and transform themselves from direct producers into entrepreneurs. As Marx points put in a perceptive comment on our passage, Plato's point of view and that of other classical authors (he quotes also Thucydides and Xenophon) differ profoundly from that of "modern political economy" whose spokesmen (Adam Smith & co.) see in the division of labor "only the means of producing more commodities with a given quantity of labor and, consequently, of cheapening commodities and hurrying on the accumulation of capital."[7] In Plato's picture of the economy of protopolis, capital does not appear as such. The making of agricultural and industrial tools is noticed (370c–d) but is not described as production of capital goods. There is nothing here answering to entrepreneurial activity by capitalists making investments, i.e., foregoing consumption for the specific purpose of devoting wealth to operations designed to increase it. Money functions only as a medium of exchange, and the merchant only as a middleman (371b–d).[8] Only later on, when protopolis, with its healthy simplicity, is succeeded by the luxurious "fevered" [175] city, do men "turn to boundless money-making, over-passing the bounds of the needful" (373d).

To be sure, one thing is said in the account of protopolis which may suggest the profit-seeking which is the *primum mobile* of a capitalist economy. Socrates asks:

> And in the give-and-take, whether one gives or takes, does not one act in the belief that this would be better for oneself? (369c6–7)

In the Cross-Woozley commentary, Plato is seen as maintaining here that these people are acting "entirely selfishly."[9] I submit that this interpretation, though plausible, is unwarranted. Everyone's seeing that cooperative reciprocity is "better for himself"—better than isolationist self-sufficiency—does not itself preclude his seeing also that it is better for the others too, the enhanced benefit to himself being so connected with enhanced benefit to them that neither could occur without the other. Why then should each one's motivation be *entirely* self-regarding? Why should it not be self-regarding and

---

[7] Karl Marx, *Capital,* ed. Friedrich Engels; translated by S. Moore and E. Aveling (New York: Modern Library), chap. 14, sec. 4, pp. 400–401 and nn.

[8] There are some hired laborers (371c–d), but presumably only as aids to self-employed producers. For entrepreneurs as such, no place whatever is made in this primitive economy.

[9] R. C. Cross and A. D. Woozley, *Plato REPUBLIC: A Philosophical Commentary* (London: Macmillan, 1964), p. 80.

other-regarding too?[10] There is no reason why it should not. Why then does not Plato say so? Why should he say only "because it is better for himself"?[11] A fair guess would be, Because he does not want to get ahead of himself in his construction. The time will come when he will want to tell us that the partners in a mutual benefit association will have a fraternal feeling for each other.[12] He may be already hinting at something of the kind even at this stage of the construction, when he speaks of these people a little later (327b) as "living in pleasant fellowship with each other."[13] But that this will be their attitude toward each other is not *entailed* by the pattern of interdependent economic activity he has laid down. The norm of just social relations remains underdetermined at this point.

It also remains underdetermined at another, not unrelated, point: no provision has yet been made to indicate at what ratios the producers would exchange their products. What is there, then, to preclude gross inequalities in these ratios which would be hard to reconcile with one's intuitive sense of justice, be this ours or that of the Greeks, for, as I pointed out in *SJR* (18–19) ⟨**2.84⟩,[14] [176]

---

[10] The first sense listed for "selfish" in the *OED* is "deficient in consideration of others," and this is surely by far the most common use of the word. In a community of "partners and helpers" (369c3), where everyone is willing and able to pull his weight, there would be no special reason why everyone should be "deficient in consideration of others": everyone would be in the happy position of seeing that others benefited as much from his labor as he did from theirs.

[11] This is the strength of the Cross-Woozley ⟨above, n. 9⟩ interpretation. Italicizing the phrase that Plato uses in 379c7, "thinking it is better for himself to do so," they gloss (at p. 80):

> The attitude which Socrates ascribes to each of his imaginary citizens is that of putting into the common stock . . . whatever he must in order to get out of it what he wants. That another man might have need of what you produce would not be regarded by you as a reason for your supplying it, unless you yourself had need of what he produces.

This is perfectly true, but all it entails is that these people are not being described as altruists— from which it does not follow that they are being portrayed as egoists. What does follow is that, they, any one of them, *could* be an egoist, if so inclined, and get along quite well in that society— which is not to say that this is what all, or most, of them would have to be or what Plato expects them to be.

[12] The Myth of Metals begins, "All you are brothers in the polis . . . " (415a); the soldiers "must think of the other citizens as brothers . . . " (414e). And see the development of this theme in 461–464b, and the brief, but highly significant, reassertion of *philia* (in this case specifically between the intellectual and the manual worker) at 590d5–6.

[13] Cross and Woozley, ⟨above, n. 9⟩, pp. 91, 93, quote the later phrase, admitting that it does not sit well with their interpretation. That Plato himself should feel no strain between that phrase and the one he had used at 369c7 gives some indication that the earlier characterization had not been meant to imply that the cooperative conduct was "entirely selfishly" motivated. Some indication of the same thing had also been given in 369c3 by the description of its people as "partners and helpers."

[14] Cf. n. 2 above. For this use of *isos*, see LSJ, *s.v.*, sense II, 1–3, and PS, 184–85n. 78.

the linguistic bond of justice with equality was even closer for the Greeks than it is for us: *to ison, isotēs* ("the equal," "equality") would be the very words to which they would turn for a natural, unstrained, one-word variant for *to dikaion, dikaiosunē* ("the just," "justice"). . . . (It) leads Aristotle to declare (*E.N.* 1130b9) that "justice *is* equality, as all men think it, even apart from argument."

Let me suggest a scenario. Suppose that one man in this settlement has a natural monopoly on some skill: he can make fine wooden flutes, an article which is much in demand in this community and can only be made by someone who has an ear with "perfect pitch" and manual skill to match; only this fellow has this capacity, and being a fast worker he can turn out a flute in four hours. So working four hours every fourth day, turning out ninety flutes per annum, and charging in exchange a share of the goods produced by others which is twice as large as that of everyone else, his position relative to all the others is enviable indeed: working one-eighth of the time the others do, he gets twice as much as they; one hour of his working time is being paid as much as sixteen hours of theirs. Is there anything in Plato's description of the protopolis to rule out this kind of inequality? Nothing, so far as I can see. Assuming that those people prize a perfectly pitched flute as you and I might value a fine antique or a Picasso, why shouldn't each feel that it is "better for himself" to have this character in their group, in spite of his getting away with so little work for so large an income? Aren't all the others better off with him in the group than they would be without him?[15] So what is wrong with his being so much better off than any of them? If it grates on our sense of justice, why should it?"[16] May it not be only vicarious envy that makes us feel mor-

---

[15] "Pareto optimality" would be preserved, and would be still, even if the inequalities were immeasurably intensified, as they might in given circumstances if the natural monopoly enabled its holder to perform a service of such importance to others that they would be prepared to give almost anything in exchange for it. Thus suppose that someone in protopolis had a unique medical skill, and his price for exercising it would be that the patient, on recovery, would give to him (or to one of his friends) a whole year's full-time personal service. If people were willing to accept these terms (their regular workload being shifted to friends of theirs willing to work overtime for their sake), Plato's stipulation that each would reckon the exchanges "better for himself" would be sustained and Pareto optimality would be preserved: judging the benefit to each by what he and his friends are prepared to pay in a legally unconstrained bargain, we would have to say that the community is better off paying this tribute to their medico than they would be by foregoing his service to them.

[16] It does on mine, and I leave it to the reader to judge whether or not it does on his. I write in full view of a current conception of justice whose proponents could swallow without discomfort the example in the text above and, if they have strong stomachs, even the one in the preceding note. So, I assume, would Robert Nozick, if he adhered consistently to the views he expounds in his remarkable book, *Anarchy, State and Utopia* ⟨above, n. 1⟩: if, as he holds, everyone has exclusive right to the exploitation of his own individual abilities, the heroes (or villains) of each of my two examples would violate no rule of justice by acting as they do. Neither would the

ally uneasy about his ability to command terms so privileged by comparison with those of his peers? Would Plato's theory deny the justice of such an arrangement and, if so, on what grounds?

It would indeed, but not on the ground of anything mentioned or implied in the account of the protopolis. To find it we must move on, though even so we shall not get it in the form of a direct statement. We shall have to derive it from the decisions [177] governed by a new principle which is never spelled out. Let me take it upon myself to formulate it on Plato's behalf so that we can have it before us as clearly and explicitly as possible:

> All members of the polis have equal right to those and only those benefits which are required for the optimal performance of their function in the polis.

I shall call this the Principle of Functional Reciprocity. For "function" I could have used "service" or "work." Plato uses various words for it.[17] Terminological rigidity is not to his taste. Regardless of its verbal vehicle, this is the key component of his concept of the justice of the polis, as is made abundantly clear at various points. Thus it turns up in the final definition of the justice of the polis which is meant to crystallize the cumulative insight gained in the preceding inquiry. The abbreviated formula at 433b, "doing one's own," is a contraction for "doing one's own work" or "performing one's own function." In its expanded form in the preceding sentence (433a5–6) it reads (in one of the possible translations),

> each single person pursuing that single practice pertaining to the polis which his own nature is best fitted to pursue.

A still more complete description of it, expanded to include additional items introduced at various points in the preceding account, might run:

> A politically assigned life-long work role—for which one qualifies by natural aptitude, by politically provided education, and by excellence of performance—which

---

discoverer of a cure for cancer whose formula, if made public, could be mass-produced to cure thousands, but who prefers to keep it secret and its production scarce to enhance thereby the financial returns to himself: cf. Nozick's own discussion of related (if less gruesome) examples, on pp. 181–82 of his book.

[17] *Ergon* ("work," "function") and the verb *ergazesthai* (369e, 374a–c, 406c, 407a1, 434a); *epitēdeuma* ("practice," "occupation," "pursuit"), and the verb *epitēdeuein* (374e, 394e, 359c, 433a, 454b–455b, 457b); occasionally also by *technē* ("art," "craft": 370b; 374a, c, e), which had been frequently interchanged with *ergon* in Book 1). *Dēmiourgos* ("craftsman") is used repeatedly of the rulers (395b, 421c, 500d) in defiance of the fact that these people are rigorously excluded from the *manual* crafts for which *dēmiourgos* and *dēmiourgia* were commonly used (and are so used by Plato in the same books of the *R.*: 371a, 406c, 468a).

constitutes the unique vehicle for one's optimal contribution to the happiness and excellence of the polis.[18]

To comment on each of the items in this description would call for another essay. The two things I would emphasize the most if I were doing that job would be, on one hand, the terms "politically" and "polis," and on the other, "excellence of performance." The first explicitly identifies function in reference to the polis, no longer now a euphemism for the purely economic association with which we started in the protopolis, but a full-blooded state, and indeed much more than that by modern notions [178] of the state—not only complete with apparatus of force and law, but bloated to include every single other public institution, educational, cultural, and religious, and exercising control over the whole life of the citizen, including his private life and that of his family, if he is allowed to have one. The second is best conveyed by the alternative term Plato sometimes uses to describe the citizen's function: *technē,* "craft,"[19] conceived in the typical Greek way, which thinks of a craft *as* an "art"—the other sense of *technē*—placing as high a premium on the beauty as on the utility of what a craft creates,[20] expecting from the craftsman something of that striving for perfection which had produced in Athens such marvels of workmanship by common craftsmen as the curvature of the stylobate and entasis of the columns of the Parthenon, or those sixth- and fifth-century vases, some of them made by slaves, which are now counted among the world's masterpieces of design. Plato extends this conception, making it cover not only the craftsman's product but also the character of the craftsman himself: he is expected to make of his own self also something beautiful, as well as useful, for the polis.[21]

But I cannot afford to expand on this. I must content myself with a remark on the only immediately relevant feature of this function: the one which ties it directly to the concept of justice and of rights: one's function, as Plato conceives of it, is both the citizen's master-duty and, at the same time, his master-right. The first is emphasized both in the "doing one's own" formula, where "doing" clearly refers to a duty, not to a right, and in sundry ad hoc statements, as when it is said of the guardians that their function is to constitute the "one goal in life with a view to which they do everything they do, both in private and in public" (519c), and that they "must practice nothing which does

---

[18] For textual documentation see the passages adduced in support of a similarly expanded description in PS, 119.

[19] See n. 17 above.

[20] Plato repeatedly uses the adverb *kalōs* ("beautifully") to refer to excellence in the performance of social function, as, e.g., at 370b, 374a, 394e.

[21] Thus the philosopher-ruler is described as a "craftsman" (*dēmiourgos*) who "molds himself" (no less than the polis) in the image of his ideal vision (500d).

not conduce" to this single goal (395b–c). But this is only one side of the coin. The other is that the discharge of this function is for each of these people a privilege, an infinitely precious one, the basis of the worth and meaning of their life, so much so that if through some calamity they were to become unfit to do their work, life would lose its value for them: if they cannot do their function, they would just as soon be dead. Socrates brings this thought into his construction by a digression on the culture-hero Asclepius, boldly recondi-tioned by Plato's work-ethic to believe [179]

> that it was not right to give (medical) treatment to a man who could not live in his established round of duties; this would not be profitable either for the man himself or the polis. (407d–e)

The implication is that the polis would not grant him the right and, if he were self-respecting, he would not claim it. A carpenter, offered extended house-bound treatment by an unpolitical doctor, turns it down, replying that "life is not worth living in that way, keeping his mind on his illness and neglecting his proper work." So he goes back to his job where he either regains his health or "if his body will not stand the strain, solves his troubles by dying" (406d).

So much for the term *functional* in my label for Plato's principle. What of the other term, *reciprocity?* This reaffirms the conception of the polis as a mutual benefit association where everyone, by performing his own function, benefits everyone in the polis, counting on everyone else to benefit him along with the rest as each performs his proper task. And this conception is tight-ened up far beyond its first appearance in protopolis. The *only* benefits one is now allowed of right from the cooperative interchange are those which are required for the optimal performance of one's function. What difference this makes will be made clear shortly. But first I must ask how reciprocity, thus maintained and intensified, will relate to equality,[22] on whose intimate con-nection with the idea of justice in Greek speech and thought I remarked above. To press this question on Plato's text is to become aware of a remark-able fact to which I drew attention in *SJR*:[23] that the words *equality* and *equal* are consistently avoided throughout the whole of the construction which cul-minates in the definition of justice in the middle of Book 4 and then resumes in Book 5 to produce there a ringing manifesto of equality between the sexes

---

[22] I take equality and reciprocity as entirely distinct notions and will so use the terms in this paper. The warning is necessary since "reciprocity" is sometimes used in moral contexts so as to *entail* equality: so, for example, in Jean Piaget's admirable study, *The Moral Judgment of the Child*, trans. M. Gabain (New York: The Free Press, 1965), where it occurs interchangeably with "equality" and "equity"—understandably so, perhaps, since the only kind of reciprocity Piaget considers relevant to the moral education of the subjects of his study (children nurtured in a Western democracy imbued with a liberal ethos) is *equalitarian* reciprocity within the children's peer group in contrast to their submission to authoritarian standards imposed on them by adults.

[23] *SJR*, pp. 19, 22 ⟨**2.84–85, 87⟩.

within the guardian class, without a single use of the word *equality,* without so much as an allusion to it. From the philologist's point of view, whose concern is at least as much with words as with thoughts, and with words avoided no less than with those used and overused, this is, at first sight, startling. It is unparalleled in the whole of the Platonic corpus or in that of any other Greek philosopher, to my knowledge. How could Plato have wished to freeze out of his discussion [180] of justice a word which functioned in his mother tongue as a virtual synonym of "justice"?

A part of the answer is that equality was too much of a political hot potato. For Plato's public the question concerning the rights of persons whose urgency remained paramount over that of all other public issues concerned the just allocation of political rights which, for the Greeks, meant the right of direct participation in functions of government and therewith a share in the control of the state. Democracy and oligarchy were the main options—the only ones, where tyranny had not preempted them. Equality was the democratic watchword. This, needless to say, was not all-around equality: the re-division of property, the liberation of women, the abolition of slavery were never seriously at issue in the debate. Democracy stood for substantive equality in the political sphere: the equal right to sit in the Assembly and, through the lot, the equal chance to serve on the Council, the discasteries, and on one or more of the multitudinous magistracies. Oligarchy stood for the contrary, that is to say, in plain language, for political *in*equality. But given the ancient ties of justice with equality in the language, conservative critics of democracy and advocates of oligarchy could hardly make "inequality" their battle cry. So the notion of "proportional equality"[24] was evolved—a brilliant piece of verbal *legerdemain,* keeping the word while denying its substance. "Equalizing" rights by proportioning benefits to merit would call for any degree of inequality that could plausibly be thought to comport with unequal merit; so the propertied classes, with the higher merit they could claim for themselves on the strength of their wealth and breeding, would find it natural to believe that they, and they alone, had the right to participate in the effective control of the state.

Where would Plato stand in this debate? Since in the *R,* he puts oligarchy above democracy in the gradient of political degradations,[25] he makes it clear enough that if he had to choose between oligarchy and democracy in the political arena, his choice would be for oligarchy, and that he would prefer the still more restricted form of oligarchy he calls timocracy—a constitution of the Spartan type. But there could hardly be a graver misunderstanding of his conception of the justice of the polis in [181] the *R.* than to see it as a defense of oligarchy against democracy. Plato had an unusually clear-eyed view of the

---

[24] For references see *SJR,* p. 22n. 79.
[25] *R.,* 544c and ff.

economic basis of this political conflict. He sees it as, at bottom (and all too frequently on the surface, too), a conflict between the "two poleis," "the city of the poor, and the city of the rich" (422e–423a).[26] And he regards this very division as the disease of the city-state, chronic, endemic, and certain to prove fatal unless a cure is found. The cure is to be his functional state, where classes are articulated along functional lines, and the social differentiations are not divisive but integrative. How then could he think that the justice of this polis could be expressed in terms of the slogans of either of the contending parties? That is why, perhaps, Plato shies away from the word *equality* in his construction of the ideally just polis. That he would think the democrats' "arithmetical" equality anathema is only too clear. Could he, then, content himself with its oligarchic counter-slogan, "proportional equality?" How could he, when he thinks the oligarchic constitution a disease, less painful than democracy, but no less of a mortal illness of the body politic for all that? This, I think, is a possible explanation of why this question is never raised in Books 2 to 5 of the *R.*, and why Plato walks so gingerly around all kinds of topics that would provoke it.

But there are some questions one cannot avoid, no matter how hard one may try. Equality is such a one for a philosopher who has undertaken to determine what an ideally just polis would be like. Sooner or later he must confront the question whether or not his society can be ideally just unless in some important ways it proves ideally equal in the full sense of that term, i.e., unless its members have the *right to derive equal benefits* from its cooperative give-and-take and also the *right to an equal voice* in decisions affecting the direction of their joint activity.[27] In opting for functional reciprocity, Plato emphatically rejects equality in this ideally full sense; if the members of the polis are to have only those rights which are required for the optimal performance of their respective function, their unequal capacities will dictate unequal rights to share in the distribution of the goods produced and in the governance of their common life. Yet even so, the principle of functional reciprocity, as used by Plato, while precluding equality in the sense defined, will still operate as an [182] effective constraint on permissible inequalities, blocking those for which a functional justification cannot be found. In this way functional reciprocity does work for Plato of a radically different nature from what the principle of "proportional equality" would have done. On the surface the two principles may seem very similar. But when put to work they give different results. Functional reciprocity will block inequalities which would have passed through proportional equality like a sieve. Let me illustrate by harking back to the flute-maker in protopolis discussed above.

---

[26] And cf. his description of how oligarchy breeds within it the forces which will destroy it and bring in democracy: 551c–556e.

[27] That is to say, substantive, as distinct from merely formal equality. Cf. *SJR*, p. 20n. 69 ⟨**2.85 n.69⟩.

To justify by the principle of functional reciprocity (hereafter "FR") those handsome privileges he has carved out for himself, he would have to make a case that they are required for top performance at his job. It is hard to see how he could do that. Is there any good reason to think that he can't make as many flutes of as good quality unless he is fed, clothed, shod, housed, etc., so much better than the rest of the folk? No. Or unless his work load is such a tiny fraction of theirs? No. So he must climb down from his high horse and put in a longer working day at lower real wages. If no more flutes are needed, there are plenty of things a man with his fine ear can do to enrich the services supplied to the community. He might, of course, refuse, threatening slow-down or work stoppage unless he is given those fancy terms. But this would be construed as flagrant violation of his master-duty, and a community run on Platonic lines would rather do without flutes than tolerate a moral viper in its bosom. So the FR principle has a good cutting edge. Would the principle of proportional equality (hereafter "PE") serve as well? So far as I can see, it would be of no use at all. Why shouldn't the flutemaker claim that the merit of his superior talent is so much greater than of mere shoemakers and the like that it entitles him to vastly greater social benefits? The notion of merit is so soft, it is impossible to see how claims for the superlative merit of his work could be refuted in the face of the fact that he, and no one else, can make those delectable flutes for which the other workers are willing to exchange such big chunks of their earnings, however bitterly they may resent his extortionate terms.

Let me consider now decisions made by Plato himself concerning rights of persons. I want to show how the FR principle, though never formally stated, is in fact used. I pick out for this [183] purpose two such decisions which affect profoundly the whole design of the ideal polis. I shall argue that both are understandable only as applications of the FR principle: the PE principle would not have led to the same results. The examples are the rights of women within the guardian class, and the rights of the guardian class taken as a whole against those of the producers.

If we were to mean by "feminism"—as we could without eccentricity—the view that the rights of women should be equal in every way to those of men, then Plato must be counted as the first Western philosopher to implement a radically feminist position within an important segment of society; and not only the first, but, for more than two thousand years, the only one.[28] To find another major philosopher who qualifies, we would have to go to John Stuart

---

[28] Plato's feminism is ably defended in the following recent papers: Dorothea Wender, "Plato: Misogynist, Paedophile, and Feminist," *Arethusa* 6 (1973): 75ff.; Christine Pierce, "Equality: *Republic* V," *Monist* 57 (1973): 1ff.; W. W. Fortenbaugh, "On Plato's Feminism in *Republic* V," *Apeiron* 8 (1975): 1ff.; Brian Calvert, "Plato and the Equality of Women," *Phoenix* 29 (1975): 231ff. My own argument for the thesis will appear in a book on Platonic Justice that I hope to publish shortly. ⟨This was never published—ed.⟩ For the best argument on the other side, see Julia Annas, "Plato, *Republic* V, and Feminism," *Philosophy* 51 (1976): 307ff.

Mill. To be sure, Plato's feminism was only for the elite. How women are to fare among the producers in his state remains obscure. Since the nuclear family survives in their case, some (at least) of the disabilities of women that had been built into that institution would undoubtedly remain. But that is no reason for failing to give proper recognition to the fact that in the part of his society which Plato thought all-important—where all the creative thinking, planning, and deciding would be done and where all the power would be concentrated—there women would be admitted on a par with men and treated as the absolute equals of men.[29]

The contrast between the status of the women guardians in Plato's polis and that of the women in contemporary Athens—of all the women there, but especially the middle- and upper-class women, on whom the segregationist constraints bore down most heavily of all—is polar. Here is a rundown of the main points in a vis à vis comparison:

1. Right to education. Schools, gymnasia, palaestrae, a male monopoly in Athens, are open without distinction to both sexes among Plato's guardians.

2. Right to vocational opportunity. Above the proletarian level, none in Athens. In Plato, career is open to talent of both sexes on equal terms.

3. Right to unimpeded social intercourse. Except at the proletarian level, the Athenian woman is born, lives, and dies [184] in a domestic ghetto. In Plato her living space is the same as man's in the upper two classes.

4. Right to heterosexual choice. This is grossly unequal as between men and women in Athens, both before and in marriage. Among Plato's guardians it is strictly equal: equally restricted for men and women within the reproductive age, equally unrestricted for both thereafter.

5. Legal rights. In Athens a woman is the legal ward of her nearest male relative. In Plato a woman guardian would be as much of a legal person as would a man.

6. Political rights. None for women in Athens, the same for women as for men among Plato's guardians.

What took Plato to this position? Certainly, nothing personal—there was no Harriet Taylor in Plato's life—nor yet any kind of compassionate response to the deprivations that were the daily lot of women: when he refers to the deplorable effect which social, cultural, and vocational segregation has on

---

[29] This becomes most strikingly clear in a passage at the conclusion of Book 7, which seems to have escaped the notice of Annas in her otherwise well-documented paper mentioned in the preceding note: Socrates speaks of the guardians who "have survived the tests [for sagacity and virtue] and have excelled in all things in action and knowledge," have come to know the form of the Good, have taken their part in governing the polis, and at their death received quasi-divine honors from the polis. When Glaucon remarks, "You have made your men-rulers [*archontas,* the masculine form] surpassingly beautiful, as in a work of art," Socrates retorts:

Yes, and the women-rulers [*archousas,* the feminine form] too, Glaucon, for you must not suppose that my description applies to men any more than it does to all the women who arise among them with the adequate natural endowment. (540 c3–6)

women's intellect and character in Athens, there is no gleam of sympathy for the victims—only regret for what is lost to the polis by the failure of half its adult members to realize their intellectual and moral potential in its service.[30] As is clear from the text of Book 5 of the *R.*, Plato's feminism is a direct result of his theory of justice and, more particularly, of that component of the theory which answers to the FR principle. That membership in the guardian class should be as open to women as to men is argued for solely on the ground that biological femaleness is irrelevant for good performance in any recognized work role.[31] Though Plato believes that within any given function women are somewhat inferior to men on the average, he reckons the degree and distribution of that difference to be such as to enable many women to qualify for admission to all of the higher work roles and for performance there at a level superior to that of many men. Could he have got the same result from PE? We can see what happens to the rights of women in the *Laws* where PE is hailed as *the* principle of justice (757c) and FR is ignored. When that occurs, women's rights take a beating. The gains they had made in the *R.* in respect of educational opportunity and unimpeded social intercourse they retain. But they lose their gains on [185] three other fronts: legally, politically, and vocationally they are virtually back in their traditional inferior Athenian status.[32] How exactly Plato would have thought that the justice of these inequalities is validated by PE is unclear. What is clear is that this principle is so vague and loose that it can offer no resistance to them, while if FR were being applied it would have ruled them out as firmly here as previously in the *R.* Plato could hardly have shed his belief that some women are better than many men at many tasks. How then could he have denied them access to all except household tasks consistently with the FR principle?

Now, last, a quick look at what is, after all, the most important single decision concerning the rights of persons in the ideally just polis of the *R.*: that the great bulk of the civic body are to have no political rights—no right to participate in any of the deliberative, legislative, judicial, or executive functions of government: these are to be reserved to a tiny elite. Since the Platonic polis possesses its members body and soul—their mind, sensibility, religious feeling, conscience—the power over the masses which is now vested of right in the governing group is immense. A more extreme inequality in the tenure of political power has never been conjured up by the Greek imagination. And it is justified solely by the claim that governing is a function whose optimal performance Plato thinks only philosophers can achieve.[33] Could it then be

---

[30] A point well brought out in the paper by Annas.

[31] *R.*, 451d ff.

[32] See, e.g., G. R. Morrow, *Plato's Cretan City* (Princeton: Princeton University Press, 1960), the references to "women" in the general index to this book.

[33] *R.*, 428a11–429a3. The basic qualification for the function of governing, "knowledge" or "wisdom," is announced at this point. The central books of the *R.* (475b to the end of Book 7) fill

seriously argued that even here, in what has all the earmarks of a colossal rip-off, the FR principle nonetheless supplies a constraint on the ensuing inequalities? It can. Those vast powers that are accorded the philosophers they must earn by submitting to harsh institutional restrictions on their personal life, designed to block any nonfunctional, self-indulgent use of their powers. Hence private property and private family are denied them—deprivations whose severity has no precedent in the regimen of any ruling class recorded in Greek history or pictured in Greek fantasy. Moreover, they are required to make large sacrifices of another sort. For fifteen years they are required to give up from their studies as much time as will be needed to carry the burden of the day-to-day administration, instead of having the bulk of it done for them by subordinates co-opted for this purpose from the lower orders.[34] The rationale of these constraints is clearly dictated by FR, while contrariwise it could [186] not be by PE: there is nothing in the notion of "merit" to prescribe similar or equivalent constraints.

Nor is it clear how PE could have sustained the sense of affectionate partnership between the powerful elite and the powerless mass which Plato is counting on to provide the morale of the just society. He refers repeatedly to this in the *R.*, but most revealingly in that passage near the end of Book 9 (590c–d) which I discussed at length in *SJR*.[35] The producers' total exclusion from any right to share in the government is acknowledged in a word the Greek reader would have thought shocking to see applied to freemen, even if only metaphorically, and with benign intent: *doulos* (slave). Affirming in this way the producer's total subjection to the philosopher, Plato still insists that the relation is beneficent and will be felt as such, for through it the two will become "alike" (*homoioi*),[36] and *philoi*. *Philoi* I rendered "friends," but only for want of a stronger word that does not go all the way to "lovers." Much earlier, in the Myth of Metals (414ff.), Plato had said, "All of you are brothers

---

out the import of this vast claim. Cf. *also Politicus,* 292c5ff. on "the most difficult and greatest" knowledge, the basis of the statesman's authority, which barely fifty out of a thousand citizens could hope to have—perhaps "only one or two or very few of these" (293a2–4).

[34] Imputing to his philosophers his own boundless enthusiasm for [199] intellectual work, and his distaste for managerial office, Plato feels that this political work will be a grave sacrifice of personal happiness for the good of the commonwealth and argues earnestly that it is just to impose this painful duty on them (519c–521b).

[35] *SJR,* pp. 28–30 ⟨**2.92–94⟩.

[36] That this is the correct rendering of *homoioi* in this context I have explained in PS (p. 13n.34). Cornford's "equals" would be too strong as a translation, though one can sympathize with his reasons for so rendering it: equality is not too far from the word's ambience, as shown by the common use of *homoioi* for the "peers" at Sparta (all of them equally privileged by contrast with the legally underprivileged rural population, the *perioeci,* and the cruelly oppressed Helots), and by Plato's association of it with the leveling of social ranks which he thinks characterizes democracy (562d8 and e7.) Cf. also the use of *homoioi* in Thuc. 1, 34, 1.

in the polis" (415a).[37] Fraternal solidarity is what he has in view, affection generated in a working relationship where the sense of interdependence is heightened to the nth degree as each of the partners feels that his own work gets the benefit of the best that the others have it in them to give. It is the FR principle that provides the basis for the emotional unity of the class-stratified Platonic polis.

My presentation of Plato's theory has been sympathetic. I have seen no need to regurgitate familiar critiques of it. Here, as in *SJR,* I have thought it more profitable to try to show what there is in this theory which, in spite of everything that can be said against it, is still, quite recognizably, a theory of *justice,* and this in spite of the fact that in his exposition of it Plato chooses to isolate it from the notion of equality. My argument in both essays has been that this occurs only on the surface—that, if one looks at the way the theory works, one will find that equality still does considerable work in it. In the earlier essay I stressed the work which formal equality, i.e., impartiality, does in shaping Plato's vision of a just polis. Certainly this is important, and quite sufficient in and of itself to undercut the most virulent of the critiques of Plato's theory of justice that has been published in [187] my lifetime— Popper's.[38] However, I failed to indicate in that paper that while impartiality is indeed a necessary condition of justice, it falls so far short of being a sufficient condition that there are many circumstances in which its exercise may even confirm, instead of blocking, injustice. If the prevailing allocation of rights is itself unjustly unequal, those who act with impartial regard for those rights may be thereby only abetting and consolidating the injustice. White persons acting with scrupulous impartiality to respect the rights assigned to whites and blacks under the segregation laws of South Africa may make it only more certain thereby that blacks will be kept out of the jobs, schools, living space, etc., from which they are being excluded by those laws. So if Plato offers a theory of rights of persons within the polis which, however different from ours, is still a *bona fide* theory of justice, he must be putting into it something more than formal equality: he must be injecting a measure of equality into its content as well. This is what I have located in the FR principle, and I have sought to show how this operates as a constraint on unjust inequalities, thereby producing a design for the ideally just polis that is noticeably closer to our own sense of justice than it would otherwise have been.

However, what the FR principle cannot provide is a basis for substantively equal "human" rights. It will justify equal rights only in those special cases in which the differences between groups of persons (such as differences of sex) are judged to be irrelevant to the value of their respective contributions. When

---

[37] And cf. the other references in n. 12 above.

[38] Karl Popper, *The Open Society and Its Enemies,* 4th ed. (New York: Harper Torchbook, 1962).

these differences *are* relevant, rights cannot be equal: this is the inexorable implication of the FR principle. Inequalities in congenital capacity as vast as those between philosophers and producers thus entail correspondingly vast inequalities of right—inequalities so extreme that Plato finds it perfectly natural to represent the relation as idealized slavery. Here, if anywhere, one feels, something has gone decidedly wrong. What?

One way to go in looking for the answer would be to probe the metanormative foundations on which the moral theory rests—to examine the empirical and logical soundness of its psychological, metaphysical, and epistemological supports, all of which are so essential to it, that if even one of them cannot bear its due [188] measure of structural weight the whole edifice will come tumbling down. In *SJR* I pointed out that Plato himself came to see, later on in his life, that two, at least, of the psychological assumptions were rotten and that this new insight doomed his earlier faith in the realizability of the ideally just polis.[39] In the *R.* Plato had believed that men deprived of every right to political freedom could coexist with their masters in affectionate solidarity. In the *Laws* he has come to see that this would be a mirage. He now confesses that "slaves and masters could never be friends" (757a). In the *R.* he had scorned the Herodotean insight that autocratic power corrupts the autocrat.[40] In the *Laws* he has rediscovered that truth. He now concedes that it is simply not within men's capacity to live in absolute command of the bodies and souls of their fellows without "becoming filled with *hubris* and injustice" (713c), and thus unfitted for the function which, on his own view, only incorruptibly good and wise men could justly discharge.[41] So if one were only interested in showing Plato that the theory that led him to deny human rights to the mass of the civic body was disastrously wrong, it would suffice to elaborate just these considerations. Any theory of justice which is predicated on an erroneous estimate of human capacity can be rejected on just that ground.

But such a line of refutation could only show that Plato's theory was unworkable. That it was also unacceptable on moral grounds—that its vision of ideal justice was itself flawed—it would not show. Can we convict it of this deeper failure without indulging in moral parochialism, faulting it simply for enunciating principles of justice that disagree with ours? I believe we can. We may appeal to the common morality of his own time and place. This matches ours—and indeed every other single-standard morality known to me—in being equalitarian through and through in one fundamental respect: its basic rules confer on all members of the community rights which are equal in a sense approaching the ideally full sense defined above (p. 114):

[39] *SJR*, pp. 36–37 and Appendix C ⟨**2.98–99, 102–3⟩.

[40] Herodotus puts this in the mouth of a Persian opponent of tyranny who indicts it by observing that "even the best of men placed in such a position of [absolute] political power would be changed from his wonted mind" (3, 80, 3) and would be unable to hold back from *hubris* against his subjects.

[41] The same thought in 691c and 875a–d.

1. all have equal right to share in those benefits which accrue to individuals from the general observance of moral rules, and, moreover, [189]

2. all have equal right to share in making the judgments of praise and blame which guide the conduct by which these benefits are produced.

To see the import of (1), consider the benefits we all derive from the observance of rules interdicting murder, theft, kidnapping, blackmail, rape, slander, insult, and the rest. To realize how enormous are these benefits to each of us, we need only imagine what life would be like in a society where the rule "Thou shalt not kill" was not in force, so that forbearance from murder had to be purchased individually from those around us. What price would we be prepared to meet if they were driving a hard bargain? Would one million dollars to each be too much if we had the funds? The same—crudely melodramatic, but still true—line of reflection, applied to each of the other rules, will bring home the immensity of the benefits we derive gratis from the general adherence to the elemental moral interdicts on certain lines of socially injurious conduct. In entitlement to these benefits, all members of the community are on a par: one person's right not to be murdered, robbed, kidnapped, etc. is exactly the same as that of anyone else. The smart and the dull, the productive and the unproductive, the moral and the immoral, have exactly the same right to be shielded from such assaults on their welfare, freedom, and dignity. When Rashkolnikov excuses his murder of old Alëna with the thought that humanity would be none the worse for being rid of such a miserable specimen—no one would miss that human louse—he violates the spirit, as well as the letter, of the moral law.[42]

To see that (2) is true, one need only consider the fact that the individual judgments that guide the rule-observing conduct by which those benefits are produced consist in the main of that praise or censure which every person is entitled, equally with every other, to pass on his own personal conduct and on that of his fellows in respect to its conformity to the rules. This precious right is not reserved to a conclave of moral pundits. Though the judgment of persons known for their moral sensitiveness and sagacity may well be entitled to high respect, still, in the last analysis, each moral agent must make his own judgment, incorporating whatever insight he derives from others but judging [190] ultimately for himself.[43] No matter what may be the role of leaders credited with special moral insight on certain questions, the judgments that guide conduct in the community have to be made by the people themselves

---

[42] "But I only killed a louse, Sonia. A useless, nasty, harmful louse" Fyodor Dostoyevski, *Crime and Punishment*, trans. David Magarshack (London: Penguin Books, 1966), p. 84.

[43] This is the sense in which moral autonomy is absolutely indispensable to the morality of an adult person. To be denied this right is to be denied full moral capacity, which includes what Gerald Dworkin calls the right to "critical reflection"—the right to an independent examination of any expert ("Moral Autonomy," ⟨in H. T. Englehardt and D. Callahan, eds., *Morals, Science, Society* (Hastings-on-Hudson, N.Y., 1978⟩ para. 47).

whose lives *are* the life of the community, the ones who act and are acted upon, and whose approvals and disapprovals shape their own actions and those of their fellows: morality, if it works at all, will only work in that way. To pass such judgments all persons are equally entitled: the right of Sonia, the prostitute, to give Rashkolnikov her own direct, spontaneous verdict on his crime is the same as that of anyone else.[44]

By confronting Plato with these two considerations, we could show him that his adherence to the view that only functional rights exist puts him at odds with the morality of his own society, not merely with our own conceptions of what is just and right. Thus, in taking this view in respect of (1), he is implicitly denying that persons have certain basic rights conferred on them solely by the moral rules. And to deny this is to give up the commitment to the single-standard morality which confers those rights. Plato does this openly in the case of the interdict on lying. His acceptance of a double standard here is blatant. The duty that subjects have to refrain from lying when addressing their rulers is not reciprocal: rulers have the right to lie to their subjects whenever they judge this would be good for the state.[45] Moreover, in respect of (2), Plato's theory gives the elite a monopoly on authoritative moral judgment. Their subjects will, naturally, be making moral appraisals of each others' acts as they live their lives from day to day. But in so doing they will be either repeating the ones inculcated in them by the philosophers or, if they try to do more, will be only hazarding verdicts whose validity will be worthless until stamped "valid" by higher authority. Thus, even within their own circle, these people will be in no position to make authentically personal moral judgments; their conscience will be a shadow-conscience, of no account except insofar as it mimics or anticipates that of their rulers. It follows *a fortiori* that the populace has absolutely no right to pass moral judgment on the most important by far of all the actions taking place within their polis: those of their rulers, which may affect in minutest detail the life of every citizen. So the philosophers are [191] beyond everyone's moral judgment except their own; morally they are a law unto themselves.

Should Plato be troubled by the fact that his theory clashes in this way with assumptions deeply entrenched in the morality of his own time and place? He should. For he knows his own dependence on that morality. Though he thinks its precepts "vulgar," he cannot ignore his debt to them.[46] He speaks of them with affectionate reverence: "They have been like parents to us; we have obeyed and revered them."[47] He is caught in a bind here. For he must know that the validity of those unreasoned precepts is presupposed by his own reasoned

---

[44] She gives it without "critical reflection" and in less than a sentence in her instant response to Rashkolnikov's remark in n. 42 above: "A human being—a louse?"

[45] *R.*, 389b–d; 414b–c.

[46] *R.*, 442e.

[47] *R.*, 538c.

conception of the justice of the mutual benefit society. They are the indispensable, though unacknowledged, base on which his whole construction rests both at the first level of the protopolis and at the highest level of the fully developed ideal polis. At the former the dependence is only implicit but nonetheless real: were it not for the general observance of the rules of common decency, the life of protopolis would quickly degenerate into a jungle of fraud and violence. The dependence comes close to becoming explicit at the higher level. Since he insists that the ideally just man of the ideally just polis is bound to observe the "vulgar" standards,[48] Plato must have some awareness of the fact that the practice of justice as defined by himself requires fidelity to the common precepts of morality. But he never confronts directly this all-important fact and hence is never impelled to explore its limitations.

The failure may be traced back to the very method he employs to discover the rights of persons in the polis. The purely a priori method by which he constructs the "perfectly good" polis, abstracting systematically from all empirical data, including those constituted by the precepts of the prevailing morality, relieves him of the obligation to explain and justify the multitude of bonds which must exist between his new conception of justice and the one embedded in common opinion. Had he shouldered this task, he might have seen that the base on which his whole construction rests already accords to persons in the polis a complex of substantively equal rights which are totally independent of differential ability to excel in socially productive roles. He might then have sensed the one-sidedness of his theory of justice. What it offers is an idealization of the justice of the work-ethic—the [191] domain in which, generally speaking, persons must earn their rights through their productive labor. What it fails to recognize is that persons are also related to one another as persons, not merely as functioning units in a productive enterprise, and that as so related they have already as their birthright in their common morality substantively equal rights and may claim for the like reason substantively equal rights to participate in the governance of the polis.[49]

POSTSCRIPT ON THE USE OF *RIGHTS*

I have not felt it necessary to introduce my use of this term in this essay by way of a moral analysis; its preanalytic use has served my purposes

---

[48] *R.*, 442e–443b.

[49] Translations of the *Republic* which I have used above:

Bloom, A. (New York, 1968)
Cornford, F. M. (New York, 1945)
Grube, G. (Indianapolis, 1974)
Lindsay, A. D. (London, 1935; originally published in 1906)
Shorey, P. (London and Cambridge, Mass.: Vol. 1, 1930; Vol. 2, 1935)

well enough. However, it may be well to indicate summarily my general understanding of this term, reserving its exposition and defense for another occasion. Accordingly, I submit the following contextual definition: A substitution-instance of the sentence form "A has the right to X against B" will be true for persons bound by a given moral or legal code if and only if B is required by the norms of that code to engage in X-supporting conduct (action or forbearance) demandable of B by A and/or others acting on A's behalf. The norms of Plato's ideally just polis would satisfy this condition. In so doing, they would confer rights ipso facto, that is to say, without anything having to be said about rights in its code or in talk about it. If persons in the polis, or others acting on their behalf, are in a position to demand rule-mandated conduct beneficial to those persons, then they *have* rights under its code, regardless of the words at their disposal for naming or describing rights. I emphasize this point because there is no special word for *rights* in Plato's mother tongue—no word which corresponds exactly to ours, behaving as it does in all the contexts in which we speak of rights. To express the same notion, one would resort to a variety of makeshifts: (1) "what is due to one" (*ta opheilomena*), as in the definition of *justice* ascribed to the poet, Simonides, in *R.* 331e, "rendering to everyone his due"; (2) "the just" (*ta dikaia*), as in Demosthenes 15 (*Rhodians*), 29, "in commonwealths the laws have made participation in private rights (*idiōn dikaiōn*) common and equal for the weak and the strong"; (3) "one's [193] own" in the phrase "to have one's own" (*ta hautou echein*), as in the definition of *justice* in Aristotle's *Rhetoric* (1366b9–10), "the virtue because of which each has his own and in conformity with the law."

In an influential paper ("Are There Natural Rights?" *PR* 64 [1955]: 179–91), H.L.A. Hart has maintained that the existence of rights is a contingent feature of a moral code. He writes:

> There may be moral codes quite properly termed moral codes . . . which do not employ the notion of a right, and there is nothing contradictory or absurd in a code or morality consisting wholly of prescriptions or in a code which prescribed only what should be done for the realization of happiness or some ideal of personal perfection. (p. 176)

I would maintain that, on the contrary, any moral or legal code necessarily confers rights if it satisfies the elementary condition I have specified above, which all historical codes known to me do satisfy, not only those of classical Greece but even those of the very earliest forms of social organization: see, e.g., E. Adamson Hoebel, *The Law of Primitive Man* (Cambridge, Mass.: Harvard University Press, 1954), a study of the legal-moral codes of conduct in a variety of "primitive" societies (several of them having prepastoral economies), in all of which the concept of rights is profusely instantiated and, indeed, proves the fundamental concept required for the description and analysis of the empirical data.

Ignoring empirical findings such as those presented in Hoebel's study, Hart adduces the Mosaic Decalogue as a historical example of his thesis. He claims that it cannot be interpreted as conferring rights because

> in such an interpretation obedience to the Ten Commandments would have to be conceived as due or owed to individuals, not merely to God, and disobedience not merely as wrong but as a *wrong to* (as well as harm to) individuals (p. 182).

Accepting the implied criterion for the existence of rights in a given code, I would expect it to be satisfied perfectly in the case of the Ten Commandments. Thus, consider someone who was [194] cheated out of his patrimony by false witness. To concur with Hart, we would have to believe that it would be possible for the *general response* to such an event (i.e., not the response of some obsessive fanatic, but that of the average Israelite) to include awareness of the crime as (a) sinful and wrongful disobedience to the code, while excluding awareness of it as (b) a *wrong to* the victim. If Hart has any evidence that the ancient Israelites were capable of making habitually the extraordinary abstraction of (a) from (b), he fails to allude to it. I know of none in the pages of the Old Testament or of any other record of human experience.

9

THE VIRTUOUS AND THE HAPPY: IRWIN'S *PLATO'S MORAL THEORY*

TERENCE IRWIN is a superbly talented young scholar. His knowledge of Plato's text (and Aristotle's too, with which he often makes comparisons) is exact. He is abreast of the work of multitudes of other scholars on the texts he studies. There are nearly three hundred titles in his bibliography, many of them books and journal articles on Plato. He reports their views with pith and accuracy, explaining tersely why he agrees or dissents. He has expert command of the moral philosophy of the modern period, from Hume and Kant to the present, and uses it to good advantage to gain perspective on the substantive issues with which Socrates and Plato are concerned. And he has a flair for resourceful and tight argument which most of his seniors in his field might envy him. His style is not appetizing. Though clear in sentence-structure, it is flat, bookish, repetitious, and thick with technical terms of his own invention, often replaced by alphabetized abbreviations. Intellectual nutriment is purveyed in a form which has the bleak wholesomeness of granola. But this is a trifling hardship to put up with in a work which is rich in philosophical erudition, arresting in its claims, and powerful in its reasoning.

Its major claim is that the ethical positions of Socrates and Plato are polar opposites within the "eudemonist" view they both held in maintaining that the only complete and final good for man is happiness. For while moral virtue is for Plato a part of that final good, a constituent of it, and is therefore good in itself, for Socrates virtue has an altogether different status: it is external to happiness, a mere means to it, of no value in and of itself, preferable to vice only because it is a more efficient happiness-generator than its rival. A related difference is that while for Plato happiness is an "indeterminate" end, for Socrates it is a "determinate" one, having the same "fixed content" for any two persons picked at random: their descriptions of it may be different but the reference would be the same. (All terms within quotation marks in this paragraph are Irwin's). Thus Socrates is supposed to hold that the virtuous and the vicious man are pursuing the same end, differing only in their choice of means, and that the moralist's task is simply to enlighten that choice. This

Review of Terence Irwin, *Plato's Moral Theory: The Early and Middle Dialogues* (Oxford: Clarendon Press, 1977). From *TLS*, No. 3,961, Feb. 24, 1978, p. 230–31. Used by permission. Minor changes have been made in punctuation and spelling.

requires translating the language of moral commendation into the neutral language of utility. The programme is reductionist. Moral knowledge is only "technical" knowledge—knowledge of means. This, Irwin holds, is the point of the "craft analogy" which plays so large a role in the earlier dialogues. Only if moral knowledge were as "technical" as is the carpenter's, the cobbler's, the navigator's, and the like, whose claims can be established by "measurement," will it count as knowledge for Socrates, the sort of knowledge which will "eliminate disputed terms" from its canonical sentences and enable moral disagreements to be settled by a procedure which is, in principle, value-free.

Not so for Plato. For him happiness is a variable term, differing for persons of different character, experience, and insight. Hence to persuade us that moral conduct "pays," i.e., pays off in happiness, his strategy will be the antithesis of the one Socrates would have followed. Socrates would be content to make us see the moral virtues as means to happiness. Plato would be as concerned to enlighten our conception of happiness as our idea of virtue. This is how Irwin interprets the strategy of the great argument that "justice pays" in the *Republic*. That the notion of justice with which the interlocutors begin will have to be overhauled is explicit enough in Plato's text. At the start they are not supposed to know what justice is; they must discover it. and when they do find it at long last, it turns out to be wonderfully different from what they had previously believed.

But *pari passu* with this reconstruction of their idea of justice, Irwin points out, the argument has been transforming their conception of happiness. Plato does not say that he is doing this, but he does it all the same, and his argument succeeds only to the extent to which it achieves this effect. When we have been brought to see what our soul would be like if it were Platonically just (intellect, emotion, and appetite rationally harmonized in friendly, nonrepressive, order) and what our *polis* would be like if it were Platonically just—(its three classes analogously harmonized in friendly union under the hegemony of philosophic reason), we shall have gained a new vision of happiness, which only that kind of soul, ideally living in that kind of society, could realize. When we have exchanged our vulgar view for this Platonic happiness then, and only then, does Plato expect that we shall be persuaded that "justice pays."

What I have offered here is, in barest outline, the main plot of Irwin's story, without a word on its subplots—its numerous collateral and ancillary theses —nor yet on its analyses of the plethora of individual arguments, many of them self-contained, which form the substance of the dialogues, their flesh and bone, all but their skin of graceful chatter and badinage. Though this detailed work which makes up much of the book will be of greatest interest to the specialist, it would be hopeless to report, let alone appraise, it here. So my critical comment must be selective: harshly, but not arbitrarily, so, for it will focus on the tale I have sketched above, and this, were it accepted by the historians, would fix the positions of Socrates and of Plato in the development of moral theory in the West. Is that tale true?

Let me start with its second half, which concerns Plato. A case for this general view of Plato's ethical theory had already been made by scholarly work over the past generation, particularly in Oxford (Irwin's *alma mater*). It was just fifty years ago that H. A. Prichard, in his inaugural lecture as White's Professor of Moral Philosophy at Oxford, had put forwards the startling claim that Plato's moral position was utilitarian. The claim seemed false on the face of it, since the explicit thesis of Plato's argument that "justice pays" is that justice is good in itself, not merely in its consequences.

But Prichard's tour de force of acute and stubborn argument made his claim plausible enough to provide a series of ripostes which in the course of refuting Prichard accomplished something far more important: they separated out the notion of eudemonism from that of utilitarianism (in its consistently conse-quentialist form), with which it had been commonly confounded (for a sample of the confusion, see the section "Theory of the Good" in Henry Jackson's article on Socrates in the eleventh edition of the *Encyclopaedia Britannica,* one of the most muddled paragraphs in the whole of that admirable compen-dium of knowledge authoritative in its time). These scholars showed that justi-fying morality "teleologically" (i.e., by its contribution to happiness) need not involve a sellout of probity to expediency, as Kant and others after him had maintained: that error the teleological moralist can avoid by thinking of the moral virtues as "parts" of happiness, as "elements" or "ingredients" of it.

These quoted words and the thought itself hail from John Stuart Mill's *Utilitarianism,* the surprising source to which, as Irwin notes, this line of thought can be traced back. But in Mill's time this strain in his thought had been dismissed as an amiable indiscretion ("mere looseness of phraseology, venial in a treatise aiming at a popular style," was the phrase Henry Sidgwick had used in disposing of it). It was not applied to Plato until much later, when it was rediscovered independently by the Oxford philosophers and scholars who used it to refute Prichard's misunderstanding of eudemonism in Plato and in Aristotle. In Irwin's book this job is done up brown, yielding a more illu-minating interpretation of the central argument of the *Republic* than any we have had before.

But in its first, Socratic half, Irwin's story is not so successful. The account of Socrates as a hard-line reductionist utilitarian I do not find convincing. For there are many texts in Irwin's sources for Socrates' moral theory—the earlier Platonic dialogues—which are flagrantly inconsistent with that account. Con-sider, for instance, how Socrates explains in the *Apology* (28b) why he had acted as he did in circumstances where to stick by justice was to take his life into his hands: "A man worth anything at all should take no account of whether he is to live or die, or give consideration to anything but this: whether his conduct will be just or unjust, the action of a good or of an evil man." He cites Achilles, noblest of the heroes (strange model for a plebeian, a statuary's and a midwife's son): when his options were a base deed (*aischron*) or death, Achilles preferred death, and so do I. As Irwin recognizes, this is a far cry from justifying a choice by measuring utility in competing options. Socrates chooses the action which is good in itself—morally splendid, beautiful (*kalon*)—because it is just; nothing else matters.

Irwin sees how out of sorts this passage is with consequentialism, and so too a later one in the *Apology*, when Socrates remarks after his condemnation that "no evil thing can happen to a good man" (41d), which Irwin glosses admirably: "A good man cannot be harmed: being virtuous is not simply our best prospect for happiness, but in itself assures happiness." He dubs this "the sufficiency of virtue," a label I gladly adopt, and recognizes the same sentiment in the *Crito* and then again in a passage in the *Gorgias* (512d6–e5), where Socrates declares (in Irwin's paraphrase) that "it is living well which matters, however bad the consequences for the future welfare may be." Irwin connects this thought illuminatingly with that in the *Nicomachean Ethics* (1159a22–25) of Aristotle who, he says, "argues similarly that the virtuous man who acts for the sake of what is admirable will prefer to do a single admirable action, even with disastrous consequences to himself, than live on without having done it."

In all these passages, Irwin acknowledges that for Socrates (as for Aristotle and for Plato) living "well" (i.e., virtuously) is what makes life worth living, hence worth choosing even if the choice were to cost us every other requisite of happiness, life itself included. This is as far as anything could be from the consequentialist view which is assigned to him monotonously throughout the book. To keep this up, the "sufficiency of virtue" doctrine has to be given a curious treatment: admitted as "important to Socrates," but not allowed to control the constructive interpretation of Socrates' philosophical position.

In this, I fear, Irwin has failed to realize how central that doctrine is in Socrates' positive moral thought. The failure is palpable in the chapter on the *Gorgias*. In the course of it, we are told that Socrates "nowhere rejects" in this dialogue the view "that virtue is only instrumental means to happiness." How could he *not* be rejecting it in the passage where he maintains that "it is living well which matters, however bad the consequences?" That "nowhere" could be a slip, and I do not wish to take advantage of it. What Irwin [230] doubtless means is, nowhere in the passage we should consider controlling. But that is just where I would take issue with him. To leave out for this purpose those texts which are irreconcilable with an instrumentalist conception of virtue would be to work with a gutted dialogue. As Heinrich Maier noted long ago (*Sokrates* [1913]—a book which may be added to Irwin's vast bibliography; and its chapter on "The Moral Life and Happiness" may be read with profit, not for logical finesse, of which it has little, but for the sureness of its insight and the sanity of its judgment), the rejection is implied by the master-thesis of the *Gorgias* that in every unjust act the agent does more harm to himself than to his victim. That thesis would be wildly implausible unless virtue were being implicitly construed as no mere means to happiness but as a component of it, indeed as its supreme component, sufficient in and of itself to outweigh all possible advantages an unjust act could bag for the wrongdoer, all possible evils it could cause its innocent victim.

This implication never surfaces. But if Socrates were not counting on it, his espousal of that thesis would have been an act of folly. And that he does count on it shows up at the climax (506c–507c), where he presents *sophrosunē*, piety, courage, and justice as elements of order in the psyche which in themselves, not by causing some *further* benefit, make their possessor "blessed and happy." This is, of course, an anticipation of the argument Plato is to make in the *Republic*. The fact, on which Irwin rightly insists, that it is not nearly as successful in this first version as it will prove in the later one, is irrelevant to the only point I am making: that it is the kind of argument Socrates would not have even tried to make unless he were rejecting the view that "virtue is only an instrumental means to happiness."

So we must reckon with the fact that the strongly anticonsequentialist import of the "sufficiency of virtue" doctrine is at the center of the *Gorgias*, fully as much so as in that of the *Apology* and the *Crito*. These three dialogues are vehicles of positive doctrine *par excellence*. They are the only Socratic dialogues in which solemn moral affirmation is sustained to their very end. All three conclude on a triumphant, upbeat note, in striking contrast to the other dialogues in their group, which regularly drop off at the finish into real or simulated *aporia*. And we must reckon further with the fact that this same doctrine is the fertile source of that part of Socrates' teaching which constitutes its profoundest moral innovation: the denial of the legitimacy of returning wrong for wrong. Socrates' root-and-branch rejection of that whole rotten side of Greek morality was motivated directly by his conviction that virtue was so precious in itself that it would compensate us for all the losses we might expect to suffer when imposing unilaterally upon ourselves the constraints of nonretaliatory justice.

When we return with this in view to take a second look at the picture of Socratic ethics in this book, what will we see? An extraordinarily ingenious construct which is doubly insecure at its evidential base: first, because it has been derived by exclusion of that whole part of the evidence I have just discussed; second, because the support which can be claimed for it from that group of texts on which it is made to rest is itself questionable. That, at any rate, is the conclusion I have reached after pondering Irwin's complex and subtle argument to the contrary. This argument I cannot detail and probe here. The long and short of the matter appears to me this: There *is* a passage (*Prot.* 351b–360e) which would establish Irwin's construct beyond dispute, *if* the hedonistic doctrine on which Socrates premises the demonstration of the impossibility of *acrasia* he offers here were meant to be understood as Socrates' own view rather than only that of the *hoi polloi* on whom he foists it.

I italicize the *if* because the point is moot: some good scholars would agree with Irwin that Socrates himself is accepting the hedonist view of morality in this passage; others would disagree. And if that passage were put to one side and the acceptability of the instrumentalist interpretation were to be judged by its support from any or all of the other texts to which Irwin refers us, we would be entitled to conclude no more than this: while that interpretation is *consistent* with those data, it is not *required* by them; good sense can be made of them without assuming that they are the visible tip of a utilitarian iceberg.

In making this assertion, I am being unavoidably dogmatic. To argue for it, I would have to go through each of the relevant texts and show that while they can be read as Irwin reads them, they need not. It is possible to understand them in a way which reconciles each of them with the "sufficiency of virtue" doctrine. Though I cannot mount this argument here, I can illustrate it.

Consider the "craft analogy" to which Irwin appeals again and again in support of the instrumentalist thesis. I would argue that his confidence that the analogy has this implication is misplaced. For though Socrates certainly wants moral knowledge to be in *some* respects like that of carpenters and the like— for example, in being honest knowledge, free of rhetorician's humbug—he knows that it is radically different in others. Thus, as Irwin duly notes, Socrates insists that moral knowledge can never be misused, while the practical crafts always can be. Why then must he be assuming that it is like the crafts in that particular respect which is pivotal for Irwin's argument, i.e., that what it creates has only instrumental value? Nowhere does Socrates say anything remotely of that sort, and Irwin does not suggest that he does (there is no forcing of evidence in this book). And why should Socrates have wished to say it? Believing, as we know he does, that all crafts seek the perfection of their object, what moral knowledge would seek *qua* craft is, in the first instance, the perfection of the soul which practices it.

And since we know that perfection of soul is for Socrates moral perfection, and since we also know that moral perfection is itself what he takes to make life worth living, I would argue that the import of the analogy must be the opposite of what Irwin has taken it to be, i.e., that in the case of this craft, the only one of its kind, its exercise is an end in itself; the moral perfection at which it aims is realized in the very process which creates it. To be sure, Socrates never says any such thing. But neither does he say what Irwin understands him to mean. Since the analogy is open to both readings, we ought to prefer the one which harmonizes, instead of clashing, with the "sufficiency of virtue" doctrine.

I conclude that Irwin's account of Socratic morality needs to be drastically revised. I do not say this to depreciate its value. Those who might think I am doing so would only reveal how sadly they misunderstand the standards by which a work of pure scholarship is appraised in its own domain. If an interpretation is as clear, bold, imaginative, yet painstakingly attentive to its texts and philosophically as rigorous as is Irwin's, it has more than proved its worth. Its effect on those who work with it, testing it out, text by text and argument by argument, will be bracing, compelling them to bring into sharper focus things which had been heretofore fuzzy in their perception of what is being said in the dialogues and to explore connections they had never troubled to track down before. In this I speak for myself. Time and again, in following out one of the fine-print miniatures in his notes which lays bare the skeletal structure of a Socratic or Platonic argument, I have been led to understand its thought better. For this I am greatly in his debt, which is all the heavier because of the many pages of level-headed and level-tempered criticism his notes have devoted to my own work. I have never had more valuable help from a critic.

10

WAS PLATO A FEMINIST?

W AS PLATO A FEMINIST? Hot scholarly controversy has swirled around this question. Plato has been hailed as Ur-feminist by some, denounced as antifeminist by others. When we view such collisions between honest readers of the same texts, we may suspect that not all of three desiderata have been fully met: clarity of definition, awareness of complexity, dispassionateness of judgment.

How should we define the term? For *feminism* the *OED* lists "advocacy of the claims and the rights of women," dating the entry to 1895. This is too loose. To tighten it up, I borrow wording from the Amendment to the United States Constitution proposed earlier in the present decade (failing to pass, though strongly supported by feminists and favored by a majority of the American electorate): "Equality of rights under the law shall not be denied or abridged by the U.S. or by any State on account of sex." Dropping everything unessential for my purpose, I get a shorter formula whose scope is wide enough to cover all personal rights that may be claimed for women—not just the legal ones envisaged by the Amendment, but social, economic, and moral rights as well: "Equality in the rights of persons shall not be denied or abridged on account of sex."

Does this give a defensible definition of "feminism"? I believe so. But I shall waste no time defending it. The focus of my interest is Plato, not feminism. It suffices for my purpose, making the question under debate entirely clear: Plato will qualify as a "feminist" if his ideas, sentiments, and proposals for social policy are in line with this norm.

Well, are they? When the question is put in that way, any informed reader of the *Republic* and the *Laws* should be able to see that there is no simple answer. I would argue that it takes no less than four distinct propositions to formulate one that takes account of everything he says: 1. In the ideally best society outlined in Books 4 to 7 of the *Republic*, the position of the women in its ruling elite, the so-called Guardians, is unambiguously feminist. 2. In that same society, the position of the great majority of its free women, composing its industrial and agricultural class, is unambiguously antifeminist. 3. In the alternative, second-best, society laid out in the *Laws*, the position of free women is a hybrid, feminist in some respects, antifeminist in others. 4. In

From *TLS*, No. 4, 485, Mar. 17, 1989, pp. 276, 288–89. Used by permission. Minor changes have been made in punctuation and spelling.

his personal attitude to the women in his own contemporary Athens, Plato is virulently antifeminist.

That Plato can run the gamut of these extremes will raise hackles of incredulity. It would take a whole book, a fat one, to allay them completely. All I can do here is to show that the initial impression of inconsistency between them is false. To do this I shall have to focus sharply on the first, shortshrifting the other three. For this is the eye of the controversial storm: Plato's feminism has been denied even here. Claiming that Plato's affirmation of feminism within the ruling class of the *Republic* is the strongest ever made by anyone in the classical period, I have no choice but to defend that claim in detail, letting the other three come in for their due as I proceed.

I began by listing rights systematically denied to women in Plato's Athens, which we have reason to believe would not be denied or abridged within the Guardian class of his *Republic:*

1. Right to Education. In Athens schools, gymnasia and palaestrae were a male monopoly. In Plato's *Republic* access to them by members of the Guardian class would be the same for women as for men in all respects, down to that last detail which has drawn so many prurient smirks: exercising in the nude with men. As we know from Herodotus and Thucydides, the Greeks thought total nudity in athletics a salient feature of their Hellenic culture. Plato would not dream of rescinding it for males. To deny it to females would have been discriminatory.

2. Right to Vocational Opportunity. No secular gainful employment was open to all women in Athens, except prostitution of varying degrees of elegance or squalor. Within the lowest social strata, there were other options outside the home: working-class women could be midwives, wet nurses, vegetable sellers, chaplet makers, and so forth. Aristotle apologizes for this exception to the rule, explaining it as a product of dire economic necessity: "How could you stop the women of the indigent from going outside the house?" (*Pol.* 1300a6). In Plato's *Republic* career for highest talent is as open to women as to men. Both sexes qualify on equal terms for admission to Guardianship and therewith to all those professional occupations bundled up in that nominally single job: military to begin with and, thereafter, all political offices—executive, legislative, and judicial—and all of the assorted tasks that would come along with these: economic planning, population management, critique and censorship of literature and the arts, direction of schools and sports, supervision of the military and religious establishment—all these along with research and teaching in the sciences and philosophy.

3. Right to Unimpeded Social Intercourse. Mingling with free men other than close relatives is denied in principle to all Athenian women except priestesses, hetaerae, prostitutes, and tradeswomen. Such segregation is wiped out in Plato's Guardian class, where men and women "live in the same house, eat in common dining halls" (458c), and exercise in the same gymnasia.

4. Legal Capacity. In Athens only men have it. Women are wards of their nearest

male relative, their *kurios*. They cannot sue or be sued, and even their right to give testimony in court is marginal. Among Plato's Guardians such differences could not exist. Whatever legal capacity male Guardians have, female ones have also.

5. Right to Sexual Choice. In Athens women have little say as to whom or when they will marry. The marriage contract is negotiated between their nearest male relative and the bridegroom. To what extent, if any, this gentleman was required to take the wishes of his female ward into account is unclear. Heterosexual intercourse outside of marriage is forbidden to women with the utmost severity. The ferocity of the interdict may be gauged from this: an Athenian virgin in breach of the rule may be sold into slavery by her *kurios*. This is the only case in which the law recognizes penal enslavement for an Athenian. In the case of a married woman caught in adultery, "anyone whatsoever may do to her at will anything short of death." On men there was no counterpart constraint. They could have any sexual relations they pleased with women other than Athenian virgins or spouses without incurring any legal disability, or even any moral censure so long as they did not do it for money and did not overdo it. Among Plato's Guardians the interdict on sexual intercourse outside of the eugenic unions during the childbearing age is the same for men as it is for women. The liberty after that age is also the same for both. The double standard of sexual morality is wiped out.

6. Right to Own and Dispose of Property. Under Athenian law only men have it. Among Plato's Guardians private property is denied equally to men and to women, public support is assured equally to both.

7. Political Rights. None for women in Athens. The same for women as for men among Plato's Guardians.

Given this array of equalities of rights for women Guardians in Book V of the *Republic,* can it be doubted that Plato's programme for them is rigorously feminist in the sense defined?

To appraise its rigor, we should compare it not only with Athenian practice, but also with Athenian fantasy in Aristophanes' *Ecclesiazousae.* The two dreams of gender equality have often been compared and the question of who cribbed what from whom has been debated. But I have yet to see it noticed that the philosopher's argument is bolder than the poet's whimsy. When Praxagoras' conspiratorial women capture the state and turn their wishes into law, it never occurs to them to break up the segregated public rituals and private work-roles which had always been the lot of women. When a state banquet is laid on, only the men sit down to it: the ladies do not invite themselves to dine with the gentlemen. When Blepyros, on being informed that all of his work will now be done by slaves, asks where his clothes will be coming from, Praxagora replies, "When you wear out the ones you have, we will weave you new ones" (651–54): the women are still behind the loom, where they have been since Homer.

The most radical innovation in Plato's vision of a new society is not the extension of legal and political rights to women. That had been thought of already, though it had taken the comic genius of Aristophanes to think of it. Nor is it the liquidation of the nuclear family; for this there had been earlier models in Herodotus's album of anthropological oddities. It is the reasoned rejection of the age-old dogma, never previously questioned in Greek prose or verse, that difference of sex must determine difference of work-allocation.

Is there any reasonable ground on which the feminist intent, so thoroughgoing on the face of it, of Plato's programme for the ruling class of his utopia might still be doubted? Sarah Pomeroy has argued that there is, finding it in that curious language in which Plato speaks of the breeding unions: he refers to the women and the children as belonging in common to the men, with never a balancing allusion to the fact that the men, as also, of course, the children, belong in common to the women. Here are the suspect expressions: "community (*koinonia*) of children and wives for the Guardians" (450c); "possession (*ktēsis*) and use (*chreia*) of children and of wives" (451c). From this asymmetry of references to who-belongs-to-whom, Pomeroy infers that the female Guardians are to be the property of the male ones. The inference is unwarranted. The conclusion is not entailed by the evidence, and it is inconsistent with the following data: in any given marriage-group, every woman belongs to all the men in the peculiar, but precise, sense that, so far as she knows and so far as they know, the eugenic "lottery" might make any one of them the father of her child. *Mutatis mutandis* every man belongs to every woman in his group in exactly the same sense. And there is no other relevant sense of "belonging." So the relation cannot be ownership. It would make no sense to say that x is y's property when y is also x's property.

Why then should Plato have used that kind of language? One could reply that this is the way group-marriages are talked about: they are always viewed from the man's point of view. Thus Herodotus writes that the Agathyrsoi "have in common intercourse with the women" (4.104) and that the Namasonians "believe in having many wives and in having intercourse with them in common" (4.172.2). Aristophanes makes even Praxagora, the liberator, talk in the same arsenocentric way. Though the licensed promiscuity is perfectly symmetrical, she speaks of it as "making the young women common bedmates for the men to produce children for any man who wants it" (614). Should we be surprised that Plato should have used similar language? Verbal habits could outlast the prejudices which created them. But can we be sure that Plato has outgrown the prejudices? Some of them he must have, else he could not have written Book 5 of the *Republic*. But there are others he has not. The evidence has been surveyed brilliantly by Dorothea Wender. Here is part of it: that Plato's estimate of the common run of female intelligence is very low slips out even within Book 5 of the *Republic*. Remarking that people who desecrate enemy corpses must be acting on the stupid belief that your enemy's body is your real enemy, he says that to give credence to this notion would be "the mark of a womanish and small intellect" (469d). To distinguish the higher from the lower appetites, he says earlier on (431b–c) that the former are those "you would find among the few, those with the best nature and the best education," while their opposites "one would find chiefly in children and in women and in slaves and, among so-called freemen, in the base multitude." So too in his critique of music and of poetry. The great complaint here is that in their present form these arts weaken the controls on strong emotion which decent persons ought to [276] keep and women typically don't: "We pride ourselves on bearing up quietly in affliction, for this is the part of a man, while the other is the part of a woman" (605d–e). He refers to scenes in Homer and tragedy where heroes and other great men abandon themselves to outbursts of grief whose pathos, softies that we are at heart, we enjoy sharing vicariously, though we would feel disgraced if we had so behaved ourselves.

"The element common to all that was said of women by the Greeks," writes Kenneth Dover, "is the woman's inability to resist fear, desire, or impulse. . . . A woman, in fact, was thought to have a 'butterfly mind,' equally incapable of intelligent, far-sighted, deliberation and of foregoing the emotional reaction of the moment in pursuit of distant and impersonal aims." We may note that he is not saying that this is how individual women are always portrayed. He knows well this is not so. He says that this is how they are generalized about on the stage and in oratory, and not only by men: women too are made to say such things about themselves. From women's lips we hear in Euripides and Aristophanes that their sex is weak, weepy, impulsive, irresolute, perfidious, garrulous, gluttonous, bibulous, lascivious. What I have just quoted from Plato fits this stereotype.

And now one last item to the same effect from the venomous caricature of Athenian democracy in Book 8 of the *Republic*. Plato pictures its mania for liberty as condoning the collapse of all deference due to authority: citizens no longer obey the magistrates, nor do sons their parents, nor pupils their teachers, nor slaves their owners and "even the horses and donkeys have the habit of promenading on the street with all the rights and privileges of freemen." Just before the promenading quadrupeds at the climax of the satire (563b), comes the following: "I nearly forgot to mention how great *isonomia* and liberty have entered the mutual relations of men and women." *Isonomia* is a very strong word. It stands not just for equality before the law but for equality by means of law—for substantively equal civic rights established and maintained by law. Now if progress toward sexual equality were being currently made in Athens, the last person in the world we might expect to damn his city for it would be the author of Book 5 of the *Republic*. What then should we make of his conduct in the present passage? Must we reckon it a great man's lapse into peevishness, his hatred of democracy blinding him at this point, making him forget the feminist line he had taken just three books earlier in the *Republic?* We can make better sense of it if we connect it with the image of Athenian womanhood he must have carried in his head, judging from those chance remarks in which "womanish" stands for persons with diminutive intellects, obsessive appetites, and ungovernable emotions. If this is how Plato thought of the common run of women, he might well believe that in the present state of society continued subjection would be better for them than any degree of emancipation. Keeping them down, under their nearest male relative's thumb, he could hardly think an ideal solution, considering how benighted most of those males were on his own reckoning. But it might still strike him as the lesser of two evils: *isonomia* for creatures who cannot reason and keep their baser impulses under control would be worse.

This is the streak in Plato's thinking I had in view when putting forward the last of the four theses above. Whatever improvements had occurred within his lifetime must have been so minuscule as to leave no discernible record in Athens' legal history and provide no known relief from those massive inequalities I have detailed. That Plato should have seized on those minute changes, magnifying them in hostile fantasy, blowing them up into *isonomia,* should suffice to show that on the emancipation of women within the framework of his own society Plato's position would be not only conservative but reactionary.

But could he retain this attitude side by side with the feminism of Book 5? On the face of it, it looks as though only schizophrenia could have enabled him to do this. I want to argue that this appearance is false. Prisoner of the sexist stereotype though Plato was in his reactions to the contemporary scene, he could still take, without formal inconsistency, a radically opposite view of the place women were to have in the highest stratum of his ideal society. He could do so because the "womanish" traits he denigrates are those of the great mass of women, not of those brilliant exceptions from whom the Guardians would be recruited; and, moreover, they are the traits common to women *now,* under conditions now prevailing which do not foster the development of energetic minds and resolute characters. In the most damning of the disparaging remarks cited, it is clear that he is speaking of women as they are under present, nonideal, conditions: those motley appetites predominant in women, along with children, slaves, and men of the vulgar mass, are those, he says, "which one would find" (431c) in these creatures. What one "would find" is what is already there. And he is not saying that it is there as the permanently fixed, invariant, character of the female of the species, its nature; there is no reference to women's *phusis* in this passage or any of the others I have cited from the *Republic,* as there would have been if his point had been that those bad "womanish" traits were inherent in femaleness as such. In the absence of any such indications, the right way to read those passages is as reflections on what Plato thinks women are now, formed and shaped, deformed and misshaped, by the society which has reared them.

We should recall here his vivid sense of the power of a corrupt society to pervert the heart and conversely of the power of education to improve moral character. Putting into that context those woman-denigrating remarks, we can understand them as voicing what Plato thinks most Athenian women grow up to be in their present habitat, the domestic ghetto, which stunts them intellectually and warps them morally, robbing them of what they might have been had they enjoyed that marvelous *paideia* which both sexes are to have in the ideal *polis*.

Moreover the butts of those nasty remarks differ in still another way from the women for whom Plato reserves the feminist programme of Book 5. They are females of the common run, while those who will be Guardians are as exceptional within their own sex as the male Guardians are to be in theirs: in each case Plato is counting on paragons of intellect and character. Ad if you ask, Why should he expect the female half of the population to produce such superlative specimens? the answer is, Why not, when he expects this of its male half? If there are to be stars in the population, why should they be only male? Why should Plato have assumed that being female would decrease one's chances of turning out to be a super-person instead of a mass-person?

The Greek poetic vision of humanity would give no quarter to that prejudice. Homer and tragedy present a gallery of distinguished women who rise as high above ordinary females as do its heroic males above the mass of men. Consider Penelope. In cunning, in farsighted purpose, in composure under nagging harassment, in unrelenting steadfastness of resolve, she dwarfs the people, male or female, who crowd her world. Compared to her, the suitors are pygmies and Telemachus a likable mediocrity. Only the great Odysseus is her match. In tragedy we have Clytemnestra, the counterpart in Aeschylus's masterpiece of Lady Macbeth in Shakespeare's. That both are evil is beside the point, which is that each is as far as human flesh and blood could be from Dover's "butterfly mind." Each has the qualities which, differently used, could have produced heroic goodness. The same is true of Medea. And if we are looking for high stature in a woman who stays completely within the conventional social role, instead of breaking out of it, like Antigone, in her defiance of an unjust decree, consider Alcestis in Euripides. Of perfect outward self-possession while suffering inner agony there is no better example in Greek literature than Alcestis as she moves toward her death. Dressed and adorned as for a festive occasion, she makes the round of the altars in the palace "without a tear, without a groan, without a change of color on her lovely face" (173). So long as she remains on public view even skin-color is under control.

But there is no need to give the poets sole, or even major, credit for freeing Plato from the prejudice that an intellectual and moral elite could only be recruited from male stock. We know of two other liberating influences: the theory of moral virtue he learned from Socrates and the metaphysical theory he invented himself.

One could scarcely overstress the shattering effect in Plato's mind of Socrates' rejection of the age-old axiom that excellence of character was class-bound and gender-bound. The Socratic doctrine that virtue is the same in women as in men may seem a commonplace to us. But it flouts the certainties of his people and it outrages Aristotle, who takes their parochial intuitions for universal moral truths. Nothing shows up so well the novelty of the Socratic view as do Aristotle's remarks in Book 3 of the *Politics* (1277b20–23). To prove that virtue *is* different in women, Aristotle argues that if a man were no braver than a brave woman he would be a coward, and if a woman were as talkative as a decent (*kosmios*) man, she would be a chatterbox: female excellence, he assumes, could be no better than male mediocrity. If Plato had shared that premise, he could not have composed Book 5 of the *Republic,* even if he had written everything else in that work. He did not share it because he derived from Socrates the conviction that human excellence, intellectual and moral, is unisex. So when he designed a state where that kind of excellence would be the passport to dictatorial authority, he had to make the tenure of political power also unisex.

To his Socratic heritage Plato adds his own metaphysical theory, without which the absolute powers entrusted to his philosopher-kings would be incomprehensible. Assured of access to the world of Forms, they will come to know the Form of the Good and be themselves transformed by that knowledge. Their initiation into that eternal world Plato calls a "turn-about of the soul from a day that is like night to the true day" (521c). The change is so profound that not only the mind, but the whole psyche, down to the libido, is transformed. It is a translation into a world of the mind whose magnificence beggars the prizes of the world of sense. *Sub specie aeternitatis* sensual attractions pale: Plato's imagery makes them fugitive, flat, unsubstantial—shadows on a wall. This in the last analysis is what he expects will keep his philosophers from misusing their vast unchecked authority. Their power will not corrupt them because to denizens of eternity the bribes and lures of power are trash.

Now obviously there is nothing about maleness that fits one to experience this rebirth. What one needs is, first of all, the capacity to go through its preparatory *paideia* in one's teens—a capacity Plato must think unrestricted by sex since he prescribes that *paideia* for both sexes—and thereafter the intellectual talent and the moral fiber to survive the gruelling fifteen-year course of graduate studies in mathematics and dialectic. There is a cutoff point here that will separate the men and women who are to rule from those they are to rule. Plato has no way of specifying that point. But it is clear that he is thinking of a threshold that can be crossed by persons who, though vastly superior to the great mass, may still differ considerably in ability among themselves. He believes that when the male population, taken as a whole, is compared with the female population, taken as a whole, the incidence of ability is on the average higher among males than among females. Does he then believe that in the small subgroup which passes the tests for admission to the higher studies the same differential obtains? He may, though he nowhere says so. If so, he would believe that within the Guardian class men are on the average abler than women in each of the tasks to be performed. It would then follow that on the average there would be more men than women in the higher offices. It would not follow that there would be no women in the highest ones.

That women are expected to share in the topmost offices becomes explicitly clear at the close of Book 7. Here Socrates speaks of [288] those "who have survived the tests and have excelled in all things in action and in knowledge," have beheld the Form of the Good, taken their part in governing, and at their death received quasi-divine honors. Glaucon is moved to exclaim, "Like a statuary, you have made your men-rulers matchless in beauty." Socrates retorts, "Yes, the women-rulers too, Glaucon, for you must not suppose that my description applies to men any more than it does to all the women who arise among them with the requisite natural endowment."

If the foregoing argument has been sound, the feminist programme for the ruling elite in Book 5 of the *Republic* becomes perfectly understandable as a consistent application of Plato's theory of social justice. According to that theory the rights and duties justly allocated to citizens of the *polis* would be all and only those which would enable each of them to make the greatest personal contribution to the happiness and excellence of the whole *polis,* their own included. This is the criterion by which the abolition of private property for the Guardians is justified: Guardians must own no property because they would be "best craftsmen at their own work" (421c) without rather than with private property. The same criterion would dictate full equality of rights within the Guardian class in all of the categories I detailed at the start. Nothing less will explain the rationality of Plato's extraordinary programme, so unprecedented in Greek experience, philosophy, or even fantasy. In particular, it cannot be explained as a mere by-product of the decision earlier on in the *Republic* to deprive Guardians of private property, thereby abolishing in their case the traditional pattern of Greek marriage whose base *was* private property. The claim that this is the correct explanation has been made repeatedly in the scholarly literature. The conclusive objection is that Plato could have abolished the private family along with private property in the Guardian class, could have followed to the letter the formula "common possession of goods and wives" *without* granting equality of status to those wives. He could have made them collective consorts, nurses for the children, factotums for the men, but not Guardians, rulers of the state, sharing supreme political authority and civic dignity.

That the theory of social justice propounded in the *Republic* is the decisive reason for the feminism of Book 5 gets added support from what happens when Plato turns away from that theory in his last work, the *Laws*. That move marks a retreat along a broad front from his stand in the *Republic*. The retreat is not a rout. The equal right to education and to unimpeded social intercourse women retain in the *Laws,* and here all citizen women will have it, regardless of class. But they lose equality in vocational opportunity, in legal capacity, in the right to own property, and in choice of marriage partner. I would argue that both changes—in the theory of social justice and in the conception of the status of women—are due to the more conservative philosophical and political outlook which comes over Plato with increasing age. So if we are looking for feminism in Plato there is only one place where we do not need to invent it: in the legislation for the Guardians in the *Republic*. Among all of Plato's writings and among all the writings which have survived from the classical age of Greece, that work alone projects a vision of society in whose dominant segment the equal rights of human beings are not denied or abridged on account of sex.

This innovation owed nothing to a belief in what we have now come to call human rights—rights which belong to persons as their human birthright, without regard to their membership in any ethnic, political, economic, or religious grouping, rights pertaining to each of them individually as human beings for no reason other than their humanity. It should go without saying that Plato had no such belief. His ideal society has no place for the freedoms enumerated in the Bill of Rights: freedom of religion, of speech, of assembly, of the press. It never occurs to him that without these any attempt to apply his pattern for that society in the real world would result in the opposite of his dream of it—corruption in the rulers, oppression of the ruled. Who, man or woman, should want equality on those terms? So to think of Plato as an advocate of "Women's Liberation" would be perverse. Liberation Plato advocates for no one, man or woman. Excellence, not liberty, is his goal, and he rejects liberty as the enemy of excellence. Still less could we think of him as a champion of "Affirmative Action." Nowhere in the presentation of his programme does one catch a gleam of a desire to right wrongs sexist oppression had done to women in the past. Of compassion there seems to be all too little in Plato even for men, so how could there be for women, given those sour views of them he voices in the *Republic?*

I would not call him a misogynist on that account. Certainly those derogatory remarks of his would have warmed the heart of a real woman-hater. But they hardly warrant classifying him as such himself. If they did, then by the same token we would have to classify as woman-haters the women in Euripides and Aristophanes who say equally bitter things about their sex. And while it is not unknown for members of an oppressed group to internalize masochistically the sentiments of their oppressor, it would still be misleading to say that those women hate their sex. Anyhow, "hatred" would just misdescribe the feelings Plato harbors for the women in his world: a certain dislike perhaps, condescension tinged with disdain, though more striking is the fact that he so largely ignores them in his reflections on the state, in his analyses of moral concepts and, what may be more significant, in his references to human beauty. (In the great erotic passages in the *Symposium* (210–12) and the *Phaedrus* (245–57), human beauty is desired by men desiring boys; to females desired for their beauty by men or desiring it in one another and in men there is no allusion.) When he does encounter them on the human landscape, he seems to view them with an abstract gaze, as he would stare at members of a curious species distantly related to his own. (In all other passages where Plato's Socrates expresses or simulates sexual longing, the object is male; only in Xenophon [*Mem.* 3.11.3] do we ever see Socrates sexually excited at the sight of a beautiful female.) This is perhaps all that could be expected of a one-track paedophile deficient in that instinctual attraction which women would have had for him if he had been one of those regular Athenians for whom Aristophanes cracked his bisexual jokes.

But whatever may be the right account of his personal feeling for living women, we can be sure it was not sentiment that moved him to legislate for the ruling class of his utopia rights for women equal to those of men. If he had followed sentiment, he would have gone the other way. His achievement is all the more remarkable on that account. In a triumph of imaginative impartiality, he separated the character his inherited prejudices imputed to the mass of women in his own society from the character which, he reasoned, a few exceptional women could develop under ideal conditions of equal nurture, awarding to them what his own theory of social justice required: status commensurate with the greatest contribution each of them could make personally to their own society and *therefore* equal in all respects to that of men. Few philosophers have achieved such transcendence of personal inclination in response to the dictates of impersonal moral theory.

B. METAPHYSICS AND EPISTEMOLOGY

11

ANAMNESIS IN THE MENO

I. THE DATA OF THE THEORY

I N THE *MENO* we have a chance, rare in Greek philosophy, to compare a
philosophical theory with the data which make up its ostensible evidence.
Meno asks if there is any way Socrates can show him that "learning"[1] is
recollecting. Socrates offers to produce the proof on the spot. Meno will see
the slave-boy learning, and this will show that he was recollecting. I wish to
make the most of this opportunity to examine the presented data before considering the theory. To this I will devote the first and somewhat longer part of
the paper, where I will seek by controversial argument to establish the right
interpretation of the text.[2] While doing this, it will be convenient to use "recollection" in quotes, suspending judgment upon its philosophical implications
and even withholding attention from its dictionary meaning. Plato says the
boy is "recollecting," and so shall I of this and all other situations which are
equivalent to it in a sense which I shall make clear. When a decision has been
reached on what exactly is taking place when people are "recollecting" in this
purely nominative sense, it will be time to examine Plato's thesis that this
"recollecting" is recollecting. [143]

In *Plato's Theory of Ideas* (Oxford, 1951), Sir David Ross remarks (p. 18):

> The method by which the slave-boy is got to discover what square has twice the area
> of that of a given square is *a purely empirical one;* it is *on the evidence of his
> eyesight* and not of any clearly apprehended relation between universals that he
> admits that the square on the diagonal of a given square is twice the size of the given

From *Dialogue 4* (1965): 143–67. Used by permission. Minor changes have been made in
punctuation.

[1] *Manthanein,* which is being used in this context in the restricted sense of *coming to have
propositional knowledge.* The acquisition of inarticulate skills, though well within the scope of
the word in ordinary usage, is tacitly excluded.

[2] My interpretation has much in common with those offered by the following:

F. M. Cornford, *Principium Sapientiae* (Cambridge, 1952), Ch. 4, *"Anamnesis."*

W. K. C. Guthrie, *Plato: Protagoras and Meno* (London, 1956), 107–14.

R. S. Bluck, *Plato's Meno* (Cambridge, 1961), 8–17.

N. Gulley, *Plato's Theory of Knowledge* (London, 1962), Ch. 1, "The Theory of Recollection."

I. M. Crombie, *An Examination of Plato's Doctrines,* Vol. 2 (London, 1963), 50–52, 136–41.

To each of these works, I shall refer hereafter merely by the author's name.

square. He admits that certain triangles have areas equal, each of them, to half of the given square, and that the figure which they make up is itself a square, not because he sees that these things must be so, but *because to the eye they look as if they were.* (My italics)

I daresay that few of those who have read our text will agree with this construction of it—the "empirical" one, I shall call it for convenience. But why precisely are we entitled to disagree? Not, surely, because "no mention at all is made of sense-experience either in the dialogue with the slave or in the subsequent discussion of its significance" (N. Gulley, 11–12). This is true, but settles nothing. For it is open to the retort that Plato does not have to mention sense-experience in order to direct attention to it. Is he not doing as much, and more, by dramatic means when he keeps Socrates so busy tracing figures in the sand? Can a process of discovery which leans so heavily on seeing—not in a sublimated sense, but in the literal one—be anything but an empirical process? This is the gist of the argument by which the empirical view would be defended.

In casting about for a reply, one's first impulse is to take a leaf out of the Divided Line. There Plato says quite distinctly that when mathematicians

use visible figures and make their arguments about them, they are not reasoning about *them,* but about those things which these visible figures resemble . . . ; they use these [figures] as images, seeking to see those very things which cannot be seen except by the understanding. (*Rep.* 510d–e)

I do think this would be relevant, since Plato is talking here about the common run of mathematicians, not about those enlightened by his philosophy. And since one of his main objects [144] in this passage is to point up the theoretical crudities of these people, we may be reasonably sure that the quoted passage is not Platonic largesse but a straightforward account of the general attitude toward diagrams among practicing mathematicians.[3] And if the same attitude could be imputed to Meno's slave, we could safely exonerate him from the charge of getting the answer to a geometrical problem by looking instead of reasoning. But the *if* in this sentence marks the weakness of this whole argument for the purpose in hand: our opponent could very well say that the subject of the interrogation is no mathematician but a household slave; the sophisticated use of diagrams by experts in geometry is no index to its probable use in an ignorant boy.

---

[3] Though Greek mathematicians were occasionally misled by their diagrams to assume some proposition not listed in their axiom-set (e.g., a continuity postulate, needed for the proof of I, 1, etc. in Euclid: cf. T. L. Heath, *The Thirteen Books of Euclid's Elements,* I² [Oxford, 1925], 235 and 243), they would not dream of citing the sensible properties of a diagram *as a reason* in a proof. One cannot imagine a sentence like "This must be true because that is the way it looks (or, measures) in the diagram" in a Greek mathematical text.

Let us then try an entirely different tack. Since the empirical interpretation rests wholly on the use of the diagrams in the "recollecting" process, let us ask whether or not they are really indispensable for this purpose. I wish to argue that they are not. Plato could have exhibited this process just as well by using illustrations in which diagrams would have no place—an arithmetical one, for example: The boy, let us suppose, freshly imported from darkest Thrace, has had to be taught even arithmetic, and from the bottom up. His lessons have just started and have only taught him so far to add two numbers at a time and numbers no greater than 10. Socrates now asks him to add 13 to 7, which goes beyond the boy's lessons, and Meno is invited to watch him "recollect" the answer:

You can add 10 to 3, can't you?
Yes. that is 13.
So 13 = 10 + 3?
Yes.
So instead of asking you how much is 13 + 7, I might as well have asked you how much is 10 + 3 + 7?
But what use would that be? I can only add two numbers at a time. [145]
That will be enough. How much is 3 + 7?
10, of course.
So instead of saying '3 + 7,' we can always say '10'?
Certainly.
Then instead of asking you how much is 10 + 3 + 7, I might have asked you how much is 10 + 10?
Yes, indeed, and the answer to that I know: 20.
And we did say that to ask how much is 13 + 7 is the same as asking how much is 10 + 3 + 7. You haven't forgotten that?
Of course not. And since 20 is the sum of 10 + 3 + 7, it is also the sum of 13 + 7.

I submit that this dialogue, retouched in Plato's style but unaltered in logical content, could have replaced the interrogation of the boy in the *Meno* for the purpose of Plato's argument. This can be proved by a scissors-and-paste experiment on Plato's text: cut out the whole interrogation from 82b9 to 85b7, paste in the above dialogue in its place, and consider whether any material change will have to be made in what comes before and after. You will find that none will;[4] that the same Platonic theses would be illustrated,[5] and that they

---

[4] The *only* required changes would be the substitution of "figuring" and "arithmetic" for "doing geometry" and "geometry" at 85e.

[5] Apart from being so much drier than Plato's example, the main loss resulting from the substitution would be the boy's mistakes; but we could easily make room for these, e.g., by having him make a wrong guess to begin with and then find out by the same method that (and why) his guess was wrong. A graver defect in my example is that it would not show nearly as well as Plato's the

would be substantiated to the same degree, so that the meaning and truth-value of the conclusions Socrates draws from the dialogue at the end will be unaffected. In this fairly stringent sense my arithmetical dialogue could be said to be equivalent to the geometrical one in the *Meno;* and in this appeal to sensible objects has been dropped.

I anticipate the following objection: The slave-boy has been learning arithmetic by counting pebbles, it may be said, and has been convinced that, say, 3 + 7 = 10 not because he has seen "that these things are so, but because to the eye they look as if they were;" so the boy, who has not mastered a formal *proof* for the addition of natural integers, must be relying on the evidence [146] of his senses, merely transferring what his senses taught him this morning to the solution of the new question Socrates puts to him in the afternoon. I believe that this objection is wholly misconceived. For even if we were to grant that each of the propositions material to the above result

$$(13 = 10 + 3; 3 + 7 = 10; 10 + 10 = 20)$$

were severally established by the purely empirical method of putting x pebbles together with y pebbles and learning the sum of $x + y$ by merely counting out the number of the resulting group, the fact would still remain that the answer to the question, "What is 13 + 7?" was not obtained by running back for pebbles to find out by counting. Had the boy done anything of this sort, the objection would have had force. But this is precisely what he has *not* done in my example. What happens there has absolutely nothing to do with looking at pebbles or handling them or hearing them dropped clink-clink on a stone nor, be it noted, with remembering results of previous lookings and handlings, nor imagining the results of imagined lookings and handlings: the boy would need to do none of these things to pass from the three propositions I just enumerated to the new proposition that 13 + 7 = 20. All he would need to do would be to make inferences from these propositions, using nothing but the rule that equals may be substituted for equals and the associative law for arithmetic.[6]

Should the objector remain unsatisfied, the simplest way to proceed would be to shift to still another illustration, fully equivalent in the sense defined to the one in the *Meno,* but so constructed as to block further back the imputation of even indirect reliance on the senses: Let Socrates recite in suitably metrical Greek the familiar conundrum by which a man replies when asked what is his relation to the subject of a portrait:

---

gap that may exist between discovery and proof; finding out that 13 + 7 = 20 by the above method would bring one much closer to seeing *why* this must be so than the slave could have come to seeing the why of theorem at the end of the interrogation.

[6] That $a + (b + c) = (a + b) + c$ was used, without being mentioned, in the example.

Brothers and sisters have I none;
But this man's father is my father's son. [147]

Let the slave-boy fail to hit on the solution, as sometimes happens even among the socially elect, and then "recollect" it under Socrates' prodding. Since this would be to *solve* the puzzle, all that is needed for the "recollecting" is what is needed for the solution. This calls for no more than just these operations: Noting that "my father's son" in the second premise of the cryptic jingle must refer to either the speaker himself or to one of his brothers; eliminating the second alternative by the first premise; hence being left with the statement that "this man's father" must be the speaker himself. In all this there is no recourse to anything other than the logical relations of the concepts *father, brother,* and *son,* and the use of the rules of inference. Here there is no occasion for consulting the evidence of the senses or for recalling previous use of such evidence. Had Plato used an example of this sort in the *Meno,* no one would have even dreamed of saying that the "recollecting" process gets results by relying on the evidence of the senses. Even the much weaker claim made earlier by A. E. Taylor that the "recollecting" discussed in the *Meno* consists of "the following up by personal effort of the suggestions of sense-experience,"[7] would have been ruled out by this kind of example. There is nothing in the process of discovering the answer to the conundrum which can be called, with any plausibility, "following up the suggestions of sense-experience." If one tried seeing or imagining fathers and sons, or pictures of them, to get "suggestions" for the solution, he would be wasting his time.

This is as far as this line of argument will take us. It proceeds on the premise, which could scarcely be questioned, that the "recollecting" Plato has in mind is in no way restricted to geometry, least of all the sort of geometry done by a tyro, but could be exemplified as well by other cases where sense-experience would be demonstrably immaterial and irrelevant. From this it concludes that reliance on the evidence of the senses is not a *general* feature of [148] the "recollecting" envisaged by Plato but is, at most, a special feature of the example of it he happened to use in the *Meno.* I say, "at most," for I am not conceding that the empirical view is true of even the example in the *Meno.* Such a concession would be no small matter. For since we have no other clue to what Plato was thinking of as *bona fide* "recollection" at this time except what he put into his text, it could be argued that those features of the process

---

[7] A. E. Taylor, *Plato, the Man and His Work*[4] (London, 1937) [hereafter "Taylor"], 137. Taylor then refers to "the suggestions provided by Socrates' diagrams and *questions*" (my italics), apparently failing to realize that the logical status of suggestions provided by questions is entirely different from that provided by sense-experience. In the *Meno* Plato speaks of recollected opinions as suggested ("awakened") by questions (86a6; cf. *Phaedo* 73a7), not by sense-experience; the latter point is first made in the *Phaedo* (73c6ff.).

which are material to its instantiation in the *Meno* were thought by Plato essential for the process itself, even if in fact they are not. This is a reasonable argument and must be met on its own ground.

Let us then move directly into the text and pick out for inspection a passage where the empirical view should appear to best advantage:

> Now does this line going from corner to corner cut each of these squares in half? (84e–85a)

Since Socrates does not proceed to offer proof for the proposition that the diagonal bisects a square or to give any reason whatever but expects the boy to "recollect" the answer upon hearing his words and looking at the diagram, would it not follow that, when the boy assents instantly to the equality of the triangles, he does so not because he sees that they are equal but "because to the eye they look as if they were"? This does *not* follow. To see that it does not, let us construct a case where it would, and see what that would be like. Let Socrates draw an isosceles right-angle triangle and then, without any description of what he is doing or any other comment, let him draw a similar figure of the same dimensions in some relatively distant part of the drawing area; and let him *then* ask the boy to say whether or not the two figures are equal. Here the boy would *have* to rely on the evidence of his eyesight. What else does he have to go by? His only source of information is the sensible figure, and he can only get it by looking. How vastly different is the task which Socrates sets him: The two triangles have not been presented as two independent and undescribed constructions. They are produced by drawing a diagonal across a figure which is known to be a *square* and is said [149] to be so. Knowing that squares have equal sides and equal angles,[8] the boy could infer that two sides and the included angle of one triangle equal the corresponding items in the other. So he has plenty of clues to the equality of the two figures other than the fact that they look equal. If he followed out those clues, he would see (e.g., by the rudiments of a congruence proof by superposition) that the triangles have to be equal, even if to the eye they looked unequal, as they easily might if the figure were badly drawn.[9] Yet neither does it follow that the boy would make the judgment by merely drawing inferences in total disregard of what he sees. He might have done the latter, had he been

---

[8] The equality of the sides was mentioned at the start (82c), that of the angles was not but would have been admitted right off by the boy: the concept, *equality of angle*, would have been familiar, and Socrates would have had no difficulty in getting the boy to say that all four angles of a square must be equal.

[9] It is not unreasonable to assume with Guthrie (110) that the figure would be only "roughly" drawn, so that the two triangles would be visibly unequal. But nothing is made of this in the interrogation. Socrates has other ways of getting across the idea that the properties of the squares, triangles, etc. he is talking about are those that a figure *would* have *if* it instantiated the concept *square*. See next note.

gifted mathematically and given the proper instructions. Alternatively, he might have done the very opposite, had his instructions been to go by the look of the figures to the exclusion of any other consideration. The fact is that neither set of instructions has been given him. But looking over the whole course of the interrogation, we see that while it is never even implied that he should decide anything by merely looking, there are several times when it is definitely implied that he should judge merely by thinking—e.g., when asked arithmetical questions ("And how many feet is twice two? Figure it out and tell me," 82d).[10] That the overall effect of the questioning [150] is to set the boy thinking is clear from the boy's mistakes. His two blunders are *miscalculations,* slips of the mind, not of the eye, faulty inferences, not wrong observations: that the desired square must have double the area *if* it has double the sides; that its side must equal 3 *because* it has to be larger than 2 and smaller than 4.

So the boy is reasoning at least as much as looking. Why not then say that his "recollecting" is a mixture of both, and leave it at that? Because this compromise formula would evade the vital question of the relative importance of the two factors. We could, of course, agree that observation and inference are both occurring, without haggling over the question whether there is more of the one than of the other, if what specially interested us here were the behavior of just this boy in just this case. But then the relative incidence of the two factors, revealed by our inquiry, would be of no logical consequence; it would have only informed us of the psychological abilities and habits of this

---

[10] Subtler suggestions to the same effect are conveyed by the form in which the questions are put almost from the very start: "Now could not such a figure be either larger or smaller?" (82c2–3) puts the inquiry in the domain of possibility, where it is kept by the next question, "Now if this side were 2 ft. long and that [side] the same, how many feet would the whole be?" which puts the specification of size in the hypothetical mode and asks what would happen *if* this were the case. The same modalities are signaled by the syntactical form of the sequel: optative with *an* ("indefinite supposition") in the apodosis at 82c5–6, and imperfect indicative with *an* (*suppositio irrealis*) at c8 (cf. E. S. Thompson, *The Meno of Plato* [London, 1901], *ad loc.*). In the next question (d1–2) the *gignetai* expresses a logical consequence (this is what would result "because [on the hypothesis] it is 2 ft. long that way too"). The interrogation continues on the hypothetical plane until the second break at 84d: the question remains *what would have to be* the case to satisfy the conditions laid down at 82e1–2 and what would follow if we were to suppose with the slave that the required line is 3 or 4 feet long. After the break the syntax is again well stocked with optatives with *an* to reestablish a framework of inference (exploration of logical consequences) rather than factual observation. The English reader should remember that the modalities and logical connectives do not always come through even in excellent translations. Thus 82b10–c3 becomes in Guthrie, "It has all these 4 sides equal? . . . And these lines which go through the middle of it are also equal?" Here the *oun* ("in inferences, *then, therefore,*" LSJ, *s.v.* III) has dropped out in the first question; in the second, one would miss the fact that a participial form (*echon*) so links it with the preceding question as to keep it within the field of force of the *oun*. A more literal translation would be, "Is not a square, then, a figure having all these four sides equal? . . . And having these lines that go through the middle equal also?"

particular subject. What does affect the logic of our problem is the relative *dispensability* of either factor to the "recollecting process," for only so can we determine which of the two factors is logically intrinsic to it. Once we do put the question in this way, the answer is clear: The boy's sensory powers may be cut down drastically without impairing "recollecting" in the least, provided only we suppose his reasoning ability inversely heightened. If, on the other hand, [151] we endowed him with the best hunter's eye imaginable, but deficient in the perception of logical relationships, he would be totally unfitted for "recollecting." For the best he could accomplish by superior sensory acuteness would be to collect data of superior accuracy; but unless he could arrange and rearrange these data in the required logical patterns, they would be of no use, but a burden, for the purpose of answering Socrates' questions. Conversely, the heightening of his intellectual powers would be of the greatest use to him for this purpose and could so far compensate for sensory defects that he could go through this whole interrogation and in fewer steps even if, for example, he were blind but had the mathematical talent of a young Pascal; and to think of him as blind is to think of the factor of sensory observation reduced in these circumstances to *zero*.

But would Plato have been aware of this when he wrote the *Meno?* I think he would. The evidence is indirect, but strong. At the end of the interrogation, when the boy has found the answer to the problem Socrates had set him, we are told that this is as yet no more than a true belief in his mind;[11] but that if "one were to ask him many times the very same [sort of] questions in many [different] ways . . . he would end up at last with knowledge of such matters no less exact than that possessed by any other person," 85c10–d1. The subject-matter here is geometry.[12] To reach knowledge of it that would be no worse than that of any other person would be to master this science as the purely deductive discipline it had already become. In that second stage of his inquiry, then, the one that would take the boy from true belief to knowledge, the evidence of his eyesight would be absolutely excluded as a *reason* for any of his assertions.[13] But there is no suggestion that this would involve the slightest change of *method*. [152] Quite the contrary, it is implied that his method would be the same; for if it were going to be different he would have to be subjected to a different sort of question, while, as we have just seen, he would be asked *"the very same* [sort of] *questions."* In having Socrates say

[11] So it would be obviously wrong to say that the lad "began by not knowing something and *ended by knowing it*" (Taylor, 138, my italics), rather than that he *would have ended* by knowing it.

[12] And cf. 85e1–2: the slave-boy "will do the same thing [as he has done in the preceding interrogation] in the case of the whole of geometry and of all other sciences" ("the same thing," *t'auta tauta*, here has the same reference as the same expression at c10–11, where the reference is clearly to his performance in answering Socrates' questions).

[13] Cf. n. 3 above.

this, Plato makes it clear that he thinks of the method of discovery (that of the first stage) and the method of proof (that of the second) to be in principle the same. And this is confirmed in two further remarks: "To recover knowledge oneself [from] within oneself," says Socrates shortly after (85d6–7), "is recollection."[14] Later on, near the end of the dialogue, in a crucial passage where Socrates says that true beliefs become knowledge only when "bound fast by the calculation of the reason" (*aitias logismōi*),[15] he adds at once, "And this, my dear Meno, is recollection [153], as we agreed earlier" (89a3–8).[16] In neither of these passages does Socrates say that "recollection" occurs only at the second stage of the inquiry. This would have been quite absurd in view of the fact that the first stage—the one the boy traverses in our text—had been laid on specially so Meno could see the boy recollecting.[17] So Plato's reason for speaking only of the second stage when he comes to explain what "recollection" is, could only be that he takes it for granted that the essential components of the "recollection"-process as a method of inquiry would be the same

[14] The received translations, down to Guthrie's ("And the spontaneous recovery of *knowledge that is in him* is recollection, isn't it?"), put Plato in the position of saying that the subject already *has* the knowledge he recollects, thus flatly contradicting his earlier assurances that the boy did *not know,* and still does not know, the theorem he has discovered but has only a true belief of it (85c2–10). Surely all we can get from the wording in 85d6 is that the "recollected" knowledge is being "recovered" from inside a person's own mind—not that it is already there *as knowledge.* The commentators frequently represent Plato as holding that what we come to know by "recollecting" is already present in us in the form of *latent* knowledge. But Plato never uses this expression (or variants of it, like "potential") in the context of the theory of recollection. He does not picture our souls as being always in a state of "virtual" omniscience but as having once "learned" everything (86a8, where τὸν ἀεὶ χρόνον μεμαθηκυῖα ἔσται ἡ ψυχὴ αὐτοῦ does not mean "has been for ever in a state of knowledge" [Guthrie], but "has been for ever in the condition of *having* [once] *acquired* knowledge": cf. *memathēkuias tēs psuchēs,* 81d1), and then lost this knowledge (95c6–7, 86b2–3, and cf. especially *Phaedo* 76b5–c3), while retaining the ability to recover it. By "the truth of things being always in the soul" (*Meno* 86b1–2) and "knowledge and right reason being in" us (*Phaedo* 73a9–10, αὐτοῖς ἐπιστήμη ἐνοῦσα καὶ ὀρθὸς λόγος) Plato can only mean that all men have (i) some (not, all) knowledge, (ii) the ability to make correct judgments (= to perceive logical relations) and, therefore, (iii) the ability to extend their knowledge (by persevering in inquiry) without any preassigned limit (81d2–4).

[15] ἕως ἄν τις αὐτὰς δήσῃ αἰτίας λογισμῷ: "until you tether them by working out the reason" (Guthrie). "Cause" for *aitia* here (Jowett, Meridier, Bluck) is misleading, since modern philosophical usage reserves the term for relations which instantiate laws of nature, never for purely logical conditions. Thus, to speak of the premises of a syllogism as the *aitia* of the conclusion (Aristotle, *Post. An.* 71b22) would be the crudest sort of category-mistake if Aristotle's term did mean what we understand by "cause." In some contexts, as in Aristotle's "four causes," the canonical mistranslation will no doubt have to be perpetuated. But readers of Plato, at least, can be spared some confusion if the mistranslation is avoided when avoidable, as it is certainly in the *Meno.* To tolerate "chain of causal reasoning" for *aitias logismos,* and illustrate by a mathematical *diorismos* (Gulley, 14–15) which involves no causal reasoning whatever, is disconcerting.

[16] Cf. Bluck *ad loc.*: "No mention has been made earlier, at least in so many words, of an *aitias logismos,* but this reference is clearly to 85c9–d1."

[17] And cf. 82e12–13.

at both stages, though they would be so much clearer in the second that it would be sufficient for his purposes to refer only to that. What then are these components?

The language used in the second citation—the "binding" of true belief by the *aitias logismos*—gives us a good indication of what he thinks they are. The primary sense of *logismos* is arithmetical reckoning. It is used with this sense in the interrogation,[18] as we saw a moment ago. Elsewhere in his works Plato uses it for rational arithmetic, i.e. for number theory, and, still more broadly, for rational thought in contrast to sense-perception and for knowledge reached and justified by formal inference and analysis in emphatic contrast to sensory cognition.[19] The other part of his expression, "bound fast," would tell the same tale to anyone familiar with the philosophical literature. In Parmenides the "bonds" and "fetters" which "powerful *Anankē*" imposes on [154] Being are the constraints of logical necessity.[20] In Zeno[21] and Melissus,[22] *anankē* is the signature of a deductive inference and it is used quasi-adverbially in lieu of "it follows necessarily that . . ." In the Socratic dialogues, too, *anankē* occurs with the same force,[23] and the "binding fast" metaphor caps the long demonstration in the *Gorgias* when Callicles is told that the conclusion that defeats him is "held fast and bound by arguments of iron and adamant," 508e. Thus, to say that knowledge is true belief "bound" by the *aitias logismos* is to imply that a statement becomes known when it is seen to follow logically from premises sufficient for this purpose: to "recollect" it, then, would be to see that these premises entail it. But what of the premises? They too could be "recollected" in the same manner. But how long could this go on? The geometrical model[24] would assure Plato, as it did Aristotle after him, that there must be logically primitive propositions, whose "binding" could no longer be derived by entailment from yet others but must lie wholly within themselves. Thus there would be no question of trying to

---

[18] In the reference to *logisamenos eipe,* 82d4.

[19] Examples in F. Ast, *Lexicon Platonicum* ⟨Berlin, 1908⟩, *s.v.* λογίζομαι, λογισμός, λογιστικός. When the Theory of Ideas is introduced, *logizomai, logismos* (along with *dianooumai, dianoia*) stand for the mode of their apprehension in sharp opposition to sense-perception: *Phaedo* 65c2–3, 79a3, *Phdr.* 249b, *Parm.* 130a, *Soph.* 248a11.

[20] DK⁵, Frag. B8, 30–31. The same metaphor in lines 14 and 37 of the fragment, with *Dike* and *Moira* taking the place of *Anankē*, symbolizing the rational appropriateness of the bond, while *Anankē* stands for its inexorable necessity.

[21] Frag. B1 (twice), B3.

[22] Frag. B7 (twice).

[23] Examples in Ast (above, n. 19).

[24] I.e., of an axiomatized science. Though great progress in axiomatization was made in Plato's own lifetime, (cf. the references to Leo and Theudius in Proclus, *Comment. in Eucl.* [G. Friedlein], 66, 19–22 and 67, 12–16), there is no reason to think there had been no earlier work along the same lines. The distinction between primitive and derivative propositions in geometry would certainly have been well established by the end of the fifth century.

prove that things equal to the same thing are equal to one another. The mathematician's way with this type of proposition would be to list it as a logical primitive in his axiom-set and leave it at that. Plato presumably would go a step further, but only by showing how this and other "Common Notions" are presupposed in our "knowledge of Equality," i.e., in our having, using, and understanding the concept of equality [155].[25] Nor would there be any question of proving the *definitions*[26] of this, or any other, concept. We know how prominently these figure among the objects of Socratic search. But though Plato has said so far all too little of the methodology of the "What is X?" question, it is clear from what he says in the *Meno* itself that he does not think that the true answer, when found, could be proved by deduction from other premises,[27] or that it needs such proof. Thus if the boy understood what is meant by *square* and also understood what is meant by *equilateral, right-angled,* and *quadrilateral,* he would *see* that the conjunction of the last three concepts is logically equivalent to the first. If he did not, he would be revealing that he had not understood the meaning of one or more of the concepts mentioned in the formula; what would be needed then would be to elicit this understanding in his mind.

Reduced to its simplest terms, then, what Plato means by "recollection" in the *Meno* is *any enlargement of our knowledge which* [156] *results from the perception of logical relationships.* When these are interpropositional, to

[25] I am extrapolating from the line of argument followed by Socrates in the *Phaedo* (74b4ff.: from certain judgments we have been making since our childhood it is inferred that ἀναγκαῖον . . . ἡμᾶς προειδέναι τὸ ἴσον, 74e9).

[26] "Real," not "nominal," definitions, which are the prime object of Socratic inquiry in many dialogues, including the *Meno,* where Socrates starts by diverting Meno from "Is virtue teachable?" to "What is virtue?" as the logically prior one and insists repeatedly that we cannot know any of virtue's properties (*hopoion esti* or *poion esti*) until we have come to know its essence (*ti estin*): 71b3–8, 86d2–e1, 100b4–6. Cf. R. Robinson, *Plato's Earlier Dialectic*[2] (Oxford, 1953), 50–51, where the same point is made strongly and backed with a plethora of additional references.

[27] When someone proposes a false definition, there are two ways of *dis*proving it in the Socratic dialogues:

(1) Find cases which, as he admits, instantiate the definiens, but not the definiendum, or the latter, but not the former.

(2) Find propositions known to him which contradict the definition. Socrates could not hope to demonstrate the true definition by the same, or analogous, methods:

(1) He could not go through all the cases of the definiens to show they all exemplify the definiendum.

(2) A statement of what X is could not be proved by entailment from other statements about X which are known to be true, since Socrates holds (cf. the preceding note) that if the essence of X is not known nothing else can be known about X (though, of course, there could be many true beliefs about it).

Hence, though Plato does not say so, it would follow that, while argument can disprove incorrect answers to the "What is X?" question, it cannot prove the correct one.

"recollect" a previously unknown proposition is to come to know it by seeing that it is entailed by others already known. Or if the relations are intra-propositional, as in the case of the true answer to the "What is X?" question, then to "recollect" is to gain insight into the logical structure of a concept, so that when faced with its correct definition one will see that the concepts mentioned are analytically connected. In either case we are as far from the empirical discovery and certification of knowledge as we could possibly be. Sensory observation is not excluded in the first stage of incomplete "recollection" which discovers the looked-for truth but does not yet know that (or why) it is the truth. But even at that stage the use of the senses is only a contingent factor, wholly unusable in some cases of *bona fide* "recollection" and in others used only as a crutch to the imagination which must be dropped at the next stage of inquiry in which "recollection" is brought to full completion.[28] [157]

II. THE THEORY

The nearest Plato comes to telling us why the process we have been describing *is* recollection (without quotation marks) is in the two statements that

(a) had the boy continued the "recollecting" process to the finish, he would have "himself recovered knowledge [from] within himself," 85d4, and

(b) the "recovering by oneself knowledge that is within oneself is recollection," 85d6–7.

---

[28] If one rereads the interrogation in our text in the light of these two paragraphs, one will see how deductive inference and analytic insight into concepts are called into play just as far as they can within the practical limitations of the occasion (dealing with a boy utterly ignorant of the vocabulary and method of geometry, and getting results with a speed consistent with the dramatic tempo of the dialogue). Thus the correction of the two mistakes (83a–e) is for all practical purposes a *proof* that the two erroneous propositions (that the side is 4 feet or that it is 3 feet) are inconsistent with the theorem that the area of a square with side x feet long must be x^2 square feet. Given more time, Socrates could surely have got the boy to grasp a formal proof of this theorem of a sufficiently rigorous sort to pass contemporary mathematical standards. So far from giving this proof, Socrates does not even give a general *statement* of the theorem, and for the simple reason that even to get the boy to *understand* such a statement would take longer than the dramatic time-budget allows. For the same reason, he does not take time to dot the *i*s and cross the *t*s of items which are matters of conceptual insight. Thus the only feature of a square mentioned at the start is the equality of its sides, this being enough to get the boy's mind moving in the right direction toward the major objective, i.e., to come in view of the concept of superficial (in contradistinction to linear) magnitude, since everything in the sequel will depend on the boy's ability to see the difference between the size of an area, with its two parameters of length and breadth, and that of one-dimensional magnitudes. The boy cannot even *understand* Socrates' question, let alone get into position to attempt its solution, until he gets some inkling of this difference. When the question is first put to him at 82c5–6, "Now look at it this way: If this line were 2 feet long and that line also 2 feet, how big would be the whole [square, i.e., its area]?" he is stumped.

These two statements make clear the middle term Plato is offering us between the data and the theory: given, on one hand, the indisputable fact that we do acquire knowledge and, on the other hand, the proposed theory that this takes place *because* the truths we come to know are recollected, the whole burden of convincing us of this "because" falls on the contention that these truths come from "within" us. What can be meant by this contention?

Plato talks as though its meaning and truth will be obvious once it is seen that the truths learned by the boy have not been taught him by Socrates or by anyone else. Here "teaching" is being used, with typical Socratic effrontery, in a wholly untypical way.[29] How very special is this sense becomes clear when we notice that even *telling* the boy the true answer is not allowed to count as teaching it to him! To put a question to someone who has never heard the right answer, and then, noting that he has no inkling of it, to proceed and lay it out before him, saying, "This *is* the right answer, isn't it?" is not supposed to be "teaching." Why not? Because if Socrates, having said, "*p* is true, isn't it?" says no more, the judgment that *p* is true must be made on the boy's own responsibility. He cannot shift the responsibility on Socrates *because he cannot cite Socrates' attitude toward p as evidence for its truth.* Socrates [158] makes sure of this both by instructing him, "Answer just what you think," 83d2, and also by the more painful method of laying booby traps for him along the way which teach him that he cannot rely on Socrates to make the right suggestions to him: he cannot adopt toward Socrates the attitude an inexperienced mountain-climber can and does adopt toward an experienced guide. If the climber sees or guesses that his guide wants him to take a certain path, he is entitled to use this as good evidence of its being the right path. By misleading him badly a couple of times, Socrates makes the boy realize that he is not entitled to the same assumption. Thus one avenue along which he might have looked for evidence—that open to the pupil who is only told truths by his teacher and is therefore always in a position to say on empirical grounds, "This is likely to be true because teacher said so"—is decisively blocked by Socrates' tactics. The reason for any of the propositions cannot, therefore, be sought in the teacher.

Where then is it to be sought? "Within oneself," says Plato. Why so? Because "in" one are the already-known propositions from which one can derive knowledge of others, hitherto unknown, merely by seeing that they are entailed; and "in" one are the familiar concepts whose logical structure one need only understand more clearly in order to come to know axiomatic truths and correct definitions. This not only brings full lucidity to the mock-darkness of

---

[29] Untypical not only for common usage (as is obvious), but also for Plato's own: so far from thinking "teaching" (rightly understood, as dialectic incompatible with "learning," he distinguishes (*Gorg.* 454e) rhetoric from "teaching" (*didaskalikēs,* 455a1) as producing respectively "belief" (*pistis*) and "knowledge" (*epistēmē*) and, conversely (*Tim.* 51e) *nous* from true belief as produced respectively by "teaching" (*didachēs*) and "persuasion."

the claim that Socrates is not "teaching," but also lets in some light to the real darkness of the saying that what the boy is learning "he himself recovers from within himself." For "learning" here is not just a matter of increasing his stock of true beliefs, but of acquiring *knowledge,* that is to say, true beliefs logically bound to the reasons for their truth.[30] Hence the dark saying has *at least* the following sense: new beliefs become knowledge for him when *he* comes to see what is implied by propositions and concepts which were already in his mind.[31] [159] I say "at least" this sense, for to suggest that Plato means no more than this would be a travesty on his text. But this more can wait a moment longer while we explore more fully the minimum sense now before us.

The expression "within oneself," i.e., in one's mind, is significant in this context only because of the implied contrast with what is *outside* one's mind. Well, what is "outside" the boy's mind? Socrates, for one thing: if he got knowledge from Socrates, this would refute the claim that he recovered knowledge from "within" himself. But Socrates is a small, if energetic, part of this "outside," and learning from Socrates is only a local and ephemeral instance of getting knowledge from "external" sources, if such there were. For the vast majority of men who have never even heard of Socrates and for the boy himself through most of his life, the only thing seriously worth discussing as a likely source of knowledge "outside" the mind would be the whole of the physical universe as apprehended by the senses. Though the expression "the external world" had not yet been invented, philosophers had talked and thought in similar terms. Thus Empedocles, when he spoke of sight, hearing, and taste as "duct(s) for understanding" (*poros . . . noēsai,* B3,12), was evidently thinking of the sensible world as a reservoir of information outside us, whence knowledge might flow into us through the senses. With this we may compare the saying of Democritus that "for all of us belief is inflowing," (*epirusmiē hekastoisin hē doxis,* B7) and his talk of sensory stimuli as "coming upon us" (*epeisiontōn,* B9) and Plato's talk of sensory impulses "borne from the outside and falling upon" the soul (ἔξωθεν αἰσθήσεις φερόμεναι . . . προσπεσοῦσαι, *Tim.* 44A). With this conception of sense-experience as a one-way traffic from the world into the soul familiar to Plato[32] and incorporated, through the assimilation of its metaphors, into his own thought and speech, his assertion that to acquire knowledge is only to recover what is already "in" us could not but have the force of an implicit denial that

---

[30] Cf. A. E. Taylor's comment on *Tim.* 51d3 in *Commentary to Plato's Timaeus* (Oxford, 1928), 338–39.

[31] Cf. Leibniz's use of expressions like "prendre de chez soi," "tirer de son propre fonds," for our coming to know necessary truths, and of the mind (or the understanding) as the "source" of these truths: *Nouveaux essais sur l'entendement humain,* Book 1, Chapter 1, Section 5.

[32] Cf. the empiricist theory of the origin of knowledge which is mentioned as a part of the teaching of the natural philosophers in the *Phaedo* (96b).

knowledge can be acquired by sense-experience.[33] And so far as the [160] acquisition of knowledge here is the securing of evidence for propositions, the implicit part of the minimal sense of Plato's formula is equivalent to the denial that sense-experience can, or need, provide the slightest evidence for propositions known in the special way in which knowledge is here construed; demonstrative knowledge. Thus in this very dialogue and, so far as we can tell from our sources, for the first time in Western thought, deductive knowledge, broadly conceived so as to include all of mathematics and much more besides, is freed completely from evidential dependence on sense-experience.

In saying that this happens for the first time, we need not be unmindful of its antecedents nor belittle the achievements of Plato's predecessors in order to exalt his. We need only point out that, while others had prepared the way for Plato's discovery, no one had fully anticipated it. The Greek mathematicians had learned how to construct deductive proofs by the fifth century at the latest, and Plato himself gives them credit, as we saw above, for not counting the sensible properties of their figures evidence for their theorems. But it is one thing to achieve such a working method, quite another to reflect upon it so as to state its rationale and show what this has in common with formal inferences whose subject matter is as different as are the concepts of father and son, justice and virtue, from lines and numbers. A philosophical declaration of independence of rational thought from sense-experience had been made, and in the strongest terms, a hundred years before Plato by Parmenides. But he and his disciples paid a fantastic price for this emancipation. They won it by consigning to illusion not only the whole of the physical universe, but also the whole domain of mathematics[34]—a consequence seldom realized by historians of philosophy who, with unwitting irony, have often cast Zeno in the role of the purifier or even savior of [161] Greek mathematics.[35] There still remain the Pythagoreans. But before we can say that they anticipated Plato in this doctrine, we must have evidence that, at the very least, they held it them-

---

[33] This is precisely what Leibniz takes to be the point of the expressions in n. 31 above, alluding specifically to Platonic *anamnēsis:* "On doit dire que toute l'arithmétique et toute la géométrie sont innées et sont en nous d'une manière virtuelle, en sorte qu'on les y peut trouver en considérant attentivement et rangeant *ce qu'on a déjà dans l'esprit, sans se servir d'aucune vérité apprise par l'expérience ou par la tradition d'autrui,* comme Platon l'a montré [in the interrogation of the slave-boy in the *Meno*]" *loc. cit.,* my italics.

[34] This would follow, regardless of their other doctrines, from their denial of plurality.

[35] E.g., Paul Tannery, *Pour l'histoire de la science grecque* (Paris, 1877), 254; *La Géométrie grecque* (Paris, 1877), 124; H.-G. Zeuthen, "Sur les livres arithmétiques des Eléments d'Euclide," *Oversigt det Kongelike Danske Videnskabernes Selskabs,* Forhandlinger, 1910, 395ff. at 432–43; F. M. Cornford, *Plato and Parmenides* (London, 1939), 58–61; H. Hasse and H. Scholz, "Die Grundlagenkrisis der griechischen Mathematik," *Quellenhandbücher der Philosophie* (Berlin, 1928). *Contra:* B. L. van der Waerden, "Zenon und die Grundlagenkrisis der griechischen Mathematik," *Math. Annallen* 117 (1940–41), 141ff; G.E.L. Owen, "Zeno and the Mathematicians," *PAS,* 1958, 199ff.

selves. And there is no such evidence. Moreover, if they had really made such an important discovery, it could not have remained unknown to Aristotle who, given his penchant for making historical linkages and comparisons, would have left us some indication, however slight, that Plato borrowed from them the doctrine that learning is recollection. But though he is well acquainted with this doctrine, and turns aside to refute it, he ascribes it to no one but to Plato, and to him directly, referring by title to the *Meno*.[36] So those historians[37] who tell us that Plato derived this doctrine from the Pythagoreans are making excursions into historical romance.

What the Pythagoreans did hold, and not only they but Pythagoras, is the doctrine of transmigration. But the connection of this with Plato's doctrine of recollection is so loose that one can believe in transmigration without believing in anything which includes that minimal sense of recollection I have just been discussing, indeed without having the slightest inkling of it. A doctrine of recollection was a prominent feature of the Pythagorean belief [162] in transmigration, at least to the extent of crediting Pythagoras himself with the power to recover knowledge acquired in previous incarnations. (See Xenophanes B7; Empedocles B129.) And if claimed for Pythagoras, it might well have also been claimed for other charismatic figures. It is reasonable to assume that Plato knew all this and hence to say that he borrowed *a* doctrine of recollection. But what would this borrowing come to? That some great souls had the marvelous power to recollect what they had learned in former incarnations. Let us magnify this borrowing beyond anything warranted by the evidence and all it still would come to would be this: that every soul had such powers. And this would not even approach Plato's doctrine, unless we were to add that these powers were connected with *learning* in the here and now, and so connected that the acquisition of all new knowledge is recollecting. This doctrine, the only one that would deserve mention in a history of the theory of knowledge, let alone mention as a milestone in this theory, is the product of Plato's genius and of his alone.[38]

In this encounter with Pythagoreanism, I have already gone beyond what I have been calling the "minimal sense" of the Platonic doctrine. To reckon with this doctrine as a whole, let me simply itemize the main essential points:

(1) The full-strength doctrine carries not only the implication that nonem-

---

[36] *Pr. Anal.* 67a21–22; Cf. also *Post. Anal.* 71a1–b8: 99b25–34. Cf. H. Cherniss, *Aristotle's Criticism of Plato and the Academy* (Baltimore, 1944), 69ff. and nn.

[37] According to A. E. Taylor, it had been "the mathematician-saint Pythagoras" himself who had converted the theological doctrine of the transmigration of the soul "into a theory of the *a priori* character of mathematics," *Plato,* 186n. 2. For a sane discussion of the historical question, see L. Robin, "Sur la doctrine de la reminiscence," *REG* 32 (1919), 451–61; but Robin is confused on the point to which I called attention in n. 11 above: he says that Plato "suppose que nous naissons avec des connaissances toutes faites . . . les seules qui soient dignes de ce nom," 460.

[38] Cf. Gulley, 18.

pirical knowledge can exist but also, unfortunately, that empirical knowledge cannot exist. This latter thesis could be sugarcoated with the plea that since Plato is willing to admit what we call "empirical knowledge" under the name of "true belief," nothing is changed except the name. But we should give Plato credit for engaging in more serious business than the reallocation of verbal labels. In refusing the term *knowledge* to propositions of ordinary experience and of the observational sciences, Plato is downgrading quite deliberately those truth-seeking and truth-grounding procedures which cannot be assimilated to deductive reasoning and cannot yield formal certainty; and this has enormous implications—theoretical, and also practical ones—as can be seen in the exclusion of disciplines like medicine, [163] biology, and history from the curriculum of higher learning in the *Republic*.

(2) Where p, hitherto not known, becomes known through the perception of its entailment by q, the full-strength doctrine of recollection holds not only that q is known (*ex hypothesi*), but also that p is similarly "recovered from within" the soul. This is indeed the whole point of saying that p is recollected (without quotation marks). And having said this, Plato does not cast about for some way of unsaying it. He does not qualify his claim, as would Leibniz, by making p only *virtually* known at this earlier time. Nor does he try to pass it off by saying, as a modern analytical philosopher might in such a fix, that all he is pleading for is an *extension* to more complex and involved entailments of the admission, common enough for simple and direct entailments from q to p, that he who knows q can also be said after a fashion to also know p (as, e.g., if I admit that I know that Lucy is Mary's mother, I would have a hard time convincing a jury I did not know that Lucy is older than Mary). Plato gives no sign of such backing-away tactics. He is excited, not frightened, by the strange landscape to which his imagination has transported him and is more anxious to explore it further than to keep close to escape-routes back to the safety of the old world.

(3) The exploration of the consequences of the full-strength theory of recollection is so closely related to the creation of the Theory of Ideas that it can even be said to determine the main features of this theory. The first question Plato would have to put to himself when he finished writing the *Meno* is the very one raised by Leibniz:[39] to say that we acquire knowledge by recovering knowledge we acquired at some earlier period or periods, no matter how remote, is simply to raise all over again the problem how this earlier knowledge itself was gained. That Plato thinks of the Theory of Ideas as the answer to this question we know from later dialogues, e.g., the *Phaedrus* (247c–e; 249b–c). And we know of no other answer that occurred to him, or that would have been likely to occur to him at this historical stage of philosophical [164] reflection. Had he emancipated himself completely from the tendency to as-

---

[39] Above, n. 31, Book 1, Chapter 1, Section 5.

similate understanding to the pattern fixed by the model of sense-perception, and to think of general truths reaching the mind by *vision* (though purely intellectual and intuitive) *of objects* (though purely incorporeal, beyond time and space), he would have assayed other alternatives. But that emancipation was not won even by Aristotle after him, or even by Epicurus. Without it, it seemed a reasonable solution to the problem of the primordial education of the soul to construct suitable objects for the inspection of a discarnate mind. The Platonic Form is built to the specifications of this project. Then, faced with the fact that knowledge thus gained beyond the Cave is so useful when recollected within it that one who has recovered it will be able to "see a thousand times better" (*Rep.* 520c) in the Cave, once he has got used to its darkness, than those who never left it, Plato solves this problem by postulating, so very reasonably it would seem, that the world seen by the eye is an "image" of the world seen by the mind, inexact to a degree, but faithful enough to yield physical applications of ideal truths. Thus the requirements of the doctrine of recollection, once satisfied in the Theory of Forms, suggest that broad design of the Platonic cosmology; they do the same for Plato's moral theory and for his interpretation of the experience of love and of the sense of beauty in ways which will suggest themselves to those familiar with the *Republic,* the *Symposium,* and the *Phaedrus.*

(4) What made this whole doctrine possible for Plato is obviously the belief in reincarnation. Plato marks this as a religious faith on first announcing it in the *Meno* by saying he heard it from "priests and priestesses who make it their business to be able to give reason for the rites they perform" (81a). Though this does not preclude the possibility that he heard it also from Pythagorean philosophers, it makes clear that reincarnation is not for Plato a theoretical speculation. He chooses to relate it to rites of worship and invests it with that intense religious feeling that is to pulse through the myth of the *Phaedrus.* Of this faith, just three things:

(a) It is faith, not dogma, using myth as its favorite vehicle, and feeling free to create and recreate its own myth. [165]

(b) It is a personal faith, maintained in all probability without affiliation with any organized cult, at any rate in Athens.

(c) While derivative at the core, it is in important ways a *new* faith, differing from surviving samples of its source in ways which would affect profoundly the substance of its piety. It is wholly free, for instance, of the sensationalism and magic of popular Orphic practices which are denounced in the *Republic* (364b). It appears to good advantage even when compared with the most exalted surviving transcript of the faith in reincarnation, the *Purifications* of Empedocles. The commission of a horrible crime by a godlike soul to start off the cycle of rebirth, hence the conception of human existence as expiation for the delinquency of a prehuman being and the recovery of its supernatural powers—all this is lacking in Plato. Man is created man in the beginning and is akin to god not in magical power but in his specifically human attributes, his knowledge, his moral sense, his love of beauty.

The theory of recollection in the *Meno* is the work of a profoundly religious spirit united with a powerful philosophical mind. Those who come to our text without sympathy for its religious inspiration are apt to look at this union with annoyance and to think that Plato might have been a great philosopher or, at any rate, a good one, had it not been for his religion. The results of this paper, they may then think, fully confirm this feeling. For do they not come to this: that when the data of the theory are analyzed as they have been here, they exhibit a process of inference and insight which can be described very well by Plato's theory, provided only it be stripped of just those features of it which are directly assignable to its religious provenance? But before we settle on this conclusion, might we not ask ourselves this question: Is there any good reason to think that, without the special perspective of the belief in transmigration, Plato would ever have looked at those data in the particular way which issued in his epochal discovery: of knowledge which needs no confirmation from sense-experience and admits of no refutation from it? The point is not so much that others, fully familiar with such data, had failed to make this discovery, but that Plato himself had not come within sight of it, though he had been thinking philosophy [166] and writing it for a decade or more by this time according to the received chronology. The faith in reincarnation is not mentioned, or even alluded to, in any dialogue before the *Meno*. If, as seems likely, it is at or near this time that Plato came by this faith, can we reckon it a pure coincidence that the philosophical discovery is presented in the same dialogue and that the form in which it is cast is the doctrine of recollection—the full-strength doctrine of the *Meno*?[40]

[40] An earlier draft of this paper was included in the John Locke Lectures On "Mysticism and Logic in Greek Philosophy" which I delivered in Oxford in 1960 and will be eventually published. ⟨This was never published—ed.⟩ I wish to thank all those who have criticized that draft, most particularly Mr. Yukio Kachi.

12a

THE THIRD MAN ARGUMENT IN THE *PARMENIDES*

HARDLY A TEXT in Plato has been discussed as much in the last forty years[1] as the two passages in the *Parmenides* purporting to prove that the Theory of Forms involves an infinite regress, which came to be dubbed within Plato's lifetime the "Third Man" Argument. A flood of light has been thrown both on the meaning of the text and on its philosophical implications. Yet in spite of this, disagreement continues. Is the Third Man Argument a valid objection to the Theory of Forms? Did Plato believe that it was valid? One can find acute and learned critics on both sides of both of these basic questions. I write as the beneficiary of their controversies, but not in a controversial spirit. If any progress in agreement is to be made at this juncture, it must come from some advance in understanding of the logical structure of the Argument. To this end I shall pursue its analysis further than I think anyone has yet found it profitable to push it. This will be the task of Section I. I shall then consider in Section II what this may teach us about the Theory of Forms and also about the state of mind in which Plato held this theory when

From *PR* 63 (1954): 319–49. Reprinted in Allen, pp. 231–61. Expressions of the form "F$_n$-ness" were uniformly changed to "F-ness$_n$," in the reprint.

{Rereading this paper in the light of criticisms I have seen in print or heard in discussion, I still find all of its main contentions sound. But were I writing today, I would have expressed myself differently on some points. For some improvements in the analysis of Plato's argument, I refer the reader to the one offered below in the Addendum; and for degrees of reality in Plato, to an essay I am contributing to a symposium on Greek philosophy edited by Mr. Renford Bambrough (London: Routledge, 1965) ⟨= *Platonic Studies*, pp. 58–75⟩.}

[1] I list the major contributions:

A. E. Taylor, "Parmenides, Zeno, and Socrates," in his *Philosophical Studies* (London, 1934) pp. 28–90; reprinted from *PAS* 16 (1915–16), 234–89.

F. Goblot, "Le Troisième Homme chez Platon," *Revue d'histoire de la philosophie* 3 (1929), 473ff.

W.F.R. Hardie, *A Study in Plato* (Oxford, 1936), pp. 88ff.

F. M. Cornford, *Plato and Parmenides* (London, 1939), pp. 87–95.

G. Ryle, "Plato's Parmenides," *Mind*, n.s., 48 (1939), 129ff. (especially pp. 136–40).

R. Robinson, "Plato's Parmenides," *CP* 37 (1942), 51ff.

H. Cherniss, *Aristotle's Criticism of Plato and the Academy,* I (Baltimore, 1944), *passim,* but especially pp. 231ff., 284ff., 375, and 500ff.

D. Ross, *Plato's Theory of Ideas* (Oxford, 1951), pp. 86ff.

G.E.L. Owen, "The Place of the *Timaeus* in Plato's Dialogues," *CQ*, n.s., 3 (1953), 79ff. at 83.

To works in this list I shall refer hereafter merely by the author's name.

he [319] turned against it that battery of objections of which the Third Man Argument is the most interesting and the most instructive.

I. ANALYSIS OF THE ARGUMENT

A. *The First Version*, Parmenides *132a1–b2*

> I suppose this is what leads you to suppose that there is in every case a single Form: When several things seem large to you, it seems perhaps that there is a single Form which is the same in your view of all of them. Hence you believe that Largeness is a single thing.[2]

This is the first step of the Argument and may be generalized as follows:

(A1) If a number of things, *a, b, c,* are[3] all *F*, there must be a single Form, *F*-ness, in virtue of which we apprehend *a, b, c,* as all *F*.[4]

Here "*F*" stands for any discernible character or property. The use of the same symbol "*F*" in "*F*-ness," the symbolic representation of the "single Form,"[5] records the identity of the character discerned in the particular ("large") and conceived in the Form ("Largeness") through which we see that this, or any other particular has this character. On the substantive meaning of the various terms in Plato's statement and in my transcript of it, I have nothing to say just now. Plato's argument professes to be a deductive argument and I propose to treat it as a formal structure of inference from premises, stated or implied. For this reason, I raise no questions about the Theory of Forms and presume no more information about it than I can extract from the text [320] before me. And what is supplied in its first step is, I trust, fully contained in (A1):

> What then if you similarly view mentally Largeness itself and the other large things?
> Will not a single Largeness appear once again, in virtue of which all these (*sc.* Largeness and the other large things) appear large?
> It seems so.

---

[2] For this and subsequent translations I have consulted Cornford (above, n. 1) and A. E. Taylor, *Plato's Parmenides* (Oxford, 1934) and mainly followed Cornford. My main concern has been to translate as literally as possible.

[3] I say "are," where Plato's text above says only "seem." But the difference is immaterial to the argument. A few lines later, Plato speaks of the large things as "participating" in Largeness (132a11), which is his way of saying that they are large (so far as particulars *are* anything at all) and do not merely appear such. Cf. also *Parm.* 130e5—131a2.

[4] In the last clause, I merely make explicit an assumption which is implicit throughout the argument and is stated in the second step, 132a7–8.

[5] That *F* and *F*-ness are logically and ontologically distinct is crucial to the argument. Cf. below, n. 39.

Consequently another Form of Largeness will appear, over and above Largeness itself and the things which participate in it.

This is the second step:

(A2) If *a*, *b*, *c*, and *F*-ness are all *F*, there must be another Form, ⟦*F*₁-ness⟧ {*F*-ness₁}, in virtue of which we apprehend *a*, *b*, *c*, and *F*-ness as all *F*.

Now merely to compare (A2) with (A1) above is to see a discrepancy in the reasoning which, so far as I know, has never been noticed before, though it leaps to the eye the moment one takes the trouble to transcribe the full content of the two steps in symbolic form. In (A1) we are told that if several things are all *F*, they are all seen as such in virtue of *F*-ness. But (A2) tells us that if several things are all *F*, they are all seen as such not because of *F*-ness, but because of a Form other than *F*-ness, namely, *F*-ness₁. To be sure, there is a difference in the protasis of (A1) and (A2), and this is doubtless what has misled patrons or critics of the Argument: (A2) includes, while (A1) does not, *F*-ness, among the things which have the property *F*. The significance of the assumption which prompts this inclusion will be discussed directly and will indeed remain the most important single issue throughout the whole of this paper. But if we simply stick to the logical form of the two statements, the disparity of reasoning[6] as between (A1) and (A2) remains glaringly abrupt and unwarranted. [321]

---

[6] A fastidious reader may be displeased at the vagueness of this expression. I could speak more definitely of a *non sequitur* (and, to simplify matters, will do so hereafter). But this is to understate the faultiness of the reasoning, which can only be fully stated in a proposition whose assertion is not necessary to my argument in the text and whose proof would have exceeded Plato's technical resources: *The joint assertion of* (A1) *and* (A2) *implies that the protaseis of* (A1) *and* (A2) *are mutually inconsistent;* and since the Argument assumes that both of the latter *can* be asserted (i.e., that it is true that there are large particulars, and that Largeness and the large particulars are all large), the joint assertion of (A1) and (A2) is absolutely precluded. The proof of the italicized proposition is as follows:

p = *a*, *b*, *c* are *F*.

q = *a*, *b*, *c* are seen as *F* in virtue of *F*-ness.

$\sim q$ = a, b, c are seen as *F* in virtue of *F*-ness₁, where *F*-ness₁ ≠ *F*-ness.

r = *F*-ness is *F*.

s = *F*-ness is seen as *F* in virtue of *F*-ness₁, where *F*-ness₁ ≠ *F*-ness.

(It will be noticed that, to reduce the length of the ensuing proof, I have put as $\sim q$ a proposition that is not strictly the negate of q but whose truth-value is equivalent to that of the latter, since we may take it for granted that it cannot be true that *x*, *y*, *z* are seen as *F* in virtue of *F*-ness and also in virtue of a Form other than *F*-ness.)

Then, (A1) = $p \supset q$.

(A2) = $(p.r) \supset (\sim q.s)$.

But $(\sim q.s) \supset \sim q$; therefore, $(p.r) \supset \sim q$; hence, $q \supset \sim(p.r)$.

But since $p \supset q$, (A1), it follows that $p \supset \sim(p.r)$, i.e., that the protaseis of (A1) and (A2) are mutually inconsistent.

Is there then no way to get around the difficulty? There certainly would be, if (A2) could be changed to read:

(A2a) If $a, b, c,$ and F-ness are all F_1, there must be another Form, F-ness$_1$, etc.

Is there any chance that this is what Plato did say, and that I missed it in my transcript of his argument at (A2) above? I think, none. We need only refer back to the text to verify the fact that (A2), not (A2a), is the information it supplies. All it asks of us is to "view mentally" Largeness and "the other large things" and find the Form in virtue of which *all* of these "appear large." It does *not* invite us to discern a *new* character, not large, but large$_1$ (whatever this may mean), and having satisfied ourselves that $a, b, c,$ and Largeness are all large$_1$ to infer, *pari passu* with (A1), the existence of Largeness$_1$.

Now it might be claimed that though (A2a) is not what Plato said, it is nonetheless what he meant. This proposal should be advanced, and entertained, with the gravest misgivings, since Plato is anything but a careless writer, and his vocabulary suffers from no limitation which would have kept him from saying (A2a), if he had meant (A2a). Still, the issue being crucial to the whole course of the argument, let us give the proposal its day in court. Would this improvement of the text be an improvement of the argument? The answer is, surely, that it would not. For the purpose of the second step in the Argument is to convince [322] us of the existence of a new Form of Largeness, "over and above Largeness itself." This purpose would be defeated if the protasis of the second step were as questionable as its apodosis. And is not this precisely what would happen, if the proposal were adopted? The second step would then begin, "If there are large$_1$ things . . ." ; and how could we then help retorting, "If, indeed," and ask for reasons why there must? In the case of (A1), the protasis offers no trouble at all; for who would gainsay that there are (or appear to be) a number of large things? But here the matter is absolutely different. Everyone has seen large things; but who has ever seen a large$_1$ thing or set of things? If Plato had meant to offer such an assertion as the *if*-clause of an *if-then* statement, he would surely have seen that it cries aloud for justification and would never have moved on to the *then*-clause, without stopping to interpolate reasons for the *if*-clause itself. And to do this he would have had to change the whole form of his argument. The burden of the second step would have then become to establish the existence of things that have the remarkable property, large$_1$. I am not saying that such an argument could not be made.[7] All I am saying is that, had it been made, [323] the

---

[7] It could not be made at all without anticipating the results of Sec. II. If the anticipation be permitted, the argument can be reconstructed as follows: Largeness is large in a different (superlative) sense (which follows from the Degrees-of-Reality Theory in Sec. II) from that in which particulars are large. So,

(i) Largeness is large$_1$.

second step of the Third Man Argument would have been entirely different from what it is. And since my purpose is to analyze the argument Plato gives us, instead of one he might have given, I have no choice but to consign to the waste basket the suggestion that (A2a) is what Plato meant. We are then left where we started, with (A2) staring us in the face.

Now if this is all we had to go by, (A1) in the first step and (A2) in the second, could anyone say that the Third Man Argument was logically valid? Clearly there must have been something more in Plato's mind than the information supplied at (A1), which made the transition to (A2) appear to him not only permissible but plausible. What could this be? A full answer to this question would send us rummaging into other texts to discover what further assumptions Plato made about his Theory of Forms. But this would have to anticipate Section II. Let us content ourselves now with a more modest question: What are the simplest premises, not given in the present Argument, which would have to be added to its first step, to make (A2) a legitimate conclusion?

We need, first of all, what I propose to call the Self-Predication Assumption:

(A3)   Any Form can be predicated of itself. Largeness is itself large. F-ness is itself F.

I have alluded to this already. Clearly it is necessary, for were it not true, the protasis of (A2) would be certainly false; if F-ness were not F, it would be false to say that a, b, c, and F-ness are all F. The credit for recognizing that this is an indispensable, though suppressed, premise of the Third Man Argument goes to A. E. Taylor.[8] He thereby opened the way to a correct under-

---

But the large particulars and the large$_1$ Form have something in common; call this—the determinable, of which large and large$_1$ are determinates—large$_2$. It then follows that

(ii) Largeness and the large particulars are all large$_2$.

Having completed this detour, we would now have warrant for asserting a suitable variant of (A2a), which would now read

(A2a$_1$)   If a, b, c, and F-ness are all F_2, there must be a Form other than F-ness, namely, F-ness$_2$.

It will be noticed that (A2a$_1$) would no longer be the *second* step of the Argument but, at the very least, the third; the existence of the predicate F_1 would have to be proved not as the common predicate of F-ness and the F particulars, but as the distinctive property of F-ness; and the common predicate of F-ness and the F particulars would not be F_1, but F_2—all of which is a far cry from Plato's argument in the text before us, and, I trust, will convince the skeptic why it should not be taken as "the meaning" of the second step as it appears in the text.

[8] Pp. 46ff. of ⟨the reprint of⟩ his 1916 paper. Most of the later mentions of this vital point acknowledge indebtedness to Taylor, and it is probable that even those which do not are similarly indebted to him directly or indirectly since this insight is missing in any of the earlier discussions.

standing of the Argument and not only of this but of the whole Theory of Forms, though Taylor, ironically, never realized the implications of his own discovery, for he refused to admit that [324] Plato himself made so absurd an assumption. Of this more later. Here we may remark not only that this premise is necessary to the argument, but that Plato's actual wording of the second step comes as close to asserting it as one could without actually stating the Self-Predication Assumption: "Will not a single Largeness appear once again, in virtue of which *all these* (*sc.* 'Largeness and the other large things') appear large?" The second clause clearly implies that Largeness, no less than each of the particulars, "appear(s) large."

But we need also a further premise, which I shall call the Nonidentity Assumption:

(A4)   If anything has a certain character, it cannot be identical with the Form in virtue of which we apprehend that character. If x is F, x cannot be identical with F-ness.

This too, though not stated in the Argument, is certainly implied. For think of what would happen if it were not assumed to be true. The transition from the protasis of (A2), "If a, b, c, and F-ness are all F," to its apodosis, "then there must be another Form, F-ness$_1$," would then not be a logical sequence, but the wild and whimsical jump we have seen it to be above. The minimum warrant for passing from "the large things and Largeness are large" to "the Form in virtue of which we apprehend the common character of large things and Largeness cannot be Largeness," could be no less than this: If anything is large, its Largeness cannot be identical with that thing. From this it *would* follow that if Largeness is large, then *its* Largeness cannot be identical with itself and must, therefore, be a second Form of Largeness, Largeness$_1$.

In the many modern discussions of the Argument, I can find no explicit statement that this Nonidentity Assumption, or an equivalent one, is strictly required in just this way. This may be because the role of such an assumption at this point strikes critics more nimble-witted than myself as so obvious that they feel it an insult to their reader's intelligence to put it into words or symbols. However, there are times when the drudgery of saying the obvious is rewarded, and this is one of them. For if one compares (A4) with (A3) above, one will then see that these two premises, jointly necessary to the second, and every subsequent [325] step of the Argument, are mutually inconsistent, and that their inconsistency does not need to be exposed through the indirect and elaborate machinery of the infinite regress but can be shown much more simply and directly. (A3) reads: F-ness is F. (A4) reads: if x is F, x cannot be identical with F-ness. Substituting F-ness for x in (A4), we get

(A5)   If F-ness is F, F-ness cannot be identical with F-ness.

And since the consequent of (A5) is plainly false, because self-contradictory, at least one of the premises from which it follows—(A3), (A4)—must be false.[9]

Now there is one way of avoiding this particular impasse, and that is to modify (A4), restating it as follows:

(A4a)   If any *particular* has a certain character, then it cannot be identical with the Form in virtue of which we apprehend that character. If x is F, x cannot be identical with F-ness when, and only when, the values for x are particulars, a, b, c.[10]

If (A4a) replaces (A4) above, then the inconsistency with (A3) will not arise. For (A4a) does not warrant the substitution of F-ness for x, and this in spite of the fact that F-ness is F (A3). What we are now told is that the Nonidentity Assumption holds in the case of particulars; we are not told that it holds in the case of Forms and have no ground for asserting that if a *Form* has a certain character it cannot be identical with the Form in virtue of which it has (and is apprehended as having) that character. But what happens now to the second step of the Argument? It is no longer a valid inference from our premises, (A1), (A3), and (A4a). We have now no ground for saying that if a, b, c and F-ness are all F, there must be a Form other than F-ness, in virtue of which we apprehend that a, b, c and F-ness are all F; there is now nothing to keep us from saying that they are all apprehended as F in virtue of F-ness itself. The existence of F-ness$_1$ would thus remain unproved in the second step, and, by the same token the existence of all subsequent Forms, F-ness$_2$, [326] F-ness$_3$, etc., would remain unproved. The infinite regress would not materialize.

Let us now see where this analysis of the Third Man Argument has taken us: If we took the second (and crucial) step of the Third Man Argument as a mere inference from what is stated in the first step, it would be a horrible *non sequitur*. To avoid this, further premises must be supplied, and we could not determine whether the Argument is valid until they were supplied; for to say of any argument that it is valid is simply to say that its conclusions follow correctly from its premises. And we have now seen what premises would be necessary for the assertion of (A2):

the first step of the Argument, (A1);
the Self-Predication Assumption, (A3);
the full-strength Nonidentity Assumption, (A4).

Are they then also sufficient? Certainly, though in a very odd way, for we are working with inconsistent premises which, as we have seen, have already

---

[9] I am using "false" here and occasionally hereafter in the broader sense which includes "insignificant."

[10] It will be convenient to distinguish hereafter (A4a) from (A4) above, by referring to (A4) as the "full-strength" Nonidentity Assumption.

produced the self-contradictory conclusion at (A5) "F-ness cannot be identical with F-ness," and we should not be surprised to see them justify all kinds of contradictory conclusions. Since these premises warrant the proposition that F-ness is *not* identical with F-ness, they will warrant the proposition that F-ness *is* identical with F-ness$_1$, which *is* a Form not identical with F-ness, and (A2) will then follow from (A1).[11] And having thus got the existence of F-ness$_1$ at (A2), we can proceed, by the same "reasoning," to show in the next step the existence of F-ness$_2$, then again F-ness$_3$, and so on without end. We would thus get a *bona fide* infinite regress, logically vicious, since it is assumed that we discern F particulars in virtue of F-ness (A1), F-ness in virtue of F-ness$_1$ (A2), and so on *ad infinitum,* the discernment of each successive Form being required [327] for the discernment of its immediate predecessor, a requirement which can never be fulfilled, since the series is infinite.[12]

And what would we learn from this consequence? Only that one or more of our premises is false or void of sense, on the assumption that some vice in one or more of the premises is the source of the vicious consequence. We could have got the same information by a much more economical procedure: by

[11] For we know from (A1) that if a number of things are F there must be a Form, F-ness, through which they are apprehended as F. Whence it follows that

(A2b)   If $a, b, c,$ and F-ness are all F, there must be a Form, F-ness, through which they are apprehended as F.

But if F-ness is identical with F-ness$_1$, we may substitute F-ness$_1$ for F-ness in the second clause of (A2b), which will produce (A2).

[12] There is a tolerably good explanation of the fact that the Argument does not result in an (unobjectionable) infinite series but in a (vicious) regress, in Taylor, pp. 47ff., though I should take exception to the form of his application of the regress to Platonic "participation" at p. 49. The gist of the matter may be restated as follows: If the Argument simply established an indefinite series of Forms corresponding to each discernible character, no logical disaster would ensue, so long as one (or, at most, a finite number) of these Forms sufficed to do what Forms are supposed to do, i.e., enable us to discern relevant characters in the particulars and then in the first of the corresponding Forms. All other members of the series could then be ignored as a harmless surplus, though every adept in the use of Occam's razor would itch to lop them off. But what the Argument proves is much worse than this. At (A1) we are told that we apprehend particulars as F through F-ness. Now if F-ness itself must be apprehended as F, then it follows from (A2) that we must apprehend F-ness through F-ness$_1$, and so on. Whence it follows that, since we cannot complete the series F-ness, F-ness$_1$, etc., we shall never be able to apprehend F-ness in the first place and thus never apprehend the F-particulars; and this *is* disastrous. It may be objected that Plato does not *say* that F-ness must itself be apprehended as F. Of course he does not. But what he does say implies it in conjunction with Self-Predication. For if it were true that F-ness is F, how could it be apprehended except *as F?* However, it is not necessary (and is unwarranted by the evidence) to assume that this distinction between a harmless series and a vicious regress was apparent to Plato himself. He was himself convinced that there was just one Form for each discernible character or kind, and argued (*Rep.* 597c–d, *Tim.* 31a–b) that if *per impossible* there were two Forms of anything, there would have to be a third which would be *the* Form of that thing. He would, therefore, have regarded even the existence of an infinite series of Forms of any one kind as disastrous for his Theory.

simply noting the contradiction which follows from the joint assertion of (A3) and (A4), as explained above. And if Plato had even got as far as the explicit assertion of (A3) itself, he would have found good reason for rejecting it[13] and would thus have been [328] able to nail down the exact source of the trouble that is attested but not identified by the infinite regress. But even if Plato had asserted (A3), he could still have saved himself from the disaster of the regress by simply denying (A4) and saying that he had no reason for holding anything more than (A4a).

This result may be summarized, in anticipation of Section II below, as follows: If Plato had identified all of the premises which are necessary (and sufficient) to warrant the second step of the Third Man Argument, he would not have produced the Third Man Argument at all, unless he were simply pursuing a logical game for its own sake, which is not what he is doing in the first part of the *Parmenides*.[14] In stating the Third Man Argument, and in leaving it unrefuted, he is revealing (a) that he did not know all of its necessary premises, whence it would follow that (b) he had no way of determining whether or not it was a valid argument. (a) can be independently verified, and it will be in Section II.

B. The Second Version: Parmenides 132d1–133a6

This is at least as interesting on its own account; and no less so is a third version, supplied by Aristotle.[15] Lack of space forbids altogether a treatment of the third in this paper and compels me to deal more briefly and more roughly with the second than it deserves. All I shall attempt here is to show that Plato's [329] second version of the Argument is similar in logical struc-

---

[13] To avoid misunderstanding, I should underline the fact that the Self-Predication Assumption to which I refer throughout this paper is the assertion in (A3) above that *any* Form may be predicated of itself. Absurdity or contradiction inevitably results from this assertion which implies that Forms predicable of particulars are predicable of themselves, as I shall know in Sec. II-B below. Had Plato merely said or implied that some Forms are self-predicational—those predicable only of Forms, like Logical Self-Identity, Intelligibility, Changelessness, etc.—no obvious absurdity or contradiction would have arisen. On Russell's well-known theory, *any* assertion of the form "F(F)" is logically illicit: but see, *contra*, A. Koyré, *Epiménide le menteur* (Paris, 1947), pp. 36–42.

[14] For the best demonstration of this, see Robinson, pp. 58ff.

[15] In his essay *On the Forms, ap.* Alexander, in *Met.* (Hayduck), 84.21–85.11; English translation by W. D. Ross, *The Works of Aristotle*, vol. 12, *Select Fragments* (Oxford, 1952), 129; cf. Cherniss, pp. 233–34, and 500ff. I can only observe here that an analysis of Aristotle's version will show that it too involves, without appearing to notice, the same discrepancy between the first and the second steps of the Argument. While at the first step Aristotle infers the existence of F-ness from the fact that F-ness is predicated of certain things (in this case, particulars), in the second step he very surprisingly infers the existence of a Form other than F-ness from the fact that F-ness is predicated of certain things (in this case, the particulars and F-ness).

ture to his first and presupposes both of the inconsistent premises presupposed by the first.

The first step in the second version:

(B1)   The Copy-Theory: If *a* and *b* are similar (in respect of being *F*), there must be a Form, *F*-ness, in which they both participate by way of resemblance: *a* and *b* must resemble *F*-ness, as copies resemble their model.

Moreover:

(B1.1)   If *a* resembles *F*-ness (in respect of being *F*), *F*-ness must resemble *a* (in the same respect).[16]

The second and crucial step, whose reasoning is repeated in all subsequent steps:

(B2)   If *a* and *F*-ness are similar (in respect of being *F*), there must be another Form, F-ness$_1$, in which they both participate by way of resemblance: *a* and *F*-ness must resemble F-ness$_1$, as copies resemble their model.

A comparison of the above with Plato's text will show that the symbolic transcript omits nothing vital to the reasoning and adds nothing except the parenthetical statements; and these only make explicit the sense of the argument. Clearly, if *a* and *b* are similar, they must be similar in at least one respect; and my parentheses have simply specified the respect with a symbol which is the same as that used for the Form in which they participate. Thus, if *a* and *b* are both white, they resemble each other in respect of being white, the same property which is expressed by the Form, Whiteness, in which they are said to participate by way of resemblance. Again, in the corollary, if Whiteness resembles the white particular, it can only resemble it in the same respect in which the white thing is said to resemble Whiteness, namely, "white."

Now a mere glance at my transcript of the argument will [330] show the same discrepancy between the first and the second step that we encountered in the first version. From the premise that two things are similar in respect of being *F*, (B1) infers the existence of *F*-ness, while (B2) that of a Form other than *F*-ness, F-ness$_1$. To be sure, the things which are said to be similar in the protasis of (B1) are once again not the same things which are said to be similar at (B2): *a* and *b*, in (B1), *a* and *F*-ness in (B2). And this protasis in (B2) implies the Self-Predication Assumption:

---

[16] *Not* in respect of being a copy of *a* or *b*—an absurd suggestion, which, of course, is not in the text, though Taylor (p. 87) inexplicably read it into argument and, therefore, thought he could explode the argument by retorting that the model-copy relation is not symmetrical. The argument only assures (that the relation of similarity is symmetrical which, of course, it *is* (Hardie, p. 96; Ryle, p. 137; Ross, p. 89; Owen, p. 83n. 3).

(B3)   *F*-ness is *F;* for if *F*-ness were not *F,* it would not resemble *a* in respect of being *F.*

But why should the similarity of *a* and *F*-ness in respect of *F* require the resemblance of *a* and *F*-ness to a Form other than *F*-ness? A necessary reason for this is the Nonidentity Assumption:

(B4)   If *x* is *F,* it cannot be identical with the Form, *F*-ness; for if this were not true, there would be no reason at all why *a* and *F*-ness could not both be *F* in virtue of *F*-ness. But (B3) and (B4) are obviously inconsistent, and their joint assertion leads to a contradiction:

(B5)   If *F*-ness is *F* (B3), then *F*-ness cannot be identical with *F*-ness; for if anything is *F,* it cannot be identical with *F*-ness (B4).

It is worth noting that the two Assumptions of Self-Predication and (full-strength) Nonidentity which are still necessary, as they were in the first version, are still tacit, for neither of them is stated as such; but they are now much closer to the verbal surface of the Argument, for they are both logically implied and even intuitively suggested by the key-concept of the second version, the Copy-Theory of participation. For if an *F* thing participates in *F*-ness, by way of resembling *F*-ness as a copy resembles its model, then (a) *F*-ness *must* be *F,* else it would not be resembled by, and resemble, the *F* thing in respect of *F,* and (b) the *F* thing cannot be identical with *F*-ness, since a copy cannot be identical with its model. The contradiction at (B5) exposes both the inconsistency of the two tacit Assumptions and the logical vice of the Copy-Theory, for it shows that it implies both (B3) and (B4), which are mutually inconsistent. Another [331] way of stating the contradiction that follows from the Copy-Theory is

(B5a)   If *F*-ness is *F,* then it cannot be F; for the Copy-Theory which, as we have seen, requires that *F*-ness be *F,* also requires that it cannot be *F,* for, if it were *F,* it would have to be, on this theory, a copy of *F*-ness, and nothing can be a copy of itself. And it is further worth noting that the Argument could be collapsed in the second version, exactly as in the first, by rejecting (B4) in favor of

(B4a)   If any *particular* is *F,* it cannot be identical with the Form, *F*-ness.

This would avoid the absurd consequences of (B4), (B5), and (B5a) and would ruin the regress by invalidating its second step.

Having learned all this, what is there more to learn about the infinite regress that must start at (B2)? That it does start there, if (B3) and (B4) are supplied, can be easily shown, for (B2) is justified by these premises in the same queer way in which (A2) was justified above.[17] We have thus got our precious re-

---

[17] (B5) has given us the same remarkable information that we got at (A5) above: *F*-ness is not

gress once again. But what good is it? As in the first version, its diagnostic value for the logical vices of the Theory of Forms is no better than, is indeed not as good as, the simple statement of the tacit premises, (B3) and (B4), followed by the simple deduction of the self-contradictory conclusions, (B5) and (B5a) above. If Plato knew that his theory commits him to *these* premises, he would not need the regress to tell him that his theory is logically moribund and must submit to drastic surgery to survive.

II. THE ASSUMPTIONS OF THE ARGUMENT AND OF THE THEORY OF FORMS

A. *Plato's Ontology*

The question whether or not the Third Man Argument is a [332] valid objection to Plato's Theory of Forms can now be resolved into the far more precise one: Did Plato's Theory of Forms make the two tacit assumptions which are needed to produce the infinite regress? This is what we must now determine. When we have done this, it will appear, I think, that the more complex question, whether Plato himself did or did not believe the Argument to be a valid objection to his Theory, will pretty well answer itself.

The place to begin is with what Plato himself tells about the Theory of Forms, in this very dialogue, before presenting either the Third Man Argument or any of the other objections. "Tell me, Socrates," asks Parmenides at 130b, "have you yourself drawn this division you speak of: on one hand, certain Forms *separately* by themselves and, on the other, *separately,* the things which partake of them? And do you believe that Similarity itself is something *separately* from the Similarity which we possess?" Plato could hardly have been more emphatic in identifying that feature of the Theory which will be the special butt of the attacks that are to follow; and when Aristotle, in his version of the Third Man Argument, as indeed in most of his other polemic, makes the "separation" (*chōrismos*) of the Forms the most objectionable aspect of the Platonic theory, he does so with good warrant from at least this Platonic text.[18] But what exactly is Plato saying when he asserts that Forms exist "separately" from particulars? Only what he had said many times before without using the word *separately* at all. The solemn announcements of the Theory in the middle dialogues—the *Cratylus,* the *Phaedo,* the

---

identical with *F*-ness. Let it then be, once again, identical with *F*-ness$_1$, which empowers us to substitute "*F*-ness$_1$" for "*F*-ness" wherever we please. But from (B1) we deduce

(B2a) If *a* and *F*-ness are similar (in respect of being *F*), there must be a Form, *F*-ness, etc.

Substituting "*F*-ness$_1$" for "*F*-ness" in the second clause of (B2a), we get (B2).

[18] And from many others. See Cherniss, pp. 208ff., whose thorough refutation of the contrary view makes further argument unnecessary.

Republic[19]—are generally put in this form: Beauty (or Justice, or Goodness, etc.) "is something" (*ti esti*) or "is one thing" (*hen esti*). But these expressions are themselves uninformative, nor is there gain in information in doubling the emphasis on "is," by compounding the verb with its adverbial or substantival [333] derivatives, "is really" (*ontōs esti*), "is a real (thing)" (*on esti*), "is a reality" (*ousia esti*), or even resorting to other adjectives or adverbs, "is a true (*alēthes*) being," or "is truly" (*alēthōs*), "is a pure (*eilikrines*) being" or "purely (*eilikrinōs*) is."[20]

What Plato means by saying, with or without the use of any other substantive, adjective, or adverb, that "*x* is," in the strict sense of "is," becomes clear only when we see that he understands this to entail:

   (i) *x* is intelligible;[21]
   (ii) *x* is changeless;[22]
   (iii) *x* is not qualified by contrary predicates;[23]
   (iv) *x* is itself the perfect instance of the property or relation which the word for "*x*" connotes.[24]

Obviously this is not the place to expound the content of these assertions which epitomize one of the richest and boldest metaphysical theories ever invented in Western thought. Just one or two remarks are called for here.

Perhaps more important than any one or all four of the specific statements which convey the content of the Platonic meaning of the word *is* is the tacit assumption which underlies them all. Logically, this is the costliest of all the assumptions that Plato made: that the verb *is* and all its ⟦substantival, adjectival, or adverbial⟧ variants {(when used in ontological assertions)} have a *single* meaning, the one which is jointly specified by the four propositions I have just enumerated. We must not judge him harshly on this account. The Aristotelian [334] axiom that "things can be said to be in many different

---

[19] *Crat.* 439c, 440a; *Phaedo* 65d, 74a; *Rep.* 475e, 596a. I am well aware that some scholars believe that the *Cratylus* is one of the later dialogues, but this is no place to argue the point, and nothing of any consequence turns on it for my present purpose.

[20] Detailed documentation is superfluous; these expressions turn up in every context in which the Theory of Forms is asserted, including the passages listed in the preceding note. Those who, like Owen, believe that the Theory of Forms was drastically revised in the later dialogues and who deny the lateness of the *Timaeus,* might be referred especially to *Phil.* 58a–59d; there the object of dialectic, which consists of the Forms (cf. the "divine circle and sphere" is contrast to the "human circle," the "false circle and rule," at *Phil.* 62a–b), is that which "really is" (58a2–3, 59d4), in explicit contrast to "this world" of becoming (59a).

[21] In emphatic opposition to "sensible." So, e.g., at *Phaedo* 65c ff., *Rep.* 5.509d ff., *Tim.* 51b–e.

[22] E.g., *Crat.* 439d ff.; *Phaedo* 78d ff.; *Rep.* 6.484b; *Phil.* 59a–c.

[23] E.g., *Phaedo* 74c; *Rep.* 5.479a–c, 7.523b ff.; *Ep.* 7.343a–b.

[24] For this *no* documentation (in the strict sense) can be offered—a point of great importance, to be discussed shortly.

senses" was not a commonplace in its own day, but a revolutionary discovery.[25] Before Aristotle and after Parmenides all the great system-builders—Empedocles, Anaxagoras, the atomists, and Plato himself—had taken it for granted that being had one, and just one, sense, whose cardinal feature was changelessness.[26] What Plato did was to draw up a far more systematic, more thoughtful and thought-provoking list of conditions which anything must satisfy if it can be said to be in the strict sense of the word, a list which was purely conservative in making changelessness definitive of being, but which broke with Ionian and Italian *physiologia* by rehabilitating the Eleatic inference[27] that only the "bodiless" (*asōmaton*)[28] is wholly real. Plato did not thereby revert to the Eleatic view that the sensible world is wholly unreal. His view was a Degrees-of-Reality theory which permitted him, in compliance with his native tongue, to say that sensible things are,[29] as logical subjects of

[25] One which, among other things, offers a direct way of tracking down the source of the Third Man Argument, as Aristotle himself clearly saw. In his own language, the confusion of the sense which *is* has in the first category with its sense in one of the other categories is what "creates the 'third man,'" *Soph. el.* 178b37ff.; cf. *Met.* 1038b34ff.

[26] Empedocles B8: there is no "generation" (*phusis*) or "destruction"; "generation" is only a "name"; B17.35: the only things that strictly *are,* are the "roots," and they are "everlastingly in the same state" (literally, "ever continuously alike" (*ēnekes aien homoia*). Anaxagoras B17: "the Greeks," who think there is such a thing as generation and destruction, are wrong; there *is* no such thing; generation and destruction should be "correctly called" mixture and separation; hence (by implication) "things that are" (*eontōn chrēmatōn*) are changeless. In the atomists the only things which "really" (*eteēi,* Democritus B7–10) exist are (the absolutely changeless) atoms and the void.

[27] I should warn the reader that my view that Eleatic Being was incorporeal runs against the general opinion. But it is explicit in Melissus B9; see *Gnomon* 35 (1953), 34–35 ⟨**1.186–87⟩. I believe that it is implicit in Parmenides.

[28] An assumption so basic that Plato does not trouble to spell it out in the earlier statements of the theory, where he only finds it necessary to insist upon the "invisibility" of the Forms (*Phaedo* 65d9, 79a6ff.), and it is only in the later dialogues that he supplies the further premise (*sc.,* that the invisible, or not sensible, is the bodiless, *Tim.* 28b) for the conclusion "Forms are bodiless" or just states the conclusion by itself (*Soph.* 246b, the "Friends of Forms" in opposition to the materialists who "define reality as identical with body"; cf. *Polit.* 286a).

[29] And this in the middle, no less than the later, dialogues. Thus the use of "beings" (*onta*) to include the world of becoming in the *Philebus* (23c) can be matched perfectly in the *Phaedo* 79a, "Shall we then assume two kinds of beings (*ontōn*), one visible, the other invisible?" This point spoils one of the major arguments that have been offered by Owen (pp. 85–86) in support of his thesis that the *Timaeus* was written in Plato's middle period: he assumes that a strict dichotomy of being-becoming, which implies a systematic refusal to ascribe being to the world of becoming, is characteristic of the middle dialogues, has been abandoned in the later dialogues, and therefore makes a sure criterion from the earlier date of the *Timaeus*. He ignores the fact that in spite of the harsh being-becoming dichotomy of *Tim.* 27d–28a, Plato continues in the same dialogue to stretch being to include the world of becoming; so, e.g., in the psychogony at 35a, which speaks of the "divisible being (*ousia*) which becomes in bodies," and in the cosmological trichotomy at 52d, where "being, place, becoming" are said to "be" (*einai*). He also ignores the fact that the being-becoming dichotomy is plainly asserted in an indisputably late dialogue like the *Philebus* (59a).

assertions of existence [335] and ascriptions of properties and relations. They were halfway real, "between the purely real and the totally unreal" (*Rep.* 478d). The Imitation or Copy Theory incorporates this assumption that the sensible particulars are 'less real' than the Form they resemble. If the bed produced by the carpenter is not "the real" (*to on*) Bed, "but only something which is like it," then "it would not be right to say that the work of the carpenter or of any other handicraftsman is a perfectly real thing (*teleōs einai*), would it? We must not be surprised then if this too [*sc.* the physical bed] is a somewhat shadowy thing as compared with reality" (*pros alētheian*) (*Rep.* 597a).

B. Separation and Self-Predication

We can now ask whether this ontology does or does not include the two tacit premises of the Third Man Argument. That Plato assumes Self-Predication I already implied in the fourth of the conditions of Platonic being I have listed above. I gave no textual evidence that this was recognized by Plato himself on a level with the other three, for the simple reason that there is none to give. While Plato states and defends conditions (i) and (ii), and (iii), he leaves (iv) not only undefended, but unstated. But if he never stated it, what reason can be given for saying that he did make it after all? The reason is that it is certainly implied by various things he said and believed. It is implied, first of all, both by his Degrees-of-Reality Theory and by his [336] Copy-Theory of the relation of things to Forms. For if an *F* particular is only "deficiently"[30] *F*, and only the corresponding Form is perfectly *F*, then *F*-ness is *F*. Or if the *F* particular is a copy of *F*-ness and resembles *F*-ness in respect of being *F*, then, once again, *F*-ness is *F*. Moreover, Self-Predication is also implied by quite a different set of statements which are not elucidations of the Theory of Forms, but direct and, at times, casual assertions about this or that Form. Examples turn up in the earliest dialogues, long before the Theory of Forms had taken shape in Plato's mind.[31] When a man's hairs have turned white, says Socrates in the *Lysis* (217d), "they have become such as that which is present in them, white through Whiteness": the white hairs are "such as" or "of the same quality as" (*hoionper*) Whiteness; they have the same quality that Whiteness has.[32]

---

[30] *Endeesterōs, Phaedo* 74e, 75a; *endeestera, phaulotera,* 75b. Cf. *Rep.* 529d: the celestial bodies "fall far short of" (*polu endein*) the intelligible Forms whose visible likeness they are.

[31] The contrary view (cf. H. Cherniss, *Riddle of the Early Academy* [Berkeley, 1945], pp. 4–5) that the Theory of Forms is already present in the early dialogues would simplify my argument. But I do not agree with it, and I cannot argue the point here beyond stating that I cannot consider the employment of certain linguistic expressions as *sufficient* evidence of the concurrent assertion of the metaphysical theory.

[32] Self-Predication is also suggested by Plato's use of the expression "the *x* itself" for "the Form of *x*" which, as Ross remarks (88), "treats the Idea of *x* as one *x* among others, and implies an *x*-ness common to it with others." This expression occurs repeatedly in the *Hippias Major* (Ross, p. 17n.1) as well as in the middle dialogues.

Somewhat later, in the *Protagoras* (330c–d) we get an even more striking text which, since first noticed by Goblot in 1929,[33] has [337] become the star instance of Self-Predication in Plato. Here Socrates roundly declares that justice is just and holiness holy. "What other thing *could* be holy, if holiness isn't holy," he asks, indignant at the idea that anyone could gainsay that holiness is holy. These two examples would be quite enough to refute Taylor and others who, in the goodness of their hearts, press upon Plato charitable donations gathered from modern analysis. But there are others. In the *Phaedo* (100c) Socrates gives away the same presumption when he indulges in the expression "If anything else is beautiful, besides Beauty itself." And in the *Symposium,* while there is no one sentence that says quite baldly that Beauty is beautiful, the whole point of Diotima's speech is that the Form of Beauty is superlatively fair, incomparably more so than fair bodies, minds, or institutions: the universal enters into competition with its instances, and has no trouble at all winning the beauty contest.

Is it possible that a man should say, and with the greatest emphasis, "Justice is just" yet not realize that this is as good as saying that a Form which *is* a character *has* that character? It is perfectly possible. That it is possible to say *p,* which implies *q,* and not think of the implication or even of *q,* is a first principle of inquiry in the history of philosophy.[34] In this case there is a further factor, and a very prosaic one, which may blinker the logical vision of a clearheaded man. It is the fact that "Justice is just," which can also be said in Greek as, "the just is just," can be so easily mistaken for a tautology, and its denial for a self-contradiction.[35] I am not suggesting that the Assumption of Self-Predication is just a symptom of the tyranny of language over ontology. The suggestion would not even be plausible; for other philosophers, using the same language, made no such assumption. The assumption has far deeper roots, notably religious ones, which I cannot explore in this paper. What can be debited to language is simply the fact that an assertion which looks like an identity-statement may be taken as having the certainty of a tautology; and the illusion of its self-evidence [339] could very well block that further scrutiny

---

[33] P. 473n.3. Soon after it was noticed (perhaps independently of Goblot's paper) by Theodore de Laguna, "Notes on the Theory of Ideas," *PR* 43 (1934), 450–52. De Laguna saw exactly what such a statement implies (and generalized the implication, "The Platonic idea is a universal, supposed precisely and unqualifiedly to characterize itself") and what is wrong with the implication: "Justice and holiness are not moral agents; they cannot have virtues or vices." The next important use of the passage is by Robinson (pp. 62–63) in 1942. Cornford (pp. 87ff.) in 1939 had seen that Self-Predication is implied right and left in the objections against the Forms in the *Parmenides* but still followed Taylor's lead in refusing to credit Plato himself with the Assumption; so too Cherniss. So far as I can recall, Taylor, Cornford, and Cherniss do not notice the *Protagoras* passage and fail to see that the Assumption is implied by the Copy-Theory and the Degrees-Of-Reality Theory.

[34] No one has stated this so clearly and followed it so rigorously as R. Robinson, *Plato's Earlier Dialectic* (Ithaca, N.Y., 1941), pp. 2–3 *et passim.*

[35] Cornford, p. 87.

which would reveal that it implies a proposition which so far from being self-evident leads to self-contradiction. Anyhow, whether it be for this or for some other reason, there can be no doubt about the fact that Plato never asserted Self-Predication in any of his writings, and not much doubt that neither did he assert it in oral discussion in the many debates that raged over the Forms in the Academy; for it he had, Aristotle would have known it, and he was not the man to pass over the wonderful polemical possibilities it opens up.[36] Shall we then assume that Plato did know it but kept the thought locked up in the secrecy of his own mind? This melodramatic possibility can be disposed of fairly simply. Had Plato recognized that all of his Forms are self-predicational, what would he have done with Forms like Change, Becoming, and Perishing, which he did recognize as *bona fide* Forms?[37] Clearly none of these could be self-predicational, for if they were, they would not be changeless and would thus forfeit *being*. The same could be said of other Forms, not mentioned as such by Plato, but which his Theory would require him to recognize—Forms of the Sensible, Corporeal, Imperfect, indeed of all characters contrary to those which define the conditions of Platonic being. That Plato is never aware of any such difficulty shows that he was not aware of any Assumption which would have made the difficulty as obvious to him as it is to us.[38] [339]

C. Separation and Nonidentity

What of the other assumption which I have called Nonidentity in Section 1? If the question concerned only the nonidentity of particulars with their homonymous Forms—(A4a), (B4a) above—the answer would seem so obvious as to

---

[36] In Aristotle's version of the Third Man Argument, we see Self-Predication not only at his finger tips but almost in the hollow of his hand: "and 'man' is predicated both of particular men *and of the Form* . . . ," *ap.* Alex., *in Met.* 84.29. That he did not *see* what was thus within his grasp is clear from the fact that elsewhere he makes much of the point that characters predicable of Forms cannot be predicated of their particular instances; e.g., Changelessness, predicable of (the Form) Man but impredicable of any man (*Top.* 137b3ff., 148a15ff.; and cf. 113a24ff. See Cherniss, pp. 1ff., for a discussion of these passages); and at *Met.* 1059a10ff. he turns this point into an argument against the Theory of Forms. Had he clearly seen that Plato's Forms are self-predicational, he would have argued to even better effect that, on this hypothesis, the Forms which *are* predicable of the particulars *qua* particulars (e.g., perishableness, change, mortality) have predicates incompatible with their predicates *qua* Forms (e.g., imperishableness, changelessness, immortality).

[37] *Parm.* 136b.

[38] The only Form in whose case one might think that Plato did feel such a difficulty is that of Not-Being. But a careful study of his discussion of Not-Being in the *Sophist* will, I think, show that the real difficulty Plato felt about Not-Being was not *caused* by reasoning that, since all Forms are self-predicational, this Form must also be such and hence have the character of not being. The difficulty he states at 240d–241b is simply that of thinking what is not, without, by this very fact, being involved in the contradictory assumption that what is not is. His discussion of Not-Being cannot, therefore, be cited as evidence that he understood Self-Predication.

be trivial. If the Form is what we have seen it to be, how could it help being other than the particulars whose characters it enables us to discern? Indeed, it might be said that Plato is the first Western thinker to make the distinction between a character and the things that have that character a matter of philosophical reflection. For did not his Theory of Forms call attention, and for the first time, to the "reality" of universals as distinct from that of material existents? This is, of course, perfectly true. But what is no less true is that the Platonic ontology inadvertently blurs the very distinction it was devised to express. It compels Plato to think of the difference between empirical existents and their intelligible properties as a difference between "deficiently" real and perfectly real things, i.e., as a difference in degree between beings of the same kind, instead of a difference in kind between different kinds of being. To say that the difference between a white thing, like wool or snow, and the universal, Whiteness, is a difference in degree of reality, is to put Whiteness in the same class with white things albeit as a preeminent member of that class, endowed in preeminent degree with the character which its fellow members possess in variously deficient degrees; it is to think of Whiteness as a (superlatively) white thing, and thus to assimilate it categorically to white things, instead of so distinguishing it from them. For a good example of this, I can refer to the closing sentence of the statement of the Separation Assumption I have cited above from *Parmenides* 130b: "And do you believe that Similarity itself is something separately from the Similarity which we possess?" Instead of asking the simple question, "Is the property, [340] Similarity, distinct from any of the things that have that property?" Plato is misled by his Separation Assumption to ask the entirely different question, "Is the property, Similarity, distinct from the property of Similarity which is exemplified in particular instances of Similarity?"[39] To say "yes" to *this* question is

---

[39] This is why a symbolic transcript of Plato's statements must distinguish systematically between the substantival form, F-ness, and the adjectival or predicative function of the same Form, F. Thus, in transcribing the First Man Argument, it was necessary to distinguish between Largeness, as F-ness, and the Largeness of large things, as F. Similarly the Nonidentity Assumption must be rendered as, "If a is F, a cannot be identical with F-ness," (A4a), (B4a) above. Were it not for the systematic dualism of F and F-ness, it could be stated more simply as, "If a is F, a cannot be identical with F," which I take to be the correct statement of this fundamental principle. In the absence of the Separation Assumption, we would not need the two symbols, F and F-ness; the latter would be redundant. To recognize this is perhaps the simplest way of collapsing the Third Man Argument (and, unfortunately for Plato, thereby also collapsing the Separation Assumption). I may add that, though it is language which suggests the distinction between F-ness and F (by its double furniture of substantives and adjectives or predicative terms), yet neither can this distinction be observed without occasional violence to the linguistic distinction (for we are still forced to transcribe as "F" any term which refers to the property of a particular: the Largeness of large things or "the Similarity which we possess" must be taken, on Plato's own theory, as adjectival in sense though they are substantival in linguistic form). A simple linguistic explanation of Plato's theory would be only simpleminded.

to pass from the distinction between thing and property which every philosophy must acknowledge to the vastly different distinction, peculiar to Plato's
ontology, between two grades of reality in things and properties: perfectly real
things and properties in the Forms, imperfectly real things and properties in
the sensible world.

Among the unintended and unexpected consequences of this distinction is
the Nonidentity Assumption in its full-strength Form, (A4) and (B4) above,
i.e., that the nonidentity of a Form with any of its homonymous instances
holds not only when the instance is a particular but also when the instance is
the Form itself. Certainly Plato never said any such thing; indeed this is the
last thing he would have wished to say. The Separation Theory is clearly
meant to separate Forms from particulars, Largeness from large things, not to
reintroduce the separation within the formal pole of the Form-particular relation, to split [341] off Largeness from Largeness$_1$. Yet just this is the nemesis
of the Degrees-of-Reality Theory which is part and parcel of the Separation
Assumption. For if the Form, Largeness, is superlatively large, while large
mountains, oaks, etc. are only deficiently large, it must follow that the single
word, *large,* stands for two distinct predicates: (a) the predicate which attaches to the large particulars; (b) the predicate which attaches to Largeness.[40]
Call (a) "large" and (b) "large$_1$." Now since Largeness is, by hypothesis, the
Form of the predicate "large," it cannot be the Form of the different predicate
"large$_1$." There must then be two Forms, Largeness and Largeness$_1$, and the
full-strength form of the Nonidentity Assumption becomes unavoidable: not
only can no large particular be identical with the Form, Largeness, in virtue of
which it is seen as large, but Largeness itself cannot be identical with the
Form, Largeness$_1$, in virtue of which we see that it is large. The same reasoning which compelled the "separation" of any F particular from its corresponding Form, F-ness, also compels the "separation" of any Form from itself and
splits off F-ness from F-ness$_1$.

We can now see why Plato could neither convince himself that the Third
Man Argument was valid nor refute it convincingly. He could do neither without stating explicitly its two implicit assumptions. This he never did; he never

---

[40] If these two predicates were identical, the Form would be indistinguishable from the predicate which attaches to particulars, and the "Separation" would collapse: F-ness would then be the
F of F particulars, and the distinction between, e.g., "Similarity itself" and "the Similarity which
we possess" at 130b would vanish. Had Plato "believed that . . . the idea *is* that which the
particular *has* as an attribute" (Cherniss, p. 298)—a beautiful statement of what Plato's theory
should have been—the "Separation" would have never arisen. This is my main objection to
Cherniss' interpretation of the Third Man Argument (pp. 293–300): he does not see that the
"perfect reality" of the Forms is incompatible with their *being* the (imperfect) predicates of particulars. If the Forms *were* attributes of particulars, "Separation" would make no sense, and the
Third Man Argument would be not only pure sophistry but so easily refutable sophistry that it
would be impossible to understand why Plato takes it as seriously as he does yet leaves it
unrefuted.

looked at either of them in the clear light of explicit assertion, for had he done so he would have had compelling reason to repudiate both, since their logical consequences are intolerable to a rational mind. But their repudiation would have been fatal to the Separation [342] Theory and the Degrees-of-Reality Theory, which are central to his explicit metaphysics. He was thus holding consciously a metaphysical Theory whose disastrous implications were hidden from his conscious mind. He was saying and believing things which in self-consistency he would have had to take back, had he clearly understood their true logical outcome.

D. The Record of Honest Perplexity

Now it is perfectly possible to be in this state of mind and have no inkling of its insecurity. The run-of-the-mill dogmatist lives in it all his life and never feels any the worse for it. The victims of the Socratic elenchus were cheerfully confident that they knew what they were talking about, and they would have ever remained so had they recited their ignorant certainties to anyone but Socrates. But a great philosopher is not likely to be so thick-skinned and so blind. Perfect catharsis from self-deception is given to him no more than to his fellows. But he is far more likely to become aware sooner or later of the difference between those areas of his thought where he has achieved true lucidity and those where he has not. When he first projects a new theory that succeeds in solving to his immediate satisfaction hitherto unsolved problems and satisfies deep longings of his heart, delight in his creation may produce a kind of rapture that leaves little room for self-questioning. This is Plato's mood in the *Phaedo,* the *Symposium,* and the *Republic.* The Theory of Forms is then the greatest of certainties, a place of unshakable security to which he may retreat when doubtful or perplexed about anything else.[41] But as he lives with his new theory and puts it to work, its limitations begin to close in upon him. He begins to feel that something is wrong, or at least not quite right, about his theory, and he is puzzled and anxious. If he has courage enough, he will not try to get rid of his anxiety by suppressing it. He may then make repeated attempts to get at the source of [343] the trouble; and if he cannot get at it directly, he may fall back on the device of putting the troublesome symptoms into the form of objections. He can hardly make these objections perfectly precise and consistent counterarguments to his theory{.} unless he discovers the exact source of its difficulties and can embody the discovery [in the

---

[41] Transparently so at *Phaedo* 99c ff.; the "refuge" metaphor is Plato's own, 99c5. Another characteristic of this mood is the grandiose schemes which it projects, such as the hope for a complete deduction of all the Forms from the form of the Good in the closing paragraphs of Bk. 6 of the *Republic,* a scheme which is never worked out in the dialogues, doubtless for the reason that it is unworkable.

formal premises of the objections. If he fails to make this discovery⟧, the objections are likely to be as inadequate in their own way as is their target. They will be the expression of his acknowledged but unresolved puzzlement, brave efforts to impersonate and cope with an antagonist who can neither be justly represented nor decisively defeated because he remains unidentified and unseen. This, I believe, is an exact diagnosis of Plato's mind at the time he wrote the *Parmenides*.

1. THE FIRST OBJECTION, *PARMENIDES* 130e–131e

Of the three formal objections to the Theory of Forms, first has struck every reader by its patent crudity of expression: if a single Form has many instances, either the whole of the Form must be "in"[42] each of them, or only a part of the Form; if the first, the Form will be "in" each instance "in separation" from itself;[43] if the second, only a fraction of the Form will be in each instance, so that the latter will not be an instance of this Form, F-ness, but of another Form, F-ness$_1$, which will be a fraction of F-ness.[44] The words of the argument force the conception of Forms into the flagrantly inappropriate terms of quasi-physical location, separation, and division. Hence many commentators have drawn the inference that the difficulty they [344] portray is wholly fictitious and that Plato knew that it was such. But this inference is certainly wrong, since, as their critics have remarked,[45] Plato reasserts the difficulty in almost identical terms in the *Philebus* (15b–c), though this time not as an objection to his Theory but as a problem which continues to cause him extreme perplexity and to which he has still to find an answer. Certainly Plato knew that the relation of Form to instance, whatever else it might be, is not that of physical coalescence of either the whole Form or else a part of the Form with any one of its instances. And he could easily demolish Parmenides' objection by replying that its very language misdirects it against a man of straw. He did not waste a word to win this cheap dialectical victory because he

---

[42] *Parm.* 131a8, *en . . . einai*, b2, *enestai*. Plato indulged in this way of talking about instantiation in the middle dialogues, as, e.g., at *Phaedo* 103b8. The word *eneinai* had a bewildering variety of uses in common speech (see LSJ, *s.v.*). But in cosmological and medical usage, it had reached a single, definite meaning: "*x* is in *y*" had come to mean, "*x* is a physical ingredient in physical compound *y*," as I have remarked in ⟨"Equality and Justice in Early Greek Cosmologies"⟩ *CP* 42 (1947), 171 and n. 139 (**1.78 and n. 139).

[43] Here is the immediate nemesis of the *chorismos*, announced at ⟨131⟩b–e, but of an intolerably crude one, since it talks of the (physical) "separation" of particulars from one another and of the (metaphysical) "separation" of Form from particulars in the same sentence (131b1–2) as though the word had the same sense in the two cases.

[44] The analogy of the sail dots the *is* of the transposition of a metaphysical statement into a physical one.

[45] E.g., Robinson, pp. 59–60.

knew that the difficulty lay at a much deeper level, which he eagerly sought to reach, but which he failed to reach, as the phrasing of the objection shows.

What remained hidden to him becomes clear to us when we note, with Cornford (p. 87), that in illustrating the argument with the Form, Largeness, Parmenides at one point obviously assumes that Largeness is self-predicational: "Suppose you divide the Largeness itself, and each of the many large things is then large by *virtue of a Portion of Largeness which is smaller than Largeness itself . . .*" (131c–d). To say that a "part" of the Form, Largeness, is *smaller* than Largeness is most certainly to imply that Largeness is large. Less obviously, but no less certainly, the same assumption and the Separation Assumption of which it is a part are involved in, and are the source of, the whole difficulty which the objection seeks to express, and if we put these Assumptions into our question we can state the difficulty without indulging in the irrelevant language of the text: If F-ness is F and is such in virtue of satisfying requirements which no empirical particular can satisfy, how can any empirical particular be F? If it were genuinely or perfectly F, it would have to be identical with F-ness, which is contrary to the hypothesis that it is not the Form but a particular. If it were not, it could not be said to be fully F, but only "deficiently" F, or F in lesser degree; it would then be not F, but F_1, where F_1 is the lesser degree of F instantiated in the particular. This alternative obviously leads to an infinite [345] regress, symmetrical with that of the Third Man Argument:[46] for, by the same reasoning, if F_1 be a character, it can only be perfectly exemplified by the Form, F-ness$_1$, and the particular could not then be F_1, but only F_2, and so on *ad infinitum*. So stated, the objection exposes the self-contradiction of the Separation Assumption when fully explicated to involve both Self-Predication and the Degrees-of-Reality Theory. Plato could not have stated it in this way without stating one of the components of this complex premise, Self-Predication.

2. THE THIRD OBJECTION, *PARMENIDES* 133b–134e

Plato faces this one in a more hopeful mood. It could be answered, he says, but only to (and, presumably, by) an extremely competent and persistent thinker.[47] Why then doesn't he answer it? Not because he is pressed for time; the second part of the *Parmenides* shows that he has plenty of time. He doesn't, because the answer he would have given to this objection, as to the

---

[46] Each of the two regresses exposes symmetrical contradictions in the Theory which may be stated as follows:

    (a) If the Form be F, then it cannot be F, but F_1 (as we have seen at (B5a) in Sec. I, above);

    (b) if the particular be F, then it cannot be F, but F_1.

[47] *Parm.* 133b.

first, would not have solved the problem which is infinitely more important to him than the defeat of the objector. Nor could he have solved this without, once again, spotting the Self-Predication Assumption which, enmeshed in the Degrees-of-Reality Theory, greets us here at every turn.[48] The argument implied that only the Form, Mastership, can possess "exactly"[49] the [346] property of mastership and (since the property is a relational one) only in relation to the Form, Slavery, which alone possess "exactly" the converse property of slavishness; and that only the Form, Knowledge, can be "exactly" knowledge.[50] Hence, it infers, you and I cannot *be* Masters or Slaves, since we are men, not Forms, and cannot have the properties of Forms but only less "exact," or "human," properties of mastership or slavishness or anything else; nor can we have Knowledge (for this is the prerogative of the Form, Knowledge, and we are not the Form), but only something else which is less "exact" than Knowledge. Anyone familiar with Plato's Theory of the Soul, which includes his Theory of Recollection, would have known how to talk back to Parmenides at this point. One could discredit Parmenides by telling him that he grossly ignored a part, and a most important and relevant part, of the philosophy he is criticizing. But if this had silenced Parmenides, it would have left untouched the logical difficulty, which is precisely the same as in the first objection and raises the same unanswerable question: If only *F*-ness can be *F*, how can anything else be *F*?

3. THE THIRD MAN ARGUMENT ONCE AGAIN

Seen side by side with its mates, it appears to great advantage. Its language is [logically] refined in contrast to the crudity of the first, terse and precise where that of the third is loose and longwinded. The device it exploits, the infinite regress, was the prize product of Greek logical virtuosity, and Plato must have found a bitter delight in turning it against his own Theory. Yet, for all its showy elegance, it fails as a diagnostic device to locate the exact source of the logical difficulties of the Theory of Forms, for the reasons which I set forth in

[48] So Cornford, p. 98. But he naively infers that, because Self-Predication is "grossly fallacious," Plato saw that it was. Had Plato seen this, he would have said so; and for this he would not have needed "a long and remote train of argument" which Plato tells us (133b) would be required to defeat the objection; the Greek equivalent of Cornford's single sentence ("It confuses the Form . . . with perfect instances of the Form") would have been enough. And had he done so, Plato would have seen what Cornford fails to see: that this demolition of the objection to the Theory would have demolished the Theory.

[49] He introduces this term only toward the end (134c–d), but the whole argument would have gained precision had he done so from the start. The argument turns on the difference in degree between the exemplification of the Form in the Form and in the particulars: "exact" Mastership, Knowledge, etc., refers to the former against the latter, to render the sense of "perfect," "complete."

[50] Cf. *Phaedr.* 247d–e.

Section I. And it fails also in its formal purpose, which is to prove that the Theory is logically bankrupt because it involves an endless regress. It could only have succeeded in this, had it been known to be a valid argument; but it could not be known to be this, unless the tacit premises which alone can warrant the inference from its first to [347] its second step were supplied. I trust it has now become clear that Plato could not supply these and so could not know whether or not it was a valid objection to his theory. This being the case, I can now show that Plato had a perfectly good way of refuting the Third Man Argument as stated by his Parmenides.[51] All his Parmenides has to offer in place of the two tacit premises is the Separation Assumption in its explicit form, i.e., not understood to imply both Self-Predication and full-strength Nonidentity. But if these implications are not understood, the conclusion of Parmenides' argument is grossly fallacious, and Plato could easily have shown it to be such:

If the Separation Assumption is to be the reason for acknowledging the "separate existence" of the predicative Form, F-ness, from the particulars of which it is predicated, Plato could argue that the same Assumption could not require, but must forbid, the separation of the next predicative Form, F-ness$_1$, from the original Form, F-ness, of which F-ness$_1$ is predicated; and if *this* separation were to fail, the infinite regress would fail. Plato could argue that his metaphysical theory is only intended to separate Forms from particulars, since the ground of the separation is that only the Forms could satisfy the stipulated conditions of being. "If that is so," he could ask,

> what warrant is there for saying that F-ness$_1$ is separate from F-ness? Both, as Forms, fully satisfy the conditions of being, both have exactly the same degree of reality, and the ontological separation premised on a difference of such degree fails completely. Thus Beauty is separate from any beautiful thing of our common experience because its beauty is so different from theirs—an intelligible, changeless, unblemished beauty such as, alas, we have never seen in the [348] world about us and never will. In what respect then could Beauty$_1$ differ from Beauty? How could the two fail to coincide, if they both designate the highest degree of beauty?

By such a reply Plato could have stopped the regress dead in its tracks, easily in the first version of the Argument and also in the second, by merely pointing

---

[51] Other ways of reconstructing Plato's refutation of the Argument abound in the literature (e.g., Taylor, *Plato's Parmenides*, pp. 20ff.; Goblot, pp. 474ff.; Cornford, pp. 90ff.; Cherniss, pp. 292ff.), but I believe that none of them is free from one or more of the following errors: misunderstanding of the Argument; the view that Plato did not in fact assume Self-Predication; the misapprehension that an argument, somewhat similar in form to the Third Man Argument, employed elsewhere (see above, n. 12 *sub fin.*) by Plato to establish the unity of each Form, somehow explodes the Third Man Argument. Ross (p. 87) has an admirably terse refutation of this last misapprehension: "To show that if there were two Ideas of bed there would have to be a third does nothing to disprove the contention that if there is one Idea of bed, related to particulars as Plato supposes, there must be a second."

out that the model-copy relation of predicate to instance is meant to hold only when the instance is an empirical particular and not when both predicate and instance are Forms. He could thus defeat the Argument by retreating in effect to the weaker form of the Nonidentity Assumption (A4a), (B4a) above. His objection would stand unless Parmenides could then go on to show why, in spite of it, the Degrees-of-Reality Theory did imply full-strength Nonidentity, (A4), (B4) above.

It is rare enough to find a philosopher employing his best resources to construct an argument which, were it valid, would have destroyed the logical foundations of his life's work.[52] What is rarer still and, to my knowledge, absolutely without parallel in the pages of Western philosophy, is to find a man who faces such an emergency as Plato did. He had every reason to seek to demolish it, for it was believed to be valid, as, e.g., by Aristotle; and so long as he left it standing, it remained an ugly threat to his most original philosophical contribution. And he had a way and, by every rule of disputation, a perfectly fair way, of demolishing the argument, by taking it at face value and replying not to what it implies but to what it says. His reticence at this point is a remarkable tribute to his perspicacity as a thinker and to his honesty as a man. To study the Third Man Argument in this way is to see the stature of the philosopher rising far above the limitations of his philosophy.[53]
[349]

---

[52] I believe it is a mistake to think (e.g., with Ross, pp. 87ff.) that the Argument is fatal not to Plato's Theory, but to the language in which he expressed it. It should now be apparent that the butt of the Argument is no incidental expression whose excision from Plato's text would leave his Theory intact, but the literal, rock-bottom doctrine of his ontology: the Degrees-of-Reality Theory and the Separation Assumption.

[53] Max Black has given me generous help with this paper. Though he cannot be held responsible for any statement in it, his advice and criticism have saved me from many mistakes.

12b

ADDENDUM TO THE THIRD MAN ARGUMENT

IN THE *PARMENIDES*

THE FOLLOWING ANALYSIS of the Third Man Argument avoids a few technical defects in my earlier one:

1. If any set of things are F, there exists a unique Form, F-ness, in virtue of which each of them is F.

1a. a, b, c, are F.

From 1 (a fair enough statement of one of the cardinal tenets of Plato's ontology) and 1a (a commonplace), it follows that

1b. F-ness exists.

Now Parmenides goes on (*Parm.* 132a6–11) to assert that

2. If a, b, c, and F-ness are F, there exists a second Form, F-ness$_1$, in virtue of which a, b, c, and F-ness are F.

But the antecedent of this hypothetical does not follow from anything said above. 1a, 1, and 1b do not entail that F-ness is F. To derive this, we need a new assumption,

SP. The Form in virtue of which a set of things have a certain character itself has that character.

From this, given 1, it follows that

3. F-ness is F.

From 3 and 1a we can now derive the antecedent of 2,

2a. a, b, c, and F-ness are F.

Even so, the consequent of 2 does not follow: what is there to keep F–ness itself from being the Form in virtue of which a, b, c, and F-ness are F? To exclude this possibility, we need another assumption, [261]

NI. The Form in virtue of which a set of things have a certain character is not identical with any of them.

Given this, 1 and 2a, we can now infer the consequent of 2,

2b. A second Form, F-ness$_1$, exists, in virtue of which a, b, c, and F-ness are F.

The existence of a Third Form, F-ness$_2$, and so *ad infinitum* would then follow by iteration of the reasoning.

From R. E. Allen, ed., *Studies in Plato's Metaphysics* (Routledge & Kegan Paul, 1965), pp. 261–63. Used by permission.

Just three comments:

(1) I pointed out in 1955 (⟨"Addenda to the 'Third Man Argument'"⟩ *PR* 64, 442–43 ⟨**2.198–99⟩) that Plato supplies us with the materials for two distinct (but complementary) versions of the argument he puts out so briefly in *Parmenides,* 132a1–b2: an ontological and an epistemological one. The latter would run as follows (I underline those phrases which mark the differences from the ontological version I have just given above):

1. If any set of things are *F,* there exists a unique Form, *F*-ness, in virtue of which each of them is *apprehended as F.*

1a. 1b: as above.

2. If *a, b, c,* and *F*-ness are *F,* there exists a second Form, *F*-ness₁, in virtue of which *a, b, c,* and *F*-ness are *apprehended as F.*

SP. The Form in virtue of which a set of things *are apprehended as having* a certain character itself has that character.

3 and 2a.: as above.

NI. The Form in virtue of which a set of things *are apprehended as having* a certain character is not identical with any of them.

2b. A second Form, *F*-ness₁, exists, in virtue of which *a, b, c,* and *F*-ness are *apprehended as F.*

The textual warrant for this second version is very plain: "Will not a single largeness appear once again, *in virtue of which all these will appear large?*" (132a6–7). How a critic can quote these words and brush them aside with the remark that "this is not sufficient evidence" for my view (⟨A. L. Peck, "Plato Versus Parmenides"⟩ *PR* 71 (1962), ⟨159–84, at⟩ 164n. 8), I find it hard to understand. Nor can I see any justification for the view (expressed by the same critic, p. 164) that "we do not according to Plato need any Form to enable us to discern that particulars are *X.*" Plato does not, of course, tell us that we need to *know* the [262] Form, Equality, in order to discern equality in the things we see. But he does hold that we need to *have known* the Form in the prenatal state and to have retained so much of this "precognition" (*Phaed.,* 74e9) as will enable us to use the Form as the standard to which we "refer" the things we see and judge to be defectively equal (*Phaed.,* 75b). Some sort of apprehension of Equality, however imperfect, then we all must have, since we are all supposed to make such judgments. Nor does this involve Plato in any formal contradiction, since what he calls 'knowledge' is an austere accomplishment, entailing the ability to "give an account" (*Phaed.,* 76b) of the Form in statements which are "infallibly" (*Rep.,* 477e) true. So he can claim that only dialecticians have "knowledge" of Equality without denying the rest of humanity that less articulate grasp of the concept which they need to measure correctly, to calculate effectively, and the like. This is the sort of thing Plato evidently has in mind when he speaks of the Form Largeness in this argument as that "in virtue of which all these will appear (i.e., will be apprehended as) large." Were it not for the Form, things would neither be, nor appear to be, large. Both assertions are good Platonic doctrine, and Plato would have every reason for putting both into this argument.

(2) "Self-Predication." I am not enamored of this term and now use it only because it seems well-established in the literature. It should be obvious that when extended from "*white* is white" to "the Form, Whiteness, is white," *Self-Predication* is used with a certain license. Strictly speaking, what is predicated of itself is the character which things have (and are apprehended as having) in virtue of the Form.

(3) "Nonidentity." It has been claimed (R. S. Bluck, "The *Parmenides* and the 'Third Man,'" *CQ,* N.S. 6 (1956), pp. 29ff., on p. 30) that in the full-strength form (in which it applies to Forms no less than to particulars) this assumption "is not in fact involved in Plato's Theory." There is at least one passage that proves that it is: the famous argument in the *Republic* (597c) that if there were two Forms of Bed, there would have to be a third, "whose character both of them would have" (ἧς ἐκεῖναι ἂν αὖ ἀμφότεραι τὸ εἶδος ἔχοιεν). Were it not for this assumption, there would be no reason why there would have to be a *third* Form, i.e., why the required Form should not be identical with either the first or the second of the supposed Forms.

12c

ADDENDA TO THE THIRD MAN ARGUMENT: A REPLY

TO PROFESSOR SELLARS

PROFESSOR SELLARS' discussion has helped me to rethink the first version of the Third Man Argument in the *Parmenides* (⟨**2.166ff.⟩ the "TMA," I shall call it hereafter). I now understand some things about it much better than when I wrote my earlier paper,[1] as will appear in the course of Sections I and II below. But I cannot in good conscience follow up my expression of indebtedness to Sellars on this score by conceding the "confusions" with which he belabors me. To exonerate myself from his charges point by point would not be hard, but it would be a bore for the reader. Though a paper such as this cannot avoid controversy, it can at least direct it to matters of substantial and general interest, as I have tried to do here. I have accordingly devoted the last section of the paper to a critique of that very considerable part of Sellars's interpretation of Plato which is still so widespread that it may fairly be called "orthodox."

I

In Section VI of his paper, Sellars formulates what he takes to be the TMA in the *Parmenides*. What he presents is a perfectly lucid and cogent deductive argument, and also a reasonably elegant one. The only trouble with it is that it is not Plato's. The crucial difference occurs in its opening propositions, (1) and (2). Sellars's (1) reads, "If *a, b, c,* etc., are *F*, there is *an F*-ness by virtue of which they are *F*." Substituting [438] Plato's instance "large" for "*F*," the

From *PR* 64 (1955): 438–48, in response to Wilfrid Sellars, "Vlastos and the 'Third Man,'" ibid.: 405–37.

[1] It is only fair to add that I have also been helped, directly or indirectly, by comments I had previously received in correspondence with Mr. Peter Geach, Mr. Keith Donnellan, and Professor Raphael Demos, and in discussion with Professor Harold Cherniss. Geach and Donnellan had raised, though differently from each other and from Sellars, the same fundamental question on the interpretation of the first step of the TMA which will be discussed below. Donnellan had worked out along somewhat different lines from Sellars a formalization of the TMA which makes of it, as does that of Sellars, an internally consistent argument leading to an infinite series, but not involving a logically vicious infinite regress. Geach agrees with me that the TMA reveals a deep-seated incoherence in Plato's implicit premises, though his account of this is not quite the same as mine, and I have urged him to publish his highly original and illuminating reflections on this topic.

statement Sellars thinks Parmenides is making in the first step of the Argument is, "If *a*, *b*, *c*, etc., are all large, there is *a* Largeness by virtue of which they are large." I have italicized the word which makes all the difference in the interpretation. The sense of "a Largeness" is the same as "some Largeness or other"; though even this does not bring out the point at issue as well as do Sellars' excellent remarks in Section IV. "What is *F*-ness?" he asks there; is it a "representative symbol" or a "variable proper"? He decides for the latter. Thus "Largeness" in the TMA, Sellars thinks, is not to be construed as the proper name of an individual Form, but rather as a variable, and the "substituends" for it (its values), "would be designated by some such device as the use of numerical subscripts, e.g., 'Largeness$_1$,' 'Largeness$_2$,' etc." To put this in another way: On Sellars' interpretation of what is asserted in the TMA, the well-known word *Largeness,* does not refer to a unique Form but to a class of Forms, for which Largeness is the generic name and whose individual members, nameless in common speech, may be baptized for the purposes of the Argument, Largeness$_1$, Largeness$_2$, etc. The consequent of "if there are a number of large things" is not, according to Sellars's Plato, "there is a single Form, and its name is 'Largeness,'" but "there is a class of Forms, and the name of this class is 'Largeness.'" To be sure, the fact that Largeness is a class-name does not imply that the class it names has more than one member; all it implies is that it *may* have more than one member. Thus what we have in "Largeness" at the start, on Sellars' interpretation, is the name of a class of Largenesses, which might have any number of members, from one to infinity; and if, as it turns out, the class does have an infinite number of members, this in no way *contradicts* the premise stated in the first step of the Argument.

Now let us look at the text: "I suppose this is what leads you to suppose that there is in every case *a single Form:* When several things seem large to you, it seems perhaps that there is *a single Form* which is the same in your view of all of them. Hence you believe that *Largeness is a single thing.*" I have underlined the expressions, no less than three of them, one on top of the other, in all of which the word *single* appears in the translation (*hen hekaston, mia, hen to mega*). Is there any suggestion here that the hypothesis which is put forward is to the effect that wherever we find a set of things with the same character there is a class of Forms, one member of which is the required one for this set of things, or, more simply, that there is at least one Form to serve this purpose? None at all. On the contrary, it is perfectly clear in the last [439] sentence of the above text that *Largeness* is the name of a single Form that will do the job—not, as Sellars would have it, the name of a class of Forms some one or another of which will do the job. If Sellars's interpretation were correct, Plato's Parmenides would have inferred in the text above the existence of a Form which he would have had to *distinguish* from Largeness, indicating somehow or other that Largeness is *not* the name of this Form. This is the opposite of what he does, using Largeness (*to mega*) or Largeness Itself (*auto to megethos*) in the following sentence (132a6) as the name of the Form inferred at the first step of the argument. Thus on Sellars' formulation Plato has done something in this first step (the text cited above) which is not only different from, but contrary to, what he has in fact done. The first time something turns up that has to be—and is—distinguished from "Largeness" in the text is in the *second* step (132a6ff.); this is what I designate by Largeness$_1$, Sellars by Largeness$_2$. Plato uses the expression "another Form of Largeness" for this purpose, and the context immediately supplies the answer to our question, "Other than what?" "Another Form of Largeness will appear, over and above Largeness itself." This new Form is thus contrasted with "Largeness itself," which shows, once again, that "Largeness" is *not* a "variable proper" or generic name for a class of Forms, but the name of an individual Form, the first member of the series to which the second step of the Argument adds a second.

There is one more thing about the text to forbid Sellars's interpretation. Compare its opening lines, cited above, with its concluding text: "And *you will no longer have in every case a single Form,* but an infinite number (of Forms)."[2] The italicized statement is the *contradictory* of the initial hypothesis "that there is in every case a single Form." The initial hypothesis stands to the conclusion as *p* to not-*p,* and the logical form of the argument is, "If *p* [and . . .], then not-*p;* therefore, not-*p.*" Of this, the hypothetical, "if *p,* then not-*p*" is explicit in the argument and is the favorite device of Eleatic logic, the *reductio ad absurdum.* The conclusion, "therefore, not-*p,*" is not stated as such but is, of course, implied. For what is Parmenides doing here but going to work to [440] refute Plato's Theory of Forms, and what conclusion is he bent on establishing except that the Theory is false?

Where is all this in Sellars's formulation? His Argument does not have the "if *p,* then not-*p*" form; nothing in its conclusion contradicts its initial hypothesis. On this account alone it would have to be ruled out, since the contradiction of hypothesis by conclusion is large as life in Plato's text. And why has this contradiction vanished in Sellars's account? Because Parmenides' hypothesis has been reconditioned by Sellars in the manner described above. If we smooth out of the hypothesis the crucial stipulation that there is just one Form for any set of homonymous things and stipulate merely that there is at least one Form, everything will go very smoothly. Under Sellars's skillful guidance, we shall coast past an infinite number of successive Largenesses, whose endless multiplicity was not precluded by our logical starting-point. We shall thus never suffer the nasty shock of contradiction anywhere along the line;

---

[2] I have translated this sentence in such a way as to conserve full consistency with the translation of 132a1, as unfortunately Cornford's does not, rendering the expression *hen hekaston* "in each case" at 132a1 and "each of (your Forms)" at 132b2. There can be no doubt that the sense, the same in both sentences, is that there is a single *F*-ness for any given *F* (asserted in the first, denied in the second), and so long as the translation makes this clear, its precise wording is a secondary matter.

moving along a logically harmless infinite series, the unpleasant surprise of an infinite *regress* will be spared us. Why stick by Plato's Parmenides, who is going to treat us so much more roughly?

Among the various improvements Sellars brings to Plato's TMA is to remove the contradiction between the tacit premises of Self-Predication ⟨SP⟩ and Nonidentity ⟨NI⟩. In place of my (A_3), "*F*-ness is *F*," Sellars puts his (SP), "All *F*-nesses are *F*"; and for my (A_4), "If *x* is *F*, *x* cannot be identical with *F*-ness," Sellars has his (NI), "If *x* is *F*, then *x* is not identical with the *F*-ness by virtue of which it is *F*"; and the result of the substitutions is certainly, as Sellars says, that "the inconsistency vanishes." He feels very happy about this, and not without good reason, for who would not be relieved if Plato could be exonerated from the muddle of keeping two incompatible premises at the back of his head? The historian, unless venting his personal frustrations in aggressions against his subject, would like to think as well of Plato's thought as the facts will allow; and he would be as pleased as anyone if he could believe that Plato found his way to true consistency in this as in other matters. But the facts in this case are the texts; we can only reconstruct the form of Plato's true implicit premises from the form of Plato's explicit premises as stated by himself; and this, unfortunately, requires us to believe, for the reasons given above, that "Largeness" (and so "*F*-ness") is not a variable but the name of an individual Form, contrary to the assumption which is built into Sellars's (SP) and (NI). We must, therefore, harden our hearts and withhold from Plato this particular benefit with which Sellars would endow him. [441]

II

Now for another point about the TMA, the first one Sellars raises in his paper. It concerns the underlined words in my (A1): "If a number of things, *a, b, c,* are all *F*, there must be a single Form, *F*-ness, in virtue of which *we apprehend a, b, c, as* all *F*." Sellars says that the text can be so taken as to replace "we apprehend . . . as . . ." by simply "are"; i.e., that a reference to the apprehension of *F* things as *F* in virtue of *F*-ness does not really belong in Plato's argument; or, to put it differently, that Parmenides' argument deals only with the ontological thesis that *F* things imply the existence of *F*-ness and not at all with the epistemological thesis that the apprehension of *F* things implies the apprehension of *F*-ness. I was too excited over other things when I wrote my paper to anticipate this particular question, and I am grateful for the opportunity to deal with it now.

First of all, what does the text say? In the first step (132a1–4, cited above) it is admittedly ambiguous on this point. Its references to "seeming" and "viewing" could be taken, as Sellars observes, "to pertain to the *discovery* of the principle which is to function as a premise of the TMA, rather than as constituent elements in the principle itself" (p. 406). But look now at the text when it moves on to the second step of the Argument at 132a6–8: "What then if you similarly view mentally Largeness itself and the other large things? Will not a single Largeness appear once again *in virtue of which all these appear large?*" If Sellars has noticed the italicized words here, he says nothing about them. Don't they make it clear that Plato *is* thinking of the epistemological function of the Form in the course of his argument? For if not, why should he say that it is in virtue of this (second) Largeness that large things *appear* large, instead of just saying that in virtue of it they *are* large? *Here* the epistemological function is quite explicit in his mind. But a few lines later, he does shift to an expression which does *not* contain this epistemological reference: "and, covering all these, yet another (Largeness) by virtue of which they will all *be* large."

What are we going to make of this state of affairs? We can really get *two* arguments out of the text; (1) One, as formulated in my previous paper, but with no reference to the epistemological function of the Form.[3] (2) Another in which this reference is preserved. [442]

The difference in logical form between (1) and (2) would be considerable. (1) would *not* be an infinite regress, though, as I explained above, it would be a *reductio ad absurdum.* An infinite regress arises when, and only when, the truth of a premise, *P,* implies the fulfillment of a condition, *c;* which is such that the first step required to fulfill it cannot be taken unless a second step has first been taken, nor the second unless a third, and so on throughout an infinite series of subsequent steps, a series which, being infinite, can never be exhausted; whence it follows that the first step can never be taken and, hence, that *c* cannot be fulfilled, and hence, finally, that *P* is false. This is clearly a special case of a *reductio ad absurdum.* Now the only way we can get an infinite regress out of the TMA is to include in all of its relevant statements a reference to *F*-ness as the Form by virtue of which we apprehend *F* things as *F;* and this is what we do have in (2). Thus in (1) and (2) we have two distinct arguments, whose premises differ by the addition in (2) of a premise, absent from (1), to the effect that any *F* thing is apprehended as *F* in virtue of *F*-ness. The targets of (1) and (2) are Plato's ontology and epistemology respectively. Each of them, if valid, is a fatal objection to views which are elsewhere asserted by Plato: (1) to the view that for any set of *F*s there can be only a single Form; (2) to the view that the apprehension of any *F* thing implies the apprehension ("recollection") of *F*-ness. The TMA *can* be taken as through it were nothing but (1), and I have so taken it in the preceding section, for Sellars's version of the TMA deliberately ignores (2) and is sufficiently refuted by evidence that nothing less than (1) will fit the text. But it would not

---

[3] I.e., substituting "in virtue of which . . . are all *F*" for "in virtue of which we apprehend . . . as all *F*" at (A1) and (A2), and similarly "in virtue of which it has that character" for "in virtue of which we apprehend that character" at (A4).

be right to suggest that (2) can be left out of a *complete* account of Parmenides' argument. On the contrary, I am convinced that, on the evidence, what Plato intends here is an infinite regress which, of course, can only be rendered at (2). For had he intended no more than (1), the demonstration that there is an *infinity* of Forms of Largeness would be strictly supernumerary to his argument. For the purposes of (1), he would not need to prove that there is an infinite number of Largenesses; it would have been amply sufficient to prove that there are two. This consideration is, of course, not conclusive by itself; it only proves that if the TMA were just (1), it would be uneconomical; and certainly Plato could have allowed himself some logical extravagance from time to time, though the extreme terseness of the text suggests that here Plato is husbanding his logical resources with the utmost economy. What clinches the point is the textual evidence at 132a8, cited in the preceding paragraph, where a reference to the epistemological function of the Form is unambiguous and explicit. [443]

III

In the second part of his paper (Sections VIIff.), Sellars attempts to show that Plato's thought was not burdened with Self-Predication. His argument is a welcome defense of a well-known position, like that of Taylor and Cornford, which is doubtless still held and will continue to be held. All I can do within the limits of this paper is to deal with three of the props of the interpretation he offers. But since these, or their equivalents, are essential to uphold it, it is sufficient for my present purpose to show briefly how very shaky they are.

A. *Self-predication*[4] *in the Parmenides.* By the time he wrote this dialogue, says Sellars, Plato "had faced up to the question, 'Is, e.g., The Large Itself large?' and answered it in the negative"; indeed, "the first part of the *Parmen-*

---

[4] Sellars offers the following as the "correct" formulation of Self-Predication: "The adjective corresponding to the name of any Form can correctly be predicated of that Form." I have no objection to this as such. What I do object to is his preceding statement, "that it is not Largeness which is predicated of Largeness, but rather 'large' or (material mode) *being large.*" He says this is "obvious"; but it is not even true. Anyone who asserts that "Justice is just" *is* predicating Justice of Justice, since in any statement of the form "*x* is just," the character expressed by the predicate is predicated of the subject, whether the predicative expression be construed as an adjective, "being just," or as a substantive, "justice." Now there is a difficulty for Plato here, but it goes much deeper than the one which seems to worry Sellars and would remain if we were to give Sellars all that he asks and settle for his own statement as the completely and uniquely correct formulation of Self-Predication. The trouble issues from Plato's Separation and Degrees-of-Reality Theory, which imply that the *F* of the Form is *not* the same as the *F* of its homonymous particulars, whence it would certainly follow that if "large" is predicated of particulars (and who could deny this?) then it cannot be predicated of Largeness; so "being large" *cannot* be predicated of Largeness, after all. What happens then to Self-Predication even as formulated "correctly" by Sellars? This is, of course, only another aspect of the inconsistency which showed up in my paper as the formal contradiction between (A3) and (A4) at (A5).

ides is a deliberate and sustained critique of Self-Predicational interpretations of the Ideas." But neither Sellars nor those who would agree with him would suggest (they could not with the least plausibility) that Plato ever so much as stated Self-Predication in his writings. Isn't this very odd? Why should Plato wish to conceal his target? Is there any parallel in Plato of such secretiveness? Is there any in the whole history of philosophy? There have been philosophers who believed certain things but preferred for one reason or another to keep their opinions to themselves. But where would we find a philosopher who, knowing that a certain misinterpretation of his [444] doctrine was about, wrote a "deliberate and sustained critique" of it but carefully refrained from mentioning it and tucked it away instead among the tacit premises of his Argument, where no one, so far as we know, was able to spot it until well over two millennia after his death?

B. *Self-predication and imitation.* Sellars observes, quite rightly, that the mere fact that Plato used language which suggests Self-Predication is insufficient evidence for saying that he held it, and that to find evidence for this "one would have to show that Self-Predication plays a role in the *philosophical* use to which Plato put the language of the theory." But we do have such evidence in the Imitation- or Likeness-Theory of the relation of particulars to Forms. To say that an F particular is a copy or likeness of F-ness or, conversely, that F-ness is the model of the F particular, or that the two are similar, is to imply that F-ness is F. Can a particular be "like" a Form C-ness in respect of a given character, C, unless C-ness *has* the character C? Sellars seems to think that it can, though on what grounds he can think this I cannot imagine.[5] He never gives his grounds. When he comes to the point, or close to it (Section X, p. 432), he says "it just won't do to jump from the fact that Plato uses language with Self-Predicational implications [when he talks of the relation of Becoming to Being as that of imitation to original] to the conclusion that Plato thought of the ideas in Self-Predicational terms." But he does not say why this is a "jump" instead of a justified inference. His reason, I suppose, is that he discounts Imitation as mere "language." He is not the only one to take this line. It is a very common practice in the interpretation of Plato to explain away a troublesome feature by writing it off as due to his language and, for

---

[5] Naturally, if Imitation meant *no more* than "dependence," as he seems to suggest (Section X), Self-Predication would not be implied. But I cannot take this suggestion seriously. For when Sellars tries to explain what sort of "dependence" Plato himself had in mind, he *returns* to Imitation: "It [dependence] finds its clearest expression in the Analogy of the Line, where the relation of Becoming to Being is compared to the relation (within the world of becoming) of shadows and reflections to physical things" (p. 431). It is labor lost to try to exonerate Plato from the Self-Predicational implications of Imitation by saying that the latter means no more than dependence, only to find the "clearest expression" of dependence in the thing-shadow relation, which, of course, Plato does take to imply the likeness of shadow to thing shadowed and therewith to involve Self-Predication where the thing shadowed is the Form.

that reason, irrelevant to his doctrine. But the fact that this practice is followed often and by highly reputable interpreters does not excuse it. Responsible exegesis of a historical system should follow rigorously the rule that every philosopher must be held responsible [445] for the logical implications of his own statements, unless he gives definite evidence that these implications are adventitious features of his language and are not involved in what he is asserting by means of this language.[6] For once we cut loose from this rule, our own preconceptions of what it would be reasonable for Plato, or any other thinker, to believe become the final criterion for deciding what he did believe, and if we are brought to this pass, we might as well confess that the *history* of philosophy is only a euphemism.

Now I should have thought that Sellars would be the last to make Plato's language the scapegoat of his logical sins. A few lines before the statement I have just cited, he makes another which, so far from implying a dualistic view of the relation of language to doctrine, seems to imply an extremely monistic view of the relation: "The creation of the Theory of Ideas was identical with the creation of the language of the Theory of Ideas." This seems to me to go much too far in the other direction; whatever may be the true relation of the creation of a philosophical theory to that of its linguistic vehicle, it is certainly not identity, in my opinion. But the relation is close enough in any case, and Sellars must think it so. If so, how is it that the Imitation language, introduced in the first full-fledged statement of the Theory of Forms in the *Phaedo,* is retained not only in other "middle" dialogues but even in one of the latest, the *Timaeus?* Imitation is, of course, the bull's eye of the target to which the second version of the TMA is directed. Had Plato been persuaded that the use of this language exposed him to needless embarrassment, he would have had all the time in the world to shed it by the time he came to write the *Timaeus.*

Finally, in the latter part of his paper (Section X, p. 433) it becomes evident that Sellars himself does think Imitation a philosophical doctrine after all. For he now says that, according to the *Timaeus,* physical things "consist" of imitations of the Forms and it is for this reason that Plato is able to dispense with a substratum. What this means, if anything, or whether Plato believed any such thing, I shall [446] not consider. But in assuming that this view is significant and can be truly imputed to Plato, does not Sellars promote Imitation to respectable doctrinal status? I don't suppose he would refuse this status to a

---

[6] The common device of taking this or that philosophical expression as a metaphor should not, of itself, allow the suspension of this rule. For what is asserted by means of a metaphorical expression, if it has philosophical sense at all, must have logical implications and the philosopher who employs it must be held responsible for the latter. In the case of Imitation, whatever may be the exact sense of what it asserts, the similarity or likeness between the material "copy" and its ideal original is part of what is explicitly asserted by Plato; and since it is *this* relation that implies Self-Predication, the metaphorical nature of Imitation does not in the least exonerate Plato from the assumption of Self-Predication.

belief in a substratum; by the same token he could not refuse it to what, he here informs us, enabled Plato to do without this belief and give an alternative answer to the question, "What do physical things consist of?"

C. *Self-predication and the Degrees-of-Reality Theory.* Sellars does not question that Plato held the Degrees-of-Reality Theory. What he denies is that Plato held the special form of this Theory which would commit him to Self-Predication. He states this somewhat facetiously, but still well enough for my purpose, as the view which "involves that the Form *F*-ness is *superlatively F*, particulars being by contrast *humdrumly F*" (Section II). Admittedly, it is logically possible to hold a Degrees-of-Reality Theory which involves no such commitment. "One of the many Bertrand Russells" may have done so, as Sellars says. What is more to the point in this discussion, one can find contexts in Plato himself where the degrees of Reality are asserted or implied without such a commitment. Thus the view, which Plato did believe to be true, that minds are more real than bodies, if significant, does not of itself imply Self-Predication in the least. For it does not of itself assert or imply that the two terms of the comparison have one or more of the same characters, exemplified more perfectly in the "more real" of the two. But aside from such special contexts, the form in which the Degrees-of-Reality Theory has been held by Plato himself and by many after him—notably the neo-Platonists and some of the great scholastics—has just this implication. At the least, this tradition asserts that Being is itself the most real thing there is, and that less real things derive their reality by some kind of emanation from or participation in Being; from this it follows that Being has the property of Being, and more perfectly than does anything else. And in Plato it is not only the property of Being, but every property, which is supposed to be realized perfectly in the most real things, the Forms, imperfectly in sensible particulars. One could give many instances of this line of thought in Plato, but one could hardly do better than stick by the one to which I referred in my paper (p. 336 ⟨**2.180⟩): The real bed—"that which, we say, *is* Bed"—is the Form, Bed; the bed made by the bedmaker cannot be said to be "perfectly real" (*Rep.* 597a). Is there any doubt that what Plato here says of Bed and bed he would also say of *F*-ness and *F* particulars generally? Sellars, I take it, would agree that there is none. What then is the substance of his objection to my view? He states it at [447] pp. 426, Section IX: "To say that *the* difference between an *F* particular and *F*-ness is a difference in degree of reality is indeed tantamount to saying that the *F* particular and *F*-ness are both *F*." But there is no reason to suppose, he continues, that Plato believed that this is *the* difference in question; "and without this premise, the argument doesn't get off the ground." The reasoning is fallacious. To say that Self-Predication is implied by the foregoing Platonic doctrine does not require one to hold that *this* difference— difference in perfection of realization of a given character—is "the," i.e., the only, difference between a Form and one of its instances, or the only difference that is asserted in Plato's Degrees-of-Reality Theory. There may be umpteen such differences. But if there is this one, the one asserted above, it would suffice to establish that Plato's Degrees-of-Reality Theory implies Self-Predication.

12d

POSTSCRIPT TO THE THIRD MAN: A REPLY

TO MR. GEACH

I FEEL EXTREMELY fortunate to have the benefit of comments as acute as those with which Mr. Geach now follows up those previously given me by Professor Sellars ("Vlastos and the 'Third Man,'" *PR*, 64 [1955], 405ff.). [How much] I have learned {much} from both [of them will be evident in a revised version of "The Third Man Argument in the *Parmenides*" which, I trust, will appear shortly. ⟨Note: This promise was never fulfilled. But see Vlastos 1969b in Bibliography to this volume.⟩ Meanwhile,] I should like to return the compliment to Mr. Geach, telling him, in Section I, what I believe is wrong with his analysis of the *TMA* and, in Section II, what I think both sound and penetrating in his insight into the Platonic Theory.

I

For the imaginative originality and technical ingenuity of the formal argument which Geach presents in the second part of his paper, I have great admiration. But it does not satisfy me as a reproduction, or a restoration, of *the TMA*—the one which, for better or for worse, Plato wrote down in the *Parmenides*. To be sure, some deviation from the text is inevitable since, as we agree, something must be inserted between the first and second steps of the argument recited by Plato's Parmenides (132a1–4 and 6–11, respectively) to justify the transition. But I wish we could also agree that this expansion of the argument must be kept down to the bare minimum required to span the logical gap; and that the materials should be taken, if at all possible, from the quarry which we know Plato used in other contexts, so that the result will have the best chance of matching what Plato himself would have done, had he been able to do the job. When I look at my own efforts through the eyes of the man with the most sensitive conscience in such matters—the philologist—I feel none too confi-

From *PR* 65 (1956): 83–94, in response to P. T. Geach, "The Third Man Again," ibid.: 72–82. Reprinted in Allen, pp. 279–91. {Additional Note (1965). I now think I erred in endorsing Geach's elucidation of *auta ta isa* (Allen, pp. 287–89 ⟨**210–12⟩). The correct explanation is the one given in (ii), p. 289. For an even better example of the plural neuter used in a perfectly matter-of-fact way to replace the singular form for an abstract, see *Rep.* 520c5–6 and 538c6–7 (cf. d7 and e2).}

dent of my success in preserving the simplicity of the original. But at least I tried to keep intact those chunks of the *TMA* which are in Plato's text and can be transferred to one's own reconstruction with almost no alteration, save that of generalizing the statements by utilizing symbols wherever possible. Geach seems to have felt no obligation to do the same. There is nothing in his account to answer exactly to the first step in the text. The nearest thing to this is his (5). But this states quite explicitly the assumption of Self-Predication, which is not even implied in the first step of the text. [83] And the reason given in the text why there must be a single Form is not good enough for Geach; so instead of reproducing Plato's reason for it (132a2–3), he postulates a couple of tacit premises (2 and 4a) and deduces it from *them*. In the case of the second step, Plato explicitly presents *its* conclusion (the crucial statement that "another Form of Largeness will appear") as an inference from an explicit statement *in* the second step which, in turn, harks back to the first:

> "If you *similarly* view mentally Largeness itself and other large things . . . , a single Largeness will appear once again, in virtue of which all these appear large."

I italicize *similarly* because this is what links the second step inferentially with the first. In Geach the second step is swallowed up in the proof of (6a). This is not so objectionable in itself, since (6a) is how Geach writes the conclusion which Plato draws from the second and subsequent steps; so there is some warrant for ingesting the second step in this manner. What is unfortunate is that the explicit inferences which *Plato* makes in arriving at the conclusion of the second step are now lost. The result is that instead of bringing in tacit premises to *supplement* Plato's own explicit premises, Geach constructs an argument whose *only* premises are supposed to have been tacit in Plato's argument. But to say that everything is inferred from unstated premises is as good as saying that nothing is explicitly inferred. A strange argument this would be.

My second and more important objection is directed not so much to the general form of Geach's analysis as to a matter of substance, a notion which turns up all over his formalization, most conspicuously at (3) and then later at (7). It makes its first and most innocent appearance at (1), "There is a set consisting *just* of the many Fs that are not Forms." Geach says this "comes out in his (Plato's) speaking of 'the many large things' (*ta polla megala*)." {He takes this from an earlier portion of the text (*tōn pollōn megalōn,* 131d1).} What I find in the {present} text {(that of the *TMA*)} are not the quoted words but "several large things" (*polla atta megala*) or, more exactly "several things (which) seem large to you" (132a2). But this may be of no importance. What is important is the question whether the reference to (i) "several large things" in the text would warrant the statement that Plato assumed (ii) that there is a set consisting of several large things. I should have thought so. But this is not to the point, for this is Geach's axiom-set, and it is what he thinks its statements mean that counts. Now he evidently thinks there is a vast difference between (i) and (ii). He must, else he would not hold that one can "break the back" of the *TMA* by dropping (3) to pick up (7). For (3) affirms, while (7) denies, that if a [84] Form, *w*, is an *F*, and a lot of particulars are *F*s, there is a set consisting of *w* and the particulars. Suppose, for example, there were just two *F* particulars, *a* and *b*, and an *F* Form, *w*. We would then have three *F* things. Thinking of them, we might remark, (i) "There are three *F*s," and then again (ii), "There is a set of three *F*s," believing, in our innocence, that (i) would be quite enough to justify (ii), unless there were some very special reason to the contrary. But Geach would then tell us we have made a blunder. There is all the difference in the world between (i) and (ii), he would say: (i) could be true, while (ii) is false; knowing that (i) is true, we wouldn't have the least warrant for holding that (ii) is also true, unless we are *told* so, as we are at (3). If we weren't told so, then, according to Geach, the contradiction would *not* materialize.[1] So the difference between (i) and (ii) makes all the difference between logical solvency and logical bankruptcy for Plato. But if there is all *that* difference between them, how could we possibly take (i) in the text as evidence for Plato's assumption of (ii)? And if we can't, what other evidence is there to bear out the claim that Plato did assume (1)? None. And what evidence in the text that Plato assumed (3)? None.

I have so far asked only for evidence in the text of the *TMA* itself to warrant Geach's claim that the questionable assumption he imputes to Plato *in* this argument is Plato's.[2] But let us now broaden the scope of the inquiry. What is there in Plato's work—all of it, not just this text—to correspond to the notion of the great difference between (i) and (ii) above which leaves one free to affirm or deny at pleasure that an *F* Form and *F* particulars may be joined in a set? I should be inclined to say, Nothing. Plato never says *that* this or anything like it is true. Indeed, I don't know *how* he would have said it, for the corresponding terms are not in his logical vocabulary. But I don't [85] want to be wooden in a matter as difficult and elusive as this. Even if Plato never talks about sets, does he say anything which *we* could interpret along the lines proposed by Geach? Geach says two thing which raise, then dash, my hopes of encountering something of this sort:

---

[1] I say this, judging him by what he does rather than by what he says, for he hasn't quite got the two together. At one point he says he would "still maintain . . . that failure to formulate and distinguish (4a) and (4b) was what made Plato unable to locate the source of the contradiction." This must be a slip or a hang-over from his former view. For he now *uses* both (4a) and (4b) in his deduction of the proposition (7) which clears Plato of the contradiction. Thus, on his own showing, Plato could have formulated and distinguished (4a) and (4b), and asserted them to boot, and still kept clear of the contradiction, so long as he refrained from asserting (3). Geach then *must* hold that (3) is "the source of the contradiction."

[2] He prefaces his axiom-set by saying, "I shall now state in an abstract way what seem to be Plato's implicit assumptions in the *TMA*" and makes an effort to connect his (1) and (2) with the text of the *TMA;* but the effort seems to give out after this point.

(A) He says that (7) might count as a precise formulation of what Plato meant by Forms' being "separate." Now what Plato means by the latter expression, though not easy to determine, does admit of investigation. The answer I have so far reached was sketched in my original article (pp. 333ff. ⟨** 177ff.⟩). To say that a Form "exists separately from its homonymous instances is to make several statements about it" (I listed four), only one of which need be considered here:[3] that the Form, x, "is itself the perfect instance of the property or relation which the word for x connotes"; e.g., that justice is just and preeminently so. But how could *this* be "precisely formulated" (I should be satisfied with much less) in the statement that Justice cannot be grouped with just men, or be joined with them in a single set? If we want to prevent this illicit union, what we surely have to do is to distinguish the respective logical types of Justice and just persons-acts-institutions; and if we do this, what temptation could we possibly feel to join such disparate terms in sets or groups? Geach's (7) would then be at best an innocuous formality; its only use would be against the logical prankster, for no one else would dream of doing what it solemnly forbids. But instead of doing this, Plato's Separation Theory does the opposite. In saying that Justice is preeminently just, it requires us to do the very thing Geach's (7) is devised to prohibit: to think of Justice as the outstanding member of the class of just individuals.

(B) In the next paragraph Geach says, in effect, that Plato's theory is best understood as saying that a Form is "only analogously" F, and that this *would* make (7) a reasonable assumption. But this contention leads to a dilemma, of which Geach is aware; he put a tolerably good statement of it in the mouth of an objector in the antepenultimate paragraph of his paper. It could be made a little more strongly: The difference between ". . . is F" and ". . . is only analogously F" is such as to either (a) permit or (b) forbid statements to the [86] effect that this Form and that particular are both F. (a) If it permits them, we have still to find the reason for the mysterious unjoinability of the F Form and the F particular, and for evidence that Plato believed any such thing. (b) If it forbids them, then the mystery is solved indeed, but at the price of calling for drastic changes in our axiom-set. Every reference (open or tacit) to the fact that the (any) Form is F must now be amended to read that the Form is "only analogously F" or "F by analogy." And this will gum up hopelessly the deductive machinery of the axiom set.[4]

---

[3] Because this all by itself is sufficient to show that "separation" does the exact opposite of what Geach seems to think it does. I suspect he is misled by the *word*, which admittedly is confusing. But it may be worth recalling that Plato scarcely uses it himself; neither the substantive nor the corresponding adjective occurs in his text, but only the adverbial *separately,* and this rarely (*Parm.* 129d, 130b–d).

[4] Just look, for example, at Geach's first theorem, (5), which must now read, 'There is just one analogously F thing that is a Form by which all Fs are made to be Fs." How much of the proof of (5) can now be salvaged? It began, "By (4a) there is at any rate one such F." But (4a) must now

At this juncture Geach refers to the extremely interesting analogy of the Standard Pound. But the point of the analogy can hardly be that this and the Platonic Form are "only analogously" F. To say that the Standard Pound is "analogously a pound" is scarcely permissible in the prose of philosophical discussion except as a preliminary to analysis, and the sort of analysis which would reveal *some* sense in which ". . . is a pound" (*without* the *analogously*) can be said of the Standard Pound. That the ordinary sense will not serve this purpose is obvious. If "x is a pound" is to be a statement of weight established by means of the operation of weighing x against the Standard Pound, then clearly it would be senseless to say this of the Standard Pound, for it would presuppose the necessarily false statement, "The Standard Pound has been (or, can be) weighed against itself." The illusion that it has sense would lead one to reenact the plot of the *TMA*, conjuring up Standard Pound$_1$ against which to weight the Standard Pound, and so forth. So unless we can find something else to justify saying, "the Standard Pound is analogously a pound," we would do well to drop it in the interests of clear thinking; since in the ordinary sense of ". . . is a pound" the Standard Pound is *not* like other objects; and the clean-cut way to say so would be to say that it is *not* a pound—where "is not" means, of course, not that it would be materially false to say [87] that it is, but logically senseless,[5] like saying "the number, Three, is a pound," or "cheerfulness is a pound."

Nevertheless I would strongly sympathize with those who feel that this cannot be one's last word on the subject, and that to say "the Standard Pound is a pound" is not *exactly* like—not half as shocking and inexcusable as— saying "the number, Three, is a pound." The thing to do then is to find the respect in which the Standard Pound is like a pound of coffee, while the number, Three, is not. Obviously this is weight, a property which the Standard Pound does share with every material object. It would have this property even if no one had thought of conferring on it the dignity of its legal office; and the relative magnitude of its weight to that of other objects would be exactly the same[6] and could be determined perfectly without reference to its

---

become, "Something which is only analogously F is a Form by which all Fs are made to be Fs." Can we then continue with the proof, "Suppose, if possible, that there are two, x and y, and each is other than the other. Then, since each is other than the other, it follows from (4a) that x is made to be an F by the Form y, and y, by the Form x . . ."? We cannot. For what we now have to show is that there cannot be two different things, x and y, which are both "analogously F"; and (4a) as now revised is of no help for this purpose: it permits no inference that here x is made to be analogously F by y, and y by x.

[5] This I take to be Wittgenstein's view, when he remarks that of the standard metre in Paris "one can say neither that it is one metre long, nor that it is not one metre long" (*Philosophical Investigations*, Para. 50).

[6] I feel uneasy with the statement that the Standard Pound "weighs a pound, no matter what it weighs" because it might convey the suggestion (doubtless not intended by Geach) that something

conventional status. Thus one could know that this platinum cylinder weighs the same as this bag of coffee without ever having heard of pound units or, for that matter, of any conventional unit of measurement. However, though we could determine this fact, we could not express it in terms of ". . . is a pound" without going back to Standard Pound as the unit of measurement after all. The best I can do under the circumstances is to accept this necessity and offer the following sense for ". . . is a pound," to fit our Standard Pound: ". . . has the same weight as that of objects which have been (or, can be) found to weigh the same as the Standard Pound." Since the latter are a pound in the ordinary sense (call this "pound-*a*"), the Standard Pound could be said to be a pound in the derivative sense (call it "pound-*b*") of having the same weight as theirs. Is this a good sense for ". . . is a pound"? I feel no missionary zeal to propagate its use. It just happens to be the best I can do to give substance to the persistent feeling one has that there is some sense in which the Standard Pound is a pound after all. But the point of my argument does not depend on [88] the acceptance of this sense, or of any other. What I am arguing for can be put in the form of a second dilemma: Whether or not there is a sense in which it is a pound, the Standard Pound will not provide a parallel for something which *is* an *F* but may *not* be joined with other *F* things. For if there be no such sense, the Standard Pound will not be *F,* and the problem will not arise. And neither does it arise if there be such a sense. For there would then be two sets: one into which the Standard Pound does not go because it is not a pound in the same sense as other objects (the set of pound-*a* things on the above analysis); another into which it does go, because it is a pound in *that* sense (the set of the pound-*b* things, above).[7]

---

could be the Standard Pound without having a fixed weight in two quite definite ways: (a) the *substance* of which it is made maintaining a physically constant relation to the weight of other objects; (b) the *object* made from that substance and officially named "the Standard Pound" suffering no change of *its* weight (e.g., by having bits of it chipped off by burglar-tourists). Both (a) and (b) are presuppositions of its *being* the Standard Pound.

[7] I may anticipate the following objection: "That the Standard Pound is a pound-*b* is a necessary statement, while that anything else is a pound-*b* is contingent. It follows that the Standard Pound is not a pound-*b in the same sense* as other objects." Suppose this *did* follow; we would then be right where we started from, with no sense of ". . . is a pound" common to the Standard Pound and other objects, and the statement that the Standard Pound is "analogously" a pound still unaccounted for. But *does* it follow? Surely a predicate can have the same sense in a necessary and a contingent statement: "two" in "a square has two diagonals" and "Zebedee has two sons." If identity of meaning in our predicates did not persist through change of modality in statements in which they are used, how could we draw inferences from modally mixed premises as, e.g., "All *A* is *B*" (Necessary), "This is *A*" (Contingent), Hence, "This is *B*" (Contingent)? Naturally, if one is bent on getting two different senses for pound-*b* here, one *can* concoct two different predicates, "necessarily pound-*b*" and "contingently pound-*b*." But so long as one keeps to "pound-*b*" without working the modal qualifier into the predicate, I can see no objection to saying that there is *a* sense, "pound-*b*," which is the same for the present purpose.

II

The foregoing might give the impression that I have nothing but fault to find with Geach's paper. Let me do something to correct this impression, for even in the matter in which I have criticized him most vigorously the area of agreement is far wider than might appear. That the Form and its homonymous particulars are treated in the *TMA* as forming a single class, seems to me a true and penetrating way of getting at the source of the contradiction; and I quite agree that if this assumption were dropped the contradiction would not arise. All I am arguing for is a procedure for implementing this analysis: Find a sense for *F*—call it *F-a* by analogy with pound-*a* above—in which the Form is not *F*, and present Plato with this sense, telling him that if he will only remember to deny systematically that the Form is *F-a*, [89] he will not be putting Form and particulars into an ill-formed set, and will have nothing to fear from the *TMA*. The next step (for we can't stop here, if we are going to allow Plato to keep assuming that the Form *is F* nonetheless) is to find him another sense—*F-b*—in which Form and particulars *are F*, and go into the same set without causing trouble.[8] This is what has to be done. And if we say that the Form is "analogously *F*" to announce our intention of doing this, I would have no objection to the "analogously." Who would object to a promissory note?

But Geach's paper has something far more important to say, and though this was involved in the preceding discussion it deserves to be noticed on its own account. It is that the Platonic Form is essentially a "standard" and therefore "nothing like what people have since called an 'attribute' or 'characteristic.'" The truth of the matter, in my opinion, is that (within certain limits) Plato wants his Forms to be *both* attributes and standard objects and that their logical distress is mainly the outcome of their having to complete this impossible assignment. But in highlighting one side of this picture, Geach performs an extremely useful service. He succeeds at the very point at which free and easy guesses as to what Plato "must have meant" fail: in producing good exegesis, illuminating in a new and exciting way some portions of Plato's text.

His account of Plato's use of the expression "the equals themselves" (*auta ta isa, Phaedo* 74c) in contrast to sensible instances of equality, is the most ingenious and plausible explanation of this puzzling expression that has yet

---

[8] But before even starting to look for such a sense (and, more generally, to justify Self-Predication along these lines), we would have to assume that the Platonic Form matches in its own way the crucial feature of the Standard Pound, i.e., the fact that the latter must be a physical object and *have* weight as a condition of serving as a standard of weight. Thus, to get a just-*b* sense, corresponding to pound-*b* above, we would have to assume that Justice names a moral individual and/or a moral institution. I fail to see how we can do this without going further in the direction of particularizing the Form than Plato ever did. This way of getting Plato out if the frying pan of the *TMA* might get him into something worse.

been offered. The only other that does justice to the plural is the one whose latest sponsor is Ross: "an allusion to mathematical entities which are neither Ideas nor sensible things."[9] [90] But that the expression does refer to the Form, Equality, is proved by the sequel in the text: From the premise that "the equals themselves" never even appear unequal, while sensible equals sometimes do, Plato infers that "these equals [*tauta ta isa,* the sensible ones] and the equal itself are not the same." Here "the equal itself" *must* refer to exactly the same thing as does "the equals themselves" in the premise, else the premise would not justify the conclusion.[10] And since "the equal itself" obviously refers to the Form, "the equals themselves" must do so too. Some other interpretation must then be found, for the plural in "the equals themselves" is not only inconsistent with Plato's linguistic usage (the normal expression for a Form is in the singular) but seems to contradict the doctrine of the *unity* of the Form. Geach's interpretation fills this gap better than any yet offered: it accounts for the plural without imputing to Plato a breach of his own doctrine, for it suggests that if Plato thought of Equality as a "standard," he would have to think of this *one* Form as consisting of at least *two* equal things. I should like to accept Geach's interpretation, but with two reservations:

(i) I would not wish to say that Plato ever made this thought explicit, i.e., that he ever said any such thing as "Equality consists of two things." For had he done so, he would then have had ample reason to ask himself whether by the same token the Form Three consists of three things, the Form Half of half a thing (half of what?), the Form "Greater Than" (*Phaedo* 75c9) of a greater thing (greater than what?), and so on. I cannot pursue this line of thought here. But it is clear that it calls for serious qualification of the thesis that Plato thought of the Forms as "standards" in Geach's sense. He did, and he didn't— as one can, and does, in the twilight zone of consciousness where one's ideas do not reach clear-cut, hard-edged shape and are not controlled, or are imperfectly controlled, by reflection about them.

(ii) There is another explanation of "the equals themselves" here, not inconsistent with Geach's but complementary to it and logically [91] independent of

---

[9] *Plato's Theory of Ideas* (Oxford, 1951), p. 25, and cf. p. 22; but cf. p. 60, where it becomes uncertain whether Ross means to say this after all: cf. Ackrill's comments, *Mind* 62 (1953), 553. Burnet's commentary (on Plato's *Phaedo* [Oxford: Clarendon Press, 1911]) gives us the cheering remark that "there is no difficulty about the plural" and proceeds to gloss Plato with Euclid; presumably Burnet means that "the equals themselves" are mathematical equals. This is also the view of the latest commentator, R. S. Bluck, in *Plato's Phaedo* (London, 1955), p. 67n. 3; he doesn't think these would be intermediate between Forms and particulars, but neither does he see that the plural *equals* does refer to the Form, Equality. The most attractive statement of the interpretation of "equals themselves" as referring to mathematical equals is in Cornford (*Plato's Parmenides* [London, 1939], p. 71): "Here 'equals' means quantities of which nothing is asserted except that they are simply 'equal.'"

[10] There is no suggestion that the argument is elliptical. Socrates is being very explicit throughout this passage.

it. Greek usage does permit the use of the plural form of the (neuter) adjective with the article to signify the corresponding abstract—i.e., as roughly equivalent to (a) the abstract noun and (b) the same adjectival form in the singular: thus *ta dikaia* ("the just," in the plural form) can be used to express the same thing as *dikaiosunē* ("justice") or *to dikaion* ("the just," in the singular). Socrates in the *Gorgias* (454e–455a) shifts from περὶ τῶν δικαίων τε καὶ ἀδίκων ("about the just and the unjust," in the plural)[11] to περὶ τὸ δίκαιόν τε καὶ ἄδικον ("about the just and the unjust," in the singular) and back again, obviously using them as interchangeable expressions. "The equals" then as an alternate for "the equal" would be good idiomatic usage, and this would be *one* reason why Plato could slip into it.[12]

I would say the same thing about Geach's parallel interpretation of the plural "the similars themselves" (*auta ta homoia*) and "the many" (*ta polla*) as variants for "similarity" and "multiplicity" respectively. And Geach's exegesis of "mastership itself of service itself" at *Parm.* 133e3–4 deserves credit not only for offering a solution (a completely adequate one, to my mind), but also for being the first to notice that there is a problem to be solved, i.e., that (and why) there is something logically odd about the *expression* (quite apart from the implied *doctrine*) "mastership itself of service itself," instead of "mastership itself of *a* servant (or 'servants')."

Geach's thesis leads him to make another original observation of great merit: that the common noun (*Man, Fire*) brings out the assumptions of the Platonic Theory (it would be more exact to say: some of them) much better than does the abstract noun (*Humanity, Justice*). His remarks about "the Lion" are a suggestive gloss on Plato's talk about the Form, "Animal" (or "Living Creature") all through the opening part of the *Timaeus,* as well as on "Bed" in the *Republic* and "Shuttle" in the *Cratylus.* On the other hand, if Geach is looking for the "idiom in Greek . . . (which) influenced Plato's way [92] of thinking about Forms" (and he is), he should have thought of something else whose influence on the Platonic Theory must have been far greater, *sc.* the use of the adjective with the article to designate Forms ("the Just," "the Beautiful"). We meet this idiom in extreme profusion in Plato's formative (Socratic)

---

[11] I am not forgetting that he gets the cue from Gorgias' earlier reference to "those things which are just and (those which are) unjust," 454b. The fact remains that Socrates uses "the just and the unjust" in the plural to mean the same thing as the same expression in the singular, i.e., justice and injustice.

[12] It may be asked whether this explanation does not make Geach's redundant. It would, *if* this passage were the *only* evidence Geach could offer for his thesis that Plato thinks of the Forms as "standards." But since he has, or could find, quite a lot of other evidence for it, one may very well hold that the explanation in (ii) *reinforces* Geach's: the fact that Plato could *speak* of a singular abstract in the plural would make it all the easier for him to *think* of Equality as a pair of two things. {See the Additional Note ⟨appended to the first, unnumbered note to this article⟩.}

period to designate the "*X*" of the "What is *X?*" question. It is hardly less frequent in the "middle" period when the Socratic *difiniendum* has been elevated into a Form. In both periods Plato's attention is fixed mainly on moral terms (with mathematical ones moving up as close seconds in the middle period); and these, of course, *could not* be expressed by common nouns. Hence *this* idiom is not likely to have influenced appreciably Plato's thinking as he hammered out the Theory and put it to use most confidently and systematically. Forms whose linguistic vehicle is the common noun occur rather infrequently[13] and seldom move into the focus of Plato's thought in the "middle" period.[14] A fair commentary on their marginal status in his thought is that at the end of this period: in the *Parmenides* (129b–d) Socrates affirms unhesitatingly the existence of Forms like Similarity, Justice, Beauty, Goodness but says he is "puzzled" as to whether there also exist Forms of Man, Fire, or Water. These are the least securely grounded, for they are shaken by the first tremor of doubt that leaves the others undisturbed. Geach might then have asked himself whether the use of the adjectival form of expression ("the beautiful," etc.) does not exhibit the same assumptions which he thinks are conveyed by the use of the common noun. The answer, of course, is Yes, and for two main reasons: [93]

(i) A grammatical form like "the beautiful" expresses the notion of beauty by way of referring to a standard member of the class.[15]

[13] Thus, of all the different instances of Forms mentioned in the *Phaedo* (seventeen on my count), only three are designated by common nouns: Snow, Fire, Soul.

[14] On just three occasions of any consequence: the discussions of the Form of the Shuttle, *Crat.* 389; of Bed and Table, *Rep.* 596–97; of Fire, Snow, Soul in the *Phaedo* (103c ff.). I stretch a point to include the ones from the *Phaedo*. No Forms of this kind are mentioned when the Theory is first announced at 65d and reaffirmed with a great roll of drums at 75c–d and 76d. It is only in the last of the arguments for the Immortality of the Soul that Snow, Fire, Soul come in, and even so they are not *tagged* "Forms." D. J. Allan even goes so far as to say that "on the whole" they are not "treated as forms" (Review of W. D. Ross, *Plato's Theory of Ideas*, *PQ* 2 [1952], 369–70); but I take it as certain that Plato assumes that they are (cf. the introduction to this argument, 102b1–2). As for the *Republic*, the epistemological and metaphysical heart of the dialogue (Bk. 5, 475e ff. to end of Bk. 7) does not include the mention of a single Form designated by a common noun. It is only the appendix at Book 10 that brings in Bed and Table, and this not so much to illustrate the Theory of Forms as to offer a handle for disparaging the artist at the expense of the artisan.

[15] Cf., T.B.L. Webster, "Languages and Thought in Early Greece," *Memoires and Proceedings of Manchester Literary and Philosophical Society* 94 (1952–53), no. 3, p. 8: "In its full development . . . the definite article with the neuter participle or adjective signifies (a) a particular member of a class, (b) any member of a class (and therefore all members), (c) a standard member of a class (and therefore very nearly the quality by virtue of which it is a member of the class)." Webster is not thinking of Plato at all in this connection; he is describing the usage of "the early Hippocratic writings, Anaxagoras, and Thucydides." His statement is all the more valuable on that account; it outlines the possible senses of this grammatical form in contemporary (or some-

(ii) The "hypostatizing definite article," as Geach calls it, is even more in evidence: though the article is not always used even in the adjectival form, it is certainly far more frequently used in this than in the case of the common noun.[16]

---

what earlier) usage; and the only one of these that will approximate Plato's (c), is the very one that would give grammatical support to the tendency to think of the Form as Self-Predicational. Cf. Bluck (above, n. 9), pp. 174ff.

[16] The article is absent in "Form of Man, Fire, or Water" and of "Hair, Mud and Dirt," *Parm.* 130c; it is omitted in a ratio higher than 5/1 in reference to Fire or Snow, *Phaedo* 103c–d and 105c; it is hardly used at all in references to the Forms of Bed and Table in *Rep.* 596b ff.; it is wholly omitted from significant expressions, "that which *is* Bed," "Bed which really is," *Rep.* 597a, c, d.

13

ON A PROPOSED REDEFINITION

OF "SELF-PREDICATION" IN PLATO

H OW SHALL we read those perplexing sentences—"Justice is just," "Beauty is beautiful," and the like—which have occasioned so much controversy in discussions of Plato's metaphysics in recent decades? Shall we assume that they are ordinary predications, asserting their predicate-term of the Form named by the subject-term?[1] Or shall we hold, more charitably, that they are identities?[2] Or should we, as charitably, opt for a third reading which understands them to assert their predicate not of the Form but of its instances, if any?[3]

In an important paper,[4] remarkable for the boldness of its attack on fundamental problems of Platonic ontology, Professor Alexander Nehamas puts forward a formal redefinition of "self-predication" which is meant to be a fourth way of reading such sentences in Plato, distinct from each of the three I have just set forth.[5] He proposes "the following analysis of self-predication:

From *Phronesis* 26 (1981): 76–79. Used by permission. Minor changes in punctuation and minor corrections have been made.

[1] When these Platonic sentences first came under close scrutiny, it was taken for granted that only this could be their right interpretation. Thus R. Hackforth (*Plato's Examination of Pleasure* [Cambridge, 1945], 22n. 1) assumes without argument that at *Parm.* 132a and *Prot.* 330d Plato is maintaining that "each Form itself *has* the character that it *is*" (Hackforth's emphasis). The same reading of *Parm.* 132a in W. D. Ross, *Plato's Theory of Ideas* (Oxford, 1954), 319ff., again without argument. The same reading of *Parm.* 132a and also (mistakenly, as I now believe) of *Prot.* 330d is argued for in my "Third Man Argument in the *Parmenides*" (*PR* 63 [1954], 319ff. ⟨** 2.166ff.⟩), where the term *self-predication* is introduced into the critical literature to nominalize the expression "[predicates' predicable of themselves" by Bertrand Russell (*Principles of Mathematics* [Cambridge, 1903], at pp. 80 and 100ff. of the second edition [1933]) in his analysis of the logical paradoxes and, after him, by A. E. Taylor in his discussion of *Parm.* 132a–c in *Philosophical Studies* (London, 1934), 50.

[2] So H. Cherniss, "The Relation of the *Timaeus* to Plato's Later Dialogues," *AJP* 78 (1957), 225ff. at 258–59; and R. E. Allen, "Participation and Predication in Plato's Middle Dialogues," *PR* 69 (1960), 147ff. For my critique of Cherniss, see my *Platonic Studies* (Princeton, 1973), 335ff., and of Allen see ibid., 263n. 111.

[3] I have argued *for* this interpretation of "Justice is just" in *Prot.* 330c, and *against* the same interpretation of "Beauty is beautiful" in *Symp.* 211 c–d (*PS*, 252ff. and 262ff.), defending the view that Plato's use of sentences of the form "The *F* is *F*" varies from context to context and must be determined *ad hoc* according to context. For criticism of the third reading, see e.g., C.C.W. Taylor, *Plato: Protagoras* (Oxford, 1976), 118–20.

[4] "Self-Predication and Plato's Theory of Forms," *APQ* 16 (1979), 93ff.

[5] He argues against the first and the third in ibid., n. 13, against the second in ibid., n. 14.

The *F* itself is *F* = df. The *F* itself, whatever it turns out to be, is what it is to be *F*." (95b)

Dropping unessential wording from the proposed definiens, I abbreviate it to

[A] The *F* itself is what it is to be *F*.

The proposal has proved attractive,[6] presumably because it appears to offer a *via media* between the first and the second of the above readings of self-predications in Plato.[7] But this appearance is delusive, as I shall try to show. I wish to argue that when the proposed definiens is correctly analyzed it turns out to be a simple identity disguised by periphrastic grammar. If this argument succeeds, it will show that the proposal takes us inadvertently back to the second of the above readings. And I shall argue further that the author, mistaking the disguised identity for predication, is led to ascribe to Plato a metaphysical doctrine which only the strongest version of the first reading could hope to justify.

I

I wish to show how a sequence of reasonable substitutions transforms [A] into the explicit identity

[A'] The *F* itself = what it is to be *F*.

thereby resolving the syntactical ambiguity, "copula or identity-sign?" in the first occurrence of "is" in [A] and clarifying the meaning of the expression "what it is to be *F*."

Let me begin by calling attention to a simple fact of Greek (as also of English) grammar: an infinitive can be used to do the work of an abstract noun. Thus when Plato writes

To know is to get hold of knowledge (τὸ γὰρ γνῶναι ἐπιστήμην που λαβεῖν ἐστιν, *Theaet.* 209e–210a), [76]

either of his infinitives might have been replaced by the cognate abstract noun without change of sense: *to gnōnai* by *gnōsis*, and *epistēmēn labein* by *epistēmēs lēpsis*. By this rule of usage, an abstract noun in subject position is

---

[6] It is embraced with enthusiasm by Professor R. G. Turnbull in his Presidential Address to the Western Division of the American Philosophical Association (*Proceedings and Addresses of the A.P.A.* 51 [1978], 735ff., 755n. 28). He says that he owes to Nehamas "the idea of construing selfpredication in the case of forms as stating what it is to be ———."

[7] Cf. the description of them as "not just ordinary predications," yet "not pure tautologies either," in my citation below from page 96A of the paper.

replaceable by the infinitive of the copula governing the cognate adjective or common noun:

Leniency would be weakness = *to be lenient* would be weakness.
Slavery is worse than death = *to be a slave* is worse than death.

For an example in Plato, consider *Prot.* 352a1–2,

Justice and Temperance and to be pious (*to hosion einai*), in a word, human excellence . . .

Here it is transparently clear that "to be pious" is simply a stylistic variant for "Piety": the latter translates *to hosion einai* in all translations known to me.[8] The expression "to be bees" (*melittas einai*) is used to the same effect in the *Meno* (72b5–6), here pressed into service to fill the lexical gap created by the unavailability of the corresponding abstract noun (Greek, like English, lacks a cognate adjective or abstract noun for *bee* analogous to *human* and *humanity* for *man*):

Would you say that bees are many and of many sorts and differ from each other in this—in to-be-bees (*tōi melittas einai*)? or that they do not differ in this way but (only) in others, for example, in Beauty (*kallei*) or in Bigness (*megethei*) or in something else of that sort?

It should be evident that "to-be-bees" is used in a way which is syntactically parallel to "Beauty" and "Bigness"—perhaps more evident in Greek than in English, for in Greek the article which precedes the infinitive is put into the same case as are "Beauty" and "Bigness": which have three "datives of respect."

Given this background, we can transform [A] into [A'] by simple substitutions, after getting rid of the functionless *it* on the righthand side of [A]: like the *it* in "it is wrong to cheat," it has no reference, contributes nothing to the meaning of the sentence, and may be deleted (Cf. "it is wrong to cheat" = "to cheat is wrong"). Thus

[i] What it is to be *F* = what to be *F* is.

Then, since "the *F*" is a stand-in for an abstract noun (or its equivalent in Greek idiom, an articular neuter adjective in the singular), it follows from what was said in the preceding paragraph that

[ii] What the *F* is = what to be *F* is.

---

[8] For a second example, see *Euthd.* 279b5–c1: four virtues are listed, the first three are expressed by infinitive *cum* adjective ("to be temperate and just and brave"), the fourth by an abstract noun ("wisdom"). For a third cf. *Gorg.* 477d4–5 ("to be unjust and licentious and cowardly and ignorant") with 477e4–5 ("injustice and licentiousness and other baseness of soul").

We may, therefore rewrite [i] as

[iii] What it is to be F = what the F is.

And we know that

[iv] What the F is = the essence of F,

as is clear, e.g., at *Meno* 72b, "if being asked about the essence of bee, what it is . . . ," where "what it [*sc.* bee] is" is in epexegetic apposition to "the essence of bee": the expressions are synonymous; they must be such, since "the essence of bee" nominalizes "what bee is." Moreover,

[v] The essence of F = the F,

for the F *is* an essence and the essence of, say, Piety, could only be that essence which Piety is—not, absurdly, some other essence which Piety is not.[9] From [iv] and [v] we get

[vi] What the F is = the F. [77]

Since "the F" = "the F itself," [vi] empowers us to substitute "the F" for "what the F is" in [iii], rewriting it as

[vii] What it is to be F = the F itself.[10]

Since identity is symmetrical, [vii] shows that substitution of identities has transformed [A] into [A'].

II

In his paper Nehamas maintains that self-predications are "not just ordinary predications, yet they are not pure tautologies either. They are not, on any occasion, absurd: nothing is logically or metaphysically wrong with Justice, doing one's own, being what it is to be just, with Motion being what it is to move, or with Plurality being what it is to be plural" (96a). What is this

---

[9] I know of no textual foundation for R. E. Allen's view that "there is a distinction between the essence, X-ness, and the essence of X-ness" (*Plato's "Euthyphro" and the Earlier Theory of Forms* [London, 1970], 103n. 1 [his emphasis]). The only reason given is that "the question, 'What is X-ness?' must be answered by a defining formula of the essence, X-ness" (ibid.). But so must the question, "What is the essence of X-ness?" To ask, "What is X-ness?" and "What is the essence of X-ness?" is to pose identical questions calling for identical answers.

[10] Good confirmation for this result is available in the well-known synonymy of "what it is to be F" and "the essence of F" in Aristotle (see e.g., *Top.* 102a18 and *Met.* 1030a6–7, where *to ti ēn einai* substitutes for "the [definable] essence"; and *Met.* 1017b21–22: "The what it is to be, whose formula is definition—this too is called the 'essence' of a thing [in the relevant use of 'essence']"). Since "the essence of F" = "the F," Aristotle takes it as obvious that "what it is to be F" = "the F."

tertium quid—neither "ordinary predications" nor "pure tautologies"—he does not explain. That he does take them to be predications of some sort becomes evident when he proceeds to argue that "Plato follows Parmenides to the extent of thinking that *there is, strictly speaking, only one way of having a characteristic, namely, being that characteristic itself.* This is precisely what the interpretation of "*a* is F" as "*a* is what it is to be *F*" implies" (98b–99a; my italics).

I would agree that Parmenides is committed to the mind-boggling tenet expressed in the words I have underscored. I would not agree that Plato is committed to it.[11] But I do not wish to argue out that point. I merely wish to make clear that, in any case, self-predications do not commit Plato to it if they mean what Nehamas' definiens *says* they mean, as distinct from what Nehamas *thinks* they do. If we should understand "the *F* is *F*" to mean "the *F* is what it is to be *F*," then all substitution instances of it would turn out to be innocuous identities. Thus, of the three examples Nehamas gives above, the first is a definitional identity, the second and third are tautologies. The latter two are offered as substitution-instances of [A], hence, for the reasons given above, they must be likewise substitution-instances of [A'], reducing, respectively, to "Plurality = what it is to be plural," "Motion = what it is to move." The first example is saved from being a tautology only because it is a non-tautologous definitional identity, "Justice = doing one's own = what it is to be just." The reason why "there is nothing logically or metaphysically wrong with Justice . . . being what it is to be just, with Motion being what it is to move, with Plurality being what it is to be plural" is that there is nothing logically or metaphysically wrong with identities.[12]

----

[11] Neither would Nehamas, if he had not misunderstood the import of his proposed definiens. As the last quotation from him shows, he assumes that "Beauty is what it is to be beautiful" entails that Beauty has beauty as a characteristic and is, indeed, "strictly speaking," the only entity that can have that characteristic.

[12] For helpful comments on a previous draft, I am indebted to Alan Code, and also to Frank Lewis, Gail Fine, and Terry Irwin. This acknowledgment carries no presumption that any of them would agree to any of the views I express here.

C. SCIENCE

14

THE ROLE OF OBSERVATION IN PLATO'S CONCEPTION OF ASTRONOMY

I

THERE IS A famous passage in the *Republic* which has been read in drastically different ways.[1] Some have gone so far as to see in it Plato "banning sense-perception from the science of astronomy" (Heath),[2] advising astronomers "to replace observation by speculation" (Neugebauer).[3] Others have found in it nothing worse than a critique of sterile methodological empiricism and a plea for the mathematization of astronomical theory: "Plato is not objecting here to observation as a suggestion for mathematical studies but to its substitution for them" (Shorey).[4] I shall defend a *via media*. I hope to show that this passage, properly understood, permits us to recognize the positive impetus Plato gave to mathematical astronomy without requiring us to whitewash the anti-empirical strain in his whole philosophy, which shows up as strongly in this passage as anywhere in his work.

Since the whole issue will turn on seeing exactly what it is here that has provoked such diverse interpretations, and seeing it fairly in its own context, I must quote the passage in full. I give this in my own translation,[5] subjoining critical annotations in its defense at crucial points.[6] Socrates is speaking in the first person, Glaucon, his foil, in the third:

From J. P. Anton, ed., *Science and the Sciences in Plato* (Delmar, N.Y.: Caravan Books, 1980), pp. 1–31. Used by permission. Full documentation of secondary sources cited in text and notes can be found in the Bibliography at the end of the article.

[1] This paper was presented at a symposium on "Science and the Sciences in Plato," which took place on April 2, 1976, at the International Philosophy Conference at the Biltmore Hotel, Sunday, March 28 to Sunday, April 4, 1976.

[2] Thomas Heath [1913, 139].

[3] Otto Neugebauer [1958, 152].

[4] Paul Shorey [1935, vol. 2, 186]. Plato's purpose in this passage, writes Shorey, "is to predict and encourage a purely mathematical astronomy" (ibid.).

[5] Whose debt to other translations is great, not least to the one by Shorey [1935] in spite of sharp disagreements with him on the rendering of certain sentences and on the import of the whole passage. I am also indebted to the translations by Lindsay [1935], Cornford [1945], Robin [1950], and Bloom [1968]; and to Adam's invaluable commentary [1902]. I shall be referring to all of these works by author's name only, except where I need to distinguish the translation from another work by the same author.

[6] Nn. 14 and 17 below.

528e "And now," he said, "I shall not give astronomy the vulgar commendation
529a for which you scolded me just a moment ago; I shall praise it along your own
principles: It should be obvious to everyone that this [science] forces the soul
to look upward,[7] leads it higher, away from things [down] here." [1]

"Maybe that is obvious to everyone," I said, "but it is not to me. It is not
my own opinion."

"How so?" he asked.

"Because," I said, "the way it is treated now by those who would lead us
up to philosophy,[8] its effect is most decidedly to make us look downward."

"What do you mean?" he asked.

"Your notion of the study of higher things is much too fine,[9] I replied. "It
b looks as though you'd say that one who throws back his head to gaze at
ornaments in the ceiling is viewing them not with his eyes but with his
reason. Maybe you are right, and I am stupid. For I can only think of one
study that makes the mind look up: the one that has to do with the real and
the unseen.[10] But if anyone tries to learn about the things of sense, gaping up
c or squinting down, I would say that he will never learn—of things of that
sort there can be no knowledge[11]—and I would say that he is looking down,
not up, even if he were to do his learning on his back, flat on the ground or
afloat in the sea."

"You are right," he said. "Your rebuke is deserved. But how then did you
mean that astronomy should be learned, differently from the way it is now,[12]
if its learning is to be conducive to what we are talking about?"

---

[7] *Eis to anō*, "to the upper or higher [realm]." The allusion is to the Allegory of the Cave at the
start of Book 7, where the sensible world is "subterranean" (514a3) while the intelligible world of
the Platonic Ideas is high above and its discovery by the philosopher is an "ascent and view of the
upper [world]" ἄνω ἀνάβασιν καὶ θέαν τῶν ἄνω 517b4). Glaucon is given the part of the
sentimental Platonist (cf. Shorey *ad loc.*) who takes "upper" with stupid literalism.

[8] Plato may be thinking here of Hippias, whom he represents as "tak[ing] young men who have
fled technical studies [*technas*], and throw[ing] them back, against their will, into these studies—
number theory, astronomy, geometry, and musical theory" (*Prot.* 318e); the speaker is Protagoras,
who prides himself on sparing his students such technical studies. He may be thinking also of his
own contemporary, Isocrates, who praises astronomy and geometry (*Ant.* 261–65; *Panath.* 26–
27) as ingredients in the education of young men: they provide training in "subtlety" (*perit-
tologia*) and "precision" (*akribeia*).

[9] Heavy-handed Socratic irony.

[10] περὶ τὸ ὄν τε . . . καὶ τὸ ἀόρατον. For the sense I would give to *to on* in such contexts
("real," not "existent"), see Vlastos [1973, 43ff., 58ff.]. Plato, of course, does not think sensible
things *unreal.* But their reality pales by contrast with that of the Ideas, which represent reality *par
excellence.*

[11] ἐπιστήμην γὰρ οὐδὲν ἔχειν τῶν τοιούτων [i.e., τῶν αἰσθητῶν]. One of the most cate-
gorical assertions ever made in Plato's writings that sensible things cannot qualify as objects of
knowledge.

[12] We need not assume that Plato has in view here a crassly empirical astronomy. Even if he
were envisaging a heavily mathematicized astronomy, he would still be confronting a discipline

"Like this," I said. "Those ornaments in the sky, since they adorn a visible
d   [realm], should indeed be regarded as the finest and most exact things of that
sort, but as falling far short of the true [ornaments]—those motions which
the real[13] speed and the real slowness in [their] true number and in all [their]
true figures move relatively to each other and carry along whatever is in
them;[14] these things are for reason and understanding, not for sight, to discern. Or do you think otherwise?"

"By no means," he said.

---

which is not particularly conducive to the kind of philosophy he desiderates, for which the "real"
things are not the celestial phenomena (as, of course, they would be for the working astronomer)
but the "unseen" Ideal Forms (cf. 529b5). Mathematical astronomy would not of itself dislodge
the unconscious materialism of Anaxagoras and Democritus.

[13] Plato uses "true" and "real" as virtual synonyms in the *Republic* (cf. Vlastos [1973, 62n.
16]) and many other contexts. English usage presents some parallels. In some contexts these
adjectives are virtually interchangeable: "true gold" = "real gold."

[14] For the construction of this difficult stretch of Greek, I am indebted to Adam (in his long
note *ad loc.*), in spite of residual differences in my interpretation of the sense. Agreeing with
Adam that ἅς in d2 goes with φοράς in d3, I infer that, since ἅς φοράς refers to τῶν ἀληθινῶν
[ποικιλμάτων] in d1, it follows that the "true" (ornaments) are the ("true" or "real") motions of
the stars. When Adam takes τὸ ὄν τάχος and ἡ οὖσα βραδυτής as "the mathematical counterparts of visible stars," I cannot follow him: if the latter were what Plato had wanted to say, he
would have written quite simply τὰ ὄντα ἄστρα. An expression like τὸ ὄν τάχος Plato could
only have used for "the real speed"; and this could only mean for him either (a) The Form Speed,
or if used as an incomplete expression, "the real speed of *x*," then (b) the instantiation of the Form
of Speed in *x*. That (b), not (a), is what Plato has here in view is clear from the context: it would
make no sense at all to say that the (immutable) Forms of Speed and Slowness "move and carry
along whatever is in them" (φέρεται καὶ τὰ ἐνόντα φέρει); hence the subjects of these verbs
could only be the "speed" or "slowness" (i.e., the high or low velocities) of particular stars. I take
"motion which the velocity of *x* moves" to be Plato's roundabout way of saying "motion which *x*
performs when it moves at that velocity." And I take the "real" velocity of stars to be what we
would find more natural to call their "ideal" velocity, i.e., the speed imputed to them in the true
theory of their motion, which is only approximated by their observed speed.

This reading of Plato's Greek undercuts Adam's notion that Plato is postulating in this passage ideal or "mathematical" stars ("a mathematical *ouranos* of which the visible heavens are but
a blurred and imperfect expression in time and space"), thus adding to his ontology a new tier of
entities, astronomical intermediates, paralleling the mathematical intermediates, which Aristotle
imputes to Plato (*Met.* 987b14–18; other passages and references to the secondary literature in
Ross [1924, vol. 1, 166]), but which have no firm basis in the dialogues and should probably be
discounted as a variant ontology which gained some currency in the Academy but was not definitely sponsored by Plato himself. Adam appeals to *Met.* 997b12–18 to support his own ascription of astronomical intermediates to Plato on the strength of our passage in the *Republic*. He does
not seem to realize that Aristotle himself does *not* say that Plato affirmed the existence of "a
heaven over and above the sensible heaven," but that such a thing would follow "*if* one were to
posit intermediates between Forms and sensibles," and "*if* astronomy is one of these genera"
(i.e., a scientific domain, in addition to mathematics, where intermediates are to be posited); this
double conditional makes it doubly clear that what he is presenting in 997b12–18 is not meant to
be a report of Platonic doctrine but a constructive inference upon it.

"Then," said I, "should we not use those figures in the sky as models[15] for the sake of understanding *those* things [the "real" movements of the stars],

e   as if we had chanced upon diagrams drawn and perfected with surpassing skill by Daedalus or some other artisan or draughtsman? An expert in geometry, viewing such things, would deem them most beautifully crafted; but [2] he would think it laughable to scrutinize them zealously,[16] expecting to find

530a   in them true equality or duplicity or any other ratio."

"How could that be anything but laughable?" he said.

"Then don't you think," I said, "that the real astronomer will view similarly the motions of the stars? He will feel that the heavens and all that is in it has been constructed with the utmost beauty attainable in such work. But in respect of the proportion of night to day, of these to month, of month to

b   year, and of the [periods of the] other stars to these and to one another, don't you agree that he would think it absurd to expect such objects, corporeal and visible as they are, to be for ever invariant and to be absolutely undeviating, and to strive to determine their truth by every possible means?"[17]

"I certainly think so now, listening to you," he said.

---

[15] *Paradeigmata*, here in its common use of "exhibits," *not* that of "exemplars" in which Plato applies it to the Ideas.

[16] *Spoudēi*, "with grave concern," "high seriousness."

[17] καὶ ζητεῖν παντὶ τρόπῳ τὴν ἀλήθειαν αὐτῶν λαβεῖν. To translate, e.g., with Cornford, "to spend all his pains to find exact truth *in them*" would be a mistranslation: there is no Greek for the italicized phrase; Plato has not written *en autois* (as he did a few lines earlier, in 529e5, when "in them" *was* what he meant), but *autōn*, which could only be properly rendered "of them" or "about them." (Similar mistranslation in Robin, "là-dedans" for *autōn*. This construction of Plato's sentence seems to go back to Duhem [1913, 95], who paraphrases, "il regardera comme un insensé . . . celui qui s'efforce de toutes manières *de saisir la verité en ces choses* accessibles aux sens." The apologetic intent of the italicized phrase should be obvious; Duhem and those who follow him shrink from the thought that Plato would go so far as [A] to find fault with painstakingly precise observation of sensible things; so they tone down Plato's sentence, making it say [B] that the absurdity lies in expecting to find astronomical truth *in* raw phenomena (rather than in mathematically formulated laws). Plato would, of course, concur wholeheartedly with [B]. But the sentence he writes here, faithfully translated, shows that he wants to say the much stronger thing in [A]. The sense is rendered correctly in Heath [1913, 137]: "and will he not hold it absurd to exhaust every possible effort to apprehend their true condition?" The same sense is in Lindsay and, most recently, in Bloom. Shorey, who sees that the Duhem translation is grammatically impossible, tries an alternative way of exonerating Plato from the charge of denigrating observational astronomy. He forces the syntax to make the terminal clause a "trailing anacoluthon," so that the subject of *zētein* becomes "the real astronomer who, using the stars only as 'diagrams' or patterns (529d) seeks to learn a higher, exacter truth from mere observation" (186, note *a*); and Plato's sentence is thus made to say the exact opposite of what it undoubtedly means (and has been taken to mean by everyone else in the literature): Shorey has Plato saying that the "real astronomer" *will* "strive to determine truth by every possible means." This is a perverse misconstruction, a showpiece of the degree to which a magnificent Hellenist's handling of Plato's Greek may be distorted by apologetic animus. In thus reproaching Shorey, I do not wish to belittle

"It is by no means of problems, then," I said, "that we shall proceed in astronomy, in the same way as we do in geometry, and *we shall let the things in the heavens alone* (τὰ δ' ἐν τῷ οὐρανῷ ἐάσομεν) if, by doing real

c astronomy, we are to turn from disuse to use that part of our soul whose nature it is to be wise."

"You are laying down a task many times bigger than the present practice of astronomy," he said.

"And I fancy that our other prescriptions will be in the same scale, if we are to be any use as legislators." I said.

II

The puzzle of the passage is in that sentence near the end, which I italicized: τὰ δ' ἐν τῷ οὐρανῷ ἐάσομεν. What could that mean? The verb, *eān,* could mean "let alone," "let be," "let go," "put aside"; or it could carry the stronger sense "dismiss," "abandon."[18] Giving it the stronger force, many historians have read the sentence as an injunction to astronomers to dismiss celestial phenomena from the subject [3] matter of their science. I have already quoted Heath and Neugebauer to this effect at the start of this essay. Here is another part of Heath's gloss on our sentence [1913, 138]:

Says Plato with a fine audacity, we do not attain to the real science of astronomy until we have "dispensed with the starry heavens," i.e., *eliminated the visible appearance altogether* [my italics].[19]

And here is another gloss from a more recent book (Mittelstrass [1964, 122]):

Plato's *a prioristic* constructions of the motions of the stars are not to be brought

---

the difficulty of the generally accepted construction of Plato's sentence, which I have followed, requiring us to take the adjective in ἄτοπον . . . ἡγήσεται first as a masculine in ἄτοπον . . . ἡγήσεται τὸν νομίζοντα etc., and then, in the second dependent clause, as a neuter: this is certainly an awkward construction, but its correctness, as against Shorey's, is fully borne out by the parallelism between ἄτοπον . . . ζητεῖν παντὶ τρόπῳ τὴν ἀλήθειαν αὐτῶν λαβεῖν here, and γελοῖον . . . ἐπισκοπεῖν αὐτὰ σπουδῇ ὡς τὴν ἀλήθειαν ἐν αὐτοῖς ληψόμενον in 529e4–5.

[18] For the use of *eaō* with the stronger sense elsewhere in Plato, see, e.g., *Gorg.* 484c, ἐάσας ἤδη τὴν φιλοσοφίαν, "having already abandoned philosophy," and *Rep.* 490d, ἐάσας δὲ τοὺς λόγους, "if we abandoned [mere] words" (to turn to the persons to whom the words referred).

[19] Heath's interpretation of the passage is deeply influenced by Adam's comment [1902, 128–31, 166–67, 186–87], even echoing its phraseology ("fine audacity" is an unacknowledged quotation). Adam had (rightly) emphasized "Plato's unconcealed distrust of observation and the use of the senses" (168) but had not gone nearly as far as Heath does in the above quotation: "distrusting" observation is one thing, "banning" is quite another.

together with their apparent motions: *the latter should be altogether forgotten* [my italics].[20]

The crux of my objection comes to this: if Plato's proposal, so interpreted,[21] were seriously meant (and no one would doubt that he is in dead earnest), it would involve not the reform of astronomy but its liquidation. For what would be left of what the science had become, if the visible appearances were to be "eliminated altogether"? Which of its factual discoveries would survive the "banning of sense-perception"[22] from its methodology? On what ground could it hold on to the discovery of, say, the existence of such and such planets and their eastward motions in the Zodiac, if the sensible data on which these discoveries were based were to be "eliminated altogether"? Did Plato have up his sleeve some other means of assuring himself of such facts? There is no trace in the dialogues of his having ever been addicted to such a crackpot astronomy.[23] And if anything of that sort had been back of his proposal in the *Republic,* how could we explain the fact that Eudoxus, the greatest astronomer of the day, became closely associated with the Platonic circle?[24] And what would we do with the tradition that he produced his theory of

---

[20] Earlier (117) Mittelstrass had remarked:

Of a saving of the phenomena there can be no question [for Plato in this passage]: all preoccupation (jede Beschäftigung) with the phenomena is represented in advance as laughable.

This appears to be an allusion to 529e4–5. If so, it is pushing the text too hard. Plato is not saying that "jede Beschäftigung" with the phenomena, but *episkopein auta spoudēi,* "scrutinizing them zealously," is laughable; what is ridiculous according to Plato is to make much ado over the phenomena as such. *Spoudēi* does the same job in *episkopein spoudēi* as does *panti tropōi* in *zētein panti tropōi* (530b3–4), on whose sense, cf. n. 17 above.

[21] I could have cited many other spokesmen for this interpretation of the disputed sentence and of the passage as a whole (for some of them, see the references in Shorey's note *ad loc.*), but none would be as significant as Heath (the most distinguished historian of Greek astronomy in his generation in the English-speaking world) or Mittelstrass (the author of a sophisticated essay on the philosophy of natural investigation from Plato to Kepler, who is also a learned and thoughtful student of Plato's metaphysics). I should add that while I shall be arguing strongly against this interpretation, I am very sympathetic with its motivation. In their awareness of Plato's denigration of the role of empirical observation in scientific inquiry, the authors I have cited show deeper historical insight than do their adversaries.

[22] For the reference, see n. 2 above.

[23] There are some strange things in Plato's cosmology, like the sequence of numbers (two geometrical progressions in which arithmetical and harmonic means are interpolated) in the composition of the World Soul in *Tim.* 35b–36b, which is supposed to account for its harmonious structure. But this curious construction is not offered as the outcome of astronomical investigation and does not purport to eventuate in the discovery of observable physical facts.

[24] ἑταῖρος τῶν περὶ Πλάτωνα (Eudemus *ap.* Proclus *Comm. on Book I of Euclid's Elements,* 67 Friedlein). Strabo (*Geogr.* 14, 2, 5) refers to Eudoxus as "one of Plato's companions" (τῶν περὶ Πλάτωνος ἑταίρων). In the *Vita Marciana* (11, p. 99. Düring) it is stated that Aristotle "visits Plato in Eudoxus's time" (φ<οιτᾷ Πλάτωνι ἐπὶ Εὐδ>όξου) according to the virtually certain restoration by F. Jacoby. The statement has been taken to mean that the event occurred

homocentric spheres in response to Plato's challenge to "save the phenomena"?[25] To make sense of such facts, we would have to hypothesize a radical reversal in Plato's attitude to astronomy at some time after he wrote the *Republic*—a hypothesis for which I can find no support within the Platonic corpus[26] nor yet in any external corroborative testimony: there is no hint in Aristotle that Plato ever did such a volte-face, or indeed that he ever changed at all his attitude to astronomy in the course of his life, and certainly [4] no suggestion that at any time Plato had wanted astronomers to "replace observations by speculation."[27]

---

when Eudoxus was presiding over the Academy during Plato's second visit to Syracuse in 368 B.C. (so, e.g., Düring [1966, 5]; Festugière [1947, 12n. 9]; other reference in Friedländer [1958, 353–54]). Quite apart from the difficulty of taking φοιτᾷ Πλάτωνι to refer to a visit to the Academy *in Plato's absence,* the inference would be a tall tale for so slender an evidential base. But even if the emendation <ἐπὶ Εὐδόξου> meant only "during the presence of Eudoxus in the Academy," it would still be important corroboration of the natural inference one could draw from the statements in Eudemus and Strabo above, namely, that Eudoxus found a welcome in the Academy when he came to Athens and that his relations with Plato were cordial.

[25] Simplicius, *De caelo* 488, 17–24:

Eudoxus of Cnidus (as Eudemus records In Book II of his *History of Anatomy,* and Sosigenes too, who took this from Eudemus) was the first to engage in such hypotheses [of "uniform, orderly, circular motions" whose positing "would save the motions of the so-called wandering stars"]. For, says Sosigenes, Plato had set this problem to those who were engaged in these studies: What uniform and regular motions must be hypothesized to save the phenomenal motions of the planets?

For comment on the passage, see Vlastos [1975, 110–12].

[26] Heath [1913, 139–40] hypothesizes such a change between the *Republic* and the *Timaeus,* arguing that "in the Republic [A] sense-perception is only regarded as useful up to the point at which . . . it stimulates the intellect," while in the *Timaeus* [B] sight is called "the cause of the greatest blessing to us" [i.e., a very great blessing to us, *not* the greatest of our blessings]. The argument is feeble: the author of the *Timaeus* would fully subscribe to [A], where only usefulness *for the acquisition of knowledge* is in view (which obviously does not exclude usefulness for a million other things). And the author of the *Republic* would underwrite not only [B] but everything, word for word, in the lines (*Tim.* 47a1–b2) which Heath quotes: thus why should he have disagreed with the sentiment that "if we had never seen the stars and the sun and the heavens" (*Tim.* 47a4) we would have been in no position to engage in astronomical discourse? Mittelstrass [1964, 130 *et passim*] locates the alleged reversal in the interval between the *Timaeus* and the *Laws:* only in the *Laws,* he thinks, does "Plato bring his astronomy back to the heavens" persuaded at last, by the success of Eudoxian theory, that "the phenomenal celestial occurrences had a lawlike form" (ibid.). Elsewhere [1975, 99–100 and 101–2] I have argued that the statement in the *Laws* (822a) that sun, moon, and planets do not travel "in many paths" but "always on one and the same path" does not differ in substance from the doctrine of the *Timaeus,* where it is clear, by implication, that Plato has complete confidence in the regularity of all celestial motions. If so, as I have argued in n. 87 to the same Lecture, the interesting difference between the *Timaeus* and the *Laws,* which *could* imply acceptance of the Eudoxian theory, would not portend the change Mittelstrass thinks it does: it would mean finding a satisfying theory of planetary regularities, not a conversion from disbelief to belief in celestial regularity.

[27] The only sinners on this score ever named by Aristotle are "those men in Italy who are called

But even without going so far afield, we can find within our own passage—in its analogy between the visible heavens and geometrical diagrams, which dominates its thought[28]—sufficient reason to reject the proposed interpretation. The merits of that analogy I shall not discuss now—there will be time for that later on. All I wish to do for the present is to take it as the guide to Plato's conception of astronomical method, which it is evidently meant to be. How must he be viewing celestial phenomena if he holds that they are related to the truths of astronomy as would accurately drawn geometrical diagrams be related to the truths of geometry? It would have been as clear to Plato as it is to us that such visual representations, hopelessly misleading in some respects as they certainly are, may also be genuinely informative in others:

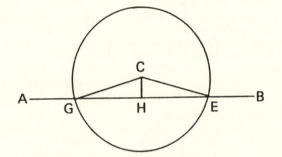

Consider a simple diagram in Euclid, say, the one above, used in the "problem"[29] in Euclid I, 12: "To a given infinite straight line, from a given point

---

'Pythagoreans' " (Philolaus): they invent a counter-earth "because they are not seeking theories and explanations with a view to the phenomena, but force the phenomena into line with theories and opinions of their own (*De caelo* 293a20–27). When he adds that "many others" share this point of view, "placing more trust in their theories than in the phenomena" (29–30), he gives no indication that Plato is one of this company. (It should be noted that he does nothing of the kind in the remark in *Met.* 997b to which I referred above (n. 14 *sub fin.*): even if meant as reportage [I argued that it was not], it would still not cast Plato in the role of "replacing observations by speculation," for it would constitute comment on Plato's ontology—not on the content of his astronomical theory.)

[28] It is no exaggeration to say that after the initial palaver, drawn out at tedious length, which corrects Glaucon's misunderstanding of the "upward" view (528e6–529c3), all the rest of the passage revolves around this analogy. Though introduced explicitly only at 529d7, its central point had been anticipated already at 529c7 in the suggestion that the visible celestial motions "fall far short" of the "true" ones (on which see n. 30 below). This proposition, developed in 529c8–d5 and accepted there as reasonable, is then used to justify the analogy (which is presented as an inference from the preceding remark: this is the force of *oukoun* in 529d7). We then have the exposition of the analogy in 529d7–530a1, its application to astronomy in 530a2–b4, and the generalized conclusion drawn from it (cf. *ara* in 530b6) in 530b6–c1.

[29] I choose a "problem," i.e., a construction-proof (cf. Proclus, *Comm. on Book I of Euclid's Elements*, 79, 3ff.) rather than an ordinary theorem, because of Plato's description of the philosopher's procedure in astronomy, as investigating "problems" (530b6). He uses the term again in

which is not on it, to draw a perpendicular straight line." Several features of the drawing misrepresent the geometrical truth. Thus AB, the stand-in for the "infinite straight line," is blatantly finite. And all the lines in the diagram are bogus, since none of them is only one-dimensional: all have breadth as well as length. But if the diagram is reasonably well-drawn, not everything in it will be askew. Some things in it will tell no lie but a sturdily honest tale—e.g., that CG = CE, and the ∠ CHG = ∠ CHE. Both of these propositions, and many others, which could be read off the diagram, will be true, though, as Plato would insist, our acceptance of their truth must be made with two fundamental provisos: [5]

(i) We must not look for *perfect* equality in either case, for we are dealing with material, sensible, lines and angles, and these are likely to "fall far short"[30] of the absolute equality we have in view in geometrical reasoning.

(ii) If our evidence for the truth of these propositions is nothing better than observation of diagrams, we cannot claim *knowledge,* but only "true opinion."[31] To turn this true opinion into "knowledge" we would have to drop the diagram ("dismiss it")[32] and look to the principles of geometry (i.e., to the Euclidian axiom-set and, for Plato, to the Forms Point, Straight Line, Angle, and so forth), deriving the propositions that CG = CE and ∠ CHG = ∠ CHE as deductive consequences of the principles, since the two lines are radii of the same circle and the two angles are corresponding angles in triangles CHG and CHE, whose congruence has been established in the proof of the "problem."

I submit that the same thing would be true for Plato *mutatis mutandis* when we use the visible heavens as a "model for the sake of understanding" the "real" movements of the stars (παραδείγμασι χρηστέον τῆς πρὸς ἐκεῖνα

---

discussing what the philosopher's procedure ought to be in harmonics, the next subject on their curriculum; he says that those addicted to the alternative, empirically oriented, procedure "seek numbers in harmonies which are heard, and *do not ascend to problems*" (ἀλλ' οὐκ εἰς προβλήματα ἀνίασιν, 531c2–3).

[30] *Polu endein,* 529d1–2. This is an important motif in Platonic epistemology, introduced already in the *Phaedo:* sticks and stones whose dimensions are equal (would be correctly so described), nevertheless "fall somewhat short" (*endein ti*) of perfect equality (74d6–7); they "resemble equality, but do so defectively" (προσεοικέναι μέν, ἐνδεεστέρως δὲ ἔχειν, 74e3–4). Plato hangs on to this conviction throughout the rest of his life. It is still in evidence in the very late dialogue, the *Philebus:* there he contrasts the Form of the Circle with the (material) circle used in construction and the industrial arts as "divine" and "human" respectively (62a4–b2); he calls the latter "the false circle" (62b5–6), evidently because it is only an imperfect exemplification of the Form.

[31] *Alēthēs doxa. Doxa* (in contrast to *gnōsis, epistēmē*), is a *terminus technicus* of the first importance in Plato. It plays a pivotal role at the start of the epistemological section of the *Republic* (see *doxa, doxazein* in 476d ff.) and again in the section on the "Divided Line," 510a ff.

[32] I offer here the clue to the correct interpretation of the sense of *easomen* in 530B7 which I shall be presenting in Section III below.

μαθήσεως ἕνεκα 529d7–8). Let us take solar motion as a case in point. Its visual representation in the cosmic mobile fashioned by the divine Daedalus of the *Timaeus*[33] is for Plato as false and misleading in some respects as is the diagram in Euclid. For example, all it shows us of the sun is a fiery disk moving across the sky. That this disk is a globe does not come through the visible model. Still less does the fact that this globe is a living creature,[34] indeed a god:[35] if what we see of it was to be believed, we could be making the blasphemous error of thinking, with Anaxagoras and Democritus, that it was a soulless mass of matter. But there are other things observable in the mobile which are as true as are the equalities observable in the diagram. Such for Plato would be the circular form of the sun's diurnal and annual tracks: if we were to plot successive positions of the sun of either track, we would find that the simplest curves joining them would be plane projections of segments of circular orbits. To be sure, here as before the same qualifications would be in order:

(i) We could no more expect perfect instantiations of circularity in our mobile than of equality in the diagram. [6]

(ii) If all we had to show for our belief that the sun's trajectories are circular were what we observe in the celestial mobile, then all we would have is true opinion, not knowledge.

Point (i) is spelled out in the passage: we should think of the phenomenal motions of the stars as "falling far short of the true [motions] (τῶν ἀληθινῶν πολὺ ἐνδεῖν, 529d1–2); it would be "absurd" to expect those corporeal and visible things in the sky "to be forever invariant and to be absolutely undeviating" (γίγνεσθαι . . . ταῦτα ἀεὶ ὡσαύτως καὶ οὐδαμῆ οὐδὲν παραλλάττειν, 530b2–3). To continue the thought: gross deviations from the circular form are ruled out, since our model is the product of consummate—divine—craftsmanship. Even so, we must be prepared for *some* discrepancies between the ideal figure and the material model. So if we learn from Euctemon that his and Meton's observations had disclosed that it takes the sun five days longer to go from winter to summer solstice than vice-versa,[36] while the two periods

---

[33] 29d ff

[34] *Zōia, Tim.* 38e5 *et passim.*

[35] *Theia onta, Tim.* 40b5; *theōn, Tim.* 40c3 *et passim.*

[36] In *Ars Eudoxi* 55 (ed. Blass [1887]) Euctemon's figures for the seasons are as follows:

92 days from winter solstice to vernal equinox,
93 from vernal equinox to summer solstice,
90 from summer solstice to autumnal equinox,
90 from autumnal equinox to winter solstice.

These observations were made around 430 B.C. (Heath 1913, 215). They could hardly have been unknown to Plato.

should be equal if it were traversing at the same speed either half of a perfectly circular orbit (as in fact it does according to Plato's theory in the *Timaeus*), we shall not be upset: if the "true number" of the sun's journey from solstice to solstice is 182.5 days each way, and observation reports it as 182.5 ± 2.5 days, that is close enough. We can ignore this as just a kink in the medium analogous to a slight irregularity in one of the lines in our diagram: our theory of the sun's "true" motion would take no account of it.[37]

Point (ii) is not worked out at all by Plato, here or anywhere else. But he has given us the materials we need to work it up for ourselves: we have his theory of solar motion in the *Timaeus*,[38] can easily figure out the methodological procedure it presupposes, and can determine which of the results Plato obtained by the procedure would qualify for what he calls knowledge as *vs.* true opinion. From astronomical observers Plato takes over the mass of empirical data which record the sun's diurnal westward motions in their ordered sequence from solstice to solstice and its annual eastward motion along the ecliptic. This is the base from which he had to start: a set of true opinions concerning the apparent motions of the sun approximating its "true" motion. Given these [7] opinions, he proceeds to do his own work, the "real" astronomy which investigates the "problem" of solar motion. He does the work by identifying the set of assumptions from which he will be able to make the deductions which will solve the "problem." These are the assumptions: that the sun's true course is a complex motion which may be analyzed into a pair of perfectly circular motions, those of the Same and of the Different, with their assumed properties (the location of each in a scheme of celestial coordinates; the angle at which their planes intersect; their relative angular velocities).[39] From these assumptions it follows by geometrical reasoning that the sun's true motion is a closed spiral tangent on the tropics at either end;[40] and this accounts for the observed phenomena.[41] In this investigation considerable

---

[37] As in fact Plato's theory in the *Timaeus* does not; as we know from Eudemus (*apud* Simplicius, *De caelo* 497, 17–22), neither did Eudoxus' theory—he too treated it as a phenomenon that need not be saved—and it was only Callippus who added two spheres to Eudoxus' three to save the phenomenal inequality of the seasons (corrected [to 90, 94, 92, 89 days respectively for the intervals corresponding to those in n. 36 above: *Ars Eudoxi, loc. cit.*] by intervening, more accurate, observations).

[38] The admissability of this material in expounding Plato's conception of astronomy in our passage may be disputed, since it comes from a later dialogue. I would reply that the circumstantial material is by no means indispensable to my argument, since it is brought in here for purposes of illustration, not proof. I could have proceeded in a more abstract vein and argued that, since we would all assume that Plato's analogy between observing diagrams in geometry, on one hand, and the visible heavens, on the other, is seriously meant, he must have counted on *some such use* of the latter, as my argument proceeds to illustrate.

[39] The theory adumbrated in *Tim.* 36b–39c. according to the standard interpretation.

[40] See, e.g., Heath [1913, 169].

[41] Lacking Plato's own analysis of what kind of accounting for the phenomena ("saving" them)

"knowledge" is won. Thus the assumption that the two component motions are perfectly circular would undoubtedly count as metaphysical knowledge;[42] and the deduction that the two motions with their assumed properties would produce the helix would represent mathematical knowledge, whose objects are the Forms of Circle, Spiral, and the like. But there would be other assumptions too which have no metaphysical or mathematical grounding but are posited *ad hoc* to explain the given data (those I called "the assumed properties" of the two component motions).[43] For this reason the final result—the explanation of solar motion, the "saving"[44] of the relevant phenomena—would still constitute true opinion,[45] though the knowledge which made that

---

his theory is meant to do, we can infer it from his geometrical analogy: when we return to the diagram with the knowledge of the demonstration, we can see, e.g., *why* the angles CHG and CHE, which do look equal, *must* look the way they do: we have an explanation of the fact. Having proved triangles CHG and CHE congruent, we know that corresponding angles must be equal; and this must show up in the diagram—if it does not, the diagram must be badly drawn. Similarly, when [26] we return to "the things in the heavens" armed with Plato's theory, we can see *why* the sun's motion must be such as it appears to astronomical observers—e.g., that its eastward annual motion must be along the ecliptic. This allows for marginal phenomena—like the inequality of the seasons—that will fall outside the scope of the explanation as theoretically uninteresting and unimportant deviations from the "true" pattern. This too fits in well with the geometrical paradigm: the demonstration does not explain all the properties of the sensible figure—only those selected properties which are adequate instantiations of the relevant geometrical truths.

[42] It is a consequence of the metaphysical doctrines that these are the motions of a divine (and hence rational) soul (34b) and that the form of motion "proper to reason and intelligence" is rotation (34a).

[43] That is why it would be wrong to think of Plato as getting his theory of solar motion by "replacing observation by speculation" or by "*a prioristic* construction." Not that there is any lack of speculative and *a prioristic* premises in the reasoning: what else should we call, for example, Plato's doctrine that solar motion must be perfectly circular because the stars are gods (nn. 35 and 42 above) and rotation is the only motion befitting perfectly rational beings (*Tim.* 34a: *Laws* 896a–b)? But all we could squeeze out of this is that the sun moves in perfect circles. That it in fact moves in circles which have the particular properties of the Same and the Different is a hypothesis whose sole justification is empirical: this is what has to be posited to account for the sun's phenomenal motions.

[44] I do not mean to suggest that the term is so used in the Platonic corpus, but that it could have been to express Plato's result. The phrase *sōzein ta phainomena* does not occur in the Platonic corpus, nor yet in Aristotle's surviving works. But "save a thesis (or argument)" (*logon, Theaet.* 164a, 167d) or "save a tale" (*muthon, Laws* 645d) does occur in contexts where "to save" is to preserve consistency, which is the root meaning of "saving the phenomena" (showing that a phenomenon which does not seem to sit well with the hypothesis is in fact fully consistent with it, the consistency being established by showing that the observed phenomenon would follow from the hypothesis in those particular circumstances). Cf. also Vlastos (1975a, 111–12).

[45] That is why astronomy, taken as a whole, would constitute "true opinion" for Plato, and his own astronomical theories are presented in a dialogue which professes to tell a "likely tale" (*Tim.* 29b–d), though this profession in no way implies that *everything* in the discourse of Timaeus is meant to be no better than true opinion: many things in it (including its metaphysical and epistemological doctrine) would certainly count as "knowledge."

result possible would be, for the philosopher, the rewarding part of the investigation, the only part of it which would feed his soul, make it look "upward" and realize its potentiality for "wisdom."

If this is even roughly correct as an interpretation of the methodology that produced Plato's own theory of solar motion, we may be certain that the idea that Plato wants the astronomers to "ban sense-perception" is radically mistaken. Had Plato done any such thing, his investigation could never even have got started, for he would have lacked the explananda, the phenomena to be saved. So whatever he may have meant by τὰ δ' ἐν τῷ οὐρανῷ ἐάσομεν, he cannot have meant that we shall "ban," "eliminate," "forget altogether" the observed phenomena. To do so would be to scrap the celestial model instead of using it. [8]

III

Now let us go over to the other end of the spectrum of available interpretations and probe one which would not only rescue Plato from the obscurantist role in which the Heath-Neugebauer-Mittelstrass line would cast him but credit him with flawless understanding of the science of astronomy and of its current needs. This has been put forward in the chapter on Plato in Dick's *Early Greek Astronomy to Aristotle* (1970, chap. 5, at pp. 106–8 and p. 234n. 139). The proposal is premised on the assumption that a great mass of observational material had accumulated by this time, so that

> what was wanted now was for astronomers to sit down and do some hard thinking about astronomical theory, so as to make the best use of the observations they already had, and evolve a mathematically based system which would take into account not only the long-known variations in the aspects of the night sky, but also the irregularities apparent in the movements of the sun, moon, and the recently discovered planets. . . .
>
> This is precisely what Plato realized, and this is why he urged the astronomers to concentrate on the mathematical side of their subject and study the real mathematical relations lying beyond the visible phenomena, to the extent even of *temporarily calling a halt to the mere accumulation of more observations.* (108)

I have italicized the phrase which contains the crux of the proposed interpretation. Dicks argues that the actual wording of the disputed phrase supports this construction; he asks us to

> note the last word: Plato does not use here the phrase *chairein eān,* "to renounce" or "dismiss altogether" (frequent elsewhere in Plato, e.g., *Phaedo* 63e; *Prot.* 348a; *Phil.* 59b), as he might well have done had he meant to imply that observation could be dispensed with entirely, but the simple verb meaning "to let be" or "leave on one

side," evidently *for the time being* while the astronomer concentrates on the mathematical side of his subject [my italics].[46]

No friend of Plato's could have asked for a more attractive interpretation. Unhappily it is not what Plato says: there is not a word in the passage to assert, imply, or even suggest, what is conveyed in the phrases I italicized— no reference there to a moratorium on observation to give theory time to catch up. Worse yet, the reasons given in Plato's text why his [9] philosophers should devote themselves to astronomical theory and "let the things in the heavens alone" have nothing to do with anything as transitory and remediable as a current lag of theory behind observation. The reasons are that the things in the heavens, being "corporeal and visible," cannot be expected "to be forever invariant and to be absolutely undeviating," nor yet to elevate the philosopher's soul to the eternal world and thus develop its innate capacity for "wisdom." For Plato these matters are ingrained in the structure of reality and of the human condition; they are ineluctable and irremediable fatalities. If these are the reasons why the philosophers should "let the things in the heavens alone" when doing astronomy, the phrase could not possibly mean "let them alone for the present."

What else then? There is a perfectly simple way to make sense of τὰ δ' ἐν τῷ οὐρανῷ ἐάσομεν which maintains consistency with everything in the passage and with all the rest of the evidence as well. This is to read it with an implied qualification, understanding it to mean: dismiss the things in the heavens *as objects of knowledge*. So taken the injunction would be a direct corollary of the fact that these things are sensible ("of such things there can be no knowledge" [529c1]), but would have no implication that they should be dismissed by one who wants to do astronomy. What will not do as *knowledge* by Platonic standards, may do famously as *true opinion;* and true opinion, though no proper part of "real" astronomy, may still be its prerequisite.[47] In

---

[46] On the linguistic remark above: I would agree that if Plato had said *chairein eān* instead of *eān tout court*, it would have been clearer that the intended sense is the stronger one. However, *eān* all by itself *could* have carried this stronger sense: cf. n. 18 above.

[47] Shorey's reading of Plato's sentence is along the same lines (cf. the quotation from him in the opening paragraph above). But his exegesis is defective in two ways:

(a) He fails to note the simple, yet all-important, fact that Plato's own methodology presupposes much greater dependence on observation than just using it to pick up "suggestion[s] for higher studies." Judging from his own practice, Plato would expect "real" astronomers to master the full dossier of observational data as *the indispensable prerequisite* to their own, purely theoretical, research: without these data they would have no "problem" worth investigating.

(b) Since what Plato presupposes in (a) he *never explicitly recognizes*, one has to *argue* for it. Indeed even the vaguer claim made by Shorey—that Plato welcomes empirical astronomical data so long as they are used only for "suggestion[s] for higher studies"—has to be argued for: on the face of it, to "let alone" the observational data expresses a purely negative attitude

the terminal part of the preceding section, I indicated what is the true relation of observation to that investigation of "problems" which Plato considers "real astronomy": the observational data merely *pose* the problems; their collection is, therefore, the indispensable preliminary to the investigation of problems and *is not counted as part of the investigation,* so that the latter is taken to consist only of the purely theoretical activity which discovers and demonstrates the solution. The vital point here—the one conveyed in the italicized phrase—is unhappily not said, nor even hinted at, by Plato in our passage. On what ground then could we impute it to him? If we had nothing better to go on, we could fall back on our confidence in his common sense. Surely he could not have ignored [10] the all too obvious fact that if we are going to set ourselves up as *astronomers* we must have some facts to begin with, facts which could only have been derived by sensory observation: how else could we have come to believe that there are such things as stars up there in the sky, millions of fixed ones, just seven "wandering" ones, etc. etc.?[48] Happily we have something better than faith in Plato's good sense to go on:

There is a passage in the *Phaedrus* (268d–e), never before connected with our passage in the *Republic* to my knowledge, which gives us pretty much what we have charitably guessed on Plato's behalf, i.e., that he is counting on having empirically established true beliefs as the prerequisites of knowledge in any given natural science. Socrates tells there how a master of musical science would talk to the practical musician who fancies himself a master of harmonics (*oiomenōi harmonikōi einai*) because he has learned such things as how to get the highest and the lowest tone from a string:

The musical man would not be so rude as to say, "Wretch, you are out of your mind." More gently, as befits his calling, he would say: "Most excellent sir, it is quite true that if one is to become a master of harmonics one must also know[49] those

---

toward observation; what warrant then does Shorey have for imputing to Plato positive interest in observation as a source of "suggestion[s] for higher studies?"

Shorey has nothing on (a); for all his bluster against the "hostile or thoughtless critics" who think Plato "unscientific," Shorey fails to indicate the depth of Plato's own debt to the observational astronomy of his own and the preceding generation. And he has nothing on (b), except to call attention to the undoubted element of hyperbole in Plato's τὰ δ' ἐν τῷ οὐρανῷ ἐάσομεν ("exaggerated Emersonian emphasis" [1927, 172]; "Ruskinian boutade" [1935, n. *ad loc.*]). He would have done well to illustrate Plato's unfortunate tendency to overstate his thesis when developing it polemically. A good monograph on Plato's faults as a controversialist (scornful of his adversaries, weakening his own case by escalating its claims beyond necessity) has yet to be written, and no one would have done it better than Shorey, if he could have brought himself to observe dispassionately the human side of his philosophical hero.

[48] Speaking from the standpoint of Greek astronomy, which knows of only seven "planets," counting the sun as a member of the septet.

[49] Note that here Plato is reverting to the common, nontechnical sense of *know* (*epistamai*). Had he been sticking to stricter standards, his epistemology would have required him to say, "You

things. But it is perfectly possible for one who has learned what you have, to be without the slightest knowledge of harmony (μηδὲ σμικρὸν ἁρμονίας ἐπαΐειν). For you know *what it is necessary* to know *before* harmonics, but not *harmonics* (τὰ γὰρ πρὸ ἁρμονίας ἀναγκαῖα μαθήματα ἐπίστασαι ἀλλ' οὐ τὰ ἁρμονικά).

By the same token Plato would have said to a purely empirical astronomer: you have learned what it is necessary to learn before astronomy, but you haven't learned astronomy. And to say this would be to make the vital concession that there are πρὸ ἀστρονομίας ἀναγκαῖα μαθήματα, namely, the ones that instruct us in the body of beliefs the sky watchers have discovered.

This being the case, what can that troublesome phrase, τὰ δ' ἐν τῷ οὐρανῷ ἐάσομεν, mean but: [i] dismiss the sensible phenomena as themselves constituting knowledge, while [ii] using them to set up the problems whose solution will disclose the sought-for knowledge? As I have already admitted, indeed emphasized, the passage in the *Republic* offers no [11] direct support for [ii]; had it done so, none of the variant misunderstandings of it would have arisen. But for [i] it does offer excellent support. Let me quote again the period in which the phrase occurs:

> It is by means of problems, then, that we shall proceed in astronomy in the same way as we do in geometry, and we shall let the things in the heavens alone, if by doing real astronomy we are to turn from disuse to use the wisdom that is by nature in our soul.

What is called "doing real astronomy" in the last sentence is described at the start as the investigation of "problems," a term borrowed from geometry, where it refers to construction-proofs.[50] And as if this were not sufficient to indicate the intended methodological assimilation of "real" astronomy to geometry, Plato labors the point, saying that "we shall proceed in astronomy as we do in geometry." Plato knows that geometrical reasoning brooks no reliance on sense-experience.[51] By the same token, neither would astronomical reasoning if its procedure is the same. In demonstrating that the appearances which constitute his "problem" follow from his proposed hypotheses, the astronomer would employ mathematical reasoning whose objects are Forms. Relying on the eternally invariant properties, he would "dismiss the things in the heavens": he would free the cogency of his argument from any dependence on the appearances.

This interpretation of the disputed sentence has put the strongest emphasis on its contextual environment, and for good reason: had that sentence oc-

---

have the true beliefs which it is necessary to have before harmonics." The readiness to speak with the vulgar upon occasion is typical of Plato; his refusal to adhere to rigid terminological rules is well known.

50 Cf. n. 29 above.

51 Cf. n. 11 above.

curred in a different context—had it been put forward as a general methodological pronunciamento—we would have had no warrant for reading it otherwise than as an interdict on sensory observation in astronomy. But the fact is that this is not what Plato gives us. *His* sentence is imbedded in a context whose syntax determines its scope by tying it to an antecedent and to a consequent. The sentence is connected paratactically to the one before it which fixes the frame of reference—the investigation of "problems" *more geometrico*—and hypotactically, as apodosis to a protasis, to the sentence which follows. Let me reverse the order to bring out better the latter syntactical bond: [12]

[A] If, by doing real astronomy, we are to turn from disuse to use the wisdom that is by nature in our soul, [then]

[B] we should let the things in the heavens alone.

[A] epitomizes the purpose for which astronomy gets into Plato's philosophical curriculum at all: its function is to get fledgling philosophers to develop the "wisdom" in their soul; and for Plato this would occur only when the soul was occupied with the strictly nonsensuous objects of genuine knowledge, the ideal Forms. So to say "if we are to achieve the goal in [A], we must heed injunction [B]" is to bind the scope of the injunction to its efficacy for just that goal; for the advancement of other goals adherence to that injunction might be useless or worse.

Now Plato's vision of philosophy so magnifies the goal in [A] as to dwarf every other. To live up to this image, one would have to dedicate oneself to the contemplative life with a totality of commitment, with an obsessive, all-engrossing abandon, which would have few parallels in recorded history, except perhaps in the annals of religious devotion and there only in its most strenuously self-denying and otherworldly forms. But for all the intensity of his longing to flee the prison of the senses,[52] the flesh-and-blood Platonic philosopher cannot deny his incarnation. Throughout its duration he must reckon with the circumstances of a soul stuck in a body which is stuck in a material world.[53] The stars are a part, albeit the noblest part, of this world and he must get the material facts about them straight, else his "real" astronomy would be only a mathematical dream. *This* purpose falls strictly outside the scope of [A] and calls for the very contrary of [B]—not to "dismiss" the things in the heavens but to take account of them. To be sure, he will do so

[52] I am conflating the imagery of the *Republic* (the sense-world, the "cave," is a prison where men are "chained," 514a ff.) and of the *Theaetetus* ("we should try to flee from this world to that one as quickly as possible; and the flight is becoming like god so far as possible . . . ," 176a8–b2).

[53] That is why, for example, he must be "compelled" to return to the Cave to rule it, much though he would prefer to spend all his time in intellectual pursuits (519d–520a; 521b).

grudgingly, for every minute he spends on "the things in the heavens" he is subtracting from commerce with the unseen things beyond, which is his paramount concern. That is why Plato had dropped, just before (530b3–4), that remark which is so shocking that some of the best translators have shrunk from rendering it into English:[54] the "real astronomer" would think it "absurd" to take the greatest pains ("strive by every possible means") to reach precise determinations of the relative [13] lengths of the periods of the celestial bodies. For the philosopher this would be a burdensome business, a kind of drudgery, which he would want to cut short; and he could not expect too much "truth" from this quarter, since the sensible phenomena are bound to be subject to "deviations" (ibid.). Anyhow there are plenty of other people in this world who can and should do whatever is necessary along these lines—the mass of empirics who have no aptitude for philosophy, who couldn't "look upward" no matter how hard they tried, and who are, therefore, properly consigned to the arts and crafts. These people, though unintellectual, need not be unintelligent. They would do jobs like navigation, medicine, construction of houses, tools, musical instruments, and the like, which call for high skills on a level of what we would call "applied science." Why should not skywatching be one of these? Plato's philosophical astronomers may then count on technicians to do, under their direction, the bulk of the necessary work of observational astronomy. To these henchmen the injunction in [B] would not apply, since goal [A] could have no relevance for them. It is only "we," the prospective philosophers, who are enjoined to "let the things of the heavens alone."

IV

Let me now pick up for brief critical comment the analogy on which I rested, in part, my case against the Heath-Mittelstrass line, i.e., Plato's claim that the visible motions of the stars are to their real motions as are the sensible properties of diagrams in geometry to the axioms and theorems of that science. On any interpretation of the whole passage, this analogy would certainly carry the burden of Plato's conception of the role of observation in astronomy. If there is a flaw in that conception, here is where it would show up. It does. There is one fundamental respect in which the analogy is radically inept and misleading: whatever truth may be pictured in a geometrical diagram, the fact that it is pictured there *has no evidentiary value*. If asked *why* CG = CE and ∠ CHG = ∠ CHE in the diagram in Euclid I, 12, no Greek mathematician would have replied at the time, "Go look at the diagram and you will see that it is true." In astronomy, on the [14] other hand, that reply would have been perfectly cor-

---

[54] Cf. n. 17 above. And cf. n. 55 below.

rect *mutatis mutandis:* what can be seen in the visible heavens is indeed a reason—in the last analysis, *the* reason—why an astronomical theory is true. Whatever knowledge of Form a theory may disclose will not, of itself, establish its claim to be true of the real movements of the stars, unless observations of the apparent movements give close enough approximations to relevant deduction from the theory. Thus, that the sun's "real" motion must be a spiral *if* it results from the concurrent motions of the Same and the Different with their assigned respective properties, does not begin to show that the motion is a spiral; to show this, we must appeal to the phenomena to see if they tally, within the permissible margin of deviation, with the consequences of the theory. In the last analysis, it will be the phenomena that must confirm or disconfirm the theory. This would be unthinkable if, following Plato's counsel, we had been investigating "problems" in the geometrical mode, where the correctness of the solution has to be proved exclusively by deduction from the axiom set, and where to look for verification in the observed properties of diagrams would be insane. What is unthinkable in Greek geometry is not only thinkable but mandatory in astronomy, where the theorist must submit his conclusions to the arbitrament of scientifically observed facts.

In so doing, the theorist may not only allow for a margin of error but may resort to simplifying assumptions which effect a deliberate idealization of the phenomena. So Plato might, when he chose to ignore the inequality of the seasons, had he claimed that his own theory, which presupposes their strict equality, is meant to present an ideally simplified pattern which the observed facts only approximate. Had Plato done so, his procedure might have been not only philosophically unobjectionable but scientifically sagacious. At a certain stage of scientific progress, this may well be the scientist's best strategy, since the demand to produce a theory which tallies more closely with the observed facts may be inhibiting, perhaps even crippling, at that particular time, when theoretical resources are unequal to the task.[55] So if this had been Plato's point, we would have had no fault to find with it. [15] But that, unhappily, is not his point. Constrained by his metaphysical and epistemological doctrine to locate truth only in ideal objects whose instantiation in the physical world necessarily involves some "falling short" of the true properties of the instantiated patterns, Plato fails to see how important it still is in astronomy that its observational component should strive to meet the highest standards of accu-

---

[55] For this insight, which has changed my outlook on the contributions to the development of scientific thought that were made by Greek philosophers from the sixth to the fourth centuries B.C., I am indebted to T. S. Kuhn's *Copernican Revolution.* I do not mean that he applies it specifically to Plato, or, in detail, to the work of any Greek philosopher-scientist. But his treatment of their theories is informed by this principle. To read him is to be freed from the all-too-easy tendency to make *unreasonable demands* on scientific pioneers—unreasonable because they could not have been met with the conceptual apparatus available at the time, so that the attempt to meet them would have led into a blind alley.

racy attainable at a given time. The failure surfaces in that remark (530b1–4) to which I referred near the close of the preceding section, that it would be "absurd" to expect the motions of the visible bodies of the stars, "to be forever invariant and to be absolutely undeviating, and *to strive to determine their truth by every possible means*." To say this is to belittle the importance of attaining the greatest possible precision in such matters,[56] and thus, unhappily, to "denigrate the role of observation in astronomy,"[57] accepting it as a necessary, but boring, work which may be left to high-grade drudges.

If Eudoxus—that marvelously gifted theorist, as great a mathematician as Greece ever produced—had shared this attitude, he would scarcely have done the work of dedicated, assiduous, observation recorded in those books of his whose very titles, *Phaenomena* and *Enoptron* ("Mirror [of the Heavens]") proclaim the observational intent of their contents,[58] work on which he built the first gigantic achievement of theoretical astronomy, his theory of homocentric spheres. One might object, borrowing wisdom from hindsight, that Eudoxus could still have produced that theory if he had had access to other people's observations, as Kepler did to Tycho Brahe's. But the objection would miss the vital point that the very ground on which Plato exempts the theoreticians from observational work would have killed the chances of such teamwork: in Plato's utopia a man of Tycho Brahe's intellectual powers would have qualified as a theorist and hence, on Plato's principles, would never have done the work of a Tycho Brahe. If the division of labor implied in Plato's theory had been clamped on the practice of Greek astronomy, it would have

---

[56] I italicized the second clause in the quotation because that is precisely where Plato reveals how indifferently he esteems the attainment of high standards of precision in observation. The italicized phrase would have had no such implication if Plato had only said that it would be "absurd" *for the philosophers* to do all that striving for exactness in empirical observation: after all, they have much better use for their time, and they would be acting irrationally if they diverted precious intellectual energy to intercourse with the sensible world. That he should not make this qualification—that he should write a sentence which declares the striving to reach precise observational truth by every possible means to be itself "absurd"—gives away the fact that he regards strict observational accuracy a matter of quite secondary importance. After all, he expects all technicians to strive for perfection in the performance of their respective tasks. Why should he not have said that while perfection in this domain would be a waste of the philosophers' energy, it should none the less be pursued conscientiously by non-philosophers who have no higher aptitudes?

[57] *Pace* Dicks [1970, 106], who says that 530b6–c1 does not "afford the smallest justification" for imputing this attitude to Plato. I agree that it would not, if we had in view the sort of denigration, rightly protested by Dicks, which is implied in Neugebauer's remark, cited above, that Plato wants "the astronomers to replace observation by speculation." But there *is* justification for it in the aspersions on observation carried by the remarks I have just cited in the text above, and in the implication in 580b6–c1 that observation is *not* "real" astronomy and does *not* serve "to turn the natural intelligence of our soul from uselessness to use."

[58] Cf. F. Lasserre [1964, 127ff.], who stresses the descriptive nature of their contents and gives good illustrations.

reduced disastrously the chances that its observational side would be done at a sufficiently imaginative and resourceful level to meet the needs of the great theorists, Eudoxus, Apollonius, Hipparchus, and the rest. [16]

POSTSCRIPT: OBSERVATION IN HARMONICS (*REP.* 530D1-531D7).

No discussion of the section on astronomy in Book 7 of the *Republic* would be complete if it did not take account of what is said in the immediate sequel, where Plato turns to its "counterpart" (*antistrophon,* 530d4) for harmonics. This passage has embarrassed even the staunchest of Plato's well-wishers. Starting with a blast at the out-and-out empirics of the science[59] (they are dismissed with the withering remark that "they put their ears above their reason," 531b1), Plato turns, more surprisingly, against another group of investigators, who are evidently several cuts above the first, but still fall far below his standards. They are described as follows:

> They measure audible concords and tones against one another—unprofitable labor, like that of the astronomers [who had been criticized in the foregoing] (531a1–3). . . . They look for numbers in those audible concords, instead of ascending to problems to investigate which numbers are concordant and which are not, and why so in either case. (531b9–c4)

Now why should Plato say that to "look for numbers in audible concords" is "unprofitable labor"?[60] Is he desiderating a purely *a priori* science of harmonics that bans sense-perception in this area as Heath & co. have supposed him to have banned it in astronomy? Such seems the obvious implication of the passage—so much so that even Shorey feels compelled to concede it, remarking ruefully at this point.

> This is perhaps one of Plato's rare errors. For though there may be in some sense a Kantian *a priori* mechanics of astronomy, there can hardly be a purely *a priori* mathematics of acoustics. What numbers are constantly harmonious must always remain a fact of direct experience. [1935, 193, note g]

Shorey here feels compelled to impute to Plato a discipline that would excogitate *a priori* such down-to-earth facts as that the octave, the fifth, and the fourth are consonant intervals, i.e., that when each of those three pairs of notes are sounded on suitable material media, like strings or woodwinds, musical concords, instead of discords, are produced.

To free Plato from this unhappy imputation, we need only recall the passage

---

[59] They "torture strings" and listen for "minims" (*puknōmata*—for the probable meaning of this technical term, see Adam on 531a4).

[60] *Anēnuta poiousi* ("useless labor," Shorey; "a waste of time," Cornford).

in the *Phaedrus* (268d–e) which proved so [17] useful in the foregoing. There Plato hands us on a silver platter what he fails to mention here, that he is counting on πρὸ ἁρμονίας ἀναγκαῖα μαθήματα—truths about the world of sound that one must learn before one can even start the theoretical investigation which, for Plato, *is* the science of harmonics. This body of information the Platonic scientist would learn from practicing musicians who had discovered it empirically; so the question of deriving it *a priori* will not arise. Why then should Plato regard "looking for numbers in audible discords" as unprofitable business? To get the answer we need only note that when he speaks here of "unprofitable labor" he adds at once, "like that of the [objectionable] astronomers": the flashback reminds us of the great to-do in the preceding passage about the liberation of the soul from this world to the "higher" one, which is, for the Platonic philosopher, the only reason for doing any science at all. So long as investigation is confined to audible concords, the investigator remains imprisoned in the world of sense; no facts discovered in this realm can of themselves yield knowledge ("of such things there can be no knowledge," 529b7–c1), thereby profiting the soul by elevating it to the eternal realm. If we did not have the *Phaedrus* passage, we might then infer with Burkert that Plato's harmonics would be a pure number theory with no interest in "audible concords"[61]—or else suppose, as Shorey does above, that he wants the scientist to derive such facts *a priori*. That Plato wants neither of these absurdities is a reasonable inference from the *Phaedrus* passage, which suggests that he thinks such facts *indispensable* (*anankaia*) and expects his philosopher-scientists to get them *pro tēs harmonias*—before entering real (i.e., theoretical) Harmonics. This inference is confirmed when we see Plato's reason for objecting to those who "look for numbers in audible concords": it is that they do not "rise to problems." What he is desiderating, clearly, is a constructive theory which will *explain* the (antecedently determined) empirical data—will show why the instantiation of such and such numerical ratios in physical sounds within the range of our hearing produces consonance instead of dissonance.

To spot investigators whom Plato would fault for *not* "rising to problems,"

---

[61] What Plato here desiderates, writes Burkert [1972, 372], "is . . . pure number theory, above and beyond experience," projecting a program which he carried out "at least by way of suggestion" in the *Timaeus* (35b–36c), "using a series of numbers derived from the ultimate principles, which arrayed themselves in a scale without audible sound." The sequence of intervals of the *Timaeus* passage, running into four octaves and a major sixth, would indeed outrun the range of tones admissible in Greek music and might thus be thought to extend to intervals "without audible sound." But what makes the passage a theory of *musical harmony* at all is the fact that a subset of its series of numbers is meant to cover the scale of Greek music; in so doing the theory would have to reckon with auditory facts which could only be derived from experience.

[62] It is widely agreed that the methodology criticized in the above quotation from *Rep.* 531a–c

we need look no further than the Pythagorean[62] [18] discoverers of such facts as that the octave, the fifth, and the fourth were produced by physical media (strings, flutes, metal disks, tumblers) instantiating appropriately the 2:1, 3:2, 4:3 ratios.[63] This could not represent anything Plato would dignify by the name of science: the observational content of these discoveries would not qualify as knowledge because of its sensory character, nor would its arithmetical content because it is grounded on nothing better than empirical correlations. Just how far Plato thought he had himself progressed in the area of "real" harmonics is not at all clear in our present passage in the *Republic*, which is purely programmatic, nor yet in the *Timaeus*, where he does present a mathematical construction of the intervals of the diatonic scale (35b–36c) but fails to connect the construction in any way with the physical theory of consonance he sketches later on (80a–b).[64] He gives no clear evidence that he himself successfully "ascended to problems" in this area, as he demonstrably did in the astronomical theory of the *Timaeus*. So we need give him no more credit here for scientific insight than he has shown us to have earned. But we can at least exonerate him from the folly of requiring the scientist to construct a theory of harmonics on purely *a priori* premises without any empirical data at all.[65]

BIBLIOGRAPHY

Adam, J. *The Republic of Plato*. 2 volumes. Cambridge, 1902.
Blass, Fr., ed. *Eudoxi "Ars Astronomica" qualis in charta Aegyptiaca superest*. Kiel, 1887.
Bloom, A. *The Republic of Plato*. New York, 1968.
Burkert, W. *Lore and Science in Ancient Pythagoreanism*. Translated by E. L. Minar, Jr. Cambridge, Mass., 1972.
Cornford, F. M. *The Republic of Plato*. New York, 1945.
Crombie, I. M. *An Examination of Plato's Philosophical Doctrines*, vol. 2. London, 1963.
Dicks, D. R. *Early Greek Astronomy to Aristotle*. London, 1970.
Duhem, P. *Le Système du monde*, vol. 1. Paris, 1913.

---

is Pythagorean. What tells for this is the remarkable fact that the *only* reference to "the Pythagoreans" in the whole of the Platonic corpus occurs in our passage: "for these [astronomy and harmonics] are sister sciences, as the Pythagoreans affirm and we too agree." So Plato here had Pythagorean thinkers very much on his mind, and it is a reasonable presumption that they are the ones who "look for numbers in audible concords," though Plato does not say this.

[63] See Burkert [1972, 373–78].

[64] An interpretation of *Rep.* 530d1ff. which has much in common with the one I have given in this Postcript is offered by Crombie [1963, 186ff.]. He refers illuminatingly to *Tim.* 67b, 80a, but fails to notice how *Phaedr.* 268d–e would have strengthened his case.

[65] I acknowledge with thanks suggestions from Alexander Mourelatos, which led me to make some corrections. [30]

Düring, I. *Aristoteles*. Berlin, 1966.

Festugière, A. J. "Platon et l'Orient," *Révue de Philologie* 21 (1947): 5–45.

Friedländer, P. *Plato,* vol. 1. Translated by H. Meyerhoff. New York, 1958.

Heath, T. *Aristarchus of Samos*. Oxford, 1913.

Lasserre, F. *The Birth of Mathematics in the Age of Plato*. London, 1964.

Lindsay, A. D. *The Republic of Plato*. London, 1935.

Mittelstrass, J. *Die Rettung der Phänomene*. 2nd ed. Berlin, 1964.

Neugebauer, O. *The Exact Sciences in Antiquity*. Second edition. Princeton, 1957.

Robin, L. *Platon: Oeuvres Complètes*. 2 volumes. Paris, 1950.

Ross, W. D. *Aristotle's Metaphysics,* vols. 1 and 2. Oxford, 1924.

Shorey, P. "Platonism and the History of Science," *Proceedings of the American Philosophical Society,* 66 (1927), 159–82.

———. *Plato: The Republic*. 2 volumes. London. Vol. 1, 1930. Vol. 2, 1935.

Vlastos, G. *Platonic Studies*. Princeton, 1973.

———. *Plato's Universe*. Seattle, Washington, 1975.

15

DISORDERLY MOTION IN PLATO'S *TIMAEUS*

S O MUCH has been written on this vexed issue,[1] that one hesitates to reopen it. Yet one has no other choice when one finds scholars accepting as generally agreed a view which rests on altogether insufficient evidence. I propose, therefore, to examine the main grounds on which recent authorities interpret the disorderly motion of *Timaeus* 30a, 52d–53b, and 69b as a mythical symbol. They are four:

    I. That the *Timaeus* is a myth;
    II. The testimony of the Academy;
    III. That motion could not antecede the creation of time;
    IV. That motion could not antecede the creation of soul.

I

In what sense is the *Timaeus* a myth? A comparison with the *physiologoi* suggests itself at once. The *Timaeus* corrects their views in their own universe of discourse. Empedocles' cosmology starts with the four *rhizōmata*.[2] Plato disagrees: "These are products, not *archai*. I cannot give certain knowledge of

From *CQ* 33 (1939): 71–83. Reprinted in Allen, pp. 379–99. Used by permission. Minor changes have been made in spelling and punctuation. Notes were not numbered consecutively in either version.

[1] For references to opposing authorities in the last century, see Zeller, *Plato and the Older Academy* (English trans., London, 1876, p. 364n. 5). Some [[postwar]] {recent} authorities ⟨subsequently to be referred to by author and title⟩ who take the view that the preexisting chaos must not be taken literally {For later works see pp. 265–66 below}:

    Wilamowitz, *Platon*, vol. i, Berlin, 1917, pp. 597–98.
    C. Ritter, *Platon*, vol. ii, Munich, 1923, pp. 415–17.
    W. Theiler, *Zur Geschichte der teleologischen Naturbetrachtung*, Zurich, 1924, section on Plato.
    A. E. Taylor, *Plato*, London, 1926, pp. 442ff., and *Commentary on the Timaeus*, 1928, pp. 66–69 *et passim*.
    P. Frutiger, *Les Mythes de Platon*, Paris, 1930, *passim*.
    Léon Robin, *Platon*, Paris, 1935, p. 191.
    G.M.A. Grube, *Plato's Thought*, New York, 1935, pp. 168ff.
    F. M. Cornford, *Plato's Cosmology*, London, 1937, pp. 37, 176, 203, *et passim*.

[2] DK B6, where, significantly enough, these physical substances are given the names of divinities. Conversely, the anthropomorphic elements, Love and Strife, are conceived as corporeal

the true *archē* or *archai*. But I can give an account which is a good deal more probable than any 〚atomist's〛 {physicist's}."³ So when he fulfills this promise, going back of the four "elements" to describe in 52d–53b the winnowing movement out of which they were formed, what he gives us is not more mythological than Empedocles' mingling of the elements in the original harmony of love,⁴ than the primordial *ēremia* of Anaxagoras' *homoiomerē*,⁵ or Leucippus' and Democritus' world-forming *dinē*.⁶

Thus the *Timaeus* is unique among Plato's myths. It is a mistake to put it on a level with the great myths of the *Gorgias, Phaedo, Republic* 10, the *Phaedrus*, {and the *Politicus*}.⁷ The *Timaeus* 〚offers no gentle disavowal of the scientific scrupulousness of the account by the literary devices used in every one of these others〛 {uses none of the devices by which all of these disavow the scientific seriousness of major features of their accounts}.⁸ The speaker is the [71] *astronomikōtatos* Timaeus (27a), who, in Socrates' estimation, has reached the highest summit of all philosophy (20a). The sober, systematic, prosaic tone of his discourse contrasts sharply with Critias' earlier reminiscences. This all but irrelevant introduction sets the fanciful myth over against the scientific myth. It is stuffed with mythological material: Atlantis, the deluge, Phaethon's flight, and the genealogy of Phrononeus, Niobe, Deucalion, and Pyrrha, which even the Egyptian priest declares to be mythology (23b).

---

forces. See Cyril Bailey, *The Greek Atomists and Epicurus*, p. 31; and Cornford, on p. 565 of vol. 4 of *Cambridge Ancient History* (Cambridge, 1926): "In Empedocles Love and Strife belong at once to the world of mythical imagery and to the world of scientific concepts." This ambivalence of myth and science, very different from didactic metaphor or allegory, is the proper mood of the *Timaeus*. It was used unconsciously by Empedocles, consciously by Plato. Cf. *muthos* in *Soph.*, 242c8ff.

³ Summarizing in paraphrase, *Tim.*, 48b1–d4.

⁴ Bailey, *The Greek Atomists*, pp. 31, 32.

⁵ Aristotle, *Phys.* 250b25, 26.

⁶ Diogenes Laertius, 9, 31, 32; Aristotle, *Phys.* 196a24.

⁷ 〚Frutiger, *Les Mythes de Platon*, classes all these together as "parascientific" myths.〛 {Anyone tempted to make much of the label "myth" might note its absence in the first two, and its very casual use at the end of the third (*muthos esōthē, Rep.* 621b–c, a quasi-proverbial expression, applied elsewhere to the "saving" of a philosophical thesis: *Phil.* 14a, *Laws* 645b, *Theaet.* 164d).}

⁸ In the *Gorgias* the story begins with ὥσπερ γὰρ Ὅμηρος λέγει (523a); Homer's witness is called in again in 525c. The story contains such figures and places as the Isles of the Blessed and Tartarus; Minos, Rhadamanthys, Aeacus; Tantalus, Sisyphus, Tityus. In the *Phaedo:* λέγεται δὲ οὕτως . . . (107d); . . . ὡς ἐγὼ πέπεισμαι (108c); λέγεται (110b); καὶ χρὴ τὰ τοιαῦτα ὥσπερ ἐπᾴδειν ἑαυτῷ . . . (114d). The detailed geography is clearly mythological. 〚In the myth of Er, we have clearly an otherworldly experience; and in the *Phaedrus* a literary exercise (257a).〛 {In the *Republic* we get an *Alcinou apologon* (allusion to the *Nekuia* of *Od.* 11: cf. Arist., *Poet.* 1455a2, *Rhet.*, 1417a13), the tale of Er, the Armenian. In the *Politicus* the reversal of the celestial revolutions is connected with the tale of Atreus and the golden lamb (268e, 269a), the age of Cronus and the *gēgeneis* (269a–b), and said to account for "innumerable other [events], still more marvellous" (269b). For the *Phaedrus* myth, note 265b6–8.}

None of this sort of thing comes into Timaeus' story; and its omission has the force of conscious restraint in view of the wealth of poetic allusions suggested by his grandiose theme.[9] When the creation of the stars forces him to say something about the popular gods, he is dry, hasty, ironical.[10] He accepts the traditional accounts in a mood that suggests Hume's, "Our most holy religion is founded on Faith."[11] Sacred mythology of this sort he treats elsewhere with the deepest respect.[12] He has no use for it here. The topography of the under-world, described in such detail in the *Phaedo,* is left unmentioned. The chthonian deities, whose worship is an integral part of the state-cult,[13] pass unnoticed. Nor is there any place here for the mediating *daimonic* entities, who figure invariably in Plato's supernatural hierarchy[14] and are conspicuous in the cosmology of the *Epinomis* (984e, 985a).

Why should the cosmology of the *Timaeus* exclude figures whose reality is vouched for by the law of the state? Because they fall below its standard of scientific probability.[15] Commentators often pick the expression *eikota muthon* out of Timaeus' epistemological introduction (29b–d) and use it as though the emphasis were on *muthon* instead of *eikota.* This is certainly wrong. *Eikos* is the important word. It is used thrice explicitly (29c2, 8; 29d2) and once implicitly (29b *eikonos . . . sungeneis*). Of these four, it is used thrice as an adjective of *logos,* once of *muthos.* In the seventeen echoes of this introduction throughout the rest of the dialogue, *muthos* is used thrice,[16] while *eikos, eikotōs,* etc., are used sixteen times.[17] *Eikota logon* is used eight times, *eikota muthon* twice. And it is a pretty commentary on the 'mythological' connotations of *eikota muthon* that it is used both times of a purely scientific opinion: 59c, of the composition of metals, and 68d, of color mixture.

[A myth is a story; whether the story is mythology or natural history de-

---

[9] Except in verbs describing the activity of the Demiurge, where he is forced into anthropomorphism, Timaeus indulges rarely in poetic metaphors. The *kratēr* of 46d is the only important one; and there it occurs with the scientist's characteristic carelessness for literary detail: he thinks he has used it before (*epi ton proteron kratēra*) when he actually has not. Expressions which he knows to be poetic Timaeus expressly qualifies as similes: *embibasas hōs es ochēma* (41e); this is a vestige of the imaginative figure of the *Phaedrus,* where it had been used *without* qualification: Ζεύς, ἐλαύνων πτηνὸν ἅρμα (246e); θεῶν ὀχήματα ἰσορρόπως εὐήνια (247b); there the mood is mythology, and to qualify would be pedantry.

[10] About irony: see especially Taylor's *Commentary,* on 40d6–e2.

[11] *An Enquiry Concerning Human Understanding,* 10, ii, 100.

[12] I.e., that he accepts the forms of traditional worship, and wishes to preserve them intact, without the slightest alteration (*Laws* 5, 738b, c; cf. also *Rep.* 4, 427b, c, and *Laws* 4, 716c–718b; 5, 759a–760a; 8, 828a–d).

[13] I.e., *Laws* 4, 717a; 8, 828c; 12, 958d.

[14] *Rep.* 3, 392a; 4, 427b; *Laws* 4, 717b; 5, 734d; 7, 818c; 10, 910a.

[15] ἄνευ τε εἰκότων καὶ ἀναγκαίων ἀποδείξεων λέγουσιν (40e).

[16] 59c, 68d, 69c.

[17] 30b, 34c, 44d, 48c, 48d, 49b, 53d, 55d, 56a, 56d, 57d, 59c, 68d, 72d, 90e.

pends on what kind of story it is. Διαμυθολογῶμεν, εἴτε εἰκὸς οὕτως ἔχειν εἴτε μή, says Socrates in the *Phaedo* (70b) of no less a matter than reincarnation.[18]] {A *muthos* is a tale. Not all tales are fictions. "What is the meaning of this *mythos?*" asks Socrates of a "Protagorean" doctrine (*Theaet.* 156c). His tone may not be free from condescension; but neither does he mean to prejudge its claim to truth. The typical *mythos* is mythological.} But there is [[no such ambiguity in]] {none of this in the discourse of} the *Timaeus* [[: here]] {where} only the *eikos* is tolerated. And what *eikos* means in [72] this context is carefully defined: the metaphysical contrast of the eternal forms and their perishing copy determines the epistemological contrast of certainty and probability.[19] Thus "the element of falsity lies, not in the mode of exposition, but in the object described, which is only a fleeting image of the real."[20] All of what we hopefully call "science," Plato regulates to verisimilitude. But verisimilitude is not fiction, for the visible cosmos is not fictitious. If within the dreamworld of the senses[21] we draw pretty definite lines between the reality of people we see and hear and, say, Hesiod's *gēgeneis* (our sanity depends on it), so scientific probability must be kept clear from didactic fictions. So the presumption must be that every element in the *Timaeus* is probable, and none fanciful, unless we are given further instructions or hints to the contrary. Of the latter there are none for the preexisting chaos. In their absence we are so far driven to accept it as a serious, though only probable, hypothesis of the origin of the material world.

II

It is not then Plato, but Xenocrates who supplies us with the suggestion that, as Aristotle put it in *De caelo* 297b32–280a1, the expressions about the generation of the world are a kind of diagram, given *didaskalias charin*. This passage of the *De caelo* is "a plain allusion to the interpretation of the *Timaeus* given by Xenocrates."[22] In none of our sources is it said that Plato thus con-

---

[18] [[Further qualified immediately by the preface, *palaios . . . logos hou memnēmetha . . .* (70c).]]

[19] The account is "akin" to the "image" it describes: *eikonos eikotas* (sc. *logous*) 20c.

[20] F. M. Cornford, *Cambridge Ancient History,* vol. 6, chap. 11, p. 330.

[21] *Tim.,* 52b, c: ὑπὸ ταύτης τῆς ὀνειρώξεως. . . .

[22] A. E. Taylor, *Commentary on the Timaeus,* p. 69. So much is clear from the Greek commentaries, listed by Heinze, *Xenokrates* (Leipzig, 1892), pp. 179–80:

Simpl. *De caelo* 303, 34–35: δοκεῖ μὲν πρὸς Ξενοκράτην μάλιστα καὶ τοὺς Πλατωνικοὺς ὁ λόγος . . .

Schol. cod. Coisl. 166: τοῦτο πρὸς Ξενοκράτη εἴρηται ἀπολογούμενον ὑπὲρ Πλάτωνος . . .

Schol. cod. Parisiens Reg. 1853: ὁ Ξενοκράτης καὶ ὁ Σπεύσιππος ἐπιχειροῦντες βοηθῆσαι τῷ Πλάτωνι ἔλεγον . . .

strued the *Timaeus,* or even that Xenocrates contended that Plato thus construed it. All we hear is that Xenocrates and Crantor, or "Xenocrates and the
Platonists," supplied this interpretation.[23] Of course, we have Xenocrates'
teaching at second, or rather at *n*th, hand. It may be that Xenocrates did make
this very claim. But this is not in our evidence. Xenocrates is, therefore, of
little help at this point. For the rest, there are excellent reasons why an apolo-
gist and systematizer of Plato's thought should wish to put just that construction upon this troublesome doctrine of the *Timaeus.* For the same reasons the
Academy would conserve it. Yet their minds could not have been altogether
easy about it, or we could hardly have had Plutarch, Atticus, and *alloi polloi
tōn Platonikōn*[24] reverting centuries later to the literal interpretation. So I
cannot put as much weight on the "all but unanimous testimony of the Academy"[25] as Professor Taylor seems to do.

On the other hand, we have Aristotle, who knows Xenocrates' interpretation and also knows something of Plato's oral teaching. So far from attributing
this interpretation to Plato, his references to the *Timaeus* imply the very opposite.[26] There can be [73] no question here of "mere polemical 'scores' got by

---

and from Plutarch, *De animae procreatione in Timaeo,* 1013a, where the reference is by implication to Xenocrates, Crantor, and their followers.

[23] ⟦It is true that we have this interpretation applied to Plato's doctrine without reference to the
mediation of Xenocrates in Theophrastus, *Phys. opin.* Fr. 11 (quoted in Taylor's *Commentary,*
p. 69n.1). But neither does Theophrastus say that this is Plato's own teaching about the *Timaeus.*
He merely records this interpretation as a possible one.⟧ {Taylor (*Commentary,* p. 69n. 1) and
H. Cherniss (*Aristotle's Criticism of Plato and the Academy* (Baltimore, 1944), p. 423n. 356) add
Speusippus and Theophrastus. The textual authority for the former is frail: the scholion in the
Parisian MS. of the *De caelo;* no mention of Speusippus in Plutarch, Proclus, or Simplicius. As
for Theophrastus, his remark, as quoted in Proclus, is τάχ' ἂν γενητὸν λέγοι σαφηνείας χάριν
and the *tacha* ("perhaps, to express any contingency from a probability to a bare possibility," LSJ,
s.v., 2), is understood by Taurus to mean "possibly" (*isōs*) in this context (Theophrastus, frag.
28). Cherniss does not explain why he favors "probably" instead (*loc. cit.,* and 610).}

[24] Proclus, quoted by Taylor, *Commentary,* 68.

[25] Taylor, *Commentary,* p. 69.

[26] I.e., *De caelo* 280a29, *Phys.* 251b14, *Met.* 1072a2. ⟦A reference to the *Timaeus* in *De
anima* 406b6ff. is interesting, even though it does not relate to the preexisting chaos: τὸν αὐτὸν
δὲ τρόπον καὶ ὁ Τίμαιος φυσιολογεῖ τὴν ψυχὴν κινεῖν τὸ σῶμα. That is how Aristotle
thinks of the Timaeus: *phusiologei.* This is important, when one remembers how *phusiologēma*
suggests the most emphatic opposition to *muthologēma.* E.g., Epicurus 2.87 . . . ἐκ παντὸς
ἐκπίπτει φυσιολογήματος, ἐπὶ δὲ τὸν μῦθον καταρρεῖ. Some contrast in Epicurus, *K.d.* 12.
One ought to think twice before ridiculing Aristotle for taking seriously the *Timaeus'* doctrine of
the soul, as does Frutiger, *Les Mythes de Platon,* p. 202. Plato, who believes, with all other Greek
philosophers, that sensation involves a physiological process, must explain how the soul is
"shaken" and "moved" in sensation (*Phil.* 33d, 34a). The theory of the *Timaeus* that the soul is a
pattern of circular motion is a serious attempt to provide such an explanation. Aristotle is quite
right in objecting that this implies a spatial conception of the soul. His objection would hold just
as much against the *Philebus* as against the "mythical" *Timaeus.*⟧ {Cf. *De anima* 406b26, καὶ ὁ
Τίμαιος φυσιολογεῖ τὴν ψυχὴν κινεῖν τὸ σῶμα, associating the account of the soul's ability to
move the body in the *Timaeus* "with the mechanical explanation of Democritus' (Cherniss,

pressing the mere words of a sentence."[27] His references are too detailed and too serious for that. He tells us that:

(a) In teaching the generation of time, Plato stood alone against the unanimous opinion of previous thinkers;[28] while

(b) he (Aristotle) was the first to teach the beginninglessness of the *ouranos;*[29] that

(c) Plato, with Leucippus, taught the everlastingness of motion,[30] yet

(d) Plato held that the world and the soul were generated.[31]

Of these statements *a* and *b* might be, and *a* and *c* or *c* and *d* would almost certainly be, taken as mutually inconsistent. To see that they are not implies conscientious recording and thoughtful distinctions. To be sure, every reference to Plato is the prelude to a crushing refutation. But crushing refutation would be singularly inept against mythology. There can be no question here either of ignorance or carelessness. If we are to discount Aristotle's testimony, we must charge him with deliberate misrepresentation. It is hard to believe that Aristotle, with all the limitations of his subtle and unimaginative mind, was capable of quite that.

III

We now come to the more difficult part of the discussion: to the contradictions in which Plato would seem to involve himself on a literal interpretation of the preexisting chaos. Here we must make sure of the canon of criticism on which we are to proceed. Shall we assume at the start that Plato's philosophy is immune from contradiction? This would be [[sheer wish-]] {wishful} thinking. Every great thinker has sought consistency, and none has perfectly attained it, except in the minds of slavish disciples who know the answers so well that they never think of the problems. One thing only we can reasonably assume about a great philosopher: that he is never carelessly or needlessly inconsistent. In the present instance, Plato himself has warned us of rough sailing ahead. This is physics, not metaphysics; his physics must have a fringe of inconsistency and inexactness (29c6), at the risk of belying the metaphysics. In fact Plato has much too cheap an insurance against misadventures in the

---

⟨above, n. 23⟩, p. 392n. 314), and thus with a genre of thought which is the polar opposite of mythology (cf. Epicurus, *Ep.,* 2, 87).}

[27] Taylor, *Commentary,* p. 69.

[28] *Phys.* 251b14–19.

[29] *De caelo,* 279b12, 13; {cf. Cherniss ⟨above, n. 23⟩, 415–16.}

[30] *Met.* 1071b31–33.

[31] *De caelo* 280a29, 30; *Met.* 1072a1–3.

Timaeus. He can always say, "I told you so. What can you expect of the image of an image that is in constant flux?" We cannot treat him quite so leniently. To meet his inconsistencies with easygoing tolerance would be as shallow as to hide or explain them away. We must insist on the question, Where is the source of the inconsistency? Is it a mere accident of the physics, or can it be traced back to a weakness in the metaphysics? And of the preexisting chaos, we must ask further: Is it the cause of metaphysical inconsistency or its symptom? If the latter, then to remove it as mythology would be needless exegetic surgery.

Let us begin with the most formidable of these inconsistencies:

> No sane man could be meant to be understood literally in maintaining at once that time and the world began together (38b6), and also that there was a state of things, which he proceeds to describe, *before* there was any world.[32]

But was the contradiction as obvious to Plato as it is to Professor Taylor? And was it avoidable? [74]

Aristotle was a "sane man." He records both of these Platonic doctrines: that motion is everlasting (*Met.*, 1071b31–33) while time is not (*Phys.* 251b14–18). He interprets the latter literally. Yet he sees no immediate contradiction between the two. He does indeed hold that "all change and all that is in motion is in time" (*Phys.* 222b30, 31), and that time has no beginning (*Phys.* 251b14–28), but he finds it necessary to establish these propositions independently.[33] They are not immediate logical inferences from the self-contradictoriness of "before the beginning of time." To convict him of inconsistency, Aristotle has to go farther afield and bring in the additional premise that Plato, who "sometimes" attributes the cause of motion to the soul, could not consistently make the generated soul cause of beginningless motion.[34] Why is it, one wonders, that Aristotle should resort to such a roundabout argument, weakened as it is by the "sometimes" in the first premise, when he

---

[32] Taylor, *Commentary,* p. 69.

[33] He proves the first as follows:

(i) *thatton* or *braduteron* is predicable of every motion;
(ii) *thatton* implies the idea of *proteron;*
(iii) *proteron* implies distance from "*now*";
(iv) "*now*" implies time (*ta nun en chronōi*) (*Phys.* 222b31–223a8).

He proves the second:

(i) time can neither be not conceived apart from "now";
(ii) any "now" is a *mesotēs* between past and future;
(iii) any past is a "now";
(iv) therefore, any past has a past (*Phys.* 251b19–26).

[34] *Met.* 1072a1, 2.

could offer the simple and fatal objection that "before time" is nonsense, since "before" presupposes time?[35]

The answer is in the "tradition running throughout the whole of Greek thought, which always associated Time with circular movement."[36] Aristotle justified this belief by arguing:

>   (a) Time is the number of motion (*Phys.* 223a33);
>
>   (b) there is only one time (*Phys.* 223b2–12); therefore
>
>   (c) time must be measured by one determinate motion (*Phys.* 223b12–18);
>
>   (d) this must be the motion whose number is "most knowable" and that is the uniform (*homalēs*) circular motion of the heavenly bodies (*Phys.* 223b18–21).

Note the implications of this argument: What would happen if you eliminated the uniform circular motion of the heavenly sphere? According to Aristotle there would be no other uniform motion.[37] Without uniform motion time cannot be numbered, and if it cannot be numbered is it still time? A number that cannot be numbered would be a contradiction in terms. Thus, if Aristotle adhered strictly to this assumption that time is the measure of a determinate motion, he should have been hard put to it to show any inconsistency whatever in Plato's doctrine that motion is eternal while time is not. So long as there is only irregular motion, there would be no time in this strict sense of the word. It is only when the regular motion of the heavenly bodies comes into being that time begins.[38] This is in fact the hypothesis of the *Timaeus*.

On this hypothesis we should have to reject the validity of the argument of *Phys.* 222b30–223a15 (summarized below, n. 1), which attempts to establish that time is coeval with motion. For the first premise in that argument is that *thatton* and *braduteron* are predicable of every motion (222b31, 32); and to define *thatton* [75] Aristotle employs the idea of uniform (*homalēn*) motion,[39] which is contrary to the hypothesis of the *Timaeus*. So Aristotle could not—

---

[35] *Phys.* 223a4–8; 251b10, 11.

[36] F. M. Cornford, *Plato's Cosmology*, 103, *q.v.*

[37] He holds that rectilinear motion is not uniform, "since (according to him) when it is *kata phusin* it becomes faster as bodies near their proper place, and when it is *para phusin* it becomes slower as the impressed force becomes exhausted. The circular motion of the heavenly bodies is the only change which by its nature proceeds uniformly." Ross, *Aristotle's Physics* (Oxford, 1936), p. 612. Hence his doctrine that ὁμαλῆ (*sc.* κίνησιν) ἐνδέχεται εἶναι τὴν κύκλῳ μόνην, *Phys.* 265b11.

[38] And we could add: If it should ever happen that the heavenly revolutions should cease, so would time. Cf. Marlowe's *Dr. Faustus*.

Stand still, ye ever-moving spheres of heaven,
That time may cease, and midnight never come.

This is good Aristotelian (and Platonic) doctrine.

[39] *Phys.* 222b33–223a2: Λέγω δὲ θᾶττον κινεῖσθαι τὸ πρότερον μεταβάλλον εἰς τὸ ὑποκείμενον κατὰ τὸ αὐτὸ διάστημα καὶ ὁμαλὴν κίνησιν κινούμενον.

and does not—use the argument of *Phys.* 222b31–223a8 against the *Timaeus*. To dislodge Plato he has to fall back on another argument: that of *Physics* 251b19–26. Here his logic is sound. But he is no longer using the same concept of time as before; he is not working with the cyclical time of *Physics* 223b12–224a2, but with the more general concept of a 'now' which is always *mesotēs* between past and present.

This excursus on Aristotle enables us to understand:

(*a*) Plato's concept of cyclical time;[40]

(*b*) how such a concept seemed compatible with the supposition of a disorderly motion going on in the absence of time.

b needs no further argument. It is a simple inference from the belief that time essentially implies periodic motion: no periodic motion, no time. *a* requires further comment. The doctrine of time in the *Timaeus* is a stronger version of the cyclical time of *Phys.* 223b12–224a2. If Aristotle takes the heavenly revolutions as a necessary condition of time, the *Timaeus* seems to identify them with time.[41] It not only tells us that sun, moon, and the other five planets were ὅσα ἔδει συναπεργάζεσθαι χρόνον (38e),[42] and were made ἵνα γεννηθῇ χρόνος (38c), but even that the "wandering" of the planets *is* time.[43] Nights, days, months, and years are "parts" (*merē chronou,* 37e),[44] and "was" and "shall be" (the most general categories of temporal succession) are "species" (*eidē,* 37e4, 38a8) of cyclical time (*Kukloumenou,* 38a8).

Now time so conceived is not the contrary of timeless eternity but an approximation to it: its likeness (*eikona,* 37d6), its imitation (38a8). Time is a finished product, the end result of a raw material which the Demiurge works over with the definite purpose of making it as much like eternity as he possibly

---

[40] {For a correction on this, see pp. 271–72 below.}

[41] [I say "the *Timaeus*" rather than "Plato," in view of *Parm.* 151e–157b, to which Professor Cornford has called my attention. There time is not conceived in the more general terms of before and after—τοῦ ποτὲ . . . καὶ τοῦ ἔπειτα καὶ τοῦ νῦν, 155d. There Plato is thinking of a different aspect of the problem: he is contrasting *chronos* as the *spread* of either motion or rest with the durationless *exaiphnēs* (156c–e), while in the *Timaeus* he is contrasting *chronos* as periodic *form* with the formlessness of random process. What the Demiurge creates in the *Timaeus* is temporal form, not temporal spread. We must not confuse the two. Contrast, for example, *Parm.* 151e7, 8, where *to einai* implies *chronon ton paronta,* with *Tim.* 37e–38b, where *to estin* implies a state to which *chronos* does not apply.]

[42] Cf. 41e5 and 42d5: *organa chronōn, organa chronou* of moon and other stars.

[43] 39d: χρόνον ὄντα τὰς τούτων πλάνας. Cf. Aristotle's statement in *Phys.* 218a34, οἱ μὲν γὰρ τὴν τοῦ ὅλου κίνησιν εἶναί φασι (*sc.* τὸν χρόνον), where *hoi men* are identified with Plato by Eudemus, Theophrastus, and Alexander (Simpl. *Phys.* 700.18–19); [(reference given in Ross's *Aristotle's Physics* ⟨above, n. 37⟩, *ad loc*). To combat this view, Aristotle has had to fall back on rather weak arguments in *Phys.* 218b13ff].

[44] {For the true sense of this and further correction, see pp. 271–72 below.}

can.[45] What is this raw material? Plato tells us in 52d3: it is *genesis*. This distinction between raw *genesis* and created *chronos* is the key to the whole account. It shows that it was just as necessary for Plato to hold that the Demiurge did not create the first, as that he did create the second. It is the nature of the Demiurge to make his work more like the eternal model, not less like it. So the one thing he could not possibly do is to bring the factor of change and decay, of "perpetual perishing," into existence. That is a necessary condition for his work. Given that, he can proceed to inform it with periodic motion. Since he did not create it, it must antecede creation. It must exist not as a bare nothing, but as change, though disordered change: κινούμενον πλημμελῶς καὶ ἀτάκτως.

But it is not utterly disordered change. Wholly devoid of form it would be, on Platonic standards, wholly devoid of Being; i.e., nothing at all. But obviously it is not that. It is something. This must puzzle Plato, who thinks of *peras* and *apeiron* as two distinct entities, requiring the imposition of the one upon the other through [76] the mediation of a third ordering entity.[46] The theme of the *Timaeus* is this informing of formless change by the Demiurge. If this dominating idea were false, the *Timaeus* would be not only mythology, but nonsense as well. Yet how conceive of *genesis* which lacks form and being altogether? The more *genesis* is denuded of stable *ousia*, the more it will be true that it *is genesis*, which sounds like a contradiction in terms. This is the deep-lying difficulty that is mirrored in the problem of pretemporal motion. Plato could not have been entirely unaware of it. In the *Sophist* he faced squarely an analogous logical difficulty and showed that *esti mē on* involves no contradiction. But the metaphysical problem he never cleared up in the same way.[47] And it is doubtful if he could, without recasting his whole

---

[45] 38b, c; also 37c, d.

[46] This idea is not peculiar to the *Timaeus;* e.g., *Phil.*, 30c: ἄπειρον . . . ἐν τῷ παντὶ πολύ, καὶ πέρας ἱκανόν, καὶ τις ἐπ' αὐτοῖς αἰτία. Notice the force of *ep' autois*. Notice also how distinct is *aitia* from *peras:* πρὸς τρισὶ καὶ τέτταρτον . . . γένος (26e). τὴν αἰτίαν ὡς ἱκανῶς ἕτερον ἐκείνων δεδηλωμένον (27b).

[47] I cannot agree with Brochard's bold attempt to identify matter with the Other of the *Timaeus* and thus with the non-being of the *Sophist* (Brochard et Dauriac, *Le Devenir dans la philosophie de Platon*, Cong. Int. de Phil., 1902). This is hardly the place to argue the matter out. But his assumption that the *koinōnia* of Being, Same, Other, Motion, and Rest in the *Sophist* covers the relation of forms to material things is effectively answered in Cornford's *Plato's Theory of Knowledge* (London, 1957), p. 297. Robin's thesis that "la distinction de l'intelligible et du sensible se fonde sur la pureté ou l'exactitude plus ou moins grandes des relations qui les constituent, et que ce n'est, par conséquent, qu' une différence de degré" ("La *Physique* de Platon," *Rev. phil.*, 86 [1918], second half, p. 398), is attractive, but, I think, much too Leibnizian an interpretation of Plato. The difficulty with it appears in such a harmless little phrase as "à la complexité infinies et perpétuellement instables" (p. 410), which Robin uses to describe sensible things. Why "instables"? Does mere increase of complexity cause instability? Why should it? To establish his thesis, Robin should be able to explain how Plato's doctrine of process can be reduced to a doctrine of increasing complexity of formal relations.

philosophy to end the ontological dichotomy of τὸ ὂν ἀεί, γένεσιν δὲ οὐκ ἔχον ⟦from⟧ {and} τὸ γιγνόμενον μὲν ἀεί, ὂν δὲ οὐδέποτε (27d–28a).

Short of such a drastic remedy, Plato had to compromise and say, The chaos is disorderly, but not altogether so; it contains "some traces"[48] of order. This is a makeshift. Even as a metaphor it is self-contradictory, for "traces" could only be a result, not an anticipation. Yet it is the best that Plato could do in the case of spatial order. And, I submit, it is the best he can do in the case of temporal order. He would have to say: Just as the preexisting chaos had "certain traces" of ⟦geometric pattern, so it had traces of arithmetic periodicity; just as these traces justify us in speaking of *hugrainomenēn* and *puroumenēn* before the formal creation of water and fire, so they might permit us to speak of a vague, indefinite priority and succession in the temporal passage which is as yet destitute of chronological order.⟧ {spatial configuration which justify us in speaking, with studied vagueness, of the Receptacle's becoming "watery" and "fiery" before water and fire had yet been created, so it might have "traces" of temporal order which might enable us to speak in similarly indefinite, uncertain, terms of priority and succession in its occurrences even before the introduction of that sharply precise chronological order for which we reserve the name of "time."}

This is, of course, a most unsatisfactory expedient. But the cause of the trouble, I repeat, is not the disorderly motion as such. It is the idea of *genesis*. *Genesis*, it now turns out, is not the protean state which Plato believes it to be, formless till it be "likened" to the model by the charitable intervention of the Demiurge. On the contrary, quite apart from any order impressed upon it by the Creator, it has a precise, inalienable order of its own: an order of before and after, inherent in the mere fact of passage. I do not see how Plato could face *this* difficulty without rewriting not only the part of the *Timaeus* which deals with the disorderly motion, but much more of the *Timaeus*, and a good many parts of other dialogues as well.

IV

We have the final perplexity: According to the well-known teaching of {*Phaedr.* 245c–246a and} *Laws* 10, all motion is caused by soul. The disorderly motion would then imply an irrational world-soul. But no such soul is mentioned in the *Timaeus*. Since this is offered as an argument against the preexistent chaos, a fair way of meeting [77] it is to ask, Just what does it mean for the contrary hypothesis (i.e., that chaos is only the residual disorder ever present in the world)? Professor Cornford answers:

---

[48] 53b2: ἴχνη . . . ἄττα.

Since no bodily changes can occur without the self-motion of the soul, the other factor present in this chaos must be irrational motions of the World Soul, considered in abstraction from the ordered revolutions of Reason. The disorderly moving mass must be conceived as animated by soul not yet reduced to order, but in a condition analogous in some ways to that of the infant soul described above (43a ff.). (*Plato's Cosmology*, p. 205)

Yet—

(*a*) Of "irrational motions of the World Soul" we know nothing in the *Timaeus*. On the contrary, we are told at its creation: Θείαν ἀρχὴν ἤρξατο ἀπαύστου καὶ ἔμφρονος βίου πρὸς τὸν σύμπαντα χρόνον (36e).

(*b*) The analogy with the infant-soul, apposite as it is,[49] is unfortunate for Professor Cornford's hypothesis: It does not tell us how an irrational soul originates irrational motions, but how irrational motions throw out of order the infant's soul. There is nothing the matter with the rationality of its soul. The trouble is with the "flowing and ebbing tide of the body" (43a, Cornford's translation), and the violent motions that break upon it from the outside.[50] As Professor Cornford himself comments on this passage: "Contrast the World Soul, which, as soon as it was joined with its body, began an 'intelligent life' (36e), not being exposed to external assaults" (*Plato's Cosmology*, 149n. 5). That is surely the difference. There are no external assaults to throw the motions of the world soul out of gear.[51] And, unlike the infant, it is free from the six "wandering motions."[52] What else could induce disorder upon it? The only other possible factor mentioned in the *Timaeus* is bad breeding (86e), which, of course, would be absurd for the world soul.

More important than any specific conclusions that we might draw from this argument is the general way in which we put the problem when we look at it through the eyes of the *Timaeus*. We have just been asking, What induces disorder in the soul? But how ask this if you assume that all motion is caused by soul? It is strictly meaningless for you, except insofar as it might suggest that disorder in one soul might be explained through disorder in some other soul. Any other kind of disorder would be irrelevant; for, on this hypothesis, there is no disorder not caused by soul. I do not see how anyone can make head or tail of the *Timaeus* on this assumption. For instead of tracing back all

---

[49] The *ataktōs kai alogōs* of the infant's disorder reminds one most forcefully of *plēmmelōs kai ataktōs* (30a) and *alogōs kai ametrōs* (53a) of the world-chaos.

[50] Note the force of τὰ τῶν προσπιπτόντων παθήματα (43b), πυρὶ προσκρούσειε τὸ σῶμα . . . διὰ τοῦ σώματος αἱ κινήσεις ἐπὶ τὴν ψυχὴν φερόμεναι προσπίπτοιεν (43c), σφοδρῶς σείουσαι τὰς τῆς ψυχῆς περιόδους (43d). Note the repetition of *exōthen* 44a1, 5.

[51] For the very good reason that there is nothing outside it. The world was made one to exclude violent incursions upon it *exōthen*, which προσπίπτοντα ἀκαίρως λύει καὶ νόσους γῆράς τε ἐπάγοντα φθίνειν ποιεῖ (33a). For *nosos* as disorder of reason, see 86b, d; 88a, b.

[52] It has only the motion τῶν ἑπτὰ τὴν περὶ νοῦν καὶ φρόνησιν μάλιστα οὖσαν (34a vs. 43b).

chaos to some spiritual source, the *Timaeus* generally assumes the opposite. This apparent contrast between *Laws* 10 and the *Timaeus* is striking, but not inexplicable. It derives from the totally different basic problems to which the two treatises are severally addressed:

Laws 10 is simply and purely an exercise in apologetics. It must establish the existence of the gods. It does not raise any issue which will not assist in the proof of this conclusion, so urgent for religion, so essential for the State. The argument turns on one question, Is soul prior to body? This question too is stripped to fighting-weight. It is not encumbered with the additional problem, What kind of soul—good or bad? Experience can decide this.[53] Only when he has proved to his [78] satisfaction that "all things are full of gods" (899b), does he feel free to broach the problem of evil. Even there his object is not to explain the origin of evil, but to provide religious comfort for the troubled soul, through the assurance of the universal plan in which all things work together for good.[54] Individual souls have in them "a cause of change" (904c); but this operates only within the framework of the universal plan already assumed. It explains the just punishment of injustice, not the occurrence of injustice itself. The ominous words κατὰ τὴν τῆς εἱμαρμένης τάξιν καὶ νόμον do slip in (904c). But what is this *heimarmenē?* Is it the will of the "king" or its limiting condition? The question is not raised in the *Laws*. But the *Timaeus* cannot avoid it.

The *Timaeus* is no manual of political theology. It is "esoteric" philosophy: the private discourse of like-minded philosophers (20a), so much more leisurely and tentative than the defensive vehemence of *Laws* 10. It can thus open up the really tough questions of theodicy, without fear of unsettling the faith of the simple or exposing vulnerable flanks to atheistic opponents. It comes soon to the creation of the soul, which the *Laws* had assumed[55] but prudently refrained from presenting as a problem. To us, with our Hebrew-Christian heritage, the doctrine of creation suggests at once the doctrine of the fall. But Plato is just as much a scientific, as a religious, thinker. He stands in a line of physiological psychologists, who have discovered that elementary cognition involves physical contact with the material world. So two difficulties must be solved at once:

---

[53] 898c. The whole of 896d to 898b is nothing more than an elaborate propounding of the question, "If soul is cause of everything, good and bad, and order implies a good soul, whereas disorder implies an evil soul, consider the *ouranos* and decide: Does it suggest the best soul or its contrary?" Therefore, it is a mistake to quote any part of this passage in support of the view that Plato believed in an evil world-soul.

[54] πρὸς τὴν σωτηρίαν καὶ ἀρετὴν τοῦ ὅλου παντ' ἐστὶ συντεταγμένα (903b ff.). It is the organic principle ("the part exists for the sake of the whole"), the same in the order of the universe as in the order of the state. Cf. *Rep.* 420d4, 5.

[55] *Laws* 10, 892a, c; 896a; 904a; 12, 967d. {And cf. p. 275n. 34, below.}

(a) How the creature of a perfect creator is so imperfect; and

(b) how an immaterial soul can be affected by material things in sensation.

Plato's solution is that {though} [[the]] soul does not consist of material articles, {it is nevertheless in} [[but of a pattern of]] motion.[56] It can move, and it can be moved. Because it can be moved, it is subject to sensation, desire, pleasure and pain, and passions of every sort.[57] And for the same reason it is prone to disease and disorder.[58] Thus [[the cause of evil is]] disorderly motion {may cause evil in soul}. To exculpate God of responsibility for evil, it is no longer [79] enough to say, *aitia helomenou*. When you find a physical cause for irrational choice,[59] you must exculpate God of the disorderly motion that has caused it. And you cannot stop short of the primitive chaos. This ultimate cause of evil must exist, uncaused by God, and (short of reopening the problem all over again) uncaused by soul.

That is why we may dispense with Plutarch's well-meaning hypothesis of the primordial evil soul.[60] Apart from his forced interpretation of *Laws*

---

[56] Soul has no part in fire, air, water, earth, the constituents of the world of "second" causes, though it does partake of the περὶ τὰ σώματα γιγνομένη μεριστὴ οὐσία (35a). That the soul is a motion is plain from the account of its creation. It consists of the revolving [[circles]] {strips} of the Same and the Other. A mental event is always a motion for Plato:

αἱ τοῦ παντὸς διανοήσεις καὶ περιφοραί (90c, d).

τὰς . . . ἐν τῇ κεφαλῇ διεφθαρμένας περιόδους ἐξορθοῦντα (90d).

στρεφομένη, θείαν ἀρχὴν ἤρξατο ἀπαύστου καὶ ἔμφρονος βίου (36e).

ἡ τῆς μιᾶς καὶ φρονιμωτάτης κυκλήσεως περίοδος (39c).

ἵνα τὰς ἐν οὐρανῷ τοῦ νοῦ κατιδόντες περιόδους χρησαίμεθα ἐπὶ τὰς περιφορὰς τὰς τῆς παρ' ἡμῖν διανοήσεως (47b).

Those who "don't use their heads": διὰ τὸ μηκέτι τὰς ἐν τῇ κεφαλῇ χρῆσθαι περιόδους (91e).

[57] ὁπότε δὴ σώμασιν ἐμφυτευθεῖεν ἐξ ἀνάγκης, καὶ τὸ μὲν προσίοι, τὸ δ' ἀπίοι τοῦ σώματος αὐτῶν *then* follow sensation, eros, and the passions (42a). In 69c, d again pleasure, passions, sensation come to the immortal soul with the subsidiary, *mortal* soul which, in turn, comes with the *mortal* body: . . . θνητὸν σῶμα αὐτῇ (i.e., τῇ ἀθανάτῳ ψυχῇ) περιετόρνευσαν . . . ἄλλο τε εἶδος ἐν αὐτῷ (i.e., τῷ σώματι) ψυχῆς προσῳκοδόμουν τὸ θνητόν. Sensation occurs when διὰ τοῦ σώματος αἱ κινήσεις ἐπὶ τὴν ψυχὴν φερόμεναι προσπίπτοιεν (43c), whence Plato derives *aisthēseis* (is it from *aissō*, which Cornford thinks the more probable of those given by Proclus? Or from *asthmainō*, suggested by J. I. Beare in *Greek Theories of Elementary Cognition*, Oxford, 1906?). See also 45d1, 2 and 64d4–6, and cf. with *Philebus*, where sensation is a "tremor" of soul and body (33d), and note its formal definition of sensation in 34a. (*Seismos* is the word used in the myth of the *Politicus* of the chaotic disorder of the counter-spin: 273a3, 6; and in the *Timaeus* of the primitive chaos: 52e, 53a.)

[58] νοσοῦσαν καὶ ἄφρονα ἴσχειν ὑπὸ τοῦ σώματος τὴν ψυχήν (86d). Further 87a: phlegms and humors blend their vapors with the motion of the soul: τὴν ἀφ' αὑτῶν ἀτμίδα τῇ τῆς ψυχῆς φορᾷ συμμείξαντες. Notice the force of *prospiptēi* in 87a5, and cf. with use of same word in 33a4, 5 and 43b7 and 43c5.

[59] E.g., in 86c, d, where we are given a definite physiological cause for *helein akairōs*.

[60] In *De animae procreatione in Timaeo*.

896d,[61] Plutarch's mainstay is the myth of the *Politicus*. Now when we examine the context of his quotations, it becomes plain that the cause of the "counter-revolution" in the myth is not soul, but body:

Ξ. . . . τοῦτο δὲ αὐτῷ τὰ ἀνάπαλιν ἰέναι διὰ τόδ᾽ ἐξ ἀνάγκης ἔμφυτον γέγονε.

Ν.Σ. Διὰ τὸ ποῖον δή;

Ξ. Τὸ κατὰ ταὐτὰ καὶ ὡσαύτως ἔχειν ἀεὶ καὶ ταὐτὸν εἶναι τοῖς πάντων θειοτάτοις προσήκει μόνοις, σώματος δὲ φύσις οὐ ταύτης τῆς τάξεως. (269d)

That is the trouble with the *ouranos*, the speaker proceeds: κεκοινώνηκέ γε καὶ σώματος (269d, e). Plutarch's strongest text is 272e5, 6. But *heimarmenē* is plainly enough the *anankē* of the *Timaeus*,[62] the realm of secondary causes;[63] *sumphutos epithumia* may only mean that the drag of the primitive disorder is *now* felt, deep in its nature, as a rebellious urge.[64] How can we then escape the plain words, *à propos* of the gradual fading of the Creator's influence upon the creature: τούτων δὲ αὐτῷ τὸ σωματοειδὲς τῆς συγκράσεως αἴτιον, . . . ὅτι πολλῆς ἦν μετέχον ἀταξίας πρὶν εἰς τὸν νῦν κόσμον ἀφικέσθαι (273b)? So far from substantiating Plutarch's hypothesis, the myth of the *Politicus* corroborates the doctrine of the *Timaeus* and the *Phaedo* that the soul's partnership with the body is the source of its aberrations;[65] though its chief value for an account of the origin of evil is the explicit way in which it traces it all back to the primitive disorder: παρὰ δὲ τῆς ἔμπροσθεν ἕξεως, ὅσα χαλεπὰ καὶ ἄδικα ἐν οὐρανῷ γίγνεται, ταῦτα ἐξ ἐκείνης αὐτός τε (sc. ὁ οὐρανός) ἔχει καὶ τοῖς ζῴοις ἐναπεργάζεται (273c).

The *Timaeus* completes the picture. It mentions circumstances in the creation of the soul which account for its susceptibility to irrational motion: ⟦the *dusmeiktos* Other⟧ and the περὶ τὰ σώματα γιγνομένη . . . οὐσία (35a) {has been built into it}. Motion is inherent in this *gignomenē ousia* which is

---

[61] This is presumably the reference of ἐν δὲ τοῖς Νόμοις ἀντικρυς ψυχὴν ἄτακτον εἴρηκε καὶ κακοποιόν, ibid., 1014e. *Per contra*, see above, n. 53; Taylor's *Commentary*, p. 116; and Robin's *Platon*, pp. 226–27.

[62] Cf. *ex anankēs, Pol.*, 269d2, 3.

[63] *Tim.* 46e. Plutarch himself puts no stock on *heimarmenē* but refers to it as *anankē*. Clearly *heimarmenē* in *Pol.* 272e cannot be the will of the "captain," for he has just let go of the helm; it is the disorder he had kept under control which is now asserting itself. That the realm of secondary causes includes a necessary element of disorder when separated from the overlordship of *nous*, is clear from *Tim.* 46e5.

[64] The same applies to 273b1, 2: the "instruction" was not given to a primitive bad soul, but to the god-made soul that marked the end of chaos and the beginning of cosmos.

[65] For the *Timaeus* see above, nn. 60 and 61. For the *Phaedo* see especially 66a–d. The soul of the philosopher must be "released" from the "fetters" of the body (67d; cf. *Rep.* 515c); it must be "purified" from the "contamination" of the body (*Phaed.* 67c5 and *Tim.* 69d6; cf. *Symp.* 211e1, 2, and *Rep.* 611c3); the body is a "tomb" (*Phaedr.* 250c; *Gorg.* 493a).

one of the soul's ingredients. One could hardly attribute the origin of *this* motion to soul without circularity. On the contrary, the *Timaeus'* mechanical explanation of [all] motion makes it quite unnecessary to postulate a bad soul to set the primitive chaos in motion: κίνησιν δὲ εἰς ἀνωμαλότητα ἀεὶ τιθῶμεν (57e).[66] Chaos [80] contains, by definition, the minimum of *homalotēs, homoiotēs*.[67] It must, therefore, and for purely mechanical reasons, be in constant motion.[68] When the creator steps in to reduce the indefinite heterogeneity of the chaos to the definite homogeneity of the five regular polygons, the question arises whether we may not get too much likeness, in which case motion would cease altogether. The Demiurge solves this neatly by [making the sizes of the atomic triangles infinitely various] {introducing variety into the sizes of the atomic triangles} (57d). Thus he never has to think of starting motion, but only to keep it going. Likewise, when he creates the "body" of the universe: there is no question of pushing it off to a start, but only of *subtracting* from it the six "wandering" motions.[69]

Is it then possible to reconcile this teaching of the *Timaeus* with *Laws* X?[70] Remembering the special limitations of the task to which *Laws* 10 is devoted, we need not find that its teaching, taken as a whole, contradicts the cosmology of the *Timaeus*. The crucial tenet of *Laws* 10, the priority of soul over all material motions, is not strange to the *Timaeus* 34b, c. Yet once Timaeus has given it fulsome acknowledgment, he makes no specific use of it. *Because* the soul is "older," the soul must "rule." Chronological priority is hardly more than a vindication of ontological priority, in line with a deep-rooted ethical and political dogma that the older must rule the younger.[71] To press it further would be embarrassing in view of the *Timaeus'* doctrine of time.

Why then does *Laws* 10 make so much of this temporal priority which seems hardly more than a pious formality in the *Timaeus?* Precisely because it has been contradicted by the atheistic materialists. It is they who make, alas, only too good sense of the temporal priority of matter. To refute them Plato must meet them on their own ground. And so he does, retaining the ambiguity

---

[66] Cornford comments in a footnote: "Obviously the mover cannot be the soul, which belongs to a higher order of existence. It could not be spoken of as either heterogeneous and unequal, or homogeneous and equal, with the moved." *Plato's Cosmology*, p. 240. Cf. also 58c2–4 and 57a2–4.

[67] Cf. the phrase of *Pol.* 273d, e, τὸν τῆς ἀνομοιότητος ἄπειρον ὄντα πόντον to which the world would revert if it persisted in its "counter-revolution."

[68] [This is not in contradiction with *Phaedr.* 245d, e, πάντα τε οὐρανὸν πᾶσάν τε γῆν εἰς ἓν συμπεσοῦσαν στῆναι. The disastrous standstill envisaged in the *Phaedrus* concerns the created heavens and earth, which do have a soul and could not move without it.]

[69] 34a: τὰς δὲ ἐξ ἁπάσας κινήσεις ἀφεῖλεν καὶ ἀπλανὲς ἀπηργάσατο ἐκείνων.

[70] {I should now [1964] make it clear that I no longer believe that the primordial motion in the *Timaeus* can be "reconciled" on these terms with the uncompromising doctrine of *Laws* 896a–b and *Phaedr.* 245c–e that soul is the "source" of all motion.}

[71] See *Rep.* 3, 412c for the axiomatic belief that the old must rule. The whole of the *Laws* is dominated by this idea.

of *archē* and *archei*,[72] and arguing its cosmic primogeniture.[73] In the course of this argument, he propounds the bare possibility that primary causation might rest with the evil soul. But this is forthwith declared to be contrary to fact, and the speaker can go on to complete the case against the atheists, without digressing to explain how primary causation through the evil soul is, in fact, inexplicable save through collision with material, secondary causes. That is why Aristotle, years later, writes that Plato *sometimes* declares the soul the *archē* of motion (*Met.*, 1071a1). The expression is a compromise between the apparent contradiction of *Laws* 10 and the *Timaeus;* [a contradiction which he must hold to be only apparent, else he would not have scrupled to make capital out of it in his usual polemic].

On this interpretation the proposition that the soul is πρῶτον γενέσεως καὶ φθορᾶς αἴτιον (*Laws* 891e) merely denotes the supremacy of the soul's teleological action *within the created universe*. Its polemic resources are fully exploited in *Laws* 10. But it is not offered as a substitute for the cosmologic teaching of the *Timaeus*. Only here, where Plato gives us a complete picture of the relations of teleology to mechanism, can we find an intelligible meaning of the "firstness" of the soul: Soul [81] belongs with the "first," good, intelligent, divine causes—not in the realm of necessity but of purpose (46e, 68e). The "worse" motions are externally impressed; the "best" are self-initiated (89a). Soul is inherently of the "best"; though it is not immune from assaults by the "worse."

This is a serious qualification of the apparent meaning of the doctrine that soul is *archē kinēseōs* (*Laws* 896b; *Phaedr.* 245c).[74] Are we mutilating the *Laws* to force conformity with the *Timaeus?* I think not. We are trying to make sense of the statement taken by itself. Forget the *Timaeus* altogether for

---

[72] E.g., 896c: ψυχὴν μὲν προτέραν, σῶμα δὲ δεύτερόν τε καὶ ὕστερον ψυχῆς ἀρχούσης, ἀρχόμενον κατὰ φύσιν, whence it follows in 896d: ψυχὴν δὴ διοικοῦσαν καὶ ἐνοικοῦσαν ἐν ἅπασι . . . καὶ τὸν οὐρανὸν διοικεῖν. Again 895b: ἀρχὴν . . . καὶ πρώτην . . . ἀναγκαίως εἶναι πρεσβυτάτην καὶ κρατίστην. The double-edged meaning of precedence is always assumed, never argued. E.g., 892a: ὡς ἐν πρώτοις ἐστί (simple assertion of precedence, immediately broken into temporal priority) σωμάτων ἔμπροσθεν πάντων γενομένη (and ontological supremacy) καὶ μεταβολῆς τε αὐτῶν καὶ μετακοσμήσεως ἁπάσης ἄρχει παντὸς μᾶλλον.

[73] *Laws* 892c: *en prōtois gegenēmenē.*

[74] I am leaving out of this discussion the additional complication that in the *Phaedrus* the idea of the soul as *archē kai pēgē kinēseōs* serves at once to prove that the soul is ungenerated: εἰ γὰρ ἔκ του ἀρχὴ γίγνοιτο, οὐκ ἂν ἔτι ἀρχὴ γίγνοιτο (245d). In the *Laws* [the meaning of the premise must have changed, else the conclusion could not have been contradicted, as it is in] {the soul is still the *archē kinēseōs* (e.g., 896b3), but the same conclusion is *not* drawn, as is clear from} the frequent references of the *Laws* to the soul as generated (see [above, n. 55] ⟨my "Creation in the *Timaeus*" ⟨** 275n. 34⟩). *Archē* is a "weasel-word" in Plato. It may mean any, or all, of (i) beginning, (ii) source, (iii) cause, (iv) ruling principle, (v) ruling power. It should be noted that the mythological interpretation of the preexisting chaos and of its associated doctrine of creation could take the chronological "firstness" of the soul no more literally; cf. Plutarch: εἰ γὰρ ἀγένητος ὁ κόσμος ἐστίν, οἴχεται τῷ Πλάτωνι τὸ πρεσβύτερον τοῦ σώματος τὴν ψυχὴν οὖσαν ἐξάρχειν μεταβολῆς καὶ κινήσεως πάσης, *De animae procreatione in Timaeo,* 1013f.

the moment. How much could Plato mean when he says that the soul is the cause of all becoming and perishing? At its face-value this asserts that the soul is itself the cause of the instability of becoming; that apart from soul reality would be untroubled by transience.[75] But this is grotesquely un-Platonic. When Plato does ask himself, "Is soul more akin to being or becoming?" he can only answer, "It is in every way more like being" (*Phaedo* 79e). The one thing he cannot mean in the *Laws* is that soul is the source of Heraclitean flux. *Genesis* must be presupposed. It must be "there," before soul can supervene to "rule" it. But if it is "there," it must involve motion of some sort; not teleological motion in the absence of soul, but disorderly mechanical motion.[76] Thus, quite independently of the description of the disorderly motion in the *Timaeus*, we should be forced to supply something like it in order to make sense of the doctrine of *Laws* 10 that soul is the first cause of becoming.

Does this clear up all the difficulties of the disorderly motion? Hardly. How does the Demiurge act upon the disorderly motion?[77] Indeed, how does any "first" cause act upon a "second" one? Aristotle's complaint that Plato gives no explanation of the soul's *koinōnia* with the body it inhabits (*De an.*, 407b12–19) can be pushed further: How is it that material impact upon the soul can and does take place,[78] even though the soul is not a material body? And, conversely, how is it that the immaterial soul acts and "masters" the discordant motions of the body?[79] How does one pattern of motion act upon another pattern of motion, though one is the motion of material particles and the other is not?

It is no accident that Plato has avoided such questions. They point to deep-lying [82] difficulties or, at least, obscurities in his categories of material reality. But their further discussion lies beyond the limits of this paper. Our task is done if it be reasonably clear that such difficulties cannot be escaped by the all-too-easy device of relegating the disorderly motion to the status of a mythical symbol.

[75] Note that the hypothesis of the universal standstill (*Laws* 895a, b), against which Plato's argument of the soul as first mover is so effective, is enemy territory. It was they (*hoi pleistoi tōn toioutōn*), not Plato who "dare" affirm it. Likewise in the *Phaedrus*, the supposition of all motion of heaven and earth coming to an absolute stop is the apodosis of a *per impossibile* hypothesis.

[76] We must never forget that Plato thinks of mechanism as disorderly, except insofar as it is teleologically ordered: e.g., *Tim.* 46e, where the "second" causes, unmistakably identified with mechanical causes in 46e1, 2, are said to be ὅσαι μονωθεῖσαι φρονήσεως τὸ τυχὸν ἑκάστοτε ἐξεργάζονται. That mechanism nevertheless does contain an order of its own is part of the contradiction in Plato's thinking noted above, pp. 256–57.

[77] An easy solution is to animate the chaos; then the Demiurge would only need to "persuade" its bad soul, and this would seem to make better sense of such expressions as 48a2, 4, or 56c5. But this is only postponing the difficulty. If the Demiurge persuades the evil soul, the reformed soul would then have to persuade its disorderly body—and the difficulty turns up again. At some point final cause must meet efficient cause. To insert intermediary souls only puts off the inevitable encounter of soul with body.

[78] See above, note[s] 50 [and 51].

[79] *Tim.* 42b2.

16

CREATION IN THE *TIMAEUS*: IS IT A FICTION?

"**D**ISORDERLY MOTION in Plato's *Timaeus*" (to which I shall refer hereafter as "*D.M.T.*") was written in 1938. It is here reprinted ⟨**247–64⟩ with minor changes in text and notes.

Five years after the appearance of *D.M.T.* came *Aristotle's Criticism of Plato and the Academy* by Harold Cherniss. This truly great work, which has enriched so many aspects of Platonic thought, dealt extensively with the topics treated in *D.M.T.*[1] Had I written after its publication, I would have been saved several mistakes. But I do not believe I would have altered my earlier conviction, developed initially in the face of stiff opposition from Cornford.[2] In any case, I have felt no inclination to change my position after absorbing all that Cherniss has had to say about it. So I shall continue to argue for it. But I would urge those who are less concerned with the fortunes of a debate than with the determination of the truth to read and weigh for themselves his side of the case, since my space here is so limited that I could not begin to deal with all he has had to say on and around this question.[3] They might also read a number of other works which have taken different positions from Cherniss on one or more [401] points relevant to this controversy.[4] The ones from which I have learned the most are "Bewegung der Materie bei Platon," by H. Herter

---

From Allen, pp. 401–19. Used by permission.

[1] For specific criticisms of *D.M.T.*, see especially nn. 314, 362, 364, 365, 366, 385, 392.

[2] *D.M.T.* was an expansion of one or two talks I had with Cornford on the *Timaeus* in the spring of 1938. The paper convinced him no more than did my oral arguments. But it was published with his encouragement.

[3] *Aristotle's Criticism*, 392–457 and nn.; "The Sources of Evil According to Plato" (hereafter "S.E."), *Proc. of American Philosophical Society* 98 (1954), 23–30; review of A.-J. Festugière, *La Révelation d'Hermes Tismegiste, II: Le Dieu cosmique* (Paris, 1960), in *Gnomon* 22 (1950), 204–16.

[4] The most important of those known to me are M. Meldrum, "Plato and the *archē kakōn*," *JHS* 70 (1950), 65–74; G. R. Morrow, "Necessity and Persuasion in Plato's *Timaeus*," *PR* 59 (1950), 147–63; A.-J. Festugière, work cited in n. 3 above, Ch. 5, and Vol. 2: *Les Doctrines de l'âme* (Paris, 1953), chs. 12–14; F. Solmsen, *Aristotle's System of the Physical World* (Ithaca, 1960), 50–51; 65n. 170; F.-P. Hager, *Die Vernunft und das Problem des Bösen in Rahmen der platonischen Ethik und Metaphysik* (Noctes Romanae, 10: Bern, 1963), 230ff.; Th. Gould, *Platonic Love* (London, 1963), ch. 7. I should also mention an older book not known to me when I wrote *D.M.T.*, P. Thevenaz, *L'Ame du monde, le devenir et la matière chez Plutarque*, (Paris, 1938), 91ff.

(*Rhein. Mus.* 100 [1957], 327–47), and "Plato's Cosmogony," by R. Hackforth (*CQ*, N.S. 9 [1959], 17–22.)[5]

I

That the cosmos was not always in existence but "has been generated, having started from some *archē*" (28b6–7), is not merely asserted in the *Timaeus*, but demonstrated, and from premises which give every appearance of expressing firm metaphysical doctrine. It is argued at 28b4–c2 that the cosmos must have been generated, because

(1) it is corporeal and as such is an object of sense perception and belief, while
(2) all such objects "are in process of becoming and have been generated."[6]

[402]

As Hackforth has pointed out (19), no metaphorical or figurative language infiltrates this sequence of propositions.[7] *Eikōs muthos* is not even mentioned until later (29d2). And metaphor does not enter the texture of Timaeus' discourse until the reference to the "Maker and Father of this universe,"[8] i.e., until after the generation of the world has been proved. So just from the opening paragraph of the discourse, we could derive a clear-cut "no" to our question—*unless* there were reason to think that Plato thinks there is something wrong about the argument: that one or both of its premises are false or that the inference drawn from them is invalid. Could this be so?

That the inference is invalid would be widely granted today. Some would

---

[5] My debt to Herter would have been more apparent if I had tried to deal with broader aspects of the topic. Hackforth's paper, published posthumously, was written late in 1956, as I know from correspondence with him. Previously he had subscribed to the mythological interpretation: *Plato's Phaedrus* (Cambridge, 1952), 67. To Hackforth's paper and to all the other works mentioned in nn. 3 and 4 I shall refer hereafter merely by the author's name.

[6] γιγνόμενα καὶ γεννητὰ ἐφάνη, c1–2. *Ephanē* ("have been shown to be," Cornford) refers to 27d6–28b7, where *genesis* has been allocated to sensible-opinables in contrast to intelligibles. The word *gennēta* is not used in this earlier passage, but *genesin schein* is used of them at b5–6, evidently with the same meaning as *gennēton einai*. *Gennēta* is rendered by "can be generated" in Cornford's translation. This cannot be right in this context. Cornford himself translated *gennētōi paradeigma* a few lines earlier (28b1) as "generated model" (not, "model which can be generated"). Cf. also *gegonen*, 28b7, in the demonstrand, taken as demonstrated (*genomenōi*) at c2.

[7] He stressed this in a letter to me: "The fact that some part, maybe the greater part, of the dialogue is in some sense a myth is irrelevant. For the passage on which the whole issue hinges, viz. 27d5–28c3, is in no sense mythical, but straightforward logical argument. . . . There is no trace of myth before 28c3."

[8] Before this we hear only of a "cause" of generation (28a4–5), and of a *dēmiourgos* who imitates an eternal model (a6–9); nothing metaphorical here, unless one takes the core of Platonic ontology to be itself a metaphor (with the *aition* here which is a *dēmiourgos*, cf. *Phil.*, 27b1–2, τὸ πάντα ταῦτα δημιουργοῦν, . . . τὴν αἰτίαν).

attack it along Kant's lines: even if both premises were true of each and every object in the world, it would not follow that the conclusion is true of the world as a whole. Others would point out, in still more modern vein, that an aggregate whose every member has a beginning need not itself have a beginning. But no one would suggest that *Plato* would have faulted the argument on these or similar lines.

Would he then have indicted the premises? Not (1) obviously. Nor can I see any good reason for doubting his confidence in the truth of (2). The only one ever offered, to my knowledge, is the following by Zeller:

> This assumption involves us in a series of glaring contradictions. For if all that is corporeal must have become, or been created, this must also hold good of Matter; yet Matter is supposed to precede the creation of the world and (30a) is represented in this its pre-mundane condition as something already visible.[9] [403]

Now Plato's cursory reference to the primal chaos in 30a as "all that was visible" is one of the most obscure of his remarks about that all too obscure concept. A little later he says flatly that nothing is visible unless it has fire in it (31b5). But chaos had only an inchoate antecedent of fire which did not have the nature of fire but only "certain traces" of it (53b2). How, and in what sense, this would, or could, be "visible" Plato does not explain. So how are we to tell if something answering to this unspecified and problematic sense of "visible" would share with "*bona fide* objects of sense-perception and belief" the property of having been "generated, having started from some *archē*"? There is good reason to think that it would not: The ground of Plato's confidence that the objects of our sense-experience have been created is that intelligible structure of theirs which, he thinks, they could only have derived from an intelligent cause; as we know from the *Philebus* (23c ff.), it is the imposition of "limit" on the "limitless" by an ordering Mind that results in "generated existence" (*gegenēmenē ousia,* 27b). But limited structure is just what fire lacked before the Craftsman "ordered [it] with forms and numbers" (*Tim,* 53b); lacking this it could not be *gegenēmenē ousia:* it would be engulfed in that limitless flux where there is process, but no generation from an *archē*. This, to be sure, is a reconstruction. Suppose then it were rejected on the ground that we do not know how Plato would have answered our question as to whether or not a thing so perplexingly "visible" as preformed fire qualifies as a proper "object of sense-experience and belief." Even so he would escape Zeller's charge by the very silence he observed on this as on so many other points relating to the primal state. We might then blame him for his silence.[10]

---

[9] *Plato and the Older Academy,* Engl. transl. (London, 1888) (hereafter "Zeller"), 365. (Cf. *Aristotle's Criticism,* n. 361.) Though Zeller speaks of a "series" of contradictions, this is the only one he mentions.

[10] I.e., for withholding information material to the adjudication of his critics' charges. In my own case, the crux of my contention is that Plato's view that all precise order in the material world

But we cannot say he contradicted himself, "glaringly" or otherwise, since all he left us is, on one side, the perfectly clear-cut statement that the cosmos "has been generated, having started from some *archē*," and, on the other [404] side, no unambiguous contradictory, but an unexplicated obscurity.

And there is a second, quite independent, reason why Zeller's charge falls flat: If it were true, it would put Plato in the position of palming off on his readers falsehoods in the major premise and conclusion of our syllogism. Believing that it is quite false that all objects of sense-perception and belief are generated, and also false that the world was generated, Plato would be making his mouthpiece, Timaeus, assert the first and join it to a true premise to engender a false conclusion. Is this at all likely in this context? At the very least, it would be singularly lacking in dramatic fitness, since his spokesman is not a sophist nor yet a philosophically naïve or confused cosmologist: when Timaeus expounds philosophy (46c ff., 49b ff., 51b6ff.), everything he says is true Platonic doctrine, with never a false note. How could he then be made to start off his discourse by asserting in a context which is solemnly, even reverently,[11] didactic, propositions which Plato believes to be the very opposite of the truth?[12]

II

But let us suppose for the sake of argument that Plato did plant a false premise into the dialogue at this point and that he went on to narrate in such detail the generation of the world, time, and soul, believing all the while that, on the contrary, world, time, and soul are as beginningless as they are endless. Since Plato cares, and cares deeply, for the communication of truth, he would not willfully mystify, still less mislead, his reader. All parties to this dispute then would agree that he would not write "*p*," while intending to get across "not-*p*" to the reader, without providing him with clear and unambiguous signs that

---

is teleologically imposed order founders on the fact that no material can be ordered teleologically unless *it already* has non-teleological order of its own (cf. *D.M.T.*, Section III, last paragraph) and that if Plato himself had made more explicit his own conception of the precosmic state he would have seen that it had to have just such order (both spatial and temporal) as the precondition of receiving the more specific order impressed on it by the Craftsman.

[11] Cf. the invocation to the gods, 27c, followed by Timaeus' vow to "give the clearest expression to [his] thinking on the subject."

[12] Zeller says that "the dogmatic form . . . argues little; for the point is primarily to show, not a chronological beginning, but an Author of the world," 305. If that is the point, why the assertion of a chronological beginning and its deduction from a false premise? Zeller cites *Polit.*, 269d–270a, ignoring the fact that everything there is premised on notorious mythology (see *D.M.T.*, Section I, p. 248n. 8), while here the premises of the argument are, to all appearance, metaphysical doctrine.

the latter is his intention. Where are these signs? I shall devote the rest of this paper to [405] just this question. Here to begin with are five supposed disclaimers of creationism which I did not take up in *D.M.T.*:

(i) The order of exposition does not always follow that of the "mythical" cosmogonic sequence.[13] But a historical account, though normally keeping pace with the events it narrates, need not always do so. Witness the backlashes in Herodotus and even in Thucydides. How then could the reader be expected to draw from the fact that items X, Y, supposed to have occurred in that order, are related in a different sequence, the inference that Plato wants him to understand that both of them are coeval with a beginningless universe? Cherniss refers us to the apology at 34c2–4 that there is "too much of the casual and the random" in our speech. But why should that be taken as an apology for any defect other than the one it mentions: the failure to put first in the story in item (the creation of the soul) which came first in the course of events?

(ii) At 42e Plato says that "having made all these arrangements" the Craftsman "continued to abide by the wont of his own disposition (ἔμενεν ἐν τῷ ἑαυτοῦ κατὰ τρόπον ἤθει)." Taking *ēthei* here (with Archer-Hind and Cornford) to mean "nature," Cherniss sees in this phrase an expression of "the doctrine that god must be unchangeable (*Rep.* 381c)," and adds that (1) "if this be taken seriously, the relation of the Demiurge to the world must always be and have been the same," which (2) would be contradicted by the very notion of his having created the world.[14] I fail to see that (2) follows from (1). The constancy of god's *ēthos* would comport with any amount of world-making, provided only his behavior as Craftsman remains consistent with his character as god. In *Rep.* 381c, the point of the statement that "it is impossible for a god to wish to change himself but, as is only right, each of them being as fair and excellent as it is possible to be, abides for ever absolutely in his own character," is not that god does not act at all, but that he does not act in undignified and wicked ways: he does not lie, masquerade, etc., like the Homeric deities; he never causes evil, only good (379b–380c). Since the world-creation is an act of supreme beneficence (30ab), it would imply no shift of nature or character in this "best of causes" (29a), but rather a fitting expression of it. [406]

(iii) The Craftsman is no doubt himself a soul.[15] Would it be a "contradiction"[16] to think of soul creating soul? I can see none that would arise in the Platonic scheme because of just this. What precisely would contradict what?

---

[13] Cf. Zeller, 364; Cherniss, *Aristotle's Criticism*, 424–25, and n. 358.

[14] *Aristotle's Criticism*, 425.

[15] Cf. *Aristotle's Criticism*, Appendix 11.

[16] *Aristotle's Criticism*, 426. Cf. Zeller, 405n. 40: he thinks there is "contradiction" (without explaining why) in supposing that the soul of the Demiurge is everlasting while all other souls are created.

Why should the Craftsman's soul-making powers be cramped by the assumption that he is himself a soul? If we are to grant him, without logical strain, so many other marvellous potencies, why should our reason take offense at this one? (And cf. pp. 276–77 below).

(iv) According to Cornford, we must understand *to gignomenon aei* at 27b–28a to mean "that which is everlastingly (i.e., *beginninglessly* no less than endlessly) in process of change."[17] But *aei* is as indeterminate as to the duration over which it extends as is the English "always" (which is the way Cornford himself renders *aei* in his translation of the phrase). In this context it could cover just as well *A*, a duration which has no beginning and end, as *B*, one which does have a beginning but goes on forever after.[18] How then could it be taken as telling the reader that the former is meant? How could Plato be expected to communicate, "*A*, not *B*," by flashing a signal which could be read as either "*A*" or "*B*"?

(v) We read at 37d2–7:

> Now the nature of *Animal* (*hē tou zōiou phusis:* "the essence" or "Platonic form") was *aiōnios* and it was not possible for a generated thing to attain this (character) fully (*pantelōs*). So he took thought to make a sort of moving image of *aiōn:* simultaneously with his ordering of the Heaven, he makes of *aiōn* which abides in unity an *aiōnios* image proceeding according to number.

Cherniss comments (I intersperse the numerals): "Since in this very sentence Plato says that (1) the copy could not be *aiōnios* as the model is (37d3–4), it appears (2) to be an undisguised self-contradiction to call time an *aiōnion eikona*, 'eternal image' (d7)." He infers that (3) Plato used this phrase "with the intention of putting special emphasis upon some characteristic of time which the form of his exposition is inadequate to describe. The [407] most obvious characteristic of this kind would be unlimited duration, i.e., duration without beginning as well as without end."[19] To begin at (1): Plato does not say that the image is not *aiōnios* but that it is not "fully" or "perfectly" so. This makes a difference. To say, "James is not fully educated" is (usually) not the same thing as to say, "James is not educated." Plato is alive to this difference. When he says in the *Republic* that no sensibles are *pantelōs* (or *eilikrinōs*)[20] beautiful, etc., he is not denying that, e.g., Helen is beautiful. There is, therefore, (2) no more of a contradiction between saying that time is an *aiōnios* image of *aiōn* than there would be in saying that Helen is a beautiful image of Beauty, immediately after admitting, indeed stressing, that she is

---

[17] P. 26. Cherniss apparently reads the *aei* at 28a1 in the same way, *Aristotle's Criticism*, 420.

[18] Cf. Hackforth, 19.

[19] *Aristotle's Criticism*, p. 419n. 350.

[20] 477a3–479d5. The two terms are used interchangeably for the purpose of the argument of this whole passage: cf., e.g., 477a3 with a7, 478d6–7, and 479d5, where the same point is being made, *sc.* that only the Form, *F*, is *F pantelōs* or *eilikrinōs*, while *F*-particulars are-and-are-not *F*.

not *pantelōs* beautiful. Hence there is no good reason for the inference at (3).[21] [408]

III

What then of motions etc., occurring before the creation of time? Is there not a deliberate contradiction here? I said no, in *D.M.T.* (Section III), and I stand by that answer. I can now make it clearer and rid it of some minor errors. I echoed there uncritically Cornford's ascription of a "cyclical concept of time" to Plato. This is a treacherous expression which can mean two quite different things:

> (i) that time is "conceived, not as a straight line, but as a circle" (*Plato's Cosmology* ⟨London, 1937⟩, 103):
> (ii) that it is "inseparable from periodic motion" (ibid.).

Here (i) is false: though time is *imaged* as a circle (*kukloumenou*, 38a8),[22] it is not so *conceived:* Plato did not believe that, e.g., yesterday's happenings will happen again at some time in the future. On the other hand, (ii) is both true and fundamental. Let me restate what this implies:

Time "proceeds according to number" (37d6–7), i.e., its passage, or flow,

---

[21] I should add that I cannot believe that Plato had now so changed his use of *aiōnios*, (cf. *methēn aiōnion, Rep.*, 363d) as to reserve it for timelessness in contradistinction to perpetual duration. Plato had indeed now glimpsed—probably for the first time in Western thought—the notion of timeless eternity (H. Cherniss, *"Timaeus* 38a8–b5," *JHS* 77, Part I [1957], 18–23, and n. 46). But there is no evidence that he has now made *aiōnios* its vehicle, any more than he has put *aïdios* to such a use: he applies *aïdios* to the created star-gods (37c, 40b) no less than to the timeless ideas (37e). *Aiōnion* is applied to the gods in *Laws* 904a8–b1, if it is read, "that (human) body and soul are (each of them: cf. b1–2), when generated, indestructible, but not (as a composite unity) everlasting, as are the legal gods," which I take to be the most likely reading: As E. B. England ⟨*The Laws of Plato*, 2 vols. (Manchester, 1921)⟩ says *ad loc.*, it is "simplest" to take καθάπεϱ οἱ κατὰ νόμον ὄντες θεοί as applying only to *aiōnion.* "The gods of the established religion were, like men, souls with a bodily shape, but in their case no dissolution was possible," referring to *Tim.*, 41b and 43a2. There is point in contrasting men with gods in this respect in this passage, where transmigration (union with different bodies in the course of a single soul's *aiōn*), a fatality afflicting men but not gods, is in the offing (904c6–905a1). It is hard to see what point there would be in coupling men with gods as indestructible-but-not-eternal, on one of the alternative readings (Bury, Diès), or in coupling men with gods as indestructible, while disclaiming eternity for men without reference to the gods (Apelt, Taylor), on the other. It is worth remembering that the sense of an extended duration (as distinct from durationless eternity) would be hard to dislodge from *aiōnios* (= "lasting for an *aiōn*"); a human lifetime had been the typical instance of *aiōn*] (cf. LSJ, *s.v.* αἰών). Cf. E. Fraenkel's gloss on τὸν δι' αἰῶνος χϱόνον in *Ag.* 554, *Aeschylus' Agamemnon*, II. (Oxford, 1950), 278.

[22] As the context shows, the "circling" is done not by time itself, but by its measures, the celestial revolutions. The same thing, in spite of some unclarity of expression, is said by Aristotle in *Phys.* 223b24–33.

can be numbered. But what does that mean? To number a discrete aggregate, like a herd of cows, is to count it. But time is a continuous magnitude. How could this be counted? Only if first broken up into discrete units. If these are contiguous and of uniform length, their count would measure the temporal length they compose. Plato gives us three sets of such units: day-nights, months, years,[23] corresponding to conspicuous heavenly periodic motions. These motions he connects so closely with time that, as I said in *D.M.T.*, he "seems to identify them with time." Cherniss objected,[24] and rightly so. When Plato speaks of the stars [409] as created "to mark off and preserve the numbers (i.e., the numerable measures) of time" (38c6), he is certainly distinguishing (though only implicitly)[25] the siderial clocks from time itself as measures from the thing measured. But neither could we ascribe to him the sort of distinction which would imply that the thing measured could exist in the absence of its measures: everyone would agree that a Newtonian notion of "absolute, true, and mathematical time, (which) of itself, and from its own nature, flows equably without relation to anything external"[26] is far from his thoughts. He could not have spoken, even loosely, of the stars "producing time" (38e4–5) or being "made that time might be generated" (38c4) unless he was taking it for granted that the very existence of uniform time-flow depends on the existence of uniform periodic motions which could serve as its measures.[27] This then is what the Craftsman brought into the world: *uniform and measurable time-flow.* Let us call this "time (U)."

Now to say that *this* is what the Craftsman created is a very different thing from saying that he introduced temporal succession, or time-flow as such, into the world. This possibility is absolutely excluded by the statement that the Craftsman made time in order to make the world "still more like the (eternal)

[23] He calls these "parts" (*merē*) of time, 37e3, meaning that any given temporal interval would be made up of the number of contemporaneous day-nights or months or years whose count gives us the interval's measure.

[24] *Aristotle's Criticism*, 418 and n. 349.

[25] The distinction becomes explicit in Aristotle: in *Phys.* 219a8–9 we have the disjunction "time is either motion or something that belongs to motion (*tēs kinēseōs ti*)," but the first disjunct is eliminated at b1–3: "For this is time: the number of motion with respect to before and after. Hence time is not motion but that in virtue of which motion has number (ἀλλ᾽ ἧ ἀριθμὸν ἔχει ἡ κίνησις)," and at 220b8–9, "But time is a number—not that with which we number, but that which is numbered."

[26] *Philosophiae naturalis principia mathematica*, Scholium to the first seven definitions, *ad init.*

[27] In this respect Plato's conception of time is vastly more modern (though also vastly vaguer) than Newton's. On the other hand, he would not have said that "the question of uniform time (is) not a matter of cognition, but of definition. . . . There is no really uniform time; we call a certain flow of time uniform in order to have a standard to which we can refer other kinds of time-flow" (H. Reichenbach, *The Rise of Scientific Philosophy* [Berkeley, 1951], 146–47). Plato would insist that there *is* uniform time—the one defined by the standard fixed for us by the Demiurge when he established the celestial revolutions. Aristotle would have agreed.

model" (37c8):[28] had there been no temporal passage before creation, matter would have been totally immune from flux and [410] would thus have had the absolute stability of the Ideas;[29] and in that case the creation of time would have made it far *less* like the Ideal model than it would otherwise have been. But *could* there be temporal passage in the absence of time(U)? Certainly. We can conceive perfectly of a state of affairs where events exhibit the irreversible order of past and future (so that, e.g., if X is in Y's past, nothing in X's past can occur in Y's future) but where uniform periodic motions are nonexistent and time cannot be measured (if A, B, C, are successive instants, we would have no means of telling if the interval AB is as long as the interval BC, or longer, or shorter). This is precisely Plato's primitive chaos: no regular motions there, hence no temporal yardsticks, hence no time(U); but there is still *irreversible temporal succession,* which we may call "time(S)." Had Plato drawn this distinction and stuck to it, he could have asserted the creation of time (i.e., of time(U)) without running afoul of that contradiction "no sane man" could commit which made Taylor so sure that creationism could not be seriously meant.[30] So far as I can see, there is no contradiction in any of these suppositions: that disorderly motions occur *in the absence of time*(U); that they occur *prior* to time(U); that time(U) was brought into existence by a creative act which did not itself occur *in* time(U).

Did Plato see all this? To be more precise: did he see, and see clearly, the crucial proposition that time(S) is instantiable in the absence of time(U)? Let me begin by pointing out that, at any rate, he *did not deny* this proposition. There is one sentence from which one might easily get the impression that he did mean to deny it: ". . . and 'was' and 'shall be' are generated characters of time (*chronou gegonota eidē*), which we do wrong to transfer unthinkingly to the eternal essence" (37e4–5). Are we to take this to mean that the difference between past and future comes into existence only when "time" (i.e., time(U)) is made? If so, we would be going beyond what the text strictly tells us: that past and [411] future come into existence when (but not *only* when)[31]

---

[28] And a "moving image of eternity" (37d5), imaging it, obviously, not in its incessant change, but in the invariance of its rate of change.

[29] A hypothesis which would violate the first axiom of Platonic metaphysics that the sensible is, of its very nature, in constant flux (reasserted emphatically in the *Timaeus* 27d6ff., 48d, 52a). So I cannot understand why Cherniss should hold that, in the absence of soul, the reflections of the Ideas on space would be purely "static" (*Aristotle's Criticism,* 454). How so, if as he himself remarks, "The continuous flux of sensible phenomena is a *datum* of Plato's philosophy from first to last. . . ." (ibid., 438, his italics)?

[30] Cf. his *Commentary on Plato's Timaeus* (Oxford, 1928), 69. Cf. p. 253 above.

[31] Not "only" in 37e4–5, nor yet in 38a1–2, "while 'was' and 'shall be' are fittingly spoken [not of the eternal essence, but] of becoming which proceeds *in time*—for they are motions." Cherniss paraphrases, ". . . 'was' and 'will be,' because they are *kinēseis*, are properly predicable only of *genesis* which goes on in time" (*Aristotle's Criticism,* p. 427n. 362); he does not explain how he got the *only.*

time does so, as attributes of time. To say that F and G come into existence as attributes of x when x comes into existence is uninformative as to any prior instantiation of F and G. The statement would be true regardless of whether F and G have been instantiated millions of times earlier (as, e.g., the sweetness and redness "generated" in this ripe cherry *and* in innumerable others in times past) or never before (as in the case of certain destructive features of the Hiroshima bomb). It is the context then that must decide for us whether by *chronou gegonota eidē* here Plato means both (*a*) "generated now as attributes of time(U)" *and* (*b*) "never generated as attributes of anything prior to time(U)," or just (*a*). The context tells for the latter on two counts:

> (i) In the preceding period (e1–3), features of time(U) which did not exist prior to its creation—day-nights, months, years—were specifically acknowledged as "not existing before the heaven was generated." Had Plato wanted to say also that past and future did not exist *prin ouranon genesthai,* he would have surely said so then or brought them in thereafter under the same description. It is most unlikely that Plato would have wanted to slip in unobtrusively a thought so novel and so momentous as that the distinction between "was" and "shall be" did not apply to events anteceding the creation of our cosmos.

> (ii) As Hackforth (22) reminded us, the purpose of the present sentence (37e4–5) is to contrast time not with the precosmic state of matter but with the timeless eternity of the Ideas; its point then could not be the inapplicability of "was" and "shall be" to antecedent occurrences (to which the sentence makes no reference) but to the eternal essence (to which the reference is direct and emphatic). Hence to stress as strongly as possible that "they are properly used of becoming which proceeds in time" (38a1–2), in contrast to the being which is not in process in time, could not be construed as saying that they are improperly used of what is in process prior to time.

There is no good reason to think then that Plato was *rejecting* the [412] instantiability of time(S) prior to the creation of time(U). But neither do we have reason to say that he *affirmed* it. He does not say so. Nor is there any evidence that he had made the analysis that would have enabled him to do this by revealing how time(U) was both different from, yet related to, time(S). He is perfectly capable, certainly, of thinking and speaking of time in other contexts in terms of the past/present/future distinction without explicit reference to measurable time-flow: he does so in the *Parmenides* (151e–157b). But there is no indication there, or anywhere else, that he saw precisely how these two concepts are related. We would do well to keep in mind that no one in antiquity succeeded in seeing this—not Aristotle, for example, who wrote more extensively on time, with greater analytical thoroughness, and with knowledge of what Plato had already contributed to the partial exploration of this difficult concept. As I suggested in *D.M.T.* (Section III), the very arguments Aristotle uses against Plato reveal the limits of his own insight. Anyone who thinks he can refute Plato's notion that time had a beginning by arguing, as Aristotle does in *Phys.* 251b19–26, that since every "now" has a "before," there could be no first "now," shows that he is unaware that this proves (at most)[32] the beginninglessness of time(S). This of itself suggests that the true relation of time(S) to time(U) has eluded him. And the suggestion becomes a certainty when we note that just before this little argument Aristotle speaks of time as "either the number of motion or a sort of motion" (251b12–13),[33] i.e., as time(U), without the slightest indication that, while this is precisely the concept of time whose beginning is asserted by Plato, the one whose beginninglessness he is about to prove is not this, but time(S).

A similar deficiency of analytic insight mars Plato's account of the creation of time. This is, of course, a far cry from that gross, blatant, and wilful contradiction which could be read by the contemporary reader as a coded message advising him to discount creation-talk as picture-talk. But it is still a blemish, as I stressed in *D.M.T.* (on the basis of a less precise diagnosis of the trouble) and wish to stress again, readverting to what I then took to be the [413] metaphysical block that helps explain Plato's failure at this point. Had he made the time(U)/time(S) distinction, he would have been able to clear up the obscurities of his account to our complete satisfaction—but, unfortunately, not to his. For the idea that the material universe could (and would) have this precise form of temporal order (the transitive, asymmetrical, irreflexive order of a one-dimensional continuum) before creation would have jarred on one of his fixed convictions: that the material universe would have been orderless were it not ordered by a designing Mind. So the most he would have been willing to admit by way of temporal order for that godforsaken nonworld would have been, as I suggested in *D.M.T.*, some sort of vague and unspecified approximation to time, "traces" of it, a quasi-time as it were.

IV

The creation of soul in the *Timaeus* is in flat contradiction with the doctrine of the *Phaedrus* (though not of the *Laws*)[34] that the soul is uncreated, and ap-

---

[32] The premise that *every* "now" has a "before" wants proof. There is no logical reason why time must extend infinitely into the past; if it did not, one "now" (the first) would have had no "before."

[33] Cf. n. 25 above.

[34] The *Laws* speaks of the soul as "the first genesis" (896a6, 899c7), "eldest of all the things that partake of generation" (967d6–7; for the sense of γονῆς μετείληφεν here, cf. γένεσιν παραλαβοῦσα 966e1–2, which makes it clear that γονῆς = γενέσεως, *pace* Cherniss, *Aristotle's Criticism*, n. 365); it says that the soul προτέραν γεγονέναι σώματος . . . , σῶμα δὲ δεύτερον καὶ ὕστερον, 896c1–2. It thus says the same thing (and in the same language) which was said in the *Timaeus* (γενέσει . . . προτέραν καὶ πρεσβυτέραν ψυχὴν σώματος, 34c4–

pears to contradict also the doctrine of [414] both the *Phaedrus* and the *Laws* that the soul is the first cause of all motion. Could either of these discrepancies be taken as "don't-believe-my-creation-talk" signals addressed by Plato to the readers of the *Timaeus?* That they could not, should be all too obvious in the case of discrepancies between the *Timaeus* and the *Laws.* Assuming that Plato knew, when writing the *Timaeus*, that *he was going* to contradict some proposition in it in a later work, he could scarcely have hoped to use this unpublished intention as a means of telling the immediate public of the *Timaeus* to disbelieve that proposition! And the chances of his counting on contradictions between the *Timaeus* and the *Phaedrus* to serve the same purpose are surely not much greater. Could anyone claim in all seriousness that Plato thought his readers would be so certain of the immutability of his philosophical views that if they should happen to find him saying *p* in one work, the mere fact that he had said not-*p* years earlier in another work would give them to understand that he did not really mean *p* when he said *p* in the later work? No one to my knowledge has made such a claim, and I cannot imagine that anyone would. Our inquiry then can be reduced to just this question: Are there any contradictions internal to the *Timaeus* which the reader of this dialogue would find inexplicable on any hypothesis other than that they were planted there to warn him that the creation of the soul is a didactic fiction? There is just one idea in the *Timaeus* that could be thought to produce such contradictions: that the soul is a "self-moving" thing. This might be taken to contradict

1. the creation of the soul, and
2. precosmic motions uncaused by soul.

I wish to argue that there is no such contradiction in either case.

The reader of the *Timaeus* who remembered how much Plato had made of the soul's power of self-motion in the *Phaedrus* would see that he continues to ascribe the same power to the soul. There are several references to it: the thoughts of the World-Soul go on within "the thing that is self-moved" (37b5);

---

5), where there can be no doubt that the meaning is that the soul *was generated* prior to the body. I cannot see how this can be explained away by arguing with Cherniss, *loc. cit.*, that, as used in the passages in the *Laws, genesis* does *not* mean "generation" but has only the weaker sense of "process": that Plato should continue to retain in the *Laws* the very language he had used in the *Timaeus* to assert *generation,* but expect it to carry an entirely different meaning which would express a thought *incompatible* with that expressed by the same words in the *Timaeus* is most improbable; I know of no parallel for such behavior in the Platonic corpus. But even if we were to accept the weaker sense proposed, it would still be impossible to see how Plato could maintain in the *Laws* that the soul is the first process, eldest of things in process, prior in process to the body, if he believed (as Cherniss holds) that both soul and body are beginningless. Moreover, *genesin paralambanein* is asserted of the "motion" of the soul in 966c1–2, and this can only mean that the motion of the soul was generated (*genesin paralambanein,* as asserted of a *kinēsis,* would be a pure redundancy, if *genesis* here meant only "process"); and since self-motion is of the essence of the soul, if its motion was generated, then *it* was generated.

vegetables are "fixed and rooted" because their psyche, passively sensitive but not actively thinking (77b5–c3), "has been deprived of self-motion" (77c4–5); a man who wants to induce the most salubrious motions in his body should remember that "the best of motions is that produced in oneself by oneself, for this is most akin to the [415] movement of thought and of the universe (i.e., of the World-Soul), while motion (produced in one) by another is worse" (89a1–3). In all three of these texts, the soul's power of self-motion is being taken for granted and used, as needed, in a very matter-of-fact sort of way.[35] The same idea is also implied in 46d–e, in that important passage where Plato reveals the methodological orientation of his cosmology:

> But the lover of intelligence and knowledge should seek intelligent causes as the first, and only as second (causes) those which, being themselves moved by others, of necessity set yet others in motion. (46d–e)

The latter—inanimate causes, exemplified by "cooling and heating, compacting or rarefying" (d2–3)—are identified as *moved-by-others*. Hence the reader of the *Timaeus* would infer at once that the intelligent causes are all *self-moved*.[36]

Would this reader then have cause to find anything which leads to either of the above contradictions? Surely not the first, unless he confused two entirely distinct propositions:

A. The Craftsman generates self-moving souls.
B. He generates the self-motions of self-moving souls.

B is obviously self-contradictory, since the very description of the motion of a given soul as a "self-motion" entails, in Plato's scheme, that it is caused by just that soul and by no other individual in the universe—hence, *a fortiori*, not by the Demiurge. But *B* is never mooted in the *Timaeus*, where the Craftsman creates souls and then leaves them alone to do their own self-moving forever after. How then could *A*, once it is clearly distinguished from *B*, involve a contradiction? What is there to keep the Demiurge (assuming he has the wonderful powers of world-creation) from creating entities that have the power of self-moving and, once created, go on to exercise this power to their heart's content?[37] [416]

---

[35] Cherniss (*Aristotle's Criticism,* 428) speaks of these three texts as "hints or veiled reminders" of self-motion; they make no such impression on me.

[36] The Aristotelian *tertium quid,* the *unmoved* mover, had not yet been invented.

[37] I cannot see, therefore, that "had (Plato) declared that the soul is self-motion, he would have ruined the whole structure and form of the *Timaeus*" (429), except (at most) for readers who would assume that he still believes everything he said about the self-motion of the soul in the *Phaedrus;* though even on readers who had such sublime faith in the unalterability of his views, the effect could hardly be catastrophic, since Plato, as Cherniss recognizes, does refer three times to the soul's self-motion in the *Timaeus.* (Such readers, if such there were, were heading for a

The possibility of the contradiction we are looking for is then narrowed down to the second (2 above). This is where it has been recently found:

> If *psyche* is self-generating motion and thus the first cause of all motion (46e1), how can the world body be in some motion, however irregular, before the *psyche* is housed in it?[38]

Must psyche be "the first cause of all motion" if it is "self-generating motion"? Plato certainly says so in the *Phaedrus* and the *Laws*. But that is not to the point here. What we are now asking is whether *the reader of the Timaeus* would have any reason to think that this is asserted or implied in this dialogue. Professor Gould evidently thinks so, since he refers us, in support, to the lines from 46d–e I cited above. But these do not say, or imply, that the intelligent causes *generate* or *originate* all the motions of those senseless, soul-less causes which we must think "second." This never happens in the case of human agency, from which Plato extrapolates his theory of cosmic causation. If the billiard player, *P,* picks up a cue, *C,* to hit a ball, *X,* and thereby cause motion in another ball, *Y,* it might look at first sight as though the "first" cause here—the self-motion of *P*'s soul—generated all the motions of the "second" causes (*X* moved by *C* moved by *P*'s hand) which serve as the *sunaitia* of the "first" cause. But though the cue and the two billiard-balls were motionless to begin with, *P*'s body was not: all [417] sort of motions were taking place within it, which the self-motion of his soul did not originate but was able to control and redirect so as to make the body execute the desired movement of the cue. What then of those cosmic "first causes" which explain the constitution of our world and all its creatures? These are presumably the self-motions of the Craftsman's soul. Are *they* supposed to originate the motions of their physical *sunaitia?* If Plato wanted to say any such thing, he could have said it perfectly within the framework of his "myth": he need only have pictured the Craftsman starting off with a motionless, inert, lump of matter.[39] He chooses instead to have this raw-material in ceaseless agitation before the Craftsman "ordered it with forms and numbers" (53b). The self-motions of his soul then,

---

terrible shock: in the *Laws,* where he is no less insistent on self-motion as the "essence" of the soul [895e–896a] than he was in the *Phaedrus,* Plato speaks of the soul as generated [n. 34 above], while in the *Phaedrus* he had derived its uncreatedness from its self-motion [246a].) In any case, Cherniss's own construction of the facts—when writing the *Timaeus,* Plato, believing that the soul's self-motion implies its beginninglessness, suppresses a declaration of self-motion which would remind the reader of this implication, expecting "that this suppression itself, especially when set in relief by his hints at the doctrine suppressed, would make the mythical character of the creation all the more obvious to his audience" (ibid., 431)—is hard to square with another fact, of which Cherniss, with admirable candor, reminds us in this context: Xenocrates, the protagonist of the mythical interpretation, completely missed this signal (ibid., and n. 366).

[38] Gould (work cited in n. 4 above), 129.

[39] As Gould himself points out, ibid. and n. 44. Cf. Herter (above, pp. 265–66) 331.

no less than ours, supervene on material motions which he does not generate but only harnesses to the fulfillment of his creative purposes.

Would we have any cause to find this in contradiction with what we were told in 46d–e? How could we? The injunction we were given there—to pursue intelligent causes as the first, and inanimate ones as the second—works perfectly within the created world, where intelligent causes are always at work. But when, at Plato's bidding, we venture beyond the world to the antecedent chaos, we see that the injunction is useless: it is no use looking for intelligent causes as "the first" in an area in which they do not exist. Here we must content ourselves with a purely physical cause of motion, *sc.* the "irregularity" (*anōmalotēs*) of the material medium. This may cause us disappointment and annoyance, since Plato's methodological maxims have accustomed us to believe that only when an intelligent cause is located will a fully intelligible explanation be achieved. But can we complain of contradiction? Has Plato told us that *every* motion admits of a fully intelligible explanation? Quite the opposite. Immediately after distinguishing the two kinds of causes, Plato went on to tell us that the causes of the second type, "when isolated from intelligence, produce particular effects which are random and without order" (μονωθεῖσαι φρονήσεως τὸ τυχὸν ἄτακτον ἑκάστοτε ἐξεργάζονται) 46e5–6. So there must be some occurrences which are not fully susceptible of rational explanation, and we are to expect these whenever the second type of cause operates in isolation from the first. And this is precisely the condition of the primal chaos, since [418] it is as "isolated from intelligence" as anything could possibly be. Hence it *must* frustrate our ideal of perfect intelligibility and *must* fall within the exclusive domain of the second type of cause. Hence the origination of its motions by the self-motions of soul, so far from being implied by what is said in 46d–e, is positively excluded by it.

In his little book *Plato* (London, 1908), A. E. Taylor had voiced the conviction that

> Plutarch is right in maintaining that the theory of the eternity of the world can only be read into Plato by a violent and unnatural exegesis which strains the sense of the most obvious expressions in the interest of a foregone conclusion. (143)

I would not myself so speak of a hypothesis which has commended itself to the finest Platonic scholarship of the second half of the nineteenth century and the first half of the twentieth. I have never thought of it as a preconception forced on the facts. I would readily grant that Zeller, Cornford, Cherniss, and others[40] gave it their allegiance only because they thought it the hypothesis which makes the best sense of our difficult textual data. All I have done here and in *D.M.T.* is to offer reasons why, for all its undoubted merits, the hypothesis is probably false.

[40] Including Taylor himself in his *Commentary*—just twenty years later!

PART THREE

AFTER PLATO

17

A NOTE ON THE UNMOVED MOVER

THE WELL-KNOWN essay by Sir David Ross on "Aristotle's Theology" in the Introduction to his edition of the *Metaphysics* ⟨2 vols., Oxford, 1924⟩, contains the following lines:

There has been much controversy over the question whether God is for Aristotle only the final cause, or the efficient cause as well, of change. There can be no doubt about the answer. "Efficient cause" is simply the translation of Aristotle's *archē tēs kinēseōs* and God is certainly this. (vol. 1, p. cxxxiv)

There is a serious slip here which unfortunately has to be noticed, as it seems to be misleading earnest students of the subject. Thus, the lines I have cited turn up in Professor Troy Organ's recent paper, "Randall's Interpretation of Aristotle's Unmoved Mover," in the October issue of this journal (⟨*PQ*⟩ at p. 302) as the (only) cited evidence for the claim that the Unmoved Mover "'causes' motion by reason of its reality as efficient and final and formal cause." May I then point out that while ὅθεν ἡ ἀρχὴ τῆς κινήσεως is a standard Aristotelian term for "efficient cause" (see, e.g., occurrences of this expression and of its variants, ὅθεν ἡ ἀρχὴ τῆς μεταβολῆς, ὅθεν ἡ κίνησις, in the passages cited by E. Zeller, *Aristotle and the Earlier Peripatetics* [Engl. transl., London, 1897; Vol. I, p. 355n. 3, and p. 356n. 1]; and cf. H. Bonitz, *Index Aristotelicus,* 22b34ff., 498b40ff.), *archē tēs kinēseōs,* without the *hothen,* can apply to *any* of the four causes, except the material (see e.g. Bonitz, ibid., 112b51ff. and, for typical usage, *Phys.* 2.1). So while *archē tēs kinēseōs could* be used to refer to the efficient cause in a given context, "efficient cause" would be as flagrant a mistranslation of *archē tēs kinēseōs* as it would be, for example, of *aition.*

To speak *ad rem:* That the Unmoved Mover does move as final cause is obvious enough. That it moves in any other way is not borne out by a single scrap of direct evidence and is flatly incompatible with the cardinal doctrine that the *only* activity of the Unmoved Mover is *noēsis noēseōs.* The latter, too well-known to be in need of documentation here, suffices to break the only argument I can think of for ascribing efficient causation to the Unmoved Mover with any measure of plausibility: the "frequent" (*pollakis*) coalescence of efficient, formal, and final cause (*Phys.* 198a24ff.). Ignoring the weakness of the argument at the base, due to the limitation of the scope of its premise

From *PQ* 13 (1963): 246–47. Used by permission.

signaled by *pollakis,* one may reply as follows: When a form functions as both a final and efficient cause, it is never, strictly speaking, the form itself, but only its actualization in some individual that performs the latter function: "a man [not the form, *Man*] [246] generates a man" (ibid.; cf. *Met.* 12.5, 1071a20–24). Now the only way in which the form, *Unmoved Mover,* could be actualized in an individual other than *the* Unmoved Mover, would be as a thought in some mind(s) other than its own (in the first instance, the mind of the "first heaven"). In that case it would be only the *latter*—the dynamic force of the thought of the Unmoved Mover in mind(s) other than its own—that would function as efficient cause. There is nothing particularly new about this remark. The gist of the matter is understood well enough in the literature and is correctly stated by Organ a few lines later when he concludes that "the only way" (p. 303) in which the Unmoved Mover moves is "by being an end aimed at" (p. 302). He thus provides his own correction to his previous claim that the Unmoved Mover is an efficient cause.

18

MINIMAL PARTS IN EPICUREAN ATOMISM

I

WHAT ARE WE to understand by the "minimum in the atom,"[1,2] its "partless"[3] parts? I know of only two plausible answers. In Section I of this paper, I shall explain the difficulties in each which have led me to search for a new solution, the one I present in Section II.

From *Isis* 56 (1965): 121–47. Used by permission.

[1] This is a partial outcome of research in the history of Greek science which was supported by a grant of the National Science Foundation. Earlier versions of the paper were circulated privately among scholars working in the same field, and I have profited greatly from criticisms they have given me. I am particularly indebted to the following: Professors S. Bochner, C. Boyer, P. De Lacy, D. J. Furley, J. Mau, J. Murdoch, F. Sparshott, Mr. Bon de Sousa Pernes, and the unidentified referee whose critical comments I was privileged to see.

[2] Epicurus, *Ep. ad Hdt.*, I, 59, τὸ ἐν τῇ ἀτόμῳ ἐλάχιστον, τὰ ἐλάχιστα (Diogenes Laertius, *Vitae philos.*, ed. H. S. Long, II, pp. 522, 5 and 10 (Oxford: Clarendon Press, 1964); hereafter I shall refer to this work by the abbreviation "DL [Long]"). Readers who are not already abreast of the scholarly literature on this subject would find the following references most useful: H.A.J. Munro, *Titi Lucreti Cari De rerum natura* (4th ed. Cambridge: Deighton, Bell, 1886) on Lucretius I.599ff. and II.478ff. (for a fuller statement of his views, see *Journal of Classical and Sacred Philology* 1, 1854: pp. 28ff. and 252ff.); Cyril Bailey, *The Greek Atomists and Epicurus* (to which I shall refer hereafter by the abbreviation GAE) (Oxford: Clarendon Press, 1928), pp. 285ff.; Bailey, *Epicurus* (Oxford: Clarendon Press, 1926), pp. 204ff.; Bailey, *Titi Lucreti Cari De rerum natura* (Oxford: Clarendon Press, 1947), Vol. 2, pp. 700ff., 882ff.; I. E. Drabkin, "Notes on Lucretius II, 479–82," *CP* 32, 1937: pp. 258ff.; and the papers of Hans von Arnim, S. Luria, and Jürgen Mau to be cited below.

[3] Epicurus, *loc. cit.*, with von Arnim's emendation (ἀμερῆ for ἀμιγῆ of the codd.), which has also been adopted by Luria and, more recently, by Graziano Arrighetti (*Epicurus, Opere* [Turin: Einaudi, 1960]; from Olof Gigon's translation, "Unteilbare," I gather that he too adopts this reading [*Epikur: Von der Überwindung der Furcht*, Zürich: Artemis-Verlag, 1949, p. 19]); von Arnim's and Luria's works will be cited shortly ⟨below, nn. 19 and 27⟩. Though my argument in this paper does not depend on the correctness of this emendation (the same expression could be recovered from Lucr., I, 601, *sine partibus* and 625, *nullis . . . partibus*, in both cases paired with *minima natura*, which corresponds perfectly with τὰ ἐλάχιστα καὶ [ἀμερῆ] in Epicurus), I am convinced that it is right, since *amigē* in this context makes (a) poor sense, but not (b) so poor that it must be retained as the *lectio difficilior*. On behalf of (a), I would argue that the notion of *unmixed* parts of atoms is quite irrelevant (contrast, e.g., ἄκρατα καὶ πρῶτα σώματα in Plato, *Timaeus*, 57c, where "unmixed" makes perfect sense, since it refers to the primary corpuscles which may be "mixed" in various proportions to account for different varieties of material stuffs; so too in ἀπάντων δὲ τῶν σχημάτων οὐδὲν . . . ἀμιγὲς τοῖς ἄλλοις, Theophrastus, *De sensu*, 67: atoms of a given shape never occur "unmixed" with atoms of different shapes). (a) is tacitly acknowledged by most of those who keep *amigē*, since the translations they offer read (at

"They Are Physically Indivisible Elements"

Suppose I were to ask, "What is the capital of a nation?" and were told, "A city in that nation." That would be true enough, but not the truth about a capital which explains what it is. Neither would the indivisibility of the minima explain what they are. For if it did, why should Epicurus [121] have invented them? In the physical system he had inherited from its founders, Leucippus and Democritus, the primary elements which were *defined* as indivisibles, and even so *named,* were the atoms.[4] Why then should he want to lodge a new set of indivisibles inside each of the old ones? Did he feel the need for a second line of defense against the horrors[5] of infinite divisibility? Why so? Was there a fear that some exceptional cosmic stress might crack the atoms? A set of more minute indivisibles would have been a childish defense against this. For if the atoms could collapse in an emergency, why should not the minima too in a superemergency? Not, surely, because they are *by definition* the smallest things that could exist. It is not Epicurus' way to settle factual questions by definition.[6] And the very problem we are now considering is fictitious. For Epicurus the atom is unalterability itself,[7] the bedrock on which the invariance of the laws governing natural change can safely rest.[8] This is the first thing he establishes in the *Letter to Herodotus,* when he has once laid down (39) the general principle of nature's lawfulness that being cannot perish into not-being (for, if it could, no law of nature would hold),[9] and that whatever is in being consists exclusively of bodies and of void:

---

best) as though their text were *amerē* after all: so Bailey, who translates "indivisible," Ettore Bignone (*Epicuro* [Bari, 1920]) "individue," (and Ernout-Robin (A. Ernout and L. Robin, eds., *Lucrèce, De la nature,* 1 [Paris, 1925], lxxiii) "irreductibles." Otto Apelt (*Diogenes Laertius* 2 [Berlin, 1955]) translates "jeder Zusammensetzung ledige" and George K. Strodach, *The Philosophy of Lucretius* (Evanston, Ill.: Northwestern University Press, 1963), p. 124, "uncompounded"; but for this Epicurus would surely have written *asuntheta.*

[4] The word *atomos* retains its literal, descriptive force in Epicurus' use of it: see the citation from DL (Long), 2, pp. 514, 1–6, a little later in the text above, and note the strong descriptive use of the word in such a phrase as "the first bodies (literally, "the principles") must be uncuttable (*atomous*) by nature" (literally, "must be natures of uncuttable bodies"), ibid., line 7.

[5] Epicurus adopts the Eleatic argument that the infinite divisibility of matter entails its annihilability, i.e., the metaphysical impossibility of the conversion of being into not-being: DL (Long), 2, pp. 521, 4–9; and cf. my remarks on this argument in my review of H. Fränkel, *Wege und Formen der frühgriechischen Philosophie* in Gnomon 31, 1959: pp. 193ff., at pp. 198–99 (** 1.171–73). His objection to the infinite divisibility of matter would be reinforced by his parallel arguments that the physical instantiation of convergent infinite sequences entailed absurdities: DL (Long), 2, 521, 3–4, 10–18; cf. the citation from this passage in Section 2 and nn. 92 and 96–99.

[6] Though the atoms are defined as indivisibles, their *existence* is not settled by definition.

[7] The atoms are "the unalterables" (DL [Long], 2, pp. 522, 13); cf. the conjunction "uncuttable and unchangeable" in the following citation in the text above—the phrase which *introduces* the atoms in this Epistle.

[8] Cf. Lucr., 1, 592–98 and 790–97.

[9] If it could, the natural order would collapse because its elements would vanish.

And of bodies some are compounds, others [the elements] from which compounds are made. And the latter must be uncuttable (*atoma*) and unchangeable, if all things are not to perish into not-being, but have power to endure through [any] dissolutions of the compounds, so full [i.e., solid] in nature that at no point in no way can they be dissolved.[10] [122]

This being the case, an auxiliary set of physical uncuttables would have been a pure redundancy. It is very difficult to see why so useless a notion should have even occurred to Epicurus and, if it did, why he should have made a place for it in his tightly constructed system.

"They Are Mathematically Indivisible Magnitudes"

If so, Epicurus would be maintaining that the physical dimensions of the minima should be recognized in geometry as its smallest admissible magnitudes. Thus, if q were to stand for their length,[11] all geometrical principles[12] and theorems relating to lines would apply only to those whose length is q or an integral multiple of q. Fractional values of q, or quantities incommensurable with it, would be absurdities,[13] to which our geometry would make no reference, except to show that they entail a logical contradiction. So too for magnitudes of two or three dimensions: only multiples[14] of q^2 or q^3, respectively, would be meant when "planes" or "solids" were spoken of in positive propositions of our system. Is this an overstatement of the position? I do not think so. This is how it should have been formulated in the first place, for this is how Epicurus would have been understood in his own time by mathematicians, or by philosophers not wholly ignorant of mathematics, if they had heard him declare himself a mathematical atomist.[15] It was unfortunate then

[10] DL (Long), 2, pp. 514, 1–6.

[11] This is the only dimension mentioned in the single passage in Epicurus where the minima are expounded (to be discussed in Section II). It is apparent that this is intended to cover all three of their linear dimensions, all three being assumed to be equal. And cf. n. 86, below.

[12] I shall be using this for the Greek *archai*, by which classical authors commonly denote the primitive propositions of a deductive system.

[13] Not innocent fictions: *if* Epicurus had been a mathematical atomist, he would have taken up this position because he thought that the arguments against infinite sequences at 56–57 were generalizable from physical to geometrical magnitudes. But note that this generalization is not made in Epicurus' text, where the magnitudes are clearly material particles, not abstract mathematical quantities: at 56 he refers to the process of division by a verb with unmistakably physical connotations (*thlibontes*, "crushing"); and at 57 he speaks of the magnitudes as *onkoi*, which Epicurus uses regularly to denote physical particles: Bailey's view (GAE, pp. 578–79) that *onkoi* is used in 56–57 as a "technical" term for the minima is sheer invention, without support from either the dictionary meaning ("bulk") or from Epicurus' known uses of the word in all other contexts (for particles in effluences of sound and smell, 52–53; for atoms [*tōn prōtōn (onkōn)*], 69; for earth particles, *Ep.*, 2, 105).

[14] To avoid unnecessary repetition, I drop (here and hereafter) "integral" when it is sufficiently clear from the context that only such multiples or submultiples are meant.

[15] Though what language he would have used to make this declaration is not quite clear. There is no exact Greek counterpart for "mathematical atomism" in our sources.

that in the first influential ascription of mathematical atomism to Epicurus—in Hans von Arnim's now classical paper "Epikurs Lehre vom Minimum"[16]—no effort was made to elucidate the crucial phrase "mathematisch unteilbar" or to show its readers the explosive implications such a thesis would have had for mathematics in its own time. This may explain how it could happen that Bailey, writing thirty years later, should speak so casually of Epicurus (GAE, p. 234) as "one who held that *area* and matter were alike a succession of *discrete* [123] minima."[17] Bailey here is evidently endorsing von Arnim's view. But is he aware of the enormous consequences such a commitment would have had for Epicurus? I doubt it. For in all of Bailey's comments on the relevant Epicurean and Lucretian passages, and in his full account of the minima in GAE (pp. 285ff.), there is no defense of this view. Bailey must have had only the vaguest notion of what it would mean to hold that every plane area is a "succession of discrete minima," else he would scarcely have pinned this thesis so casually on Epicurus, without a word of evidential support.[18]

Five years after the publication of Bailey's GAE, there appeared a fascinating monograph by S. Luria, a classical scholar who was also a learned historian of mathematics, "Die Infinitesimallehre der antiken Atomisten."[19] Here for the first time an effort was made to explain what mathematical atomism would have meant for Democritus (the principal figure in Luria's paper) and Epicurus. Though even this was not explicit enough from my point of view, it was a vast improvement on anything offered in the preceding literature. Moreover, Luria brought into his argument a mass of data which had never been exploited in earlier stages of the debate. Though most of this new evidence was tenuous, speculative, and indirect, it well deserved its day in court; and many of its items had high intrinsic interest of their own.[20] Luria's paper met

---

[16] *Almanach der Kaiserlichen Akademie der Wissenschaften Wien,* 1907, pp. 383ff.

[17] My italics. And cf. p. 315, "Epicurus apparently held that there was . . . a minimum of extension (the . . . *minima pars*) and a minimum of physical existence (the atom). . . ."

[18] At GAE, p. 234, all we are given as evidence for the cited statement is a reference to *Ep.,* I, 57, 58; but not a word there implies, or even suggests, that *area* is "a succession of discrete minima." At GAE, pp. 286–88, where Bailey deals more specifically with the minima, the claim that they represent "the minima of extension" (presumably, of geometrical, no less than physical, extension) is unsupported. Bailey does not even refer us to von Arnim's argument for this view until later (p. 315), when he comes to argue for the quite different thesis that Epicurus believed in atomic minima of time and space.

[19] *Quellen und Studien zur Geschichte der Mathematik,* B, 1933, 2:106ff. I shall refer to this paper hereafter merely by the author's name.

[20] To appreciate the merits of Luria's monograph, one might compare it with the previous ascription of mathematical atomism to Democritus in Erich Frank, *Plato und die sogenannten Pythagoreer* (Halle, 1923), pp. 53ff. and 351ff. From Frank's (or any earlier) treatment of the topic, one would have no inkling of the wealth of material which could be brought to bear on it. In spite of my radical disagreements with Luria's conclusions (and, even more, with his methods of

with a strange reception from the scholarly world in the West.[21] Though it had appeared in a journal of high eminence, and its existence was heralded to students of the pre-Socratics by Kranz's repeated references to it in the fifth[22] (and each subsequent) edition of *Die Fragmente der Vorsokratiker,* little notice seemed taken of it for fifteen years following its publication[23] and not much even thereafter.[24] But 1949 brought it at last a handsome acknowledgment: [124] Heath, who had previously argued against the ascription of mathematical atomism to Democritus,[25] now reversed himself under direct indebtedness to Luria's paper.[26] A few years later Jürgen Mau, in the most extensive treatment of this topic since the Second World War,[27] followed Luria in claiming mathematical atomism for Democritus and Epicurus, though in a more guarded manner and with a more critical treatment of the evidence. But even so, an exhaustive examination of the material in Luria's paper and of the construction he put on it has yet to be made.

It is not my purpose to undertake this here. The job would call for a paper several times the length of this one. All I wish to do, then, is to underline as strongly and as clearly as I can what I take to be the central (and, to my mind, insuperable) difficulty in the way of this view which has been defended so spiritedly by Luria and, more recently, by Mau.

---

handling evidence), I gladly record here my great debt to him. It was he who introduced me to many of the texts I shall be discussing in this section.

[21] Because of my ignorance of the Russian language, I am unable to estimate its reception in the U.S.S.R.

[22] Hermann Diels; Walther Kranz, eds. (Berlin: Weidmann, 1934–37).

[23] It was almost completely ignored. For honorable exceptions see the notice taken of it (favorably) by Wolfgang Schmid, *Epikurs Kritik der platonischen Elementenlehre, Klassisch-Philologische Studien,* Heft 9 (Leipzig: Otto Harrassowitz, 1936), pp. 29ff., and (critically) by I. E. Drabkin ⟨above, n. 2⟩ at 260–61, and by Federigo Enriques and Manlio Mazziotti, *Le Dottrine di Democrito* (Bologna: N. Zanichelli, 1948), pp. 201–6.

[24] No mention of it in the 1956 edition of Rodolfo Mondolfo's *L'Infinito nel pensiero dell' antichità classica* (Florence: La Nuova Italia), in Arrighetti (above, n. 3), in G. S. Kirk and J. E. Raven, *The Presocratic Philosophers* (Cambridge: Cambridge University Press, 1957), in the English translation of B. L. Van der Waerden's *Science Awakening* (New York: Oxford University Press, 1961), or in S. Sambursky, *The Physical World of the Greeks* (London: Routledge and Kegan Paul, 1956). However, Heath's reference to it (n. 26 below) suggests that more notice of it will be taken in the immediate future. Karl R. Popper, in *Conjectures and Refutations* (London: Basic Books, 1962, pp. 82ff.), refers to it as a "most important article" and appears to accept its interpretation of Democritus.

[25] Thomas L. Heath, *A History of Greek Mathematics* (Oxford: Clarendon Press, 1921), Vol. 1, p. 181. (Hereafter I shall refer to this work as HGM.)

[26] Heath, *Mathematics in Aristotle* (Oxford: Oxford University Press, 1949), pp. 79–80. (I shall refer to this work hereafter by the abbreviation "MA.")

[27] "Zum Problem des Infinitesimalen bei den antiken Atomisten," *Deutsche Akademie der Wissenschaften zu Berlin,* Institut für griechisch-römische Altertumskunde, Arbeitsgruppe für hellenistisch-römische Philosophie, Veröffentlichung Nr. 4, 2nd ed., 1957 (the first appeared in 1954). I shall refer to this monograph hereafter as "Mau."

By the closing decade of the fifth century (at the very latest), practicing geometricians—as distinct from sophists or philosophers criticizing geometry or dogmatizing about it[28]—must have accepted the infinite divisibility of extensive magnitudes. For this is the latest possible date for the discovery of the proof of incommensurables.[29] And once this discovery was made, [125] it would have settled forever whatever doubts mathematicians may have entertained about infinite divisibility at an earlier time.[30] For in Greek mathematical thought, the entailment of infinite divisibility by incommensurables is extremely direct and perspicuous. This is how Proclus, following Geminus, puts the point:

> For when they prove that incommensurable magnitudes exist and that not all are commensurable with each other, what would one say that they have proved but that every magnitude is divisible and that we shall never reach the partless (*to ameres*), which would be the least common measure of magnitudes?[31]

What Proclus is saying here would be known to every competent mathematician of the fourth century: that if A and B are incommensurable, their *an-*

---

[28] Such as the advocates of "indivisible lines" who are under attack in the pseudo-Aristotelian *De lineis insecabilibus;* their identity is not certainly known. Xenocrates, to whom this doctrine is often attributed and who is often held to be the butt of the polemics of this treatise, is not named in it. The only doctrines under attack in it which can be ascribed to Xenocrates with a high degree of probability are (a) the indivisible *Ideal* line (968a10–14: independently attested for Xenocrates *apud* Themistius, *Paraphrasis in De anima*, 11, 20ff. [= Xenocrates Fr. 39, Richard Heinze, *Xenokrates . . .* , Leipzig, 1892]), and (b) the priority of parts to the whole (968a15–18; that this is authentic Xenocratean doctrine is demonstrated by S. Pines, *A New Fragment of Xenocrates and Its Implications* [Philadelphia: American Philosophical Society, 1961, Transactions, N.S. 51, Pt. 2, pp. 14B ff.]). Neither of these metaphysical doctrines entails the *geometrical* atomism whose refutation is the main business of the treatise. When the latter is ascribed to Xenocrates, it is not on definite and unambiguous evidence: Proclus parrots the ascription (without citing any authority) in the references given in n. 73 below; but elsewhere (*In Platonis Timaeum*, 215F [2, 245, 29–246, 4, ed. E. Diehl, Leipzig: Teubner, 1903–6]) he says that Xenocrates' indivisible line was the "substantial" (i.e., Ideal) line, for "to think a magnitude indivisible would be ludicrous." For the same refusal to ascribe indivisible magnitudes to Xenocrates, see also Porphyry *apud* Simplicius, *Phys.,* 140, 6–18, and Simplicius himself, ibid., 142, 16–27.

[29] See, e.g., Kurt von Fritz, "The Discovery of Incommensurability by Hippasus," *Annals of Mathematics,* 1945, 46:242ff., at 243–44, on the inference to be drawn from Plato, *Theaetetus* 147d. And we may note with H. Cherniss ("Plato as a Mathematician," *RM* 4, 1951:395–425, at 412) that there is no suggestion in Plato's text that the proof (of the irrationality of the square roots of the appropriate integers between 3 and 17, implying that that of the square root of 2 had been made still earlier) was a recent discovery.

[30] In the closing decades of the sixth century and the first part of the fifth century, when Greek mathematicians were still assuming, as had their Babylonian predecessors, that all geometrical magnitudes were commensurable. Cf. B. L. Van der Waerden, "Zenon und die Grundlagenkrisis der griechischen Mathematik," *Mathematische Annalen* 117, 1940: 141ff., at 155ff.

[31] Proclus, *In primum Euclidis elementorum librum commentarii,* ed. Gottfried Friedlein (Leipzig, 1873), 278, 19–24. (This work will be cited hereafter merely by the author's name.)

thuphairesis[32] could be continued *ad infinitum;*[33] hence by means of it one could reach quantities smaller than any given quantity—hence smaller than *q,* whatever value Epicurus might wish to assign to *q.* How then could Epicurus still say that *q* was the smallest geometrical quantity? I can think of only three possibilities that might be thought to cover this point: (a) that he was ignorant of geometry; (b) that he thought geometry an intellectual frivolity, a tissue of fictions with which no sober man need seriously concern himself; (c) that he envisaged a different kind of geometry which recognized only commensurable magnitudes.

The first two of these three possibilities are worth only a moment's notice. Possibility (a) would explain nothing, even if it were true;[34] for Epicurus' [126] circle included men well versed in mathematics;[35] if one of his major tenets perpetrated a mathematical howler, he would hear of it from them at once, as he would from the people in the Stoa in any case a little later. And as for (b), had he consigned the whole of geometry to the devil,[36] he would not

---

[32] Or, *antanairesis,* sometimes spoken of as "the Euclidean algorithm" in the modern literature. As O. Becker has shown ("Eudoxos-Studien I," *Quellen und Studien zur Geschichte der Mathematik,* B, 2, 1933: 311ff.), this played an extremely important role in pre-Eudoxian mathematics: by means of this operation, *ratio* could be defined (Aristotle, *Topica,* 158b32ff.) so as to apply also to incommensurables, prior to the more sophisticated (and only perfectly satisfactory) definition formulated finally by Eudoxus (Euclid, V, Df. 5). And see von Fritz ⟨above, n. 29⟩, pp. 262–63, and his n. 87.

[33] The converse of this is proved in Euclid, 10, 2: "If, given continual *anthuphairesis* of the lesser of two unequal magnitudes from the greater, the remainder never measures what comes before it, the magnitudes are incommensurable."

[34] We do not know it to be true. There is no more reason to suppose Epicurus totally ignorant of mathematics than a proficient mathematician. For his "dislike of geometry," Bailey (GAE, p. 234) cites the references in Hermann Usener ed., *Epicurea* (Leipzig, 1887), 229a. None of these (or any other text known to me) shows that he disliked geometry more than other parts of "culture" (DL [Long], 2, p. 496, 17–18), including musical and literary criticism (Plutarch, *Non posse suaviter . . . ,* 1095c). From his dislike of these things, it would not follow that he was wholly, or largely, ignorant of all, or any, of them.

[35] Including Polyaenus, who, Cicero tells us (*Academica,* 2, 106), *magnus mathematicus fuisse dicitur.* And see the next note.

[36] Which might well have been his attitude, if we could take at face value Cicero's remark (ibid., continuation of the citation): *is* [Polyaenus] *posteaque Epicuro adsentiens totam geometriam falsam esse credidit.* Epicurus might have thought geometry "false" (and hence unimportant for the philosopher) because, on his assumptions, it would misdescribe (and so be false of) the world both in its appearance to the senses and in its atomic constitution as represented by his theory of matter (e.g., he would hold that no sense datum and no physical object answers precisely to the extensionless point of geometry). But it would be rash to infer from just this that the "falsehood" of geometry and contempt for it was a kind of "party line" mandatory for the adherents of the school. We know that within a century of Epicurus' death leading members of the Epicurean school (Basilides, Philonides) appear to have reversed the predominantly negative attitude of the Garden to geometry in the earlier period (Wilhelm Crönert, *Kolotes und Menedemos* [Leipzig: E. Avenarius, 1906], p. 88). An illustrious Epicurean of the late second century B.C., Demetrius of Laconia is known to have written on geometry (Victorius de Falco, *L'Epicureo*

have been a mathematical atomist either: to be that, he would have had to take geometry seriously enough to seek in it an application of his atomistic principles coordinate with their physical application. Then (c) is the only possibility worth serious consideration; and this is, in any case, the only one on which the defenders of this view appear to bank. Here I have three questions. First of all, I find it very hard to see what the finitist geometry to which these scholars would commit atomism, from Democritus down, would be like. It would be a system, constructed by mathematical techniques available at the time, whose elements would be exclusively discrete quantities, but would nonetheless retain sufficient contact with the mathematics of the spatial continuum to be recognizable as *geometry*. What sort of postulate set would have done this job? How many theorems now in Euclid, or what analogues of them, could it have saved? I cannot find even the rudiments of an answer to this question in Luria or in Mau. I have no idea how they would propose to meet the most elementary difficulties into which such a geometry would have run. To make any sense of their hypothesis,[37] we would have to understand that it would [127] allow no points, lines, or planes (in the strict sense of exclusively zero-, one-, or two-dimensional elements), but that all its magnitudes would be three-dimensional: a line would be a quadrangular parallelepipedal solid, whose length could be any quantity, but whose width and altitude would both be q; by the same token a point would be a minuscule cube, with side q. But how could this possibly avoid incommensurables, for example, at the diago-

---

Demetrio Lacone [Naples, 1923], pp. 96ff.: mathematical fragments from the Herculanean papyri). And I shall be arguing below that Demetrius' contemporary, Zeno of Sidon, was also a competent mathematician with a keen (and constructive) interest in the foundations of geometry. We cannot even assume that within the original inner circle geometry was thought so false as to be unworthy of serious inquiry. Demetrius of Laconia wrote a work, *Pros tas Poluainou aporias* (de Falco, *loc. cit.*): the title is conserved intact in Pap. 1429, and lines 6–13 of col. 2 make it reasonably clear that the object was to present short and "easy" solutions of the aporiae. If Polyaenus had thought geometry a mere frivolity, he would scarcely have written a treatise of "perplexities" which a later Epicurean mathematician would deem worth resolving; nor could Polyaenus' treatise have aimed to prove geometry totally false, else Demetrius would have set himself not to resolve its perplexities, but to rebut its wholesale rejection of geometry.

[37] As I have remarked above, their explanations of what an atomistic geometry would have meant to the Greeks leave something to be desired by way of explicitness. A line, on this hypothesis, would be "eine Reihe von Körperchen" (Luria, p. 156) and planes would be "Atomblättern" (pp. 144–45). The Körperchen would have the minimum length (in all three dimensions, presumably) and. And what of their shape? They are represented by tiny circles in some of Luria's diagrams; but I assume that this is no more than misleading typography, since round objects could not be expected to compose solid lines and planes of perfectly uniform thickness. Also misleading are statements which appear to say that the mathematical atoms of this theory would correspond to the differential of the calculus. (See, e.g., the citation from M. Simon, *Geschichte der Mathematik in Altertum*, p. 181, in Mau, p. 24n.4.) This is absolutely out of the question, since these atoms would have finite magnitude of constant value, as Mau himself quite properly remarks, p. 37.

nals of the squares that form all the faces of the latter solid, and two of the former, and at infinitely many sections produced by planes at angles to the base in the case of both solids?[38]

My second question is this: If there were such a mathematical system, or even fragments of it, why is there not a word about its *mathematics* in our sources? I am not asking here for philosophical opinions, speculations, or perplexities concerning mathematical indivisibles, but for some work *in* mathematics, something like a construction or a proof. Do we know of even a single item of this kind? Democritus' famous fragment on the cone is nothing of the sort.[39] In the first place, this is not work in mathematics, but philosophical reflection on its foundations.[40] In the second place, there is not a word in its text which asserts or implies mathematical atomism or shows that its author is even favorable to mathematical atomism.[41] We may [128] infer quite

---

[38] And cf. the raft of objections from "propositions demonstrated or assumed in mathematics which must stand unless they can be overthrown by trustworthy arguments" in pseudo-Aristotle, *De lin. insec.*, 969b32ff.

[39] Fr. B155. This much-cited fragment (it finds a place in every serious history of Greek mathematics) has been widely misinterpreted and even mistranslated (the mistranslation being itself a product of the misinterpretation). *Tmēmatōn* has been rendered as "sections" in every English, French, and Italian translation known to me; and in the German translations the phrase τὰς τῶν τμημάτων ἐπιφανείας has been rendered by "Schnittflächen." But the word for "section" is *tomē*. *Tmēmata* are "segments"; the word is always so translated when it occurs in Euclid, Aristotle, Eudemus, etc., by the very persons (e.g., Heath) who translate it "sections" in the case of this single fragment. Two further arguments against the latter in this context: (1) It would result in a redundancy, since in τὰς τῶν τμημάτων ἐπιφανείας the second word could only refer to *plane* surfaces (in the earlier period *epiphaneia* is commonly used for "plane": the usage survives in Euclid, I, Df. 5, and 11, Df. 2), and this would make the "surfaces" *identical* with the "sections." A sense of this redundancy has led Heath to ignore the second word completely in one of his translations (HGM, Vol. 1, p. 180), so that he renders the whole phrase by "the sections." If we give *tmēmatōn* its regular sense, there would be no redundancy: the phrase would refer to the (contiguous) plane surfaces of adjacent cone segments created in the first instance by the plane cutting the cone "parallel to the base," which is mentioned in the opening sentence and thereafter by other planes above the first, and parallel to it. (2) In the Plutarchean context (*De communibus notitiis*, 10797f, in *Moralia*, Teubner ed., 1952, Vol. 6.2) Chrysippus, as reported by Plutarch, calls the referents of *tmēmata* "bodies" (*sōmata*) while distinguishing these sharply from the plane surfaces.

[40] Mathematical (as distinct from philosophical) significance has been read into it by the assumption (for which there is no basis in the text) that the sections by which the segments are successively produced are *infinitely near* each other, so that the whole cone (it is alleged) was conceived by Democritus as an aggregate of infinitely many, infinitely thin, laminae, with important heuristic implications (see next note).

[41] The way Luria (pp. 138ff.) and Mau (p. 22) get mathematical atomism out of it is by assuming that the plane sections were atom-thin. Luria and Mau share the very widespread assumption that Democritus' discovery that the volume of a pyramid equals one-third of a prism with the same base and height and (probably) also that the volume of a cone equals one-third that of a cylinder with the same base and height (the former is stated by Archimedes in the preface to his *Ephodos* [E. J. Dijksterhuis, *Archimedes*, Groningen/Batavia: Noordhoff, 1938, p. 314] and

the contrary from the terms in which Chrysippus replies to Democritus in the Plutarchean context of the citation;[42] and Chrysippus' understanding of the sense of the fragment must be authoritative for us, since he is the original source of the citation and must have known it in its authentic, Democritean setting.[43]

The only thing on record which might be considered with any plausibility a venture in geometrical atomism is Antiphon's "squaring" of the circle,[44] and Luria has urged that we should so consider it.[45] Let us remind ourselves then what this argument was according to Simplicius (drawing on Eudemus): Inscribe a regular polygon in a circle; then double the number of the polygon's sides; as this operation is reiterated, "the area [of the circle] would be exhausted [and] in this way a polygon would be [eventually] inscribed whose

---

the latter is probably implied) was made by breaking down these figures into a very large set of appropriately graduated laminae (which, it is claimed, would tally with the serrated figure in the first arm of the dilemma in the Democritean fragment). This theory enjoys ample sponsorship, uniting those who make Democritus an infinitesimalist with their opponents who would make of him an atomist: the difference between "infinitely many/thin" and "very many/thin" collapses for the purpose of allowing Democritus at least a *heuristic* use of this type of construction. But what evidence, if any, exists for this view is not clear to me. Archimedes (our only ancient informant) tells us only *that* Democritus made this discovery, without a word as to the method, if any, Democritus used when he made it.

[42] Because, as I remarked in n. 39 above, Chrysippus refers to the sections as "surfaces" (i.e., planes) in contradistinction to the segments, which he calls "bodies." Had Democritus expounded the view of planes as atom-thin solids, which Luria and Mau ascribe to him, Chrysippus would either have *also* called the planes "bodies," after Democritus, or else would have taken Democritus to task for misconceiving planes as solids; in fact, he talks as though the only difference between him and Democritus is the following: the latter assumes that the disjunction, *equal or unequal,* holds for the (contiguous) "surfaces" (of adjacent cone segments), inferring that if the "surfaces" are equal, the "segments" must also be equal; Chrysippus, on the other hand, holds (*loc. cit.*) that the "surfaces" are *neither equal nor unequal,* and the "bodies" (=cone segments) are unequal.

[43] Chrysippus must have been a voluminous reader of original sources, for he was famous in antiquity for his quotations from them (see the remarks of Apollodorus and of Carneades *apud* DL [Long], 2, p. 379, 8–13 and p. 506, 20–23, respectively). He is known to have written a book, *On the Ancient Natural Philosophers* (ibid., p. 382, 14–15), and Cleanthes before him had written one against Democritus, who, as cofounder of atomism, must have been in any case a main target of Stoic criticism. On these and other grounds, we can assume that Chrysippus would have had good access to Democritus' books, and hence to the one from which he excerpted the present citation (Plutarch must have taken it directly from him). Nor was this particular puzzle the sort of thing that was likely to have reached Chrysippus secondhand: it neither affirms nor rebuts a "physical opinion," nor does it propound a notorious paradox, like Zeno's conundrums: no other allusion to it in ancient literature has survived. (Since these notes were written, a rejection of the mathematical atomist interpretation of the Democritean fragment has also been voiced [briefly] by Professor A. Wasserstein in his review of S. Sambursky, *Physics of the Stoics,* in *JHS* 83, 1963: 186ff., at 189.)

[44] Simplicius, *Phys.,* 54, 20ff. = Fritz Wehrli, *Eudemos von Rhodos* (Basel: B. Schwabe, 1955). 58, 1–59, 12.

[45] Luria, pp. 128–29.

sides would coincide with the circumference of the circle because of their smallness." Luria would like us to believe that [129] Antiphon thought the circle *was* a regular *n*-agon (where *n* was very large). The only evidence he cites is a remark by Alphonso, a learned Jew of the fifteenth century, that Antiphon spoke of "those particles of which the straight line no less than the circumference of the circle consists."[46] But the learned Alphonso's testimony is worth no more than that of his sources, indeed less, for there would always be some chance he might have misread them. What then were his sources? Luria does not tell us. But his only other citation from Alphonso's manuscript is not reassuring as to the excellence of this man's sources of information or of his ability to make judicious use of them: "I believe that Plato thought that bodies consisted of planes, planes of lines, lines of points."[47] This is a travesty of Plato's views on the foundations of geometry.[48] What reason then is there to think that Alphonso's remark about Antiphon is more reliable? I know of none, while there is the best of reason to think the reverse: if Alphonso were right on this point, our ancient authorities, Eudemus and Simplicius, would be wrong. For it is evident that they did not understand Antiphon in this way. If they did, they would have reported his error quite differently.[49] They would have charged him with an outrageous misconception of the "nature" or "essence" (in their language) of the circle, and not with a fallacious argument that, on the conditions of the construction, a rectilinear figure, by the mere proliferation of its sides, could be made to coincide with a curvilinear one.[50] So unless we are to put more faith in the unknown sources available to Alphonso in the fifteenth century than on Eudemus and Simplicius (the very ones, in all probability, from which Alphonso's own sources were derived at *n*th hand),[51] we can be certain that Antiphon was not a mathematical atomist.

[46] Ibid. No information as to the subsequent publication of this MS is available to me.

[47] Ibid., cited at p. 148n. 111.

[48] In the *Timaeus* (53c7–8) Plato speaks of three-dimensional elements as "contained by" (*perieilēphenai*), not "consisting of," planes, and of planes as "consisting of" (*sunestēken*) plane segments ("triangles"), not lines. In *Laws* 894a2–4, (*n* + 1)-dimensional elements are generated by the fluxion of *n*-dimensional ones; this is the contrary of the atomist view (cf. Sextus, *Adv. math.*, 3, 19–20 and 28).

[49] Simplicius, *Phys.*, 55, 22–24: "And if it [the inscribed regular polygon] were to be made [by the multiplication of its sides] to coincide with the circumference of the circle, a certain principle of geometry would be violated, which states that magnitudes are infinitely divisible. And this was the principle, said Eudemus, that was violated by Antiphon."

[50] Heath (HGM, Vol. 1, p. 222) makes the strange remark that Eudemus' objection is "really no more than verbal" and that "Antiphon in effect said the same thing," as does Euclid at 12, 2. I know of no respectable mathematician or philosopher of the fourth century B.C. who would have agreed with this estimate.

[51] The simplest explanation of Alphonso's error about Plato is that it goes back to somebody's misinterpretation of Aristotle's remarks in the *De caelo* (299a6–8), where he says that if one "constructs all bodies out of planes" (299a3) as is done by Plato in the *Timaeus,* it would follow "by the same reasoning" (*tou autou logou esti*) that "solids should be composed of planes, planes

Even so, his argument is instructive or, more precisely, the fate which befell it. Its fallacy was notorious. Aristotle denounces it as a black-market operation with which no respectable mathematician [130] would have any truck, not even for the purpose of refuting it.[52] Let us go back to Democritus then, remembering the rare respect Aristotle had for him:[53] How can we suppose that he rejected systematically in his geometry the principle of infinite divisibility, whose single infraction in Antiphon's ingenious construction elicited Aristotle's unmitigated scorn? And how could we further suppose that Epicurus, a century after Antiphon, tied the fortunes of his philosophy to a like rejection of this mathematical principle?

My third question is the complement of the second: How could Epicurus' willingness to marry his philosophy to a maverick[54] geometry be squared with the fact that those few surviving mathematical arguments which are specifically identified as Epicurean[55] in our sources (and which are definite enough

---

of lines, and these of points." Note the difference between (a) "solids [are] composed of planes" and (b) "constructing bodies out of planes": the "constructing" in (b) is not done by making solids *aggregates* of planes as would be done at (a). Only (b) is Plato's doctrine in the *Timaeus* and Aristotle does not say that (a) is *also* Plato's doctrine; he is only charging (with abysmal logic) that one who holds (b) ought to hold (a) as well.

[52] Aristotle, *Physics,* 185a14–17; *Sophistici elenchi,* 171b6–172a7. He says that the fallacies he has in view here cannot qualify as even mistaken (but authentic) geometrical reasoning [here called *pseudographein,* mistranslated as "drawing false figures (or, diagrams)" in the Oxford and Loeb translations; for the correct translation, see Heath, MA, pp. 46 and 76–77]; they are bogus geometry, "deceitful and crooked," like cheating in sport. The direct object of these compliments in *Soph. el.* is Bryson; but at the end of the passage Antiphon is put in the same company.

[53] For his physical opinions, to be sure (*De gen. et cor.* 315a35; 316a13; 325a1). But the praise would have been qualified here or elsewhere had Democritus been committed to a geometry whose first principles Aristotle thought absurdities.

[54] "Maverick" by ancient standards. The availability of finitist geometries in modern mathematics is not in question.

[55] It is arguing in a circle to classify *unidentified* thinkers as Epicureans merely because they voice opinions which are, or are believed to be, expressions of mathematical atomism. So I cannot follow Luria's use of "Epikureer" (p. 158) in referring to the unknown propounders of the puzzle in Proclus 158, 2ff., viz. that an infinite number of diameters would produce twice as many semicircles, hence a quantity twice as large as infinity. If these people were Epicureans (as they *may* have been: for Epicurean exploitation of the absurdity that would arise if an infinite set had subsets which could be said to be both equally and unequally numerous with the set, see Lucr., 1, 615–22), they were throwing stones from a house of glass: the number series (whose infinity, I presume, would not be denied by any of those persons whom Luria believes to be mathematical atomists) will give us as many sets as we please whose number can be said with equal plausibility to be larger than infinity; so will the actual infinity of the atoms, a cardinal Epicurean doctrine (e.g., by comparing the atoms in the whole universe with those in two parts of it produced, say, by dividing the universe by a perpendicular plane on the equator extending infinitely in all four directions). I would also take exception to his remark, apropos of the puzzle in Proclus 368, 26ff., "Die Wiedersacher der Mathematik, mit denen sich Proklos auseinandersetzt [viz., in this passage], sind so gut wie immer die Epikureer," p. 156. These people are evidently destructive critics of the Euclidean system (they claim they can prove that two straight

to have come from men competent in geometry) neither assert nor imply mathematical atomism but are in every single case criticisms which could have been made by persons who had not even heard of mathematical atomism? I am making a claim here whose truth has never been pointed out, to my knowledge; so I had better document it as fully as I can within the limits of this brief discussion.

The only one of these Epicurean critics whose mathematical arguments against the received geometry are reported to us along with their author's name is Zeno of Sidon.[56] This man was evidently an eminent representative of his school in the world of mathematics, else his geometrical views would [131] not have been singled out by Posidonius for extensive criticism: this is the only case in which we hear of a leading Stoic devoting a whole treatise[57] to the refutation of an Epicurean's views on mathematics. What then are Zeno's views? Proclus divides "those who took objection to geometry" into two groups:[58]

(1) The majority who "directed their doubts to its principles, seeking to show that its particular parts [i.e., the theorems] lacked foundation." In this group he mentions (a) those who controverted the principles of all knowledge—Pyrrhonians; and (b) those who doubted the principles of geometry only—Epicureans;

(2) "Those who, having already conceded the principles (of geometry), deny that the consequences have been demonstrated unless some further admission is made not previously included among the principles."

Here he names Zeno of Sidon, "who belonged to the Epicurean sect." Zeno's objections to the Euclidean system mentioned by Proclus all fall within the terms of the position, as categorized by Proclus, in the statement I have just cited: they are all objections to the incompleteness of its principles for the purpose of validating its proofs. Proclus[59] cites Zeno's objections to the first construction in Euclid (1, 1): "On a given finite straight line to construct an equilateral triangle." Zeno's point is that the received proof would not be valid unless some further assumption is made which, he contends, is not nailed down among the explicitly formulated principles of the Euclidean system: that no two lines, straight or curved, contain a common segment. Thus the first of his criticisms of Euclid's proof is that none of the previously listed principles

---

lines *AB*, *CD*, cutting another, *AC*, at interior angles summing to less than 180 degrees will not meet). But there is no evidence in Proclus that they are either mathematical atomists or Epicureans.

[56] Born *ca.* 150 B.C., "der bedeutendste der damaligen Epikureer," Eduard Zeller, *Die Philosophie der Griechen*, Vol. 3, 1[5] (Leipzig: Reisland, 1923), pp. 384–86.

[57] Proclus 200, 1–2.

[58] Ibid., 199, 3ff.

[59] Ibid., 214, 15ff.

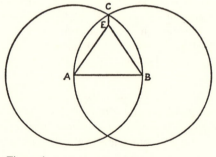

Figure 1

exclude the possibility that *AC* and *BC* might meet before *C* (e.g., at *E,* as in Fig. 1). So far as I can see, Zeno's contention is formally correct. The closest we come in Euclid to a principle that would cover the point is Postulate 2, that "a finite straight line may be produced continuously in a straight line." Heath says "this must be held to assert that . . . the produced part in either direction is *unique.*"[60] But "in a straight line" can also be read to mean "in *at least one* straight line." We could extenuate the looseness of Euclid's diction here by reminding ourselves that in such matters Greek tolerance was greater than ours; one can find other cases of it in closely reasoned Greek texts.[61] On this account one might charge Zeno with being unnecessarily difficult here. Still, he is within his rights in asking for his pound of flesh, such [132] as a modern axiom set would have given him.[62] But regardless of whether or not we honor Zeno as a pioneer of rigor in proof technique or despise him as a small-minded, carping critic, the nature of his grievance against the received geometry is clear: it is a purely methodological complaint.[63] To make this kind of

---

[60] *Euclid,* I² (Oxford: Oxford University Press, 1926), 196.

[61] Cf. "one . . . Idea" in the premise of the Third Man argument in Plato, *Parmenides* 132a: I have argued controversially that this *must* mean "just one" (*PR,* 64, 1955: 439–41 ⟨** 2.195–97⟩).

[62] E.g., that "any two distinct points of a straight line completely determine that line," in David Hilbert, *Foundations of Geometry* (English translation by E. J. Townsend [Chicago: Open Court, 1902], p. 4). This would have ruled out unambiguously the possibility that the two distinct lines, *AC* and *BC,* might have point *E* in common.

[63] And so are his further points, Proclus, 216, 1–218, 12; cf. Heath, *Euclid,* I², 196–97 and 242–43. In his discussion of Zeno, Luria (pp. 170–71) seems to miss this point completely, probably because he reads atomistic assumptions into Zeno's arguments. Thus, he takes it for granted that the supposed common segment, *CE,* of lines *AC, BC* (see the diagram in the text above) must be the length of one atom; but there is no basis for this in Proclus' text. He even goes so far as to say that *koinon to tmēma* (an expression that occurs in Proclus' account of Zeno's argument, 215, 3) is "a technical Epicurean expression" (pp. 169–70) for any point (= atom) which two lines have in common. To make good his atomistic interpretation of Zeno's points,

criticism of Euclid one does not need to be a mathematical atomist; to be a stricter Euclidean would be sufficient.[64]

The only other mention of Epicureans in the whole of Proclus' *Commentary on Euclid* is in his discussion of 1, 20 (any two sides of a triangle together are greater than the third).[65] Unnamed Epicureans are said to object that "this proposition would be clear even to an ass": given the choice of routes for getting to his hay, the straight line, *AB,* or the broken one, *AC, CB,* the ass will know enough to take the former.[66] It is a fair conjecture that what these people are driving at is that a straight line's being the shortest path between two points (listed by Archimedes as his first postulate in *On the Sphere and Cylinder*)[67] should figure among the principles of geometry. In that case Euclid, 1, 20 would follow immediately: the shortest path between *A* and *B* would obviously be shorter than the path via *C* which is not a straight line, hence, by the principle, not the shortest path between the two points. The critics would still be wrong if they claimed that Euclid, 1, 20 needs no proof: to show that it is a corollary of the principle would, of course, be to prove it. But what they probably meant is that it does not need a constructive geometrical proof [*kataskeuē*] such as it gets in Euclid: given the new principle, this would be superseded as a clumsy redundancy. In any case, the critics would be perfectly right in claiming that the proof in Euclid is not more, but less, intuitively clear than the proposition.[68] [133]

Finally, we hear in Sextus[69] that "The Epicureans" affirm that "the straight line [that extends] through the void[70] is indeed straight but does not revolve because neither does the void itself admit of motion either in whole or in part." The context in Sextus is a criticism of various definitions of "straight line" approved by "the geometers." He cites the Epicurean remark in the

---

Luria would have to be better informed of Zeno's intentions than was Proclus, who never makes the least suggestion that mathematical atomism entered Zeno's head, and documents Zeno's critique of geometry by purely methodological objections.

[64] I shall have more to say on Zeno of Sidon as a critic of Euclid in a forthcoming paper. There I shall criticize in detail the influential view of W. Crönert ⟨above, n. 36⟩, pp. 109ff., that Zeno of Sidon rejected Euclid's principles ⟨See below, ch. 19 of this volume.⟩

[65] Proclus, 322, 4ff.

[66] Cf. *Scholia in Aristotelem,* ed. C. A. Brandis (Berlin, 1836), 476b34–36, ". . . for it [the straight line] is the shortest; for asses too, say Diogenes [the Cynic], go to their food and drink in straight lines."

[67] Which Proclus (110, 10–12) takes to have been Archimedes' *definition* of "straight line."

[68] Intuitive self-evidence (*enargeia, enargēma*) plays a large role in Epicurean epistemology. It could account for any number of Epicurean criticisms of geometry that would not be grounded in their atomistic preconceptions, as should be obvious in the case of the present criticism.

[69] *Adv. math.,* 3, 98.

[70] This is misunderstood by Otto Apelt in *Beiträge zur Geschichte der griechischen Philosophie* (Leipzig: Teubner, 1891), p. 256: "Die Linie, etwas Leeres, könne, so meinten die Epikureer, überhaupt nicht gedreht werden." He took *hē tou kenou eutheia* [= the straight line of (i.e., in) a void] to mean "the void straight line"!

course of refuting two variants of one of the well-known definitions as "that which revolves evenly within its limits" and "that which, revolving about its limits, touches [its] plane with all of its parts."[71] We can be practically certain that he borrowed the Epicurean remark from a similar context: for the idea of a *line* "revolving" all by itself (i.e., not as the axis of a plane segment, or solid, in revolution) never occurs in Greek geometry except in connection with this particular definition of a straight line. Ignoring this possibility, Luria puts a peculiar twist on the Epicurean remark. He takes it to mean that a line through the void "does not exist for geometry" because, since it cannot move, "one cannot perceive any geometrical manipulations by means of it."[72] But nothing is said in our text about the "non-existence" of such a line for geometry, and quite the contrary is implied if we take account of the suggested context: the "existence" of such a line would have to be the premise of the Epicurean objection to the proposed definition of "straight line"; unless the Epicureans assumed that "straight line" is genuinely instantiable under conditions in which "revolving straight line is not, their objection to the definition would have no force. In any case, it is plain that in this, as in the preceding and in all of Zeno's objections to the received geometry—exhausting between them the criticisms of geometry, identified as Epicurean in our sources, which may be held with any plausibility to emanate from the mathematicians of the school—there is not the slightest implication that they are made by men who were themselves adherents of mathematical atomism.

What then of those other Epicureans in Proclus' group (1) above, who did doubt the principles of geometry? Proclus does not say that their doubts were prompted by addiction to mathematical atomism, and does not connect them with this point of view in any way either here or anywhere else in his writings; nor conversely, does he allude to Epicureans in those passages in which he does discuss infinite divisibility.[73] Is not this remarkable in this most erudite of our ancient historians of mathematics, who had read many earlier histories of mathematics, and in particular, as we have already seen, [134] had read one treatise by Posidonius entirely devoted to the refutation of the mathematical views of a prominent Epicurean?[74] From all this I would not infer that there

[71] A very similar definition was given by Hero of Alexandria (Heath, *Euclid*, I², 168).

[72] Luria, p. 156n.133.

[73] In the discussion of 1, 10 there is no allusion to them but only (279, 4–6) to Xenocrates: "And the Xenocratean argument which introduces indivisible lines would be refuted through this problem." Nor does Proclus refer to them in his *Commentary on the Republic,* where he says (2, 27, ed. Wilhelm Kroll, Leipzig, 1899–1901) that Epicurus "made the atom the measure of all bodies" [Proclus is obviously confusing the atom with the minimum part] and Xenocrates made "the indivisible lines [the measure] of all lines." Note that Epicurus is cited only for physical atomism. For mathematical atomism Proclus turns, as before, to Xenocrates.

[74] If Zeno had propounded geometrical atomism, this would have vexed Posidonius far more than Zeno's methodological cavils against the Euclidean system and would have drawn a major part of Posidonius' polemical fire, thereby providing Proclus with information on the details of

were no mathematical atomists among Epicurean contemners of the received geometry. From the fact that none is named it does not follow that none existed. What I think does follow with a high degree of probability—and this is all I have been contending for in the foregoing—is that such Epicureans as may have taken this line did not succeed in working out anything that could be called an alternative *geometry,* or even fragmentary sketches of it, unless their efforts were crackpot schemes unworthy of serious notice. For whenever Proclus speaks of critics of Euclidean geometry he always represents them as criticizing "geometry"; he never feels like adding (as I have been doing in the foregoing) the "received geometry," or some variant of this expression which would acknowledge the existence of some alternative system, however abhorrent to him. For Proclus there is only *one* geometry. And since we are fortunate enough to have a full-size essay by one of its critics—Sextus, *Adversus geometras* (= *Adv. math.* 3)—we can see from the very title (and everything in the essay tells the same tale) that he too shares completely Proclus' unawareness of the existence of any alternative to the Euclidean system.

This being the case, I fail to see how any interpretation of Epicurus' minima as mathematical indivisibles will square with the historical data, unless there is some alternative to the three possibilities—(a), (b), and (c) on page 291 above—I have examined here. If so, I can only hope it will be duly explained and defended. Fortunately there is no need to wait for this in order to consider on its merits the proposal I shall now go on to make in Section II. I shall contend that a correct elucidation of the text of the *Epistle to Herodotus* at 58–59—the only surviving passage in which Epicurus expounds directly his own view of the physical minima in his own words—makes no commitment, explicit or implied, to mathematical atomism. If this contention can be made good, the effect will be to cut off mathematical atomist interpretation of the minima from any support in Epicurus' own text.

II

As is well known, the word *part* is used in Euclid in two quite different senses.[75] The first, its common Greek sense, is the only one we meet in the [135] first four books. We hear of it in the opening sentence, the definition of a point as "that which has no part," and shortly after in Common Notion 5, "The whole is greater than the part." Here from "$X + Y = Z$" we can always

---

this position and with a star example of it in the person of the illustrious Epicurean, to which he could scarcely have failed to allude when he needed to document this position.

[75] See, e.g., Heath, Euclid, 2^2, 115 (on 5, Df. 1). Heath refers to Aristotle, *Met.*, 1023b12, a very clear juxtaposition of the two senses, which shows, among other things, that fourth-century philosophy was taking full cognizance of the distinction.

infer that X is a part of Z, and that so is Y. In the opening definition of Book 5, we come across something new: "A magnitude is *a part* of a magnitude, the less of the greater, when it measures (*katametrei*) the greater." On *this* sense of "a part of $X + Y = Z$" does not entail that either X or Y be a part of Z: obviously not if either is incommensurable with Z; and even if commensurable with Z, X or Y might still not qualify as *a part of Z* in this special sense: thus in Euclid's number theory, 4 would not be *a part of* 6, but only *parts of it.*[76] Nothing will count as "a part of" Z, unless Z is an integral multiple of it. To mark out this specialized sense of "part" from the more general one, let us call them part$_s$ and part$_g$ respectively.

With this in mind, let us turn to Epicurus' text. I cite the lines that are the crucial ones for our purpose, translating with brutal literalism; elegance is expendable when we are after the exact sense.[77]

> Further we must regard these partless minima[78] as limits of lengths,[79] providing from out of themselves as primary units, the measure (*katametrēma*) of the greater and the lesser for the rational apprehension of the invisibles.[80]

Ignoring for the present the rest of the sentence, let us fasten at once on "providing the measure," a periphrastic variant of "measuring" (*katametrounta*), used in an analogous manner a few lines earlier. This is the very term that occurs in Euclid's definiens of part$_s$ above. To see this is to get new light on our text. Were it not for this, we would most likely understand it to be telling

---

[76] Euclid, 7, Df. 4.

[77] Though this, and subsequent, translations from Epicurus are my own, they have been made with the help of an unpublished MS by D. J. Furley, which includes a new text, translation, and commentary on this and other Epicurean and Lucretian passages. I have also derived great help from extensive discussions I had with him shortly before I wrote this paper. In spite of serious unresolved disagreements, I feel that I have learned more from him than from any of the commentators on the ancient atomists and regret that I cannot acknowledge and discuss his views, since they are not yet in the public domain.

[78] τὰ ἐλάχιστα καὶ [ἀμερῆ] (for the latter see n. 3 above) are adjectives with the article in the neuter functioning as nouns, as is common in Epicurus; cf. W. Widmann, *Beiträge zur Syntax Epikurs* (Tübingen, 1935), pp. 24–30.

[79] I take *perata* with *nomizein* as a predicate accusative modifying τὰ ἐλάχιστα καὶ ⟨ἀμερῆ⟩: this construction in Bailey (following Giussani ⟨*Studi Lucreziani*, Turin, 1896⟩ and Bignone ⟨above, n. 3⟩); R. D. Hicks, translation of Diogenes Laertius in Loeb Classical Library (London, 1927); Gigon; and Strodach (for the references to the translations, see nn. 2 and 3 above). The alternative would be to take *paraskeuazonta* with *nomizein* ("regard . . . as providing"), as is done, e.g., by Ernout-Robin (see n. 81). This would also make good sense and would not disturb my argument. But if this were the intended construction, one would expect the infinitive, *paraskeuazein*, instead. There are many examples of *nomizein* governing an infinitive (Widmann ⟨above, n. 78⟩, p. 108), and no certain ones with a participial construction (of the two examples of the latter listed in Widmann, p. 182, one is *paraskeuazonta* here, while the other on p. 74 is not free from doubt because of the corruption of the text).

[80] Epicurus, *Ep.*, 1, 59; DL (Long), 2, p. 522, 9–12.

us that the length of the minimum is the proper [136] *unit of measurement* for atomic lengths.[81] Applying the sense of *katametrein* in Euclid, we learn instead that the length of the minimum is the submultiple of all atomic lengths. That this is the right sense is probable, quite apart from anything else, on purely linguistic grounds. The words which Epicurus uses here are not the common terms for mensuration. If this were the notion he wanted to express, he would have been likely to say simply *metrein, metron*. We can infer this from the extensive sample of relevant usage provided us in the Aristotelian corpus.[82] There *metron, metrein,* are the usual words for "unit (or, standard) of measurement" and "taking measurements." While they may also be used to express the mathematical notion of the submultiple, the converse never happens with *katametrein:* this is never used for measuring (as is sometimes done in the general literature),[83] but only with the technical sense it has in Euclid.[84] There is no reason to think Epicurus' practice would have been different.

But why make so much of this point? Would not the two senses come to much the same thing after all in this context? They would not. For while a submultiple of certain quantities *could* be used as their unit of measurement (and with one obvious advantage: this would simplify the arithmetic), the fact remains that our regular units of measurement (miles, yards, millimeters) are not submultiples of the things we measure. And there is a good reason for this: we do not expect nature to turn out all its products, like a shoe factory, in fixed sets of sizes. If we did, we would naturally have much to gain and nothing to lose by choosing submultiples of nature's handiwork for our units of measurement. I say "choosing," for even so the decision would rest with us. If we were hidebound traditionalists or arithmetical masochists, we could still keep a different system and make a go of it. Our standard of measurement is in the last analysis a matter of "convention," not of "nature," as Epicurus would say.[85] But the question of whether or not a given quantity is or is not a sub-

---

[81] As is generally assumed by the editors, some of whom even import this notion into their translations: e.g., Ernout-Robin, ". . . comme fournissant la mesure originaire dont nous partons pour déterminer les grandeurs ou les petitesses . . . ," ⟨above n. 3⟩, 1, 73.

[82] See *katametrein, metrein, metron* in Hermann Bonitz ed., *Index Aristotelicus* (Berlin: Reimer, 1870), *s.v.*

[83] Examples in LSJ, *s.v.*

[84] Euclid's usage is significant: he uses *katametrein* when introducing the notion of the submultiple in Bk. 7, in Df. 3, keeps it for two more definitions, then reverts to the shorter *metrein* in Dfs. 8 to 14. In Prop. I he uses only *katametrein,* and this again in the first sentence of his proof, thereafter dropping it for *metrein* in propositions and proofs throughout the rest of this book, and also in the next two books (which complete the number theory begun in Bk. 7). The next use of *katametrein* is in Prop. 2 of Bk. 10, where unending *anthuphairesis* is made the test of incommensurability (n. 33 above). It looks as though Euclid reserves *katametrein* for specially emphatic references to the idea of the submultiple, otherwise dropping the prefix.

[85] For the *phusis-nomos* contrast (in a legal context), see *Principal Doctrines,* 38; for the same contrast in an epistemological context, Democritus, frs. 9 and 125.

multiple of given quantities is no matter of "convention." It is something to be discovered, not decided. And where the given quantities are physical ones, fixed by nature, the discovery would be that of *a physical truth:* suppose that pebbles on the beach of a newly discovered island were measured (say, at their [137] longest and shortest diameters) and found to be invariably an integral number of inches. This would be a startling matter of fact—a fact about the pebbles on that island, not about the explorer's inch tape. If his tape had been marked off in centimeters instead, the same fact would have registered as truly, if somewhat less perspicuously: all his figures would still have been integral multiples of a fractional multiple of a centimeter.

This example is offered to illustrate one, and only one, thing in the Epicurean doctrine of the minima: that the intent of this doctrine is not to recommend a convenient mini-yardstick to hypothetical atomometrists, but to propound a truth about atoms, a law of nature. Epicurus would have spared his disciples and commentators no little confusion if he had said this in so many words, or at least had so expressed his law about the minima that it could only be read as a physical statement about the atoms. For example:

> Atoms are so constituted that variations in atomic lengths[86] occur only in integral multiples of the smallest atomic length.

---

[86] As to the interpretation of "atomic length": a parallelepipedal solid with edges of *m, n, o* minimal lengths would have just three atomic lengths, *mq, nq, oq*. Assuming (see next note) that all minima had the same shape, probably cubical, all atoms, no matter how irregular might be their contours, could be (theoretically) broken down in the last analysis into parts of parallelepipedal shape, and the atomic lengths of the whole atom would be the set composed of all the atomic lengths of these component parts. Parts having the minimal atomic length in all three dimensions would materialize in comparatively rare, but conspicuous, locations: e.g., at the vertices of a tetrahedron, each of whose peak points would be a minimal part (a cube whose upper surface is q^2 would still be needle sharp and piercing, since its dimensions would be so much smaller than those of macroscopic bodies). There could be no *atom* with atomic length q in all three dimensions, since that would mean a minimum "existing apart," which is expressly denied in Lucretius (I, 602–4) and implicitly in Epicurus, who speaks only of τὸ ἐν τῇ ἀτόμῳ ἐλάχιστον, never of ἡ ἐλαχίστη ἄτομος. On this ground I must object to Charles Mugler's statement ("Sur quelques particularités de l'atomisme ancien," *RP* 79, 1953:141–74, at 152) that the atoms are "multiples, au point de vue mathématique, d'une partie aliquote commune *qui est précisément la grandeur de l'atome minimum* distingué par Epicure" (I have italicized the objectionable clause). In other respects Mugler's statement is impeccable, and the following (p. 154) truly admirable:

> Il avait parfaitement le droit, en tant que physicien, de renchérir sur l'atomisme ancien [of Democritus] et d'introduire dans la décomposition théorique de la matière la notion de "quantum," en rendant la structure de la matière granulaire non seulement au point de vue de la séparation physique mais aussi au point de vue de quantité, en établissant une échelle discontinue des grandeurs possibles des atomes.

Here Mugler seems to realize perfectly that the minima to which Epicurus refers at 59 are not intended to function as mathematical indivisibles but simply as physical quanta. But see n. 114 below.

Let us call this "L(I)" ("L" for "law of nature").[87] The analogy with the pebbles on that beach is so far perfect: the same statement would hold [138] true, *mutatis mutandis,* in the preceding example—those unusual pebbles are so constituted that variations in their dimensions occur only in integral multiples of one inch, never in fractions or unending decimals of an inch. But in another respect there is no analogy. The way that remarkable property of the pebbles was discovered was by measuring. The record of those measurements would be the evidence the explorer would offer in support of his discovery. But Epicurus made no measurements of atomic lengths and is not making believe that he did nor requiring us to connive in such a pretense in order to concede his claim that L(I) is the truth about the atoms. We must give him credit for writing, not science fiction, but something which, if not science, is at least protoscience. Let us then see what is the process of discovery and proof that leads him to L(1):

The system he inherits—the "classical" version of the atomic theory, I shall be calling it—had maintained that (I) every kind of atomic size and (II) every kind of atomic shape exists in nature.[88] These two assertions—C(I) and C(II), let us call them, with C for the "classical" atomistic theory—had not been thoughtless guesses, but applications of one of the fundamental principles of Leucippus and Democritus: that every possibility is realized in nature unless there is a definite reason to the contrary.[89] To this principle Epicurus, a much more self-conscious empiricist, would attach an emphatic rider: 'but only if its occurrence agrees with the phenomena better than would its nonoccur-

---

[87] A second law of nature, L(II), may be derived from Lucr. 2, 478ff.; it complements L(I), stating the limits of variations for atomic shapes: *Atoms are so constituted that variations in their shapes occur only in permutations of a modular unit of invariant size and shape.* This shape is not specified. But I know of no good reason for questioning the usual assumption (e.g. Bailey, GAE, pp. 287–88, following Brieger ⟨*Jahrbuch Fleck,* 1875, 630⟩ and others) that it would be the simplest of all modular units for three-dimensional magnitude, a cube. And see n. 114 below.

[88] Simplicius, *De caelo,* 295, 7–8, "and there exist (according to Democritus) all kinds of forms (of atoms) and all kinds of shapes and differences of size." Simplicius' source here is Aristotle's treatise, *About Democritus.* In extant treatises Aristotle repeatedly ascribes infinite diversity of atomic shapes to Leucippus and Democritus, e.g., *De caelo* 303a11, *De gen. et cor.* 314a22 and 325b27. In the latter passage he contrasts Leucippus with Plato on this point, as committed to "indivisibles" of infinitely many shapes.

[89] As is noted by Theophrastus, *Phys. op.,* fr. 8, *apud* Simplicius, *Phys.,* 28, 10, in the case of C(II): Leucippus holds that "the multitude of atomic shapes is infinite, for why should an atom be of this rather than of that (shape)?" (διὰ τὸ μηδὲν μᾶλλον τοιοῦτον ἢ τοιοῦτον εἶναι). Bailey (GAE, p. 127 and n. 3) reassigns, for no good reason, the origination of this principle to Democritus, who no doubt shared it. Theophrastus also assigns to Leucippus the invocation of this principle in arguing for the existence of the void: "and further why should being exist and not not-being?" (*loc. cit.;* the same thing ascribed to Democritus by Plutarch, *Adv. Colotem,* 1109a). The argument for the infinity of matter and of worlds in Aristotle, *Phys.* 203b24, "for why should (matter and worlds) exist in this (part) of the void rather than in that? So if solids exist anywhere, they should exist everywhere," must also come from the atomists, though it is not specifically referred to them by Aristotle.

rence.'⁹⁰ He rejects both C(I) and C(II) on just this ground. Let us look at his own statement of the reasons for the rejection of C(I):⁹¹ [139]

> Moreover we must not believe that *every* size exists among the atoms, so that the phenomena may not contradict us. We must believe that there are *some* variations of size:

> [A] For if this is the case we can give a better account of what we experience and observe by the senses. But the existence of every size is of no use [for accounting] for the differences of the qualities.

> [B] At the same time [i.e., on the same hypothesis] atoms which are [large enough to be] visible should have reached us; and this is not observed to happen nor is it possible to conceive how an atom could become visible.

Of the two reasons Epicurus offers us for rejecting (C(I), the first, [A], is clear and easy to follow: since the perceived qualities of sensible things are completely determined by the unperceived properties of their constituent atoms, of which atomic size is one of the most important, our hypothesis should provide for no more atomic sizes than would be needed to account for the range of differences in perceived qualities. But the latter is strictly limited. There are not infinitely many colors, smells, etc. Why then assume the existence of every variety of atomic size? Such a supposition would be useless; it would have no explanatory value.

The second, [B], is a more complicated business. The claim made here is simple enough: that if there were infinitely many sizes, some of these would have to be large enough to exceed the threshold of visibility below which all atoms in this system are supposed to remain. But why so? Why could there not be an infinite number of atomic sizes below this threshold? There certainly could be, on either of two possibilities, neither of which has been excluded by anything Epicurus has proved up to this point, so that he would now have to eliminate both of them by fresh arguments if his present claim is to stand:

> [1] *There might be infinitely many atomic sizes between any given size, X, and zero,* as for example, if the following sequence of atomic sizes, S1, happened to be instantiated in nature:

---

⁹⁰ Contrast, for example, Leucippus' argument for the void in the preceding note with that of Epicurus at 39–40: it must exist, for if it did not, bodies would not be able to move, and they are *seen* to move (*kathaper phainetai kinoumena*). Cf. his well-known principle that where more than one hypothesis accords with the phenomena, to prefer one hypothesis to the rest is "to stop doing natural science and slip into mythology" (87). And cf. Phillip De Lacy, "Colotes' First Criticism of Democritus," in *Isonomia,* J. Mau and E. G. Schmidt, eds. (Berlin: Akademie Verlag, 1964), pp. 67–77 at 68–69 and 74ff.

⁹¹ 55; DL (Long), 2, pp. 520, 20–521, 2. C(II) he had rejected earlier at 42: the number of varieties of atomic shape are not "infinite simpliciter," though "inconceivably large." For the argument for this proposition, see n. 114 below.

$$S1: \frac{X}{2}, \frac{X}{2^2}, \ldots, \frac{X}{2^n}, \frac{X}{2^{n+1}}, \ldots .^{92}$$

Would the atomic hypothesis all by itself preclude this possibility?[93] Certainly not. Given an atom of size X, the atomic hypothesis permits us to infer only that it could not be subdivided *to generate* other atoms having the sizes defined by S1—but not that such atoms *do not already exist*. How could we possibly infer from the fact that an atom of size X is indivisible (as are all atoms, regardless of size) that there cannot exist one, or two, or a million, or infinitely many atomic sizes smaller than its own? This [140] would be a gross *non sequitur*. Hence there is nothing in the atomic hypothesis to block the possibility that infinitely many sizes intermediate between our X and zero might exist in nature.[94] To do this—as he must, else the claim he has made at [B] would be defeated—Epicurus will have to bring in some new argument. Is there any sign of that in his text? Let us read on in the *Epistle to Herodotus:*

> For, besides, neither may we suppose that, [P], a finite body could contain infinitely many masses,[95] no matter what might be their size. . . . For it is clear that [each of] these infinitely many masses has some size; no matter what may be that size, [the aggregate size would be infinitely large, and so] [Q], the magnitude [of the containing body] would have to be infinite.[96]

Epicurus here has pressed into service an old Zenonian argument against plurality,[97] endorsing in all innocence its erroneous assumption that the sum of

[92] Obviously there could be infinitely many other sequences exemplifying [1]. I choose S1 because this is the famous "dichotomy," the one most frequently used by philosophers in the fifth and fourth centuries B.C. in discussing the supposed paradoxes generated by infinite sequences converging on zero: cf. Zeno, fr. 1; Aristotle, *Phys.* 187a2–3, 233a13–23, 239b11–14, 263a4–b9; *De gen. et cor.* 316a15–317a17; Simplicius, *Phys.*, 138, 3–141, 16.

[93] As some of the commentators appear to think: cf. Bailey, GAE, p. 285.

[94] Nor could this be ruled out by objections to the "actual infinite," a concept with which Epicurus should be the last to quarrel, since the totality of atoms and worlds in his theory already instantiates the "actual infinite."

[95] The nearest I can get to *onkous* here, for whose meaning see n. 13 above.

[96] 56–57; DL (Long), 2, p. 521, 3–4 and 12–14. Epicurus fills out the paragraph with a second argument against [P] (lines 14–18): Since every finite body has an extremity we can think of [which Epicurus assumes to be itself a finite body], then, if [P], the extremity would itself have an extremity we can think of, and so on without end; whence it would follow that we could think of the whole of the infinite sequence consisting of a body, its extremity, the extremity of the extremity, etc. and thus "arrive at infinity in thought"—i.e., traverse in our thoughts an infinite series, which Epicurus takes to be a patent absurdity, whose entailment by [P] refutes [P] twice over. Cf. Plutarch, *De commun. notit.* 1078e, in *Mor.* 6.2, ed. Max Pohlenz (Leipzig, 1952), 106, 1–5; Sextus, *Adv. math.* 3, 81 (for the latter reference and for a translation and explanation of the argument in Plutarch, I am indebted to Professor H. Cherniss). I regret that pressure of space makes it impossible for me to defend my interpretation controversially against other scholars who have read this argument very differently.

[97] Zeno, fr. 1. For my analysis of it, see my review of Fränkel, *Wege und Formen*

the sequence $1/2$, $1/2^2$, . . . , $1/2^n$, $1/2^{(n+1)}$, . . . is infinite. Note that Epicurus does not get this sequence by subdividing the body with which he starts: in [P] the bodies ("masses") instantiating each member of this sequence are already present in the given "finite body."[98] If his argument were valid, it would prove that [P] entails a contradiction: that the size of the containing body is both finite, by hypothesis, and infinite, as the container of a set of bodies whose volumes sum to infinity. And if the argument did prove this, it would have demolished possibility [1]; for if that possibility were logically innocuous, no contradiction should result from the hypothesis that some body contained a set of atoms instantiating the whole of S1.[99] [141] If Epicurus' present argument were sound, it would have proved that this hypothesis leads to absurdity. It would have therefore given us the assurance that there cannot exist in nature a set of atomic sizes descending endlessly in the direction of zero[100]—an assurance without which Epicurus' claim at [B] would collapse.[101]

But there would still remain a second possibility which, if allowed to pass unrefuted, would suffice, all by itself, to falsify that claim:

---

frühgriechischen Denken, Gnomon 31, 1959: 195–99 ⟨** 1.167–73⟩ and Walter Kaufmann, ed., *Philosophic Classics* (New York: Prentice-Hall, 1962), pp. 31–34.

[98] This argument should, therefore, not be confused with the other Eleatic argument (cf. n. 5 above)—that if

[R]   a body were infinitely divisible, then

[S]   being would be reducible to not-being—

which is also brought up here (56) but is kept entirely distinct from this one, both as to premise and conclusion.

[99] For otherwise there would be no reason in the world why such a set (of appropriately selected shapes) could not be contained by any finite (composite) body. Thus suppose we had a cube of size X; a set of atomic parallelepipeds, of the same altitude and depth, but decreasing laterally to the specifications of S1, should fit quite comfortably inside the cube (provided, of course, the packing were absolutely tight). Or if the reader's imagination would feel better in a less crowded space, let him pick a much bigger container, say, an Epicurean world (huge, though finite): It should be obvious that no contradiction would result from supposing that this contained at least one of each of the sizes specified in S1, if the conception of such a set were logically innocuous.

[100] I say "would have," because the point I am making is not made in the text. All we get there is [B] *followed by* the argument that [P] entails an absurdity (in fact, two of them: n. 96 above). That Epicurus does this to show the reader that his claim at [B] has nothing to fear from possibility [1] (which he does not even mention) is no more than a reasonable hypothesis. To prove it, I would have to refute alternative ways of plotting Epicurus' line of thought in this extremely compressed and elliptical passage. I regret that pressure of space forbids this (the length of this paper has already strained editorial tolerance to its limits). All I can say here is that I cannot account for the fact that Epicurus should want to refute [P] *in this context* except on the assumption that he wants to assure the reader that an infinite sequence of atomic sizes converging on zero is out of the question, and thus to anticipate and meet a perfectly valid (and fairly obvious) objection to the claim he has made at [B].

[101] It might be thought that the other Eleatic argument (n. 98 above) would also do the same job. If it had proved the impossibility of an infinite division, would it not have shown that the

[2] *There might be infinitely many atomic sizes intermediate between any two unequal sizes, X and Y,* as, for example, if $Y = 2X$, and the sequence S2 of atomic sizes were in existence:

$$S2: X + \frac{X}{2}, X + \frac{X}{2^2}, \ldots, X + \frac{X}{2^n}, X + \frac{X}{2^{n+1}}, \ldots$$

Could Epicurus have overlooked this possibility? He goes on to give us an argument which, were it valid, would dispose of it perfectly.[102] This is [142] his famous argument by analogy from the "minimum in sensation" to "the minimum in the atom": Assuming that

(i) things must have a minimum size, if they are to be sensed at all, he infers that

(ii) sensibilia of larger size must be integral multiples of it.[103]

He then argues that

(iii) if (ii) is true of the perceived, a similar truth must hold of the unperceived: if all sensibilia are "measured" by a minimum sensible quantity, then all atoms must be "measured" by a minimal physical quantity.[104]

---

complete instantiation of S1 is impossible? It would not. All it would have shown is that if X were a divisible body its subdivision would have to stop at *some* stage. But this would do nothing to prove that there are no smaller atomic sizes than the one reached at that stage in the subdivision of X; there might be infinitely many smaller ones. This is a subtle point, and Epicurus could have missed it and therefore adduced this other argument under the misapprehension that it would lend further support to his claim that the set of atomic sizes has a smallest member. But the fact that he distinguishes the two arguments so carefully, and that he makes [P], not [R], the great contention in this section of his argument, restating it with slight modifications no less than three times—at the beginning and end of the second paragraph in 56, and then again at the start of 57—in this extremely crowded passage is a reason for exonerating him from this particular confusion and for supposing that his motive for bringing in the [R-S] argument here is more for the purpose of contrast, i.e., to get us to see that what he is offering now (in his double-barreled refutation of [P]) is something new in the *Epistle* ([S] had been asserted as far back as 41) and, therefore, uniquely relevant to his immediate concern: the proof that some smallest atomic size exists.

[102] If Epicurus had been more mathematically minded, he might have made his arguments against [1] do double duty here, since these, if sound, would have proved that an infinite sequence converging on zero entails a contradiction: the increments in S2 form just such a sequence. Conversely, a more economical argument could have been built by merging [1] and [2] through the fiction that zero is an atomic size (though this would have probably struck Epicurus as a sophistic trick). However, he is now after bigger game than the mere refutation of C(I), and the fact that the argument he is to give us now will do this other job as well would be a decisive reason for employing it.

[103] This is abundantly clear in the closing part of 58, regardless of what we make of the rest of this obscure sentence: ". . . but in their own particularity (ἐν τῇ ἰδιότητι τῇ ἑαυτῶν) [the minima sensibilia] measuring the magnitudes [of sensibilia larger than the minima], the greater more, the lesser less." "Measuring" here = "being submultiples of," as explained above. What Epicurus is telling us is that, e.g., any visible area, if examined with sufficient care with sufficiently accurate vision, would turn out to be an integral multiple of the dimensions of the minimum visible area.

[104] Note how defective is Lucretius' version of this argument by analogy (I, 749–53); all he

If this were a sound argument, it would clearly take in its stride the refutation of possibility [2]. If all sizes intermediate between X and Y are to be integral multiples of the same minimal quantity, there could not be infinitely many of them, since there cannot be infinitely many integers between any two integers. Thus this argument would round out the proof of [B]: for if we knew that neither [1] nor [2] were true, we would be assured that an infinity of sizes could only be secured by reaching into ever-higher registers of atomic size and thus exceeding the limits of visibility. Thus the refutation of C(I)—of the classical assumption that "every size exists among the atoms"—by means of arguments [A] and [B] in the above citation from 55 would have been carried out to triumphant completion.

But more ground than this would have been gained. For if the present argument by analogy in 58–59 were sound, it would have proved not only the falsehood of C(I) but also the truth of L(I), which is a far stronger proposition. Is it clear that L(I) is so much stronger than the denial of C(I)? The latter simply tells us that there is a limited number of variations in atomic size. And this leaves open a great range of possible ways in which these limited variations might be distributed. L(I) is just one of these. Were it true, no atomic length would occur which does not fit into the following sequence (where mq would be the largest atomic length in existence):[105] [143]

L(I): $q, 2q, 3q, \ldots, (m-1)q, mq$.

But why should not the true sequence be rather,

$$M(I): q, \frac{3}{2}q, 2q, \frac{5}{2}q, \ldots, \left(m - \frac{1}{2}\right)q, mq?$$

Or perhaps

$$N(I): q, \frac{5}{3}q, \frac{7}{3}q, 3q, \ldots, \left(m - \frac{2}{3}\right)q, mq?$$

---

gets out of it is that because perceptible magnitudes have an *extremum cacumen*, so must imperceptible (atomic) ones. One would have never guessed from his version that the Epicurean original included (ii) and (iii) above.

[105] I would endorse Drabkin's reasons (⟨above, n. 2,⟩ p. 261) for surmising that m would run into very large numbers: the total number of shapes is "inconceivably large" (n. 91 above), while when it comes to differences of size Epicurus does not use anything like the same expression but speaks only of "some differences" (*parallagas de tinas*, DL [Long], 2, p. 520, 21); the contrasting expressions suggest that a smaller number is meant in the latter case. To get an enormous number of shapes by rearranging the minima of a small to middling number of sizes, a huge number of minima would be needed in the larger atoms. A further, and more conclusive, reason may be drawn from the fact that round atoms can be "exceedingly minute" (Lucr., 3, 179, 187) since a sphere could only be approximated by a rather large number of cubical minima. Though differing with Drabkin on other points, I agree with him, *loc. cit.*, that it is unsafe to infer from Lucr. 2, 485ff. that atoms of "three or a few more" minima may exist: this figure is given only "by

Any number of other possibilities easily come to mind. So we must choose between L(I), M(I), N(I), O(I), . . . All of these satisfy the requirement that there should be a smallest atomic length and a limited number of variations of size; but only L(I) satisfies the requirement that all variations should be integral multiples of q. Why then should we settle on the latter, declaring that this is the general law, with never an exception to it throughout the length and breadth of this infinite universe? This question is not raised in our text. Reading it, one might form the impression that it never even occurred to Epicurus that there might be *some* alternatives to L(I) which would be also compatible with the rejection of C(I). But this would be unfair to him. It would ignore the fact that he offers us in his own text an argument which not only completes the refutation of C(I) but proves (or would, if it were sound) so very much more: nothing less than L(I).

Is then this argument sound? Alas, no. The first premise, (i), is impeccable. No one, I trust, would quarrel with Epicurus' claim that sensibilia, when ordered by decreasing size, have a determinate lower limit. But how is (ii) supposed to *follow?* Does the fact that V is the smallest visible dot imply that I cannot see another dot, U, as larger than V, unless I can see U as $2V$, or $3V$, etc.? Obviously not. It might be the case, for example, that I see U as *somewhat* larger than V without seeing it as exactly $2V$ and being, in fact, quite uncertain whether I should reckon it twice as large or only half again as large or perhaps two-thirds again as large as V. Has Epicurus conducted some research in psychometrics, presenting subjects with dots of varying sizes and asking them to report which ones they see as larger than others and by how much? It goes without saying that the very idea of such experiments never even entered his head. His bland assertion of (ii) then is just a facile extrapolation from the empirical data at his disposal[106] [144] unsupported by the *additional* empirical data that would be needed to prove it true, if true it is.

Much the same criticism could be made of the final step in the reasoning which moves (or, rather, jumps) from the supposed fact that all sensibles are integral multiples of a minimal atomic length. Clearly the former in no way implies the latter. All sorts of things are true about sensibles which (on Epicurus' theory) would be false about the atoms. Why should it be the case that *this* proposition—quantitative variations restricted to exact multiples of a smallest quantity—be true of the atoms *because* this is (allegedly) true of sensibles? It is hard to see how Epicurus, with the technical means at his

---

way of illustration (*fac enim* . . .), and the reader will better grasp the finiteness of the number of permutations when small numbers are used."

[106] The assumption he is making has considerable plausibility: that if $A + d$, or $A - d$ is perceived as different from A, then d must be perceptible all by itself. Aristotle, a shrewder empiricist, rejected this assumption (*De sensu*, 446a10–15), but only by invoking his special concept of potentiality [d is not "actually" perceptible by itself, but "potentially" perceptible— i.e., would be perceptible if added to A], which would have repelled Epicurus.

disposal, could hope to show any such thing by an empirical procedure. What kind of data could he possibly think of finding to convince us that *this* is the truth of the matter as versus competing possibilities so minutely differentiated from it as are, say, M(I) or N(I)? Here again it is evident that Epicurus' empiricism is more of a matter of sentiment than of performance; and that the proposition he thinks is proved by an appeal to the senses has, in fact, nothing more to recommend it than theoretical simplicity and economy: L(I) is indeed an elegant limitation on the "unlimited polymorphism"[107] of the atoms in the classical version of the theory, a beautifully simple way of introducing numerical and geometrical periodicity into the atomic constitution of nature. Though the difference in this respect between it and M(I), N(I), etc. is not great, it could still be preferred to them on that ground.

But after taking full account of these criticisms, let us not forget that they are made from our own quite different, and theoretically more sophisticated, perspective. We would be lacking in historical imagination if we did not appreciate the value of Epicurus' intention, however abortive, to produce an empirical argument for L(I). In an age in which questions of matter of fact could be settled in such a lordly *a priori* way as, for example, the animation of the stars by Plato in the *Timaeus,* or the existence of that fantastic "fifth element" by Aristotle in the *De caelo,* Epicurus' eagerness to determine the structure of the "unseen" only by means of analogical inferences from the "seen" commands respect.[108]

We can now return to the citation from Epicurus in the second paragraph of this second section, having answered the question: How does he decide [145] that his great proposition, L(I), is true? All that has been offered on this score may be taken as a gloss on the last words of the citation, *"for the rational apprehension of the invisibles."* Such is the intended purpose of L(I), and such we have found it to be—apprehension of physical fact (distribution of atomic lengths)[109] established in accordance with Epicurus' own standards of rea-

---

[107] I borrow the phrase from a fine estimate of the achievement of the Platonic theory of matter by Cherniss (reporting, and in this respect agreeing, with Charles Mugler, *Platon et la recherche mathématique de son époque* [Strasbourg/Zurich: Heitz, 1948], p. 81): "Plato imposed geometrical discipline upon the unlimited polymorphism of the Atomists and introduced into the physical sciences the principle of economy," p. 404 in the paper cited in n. 29 above. At this point Epicurus has actually more in common with Plato than with Democritus, though he still differs profoundly from Plato in methodology. The latter feels no compunction in settling on the four regular polyhedra as the sole shapes of the four traditional elements simply because these figures are "the most beautiful" (*Tim.* 53e) and in preferring the half-equilateral to infinitely many other right-angled scalenes for the same reason (*Tim.* 54a). By no stretch of the imagination could one think of Epicurus deciding a question of physical fact in this way.

[108] Cf. S. Sambursky (work cited in n. 24 above), pp. 117–18.

[109] As Dr. Mau points out to me (by correspondence), on this interpretation of the minimum, Epicurus is recognizing in q "a new physical constant." He adds that this "is not the only new constant introduced by Epicurus," suggesting that the absolute velocity of light and of the atoms moving freely in empty space, as well as the angle of declination in the free fall of atoms, should also be regarded in the same way.

sonableness, hence by strenuous, if at times ill-advised, efforts to ground theoretical truth on sensory data. We may now proceed to gloss the rest of the citation, working our way backwards:

". . . *from out of themselves as first*": *Katametrein* is a transitive relation; if *X* measures *Y*, and *Y* measures *Z*, then *X* measures *Z*. In geometry its relata can form sequences open at both ends. There is no more reason why a sequence in which every term measures its successor should have a first term than why it should have a last. Not so in Greek arithmetic where integers are the only numbers. There the first integer is most emphatically a *first* measure:[110] it measures all numbers, including the primes, which are measured by no other number[111] but no other number[112] measures it. From L(I) it follows that atomic length *q* plays an analogous role in Epicurus' microphysics. It stands to all atomic lengths as the Unit stands to all numbers. This is the sense in which the minima measure lengths "from out of themselves as first." Each of them is an atomic length which is a submultiple of all other atomic lengths, but there is no other atomic length which is a submultiple of theirs. And in the very same sense they are

". . . *partless* . . . *limits of lengths*": "limits," because they are the lower limit of the sequence of atomic lengths; "partless," because there is no other atomic length which can be part$_s$ of theirs, while theirs can be part$_s$ of any other atomic length. Both of these propositions follow analytically from L(I). And on reaching the second of them, we reach a precise answer to the question raised at the very start of this paper: what are we to understand by the "smallest thing in the atom," its "partless" part? We are to understand whatever L(I) gives us to understand: that *this is the smallest atomic length in existence;* that *no other atomic length exists which is part$_s$ of this.*

Compare this answer with the two that were considered in Section I, and you will see what is wrong with them as statements of what *Epicurus* teaches about the minima in his own text:[113] The one understates, the other overstates [146], the information contained in L(I). To say, (a) that they are *physically indivisible* would be miserably uninformative by comparison. Given an atom

---

[110] Cf. Aristotle, *Phys.* 207b2: in the case of number, "One is a limit in [progressions toward] the smallest."

[111] Euclid 7, Df. 11.

[112] It might be objected that the Greeks do not regard One as a number. But this is only half true. The same author who roundly declares that "the Unit is not a number" (Aristotle, *Met.* 1088a6) will not hesitate to use the expression (so common in Aristotle), *hen arithmōi*, "numerically one." The paradox is easily resolved. When the Greeks think of number as a cardinal concept, they understand it to mean "multitude" (i.e., numerousness), and they take the Unit as the contrary of number. When they revert to the ordinal concept of number, they cannot help assimilating the Unit to number after all, as the first member of the number series.

[113] Lucretius unfortunately is not nearly so clear in his conception of the minima, and most of the misapprehensions on this subject in the modern literature can be traced back to him. I have pointed out above (n. 104) his defective version of the argument by analogy, which is symptomatic of his imperfect grasp of the minima as the physical invariants of atomic size. In the most definite and informative of his discussions of the minima (2, 485ff.), he depicts them faultlessly

which is, say, a cube with edge 100q, then, since the whole atom is physically indivisible, so will be any part of it, no matter how selected: whether it be, say, either of two prisms formed by an imaginary plane cutting our cube diagonally from the right-hand edge of the top to the left-hand edge of the base; or any one of, say, one trillion little cubes of which it might please our geometrical fancy to think it composed. Any of these parts of the cube would be physically indivisible; but neither they, nor infinitely many other parts of it which we might choose to designate, would be *those physically indivisible parts of the cube which happen to be minima*. To find *these*, we need only ask, How many parts of the cube are there of q^3 size? Answer: exactly one million. And as for saying, (b), that they are *mathematically indivisible*, that would outrun fantastically the information supplied in L(I). If this were the law of nature it is meant to be, it should be compatible with *any* (self-consistent) mathematical system. If there were such a system whose elements were discrete magnitudes, all of them multiples of q, then L(I) would be compatible with it. But would L(I) *entail* that system? Obviously not. What is there about L(I) to entail that q is the smallest possible linear magnitude in geometry? Nothing.[114]

---

as the moduli of atomic shape (n. 87 above). But in two other passages (1, 615–26 and 746–53), he makes them the physical indivisibles of the theory after all, blandly ignoring his previous proof that this function is that of the atoms: see his argument (I, 499–598) that the atoms are absolutely unalterable and *a fortiori* indivisible (note especially 561, *nunc nimirum frangendi reddita finis*), and this without indebtedness to the minima, which are not introduced into his poem until after this argument has been finished.

[114] Mugler (cf. n. 86 above) recognizes (pp. 154, 156) that L(I) carries no commitment to mathematical atomism but thinks that Epicurus' belief in "the interdependence . . . between the size and the shape of the corpuscles" proves that he ascribed a "granular structure" not only to matter, but to space itself (p. 154; cf. p. 156). If Epicurus had really entertained the latter notion (a "mathematical monstrosity" Mugler calls it, p. 154), it would be most surprising that he should have kept clear of it in arguing for the discontinuity of atomic sizes and brought it in only when he came to argue for the discontinuity of atomic shapes. On what evidence are we supposed to believe that he did the latter? There is none in 42 (DL [Long], 2, p. 514, 18–23), Epicurus' only reference to the limits of variations in atomic shapes, where the argument appears to be a purely physical one. (I would reconstruct it as follows: differences of atomic shapes must be as numerous as will be necessary to account for the differences of macroscopic bodies; the former must be "not infinite simpliciter, but inconceivably numerous," because there are "that many [*tosautas:* i.e., inconceivably many]" of the latter.) Mugler's only reference (p. 156n. 2) is to Lucretius "II, 489" (by which he presumably means 485–94), where he finds the assumption that "cette juxtaposition [i.e., of minima in an atomic figure] n'est possible que d'un nombre fini de manières" (p. 156). It is certainly assumed in Lucretius' reasoning that the shape of the minima remains invariant (cf. n. 87 above) and that their geometrical conjunctions are restricted (e.g., contiguous edges and surfaces must be congruent). But where is the evidence that these assumptions are made because of a belief in "the granular structure" of space? Why should they not be made simply to keep the physical theory neat and economical? Besides, to derive this belief by arguing that it is a tacit premise of the reasoning in this passage is a more hazardous venture than Mugler appears to realize. Where only in conjunction with Q does P entail R, a man who argues "P, ergo R" may never have even dreamed of Q—especially where Q stands for "a mathematical monstrosity."

19

ZENO OF SIDON AS A CRITIC OF EUCLID

P ROCLUS DEVOTES some four pages of his *Commentary on Euclid's Elements*[1] to a report and refutation of certain criticisms which Zeno of Sidon—the eminent Epicurean whose lectures Cicero heard in Athens[2]—directed against the geometry of his time. Posidonius, Proclus tells us, had written "a whole book to show the rottenness of all of his [Zeno's] thought" (200.2–3). Since Proclus mentions this book, and since we know of no other source through which he could have got his knowledge of Zeno's geometrical opinions, we have good reason to assume that he had access to Posidonius' criticism of Zeno or at least to sizable extracts from it. As we would expect from a Stoic controverting the views of an Epicurean, and as is clear enough from the phrase I have just cited, Posidonius wrote as a virulent critic. And since Proclus' own sympathies are entirely and violently on Posidonius' side of the controversy, we may well expect some polemical bias when Zeno's position is characterized in generalities. Fortunately, however, most of Proclus' account of the Epicurean consists of detailed mathematical reasoning. And since Proclus has not only a wide knowledge of the history of geometry but a good mathematical head of his own and is perfectly capable of understanding and analyzing correctly [148] mathematical arguments before endorsing objections against them by third parties or offering us his own objections, we can read this part of his account with great confidence. We have no reason to think that Zeno's arguments as here reported are being misrepresented or distorted in any way.

Here we have an unparalleled opportunity to learn something of Epicurean work in geometry, or, more precisely, of what that work was like in the last quarter of the second century and the early decades of the first century B.C. (the period of Zeno's active life).[3] From the terms in which Cicero has Cotta

From L. Wallach, ed., *The Classical Tradition: Literary and Historical Studies in Honor of Harry Caplan* (Ithaca, N.Y.: Cornell University Press, 1966), pp. 148–59. Used by permission.

[1] I quote from the Teubner edition by G. Friedlein (Leipzig, 1873), referring to this work simply as Proclus. The relevant pages (after the introductory reference to Zeno at 199.11–200.7) are 214–18.

[2] "Zenonem, quem Philo noster [Philo of Larissa, who became head of the Academy in 110/9 B.C.] coryphaeum appellare Epicureorum solebat, cum Athenis essem audiebam frequenter" (*De nat. deorum* I.59). The speaker is Cotta.

[3] Within a century of Epicurus' death, we find leading members of the school (Basilides, Philonides) taking a great interest in mathematics (see W. Crönert, *Kolotes und Menedemos*

refer to him in *De natura deorum,* it is clear that Zeno was no deviationist but a representative, as well as a distinguished member, of his school.[4] To find then in Proclus a workmanlike account of some of Zeno's criticisms of Euclid is a piece of rare good fortune. For what does the rest of our information about Epicurean geometry come to? Three scraps that Usener put into paragraph 229a of *Epicurea;*[5] the bits of Herculanean papyri deriving from geometrical works of Zeno's contemporary, Demetrius of Laconia;[6] one mention by Proclus in the same *Commentary* of a criticism of Euclid I.20 by unnamed Epicureans (322.4–323.3); and one by Sextus of a criticism of a definition of "straight line" (not the one in Euclid; *Adv.* [149] *math.* 3.98). In sheer bulk then, as well as in lucidity of exposition and reliability of transmission, Proclus' account of Zeno is by far our richest deposit of information about Epicurean mathematics. It deserves to be studied intensively, and it is strange that as yet so little attention should have been given it.[7]

In this paper I shall restrict myself to a critical discussion of the interpretation of Zeno's views of geometry which was put forward by W. Crönert in 1906 in his celebrated monograph, *Kolotes und Menedemos.* Though brief—most of what he had to say about Zeno he crammed into one enormously compressed paragraph—it proved extremely influential in just those quarters where influence counts most of all: among specialists. Three decades after the publication of his monograph, we find his view of Zeno endorsed by authori-

---

[Leipzig, 1906], 88; I shall refer to his work hereafter merely by the author's name). Demetrius of Laconia, an illustrious Epicurean, contemporary with Zeno, wrote a work entitled "On Geometry" and several essays, *Pros tas Poluainou Aporias,* whose object was to present short and "easy" solutions of the *aporiai* concerning geometry which had been put forward by Polyaenus (the mathematician who became a convert to Epicurus' gospel and was a prominent member of the original Garden). See V. de Falco, *L'Epicureo Demetrio Lacone* (Naples, 1923), 96ff., on mathematical fragments from the Herculanean papyri. In Pap. 1429 the title *Dēmētriou pros tas Poluainou aporias* is conserved intact; and in column 2, lines 6–13, it is reasonably clear that the writer's aim is to *solve* Polyaenus' *aporiai* (present *luseis* of them), not to defend them against a Stoic critic, as Crönert (111) had surmised.

[4] In the citation above (n. 2), Cotta goes on to say that he thinks Philo advised him to hear Zeno's lectures so that, by hearing the natural philosophy of the Epicureans expounded *a principe Epicureorum*—getting it "from the horse's mouth"—he would be all the better able to refute it.

[5] To which he might have added the other scrap about Polyaenus in Cicero, *De fin.* I.20: "Ne illud quidem physici, credere aliquid esse minimum; quod profecto numquam putavisset [Epicurus] si a Polyaeno familiari suo geometrica discere maluisset quam illum etiam ipsum dedocere."

[6] Cf. n. 3, above.

[7] The main references (some of them very brief) are: O. Apelt, *Beiträge zur Geschichte der griechischen Philosophie* (Leipzig, 1891), 257–58; T. L. Heath, *The Thirteen Books of Euclid's Elements* 1 (2nd ed.; Oxford, 1925), 196, 197, 199, 242; S. Luria, "Die Infinitessimaltheorie der antiken Atomisten," *Quellen und Studien zur Geschichte der Mathematik* 2 (1933), 106ff., at 170–71; W. Schmid, *Epikurs Kritik der platonischen Elementenlehre* (Klassisch-Philologische Studien, Heft 9; Leipzig, 1936), 60–61.

ties on Epicureanism as eminent as W. Schmid[8] and the DeLacys.[9] The main reason for this success, I think, was the reinforcement of Crönert's interpretation of Zeno from an unexpected source: the appearance during the next year of another and (for historians of philosophy) much more important monograph, H. von Arnim's "Epikurs Lehre vom Minimum" (*Almanach der Kaiserlichen Akademie der Wissenschaften* [Wien, 1907], 383ff.). This was the first effective presentation of the thesis that Epicurus had applied his atomism in geometry as well as in physics, that he had taught that all geometrical magnitudes consisted, in the last analysis, of indivisible quanta. Von Arnim's argument met with huge success. Within two decades of its publication, his thesis had become widely accepted among historians of Greek philosophy. An immediate consequence of that thesis would be that the philosophy of Epicurus was committed to a root-and-branch attack on Greek geometry,[10] which was from first to last a science of continuous magnitude [150], its elements being infinitely divisible lines, planes, and volumes. In that case Zeno, as a representative Epicurean, would certainly be expected to be a destructive critic of Euclid.[11] And this is just how Crönert pictured him, though without indebtedness to von Arnim, indeed without apparent knowledge of von Arnim's hypothesis: Before assaulting the theorems of geometry, Zeno, according to Crönert, "had first attacked its foundations" (109); he had claimed that "the geometer proceeds from false presuppositions" (111).

My own inquiries in this area have led me to question and then to reject the ascription of mathematical atomism to Epicurus.[12] In the course of this work I

---

[8] ⟨Above, n. 7⟩, 62.

[9] Phillip and Estelle De Lacy, *Philodemus: On Method and Inference* (Philadelphia, 1941), 147.

[10] This conclusion was drawn (indeed, stressed) by von Arnim: "Epikurs oft bezeugte Abneigung gegen die Mathematik, die ihn von seinen Gegnern so sehr verübelt wird, seine Ansicht, dass die ganze bisherige Mathematik auf falschen Grundlagen aufgebaut sei, zu der er sogar seinen Schuler, den Mathematiker Polyän, zu bekehren wusste, ist offenbar aus seinem Finitismus zu erklären" ("Epikurs Lehre," 388). His only references for these sweeping statements (399n.11) are (1) Cicero, *Acad.* 2.106: "Polyaenus, qui magnus mathematicus fuisse dicitur . . . Epicuro adsentiens totam geometriam falsam esse credidit"; (2) the passage from *De fin.* cited in n. 5 above; (3) Proclus, 199.9–11: "τῶν δὲ τὰς γεωμετρικὰς μόνας ἀρχὰς ἀνατρέπειν προθεμένων, ὥσπερ τῶν Ἐπικουρείων." For the fact that Zeno, the Epicurean, whom Proclus proceeds immediately to mention, shows not the slightest sign of addiction to Epicurus' mathematical "Finitismus," von Arnim has no explanation; he may not even have been aware of the fact, having got the citation from Proclus only *via* Usener (who includes it in *Epicurea* ⟨Leipzig, 1887⟩, 229a).

[11] Hence one who accepts Crönert's interpretation of Zeno would naturally count on this to confirm the ascription of mathematical atomism to Epicurus, ignoring the absence of any sign of this in Proclus' account of Zeno. Luria, assuming that Zeno must have been a mathematical atomist because he was an Epicurean, reads mathematical atoms into Proclus' account of Zeno's arguments and writes them into his diagram (⟨above, n. 7⟩, 171).

[12] I offer some reasons for this conclusion in "Minimal Parts in Epicurean Atomism," *Isis* 56

was led, chiefly because of Luria's use of Zeno's supposed rejection of the foundations of the Euclidean system as a prop for the mathematical atomist interpretation of the Epicurean system, to trace this construction of Zeno's position back to its source in Crönert. I then discovered that this great papyrologist had radically misunderstood the position of the Epicurean mathematician, conflating it, on inadequate evidence, with the entirely different position represented by Sextus. The latter, as a sceptic, would have every reason to impugn both the soundness of the principles[13] of the Euclidean system and the validity of its deductions. Zeno, on the other hand, does [151] not seem to be in Proclus more than a purely *methodological* critic of Euclid, faulting Euclid's proofs but making no substantive criticisms and, in particular, none which would impugn the truth of Euclid's principles. This is what I shall try to establish, against Crönert, here.

Let us begin with the lines in which Proclus introduces us to Zeno of Sidon in the opening paragraph of the new section of his *Commentary*, where, having completed his discussion of Euclid's axiom-set, he proceeds to examine and defend the theorems which are deduced therefrom. "Of those who have raised objections against geometry (τῶν δὲ πρὸς γεωμετρίαν ἐνστάντων)," he says that

[I] the majority have directed their doubts against the principles (οἱ μὲν πρός τὰς ἀρχὰς ἠπόρησαν), intent on showing that its particular parts (i.e., the theorems) were without foundation (ἀνυπόστατα τὰ μέρη δεικνύναι σπουδάσαντες),[14] 199.3–5. These enemies of "the principles" he subdivides into
[a] those who reject the principles of all science: Pyrrhonians;
[b] those who reject the principles of geometry only: Epicureans.

Proclus then continues:

[II] But there are those who, having already conceded the principles (οἱ δὲ ἤδη καὶ ταῖς ἀρχαῖς ἐπιτρέψαντες), deny that the consequences [i.e., the theorems] have been demonstrated unless some further admission is made not previously included among the principles, 199.11–14.

To give support to Crönert's thesis, Proclus here would have to be understood to impute to Zeno not only position [II] but also position [Ib]. What reason could we have for putting such a construction on his words? These do not tell us that the proponents of [II] are a subclass of those who already hold [Ib].[15]

(1965), 121–47 ⟨**2.285ff.⟩. My present discussion is intended to supplement and support the brief remarks I make there about Zeno.

[13] Here and hereafter I use this word, for want of a better to render into English the Greek *archē*.

[14] For this sense of *ta merē*, cf. Sextus. *Adv. math.* 3.18: "For when the principles have been impugned neither can *hai kata merē apodeixeis* [= the proofs of theorems deduced from the principles] be successful."

[15] Nor are we told this in the subsequent description of Zeno's position at 214.18ff.: λέγει δὲ

If Proclus had wanted to express this [152] thought, the whole construction of his long sentence (lines 3 to 14) would have been different: Instead of the *hoi de* in [II] (line 11), to balance *hoi men* in [I] (line 4), thereby dividing the critics of Euclid's deductions at [II] from the opponents of his principles at [I], we would have had in line 11 a relative pronoun in a partitive construction to tie the group at [II] to the Epicurean sector of [I]. Moreover, the rest of his sentence would have been different: it would have conveyed the information that Zeno, having (A) already rejected the principles of geometry, went on (B) to discredit its theorems. Consider how Sextus—who, as we know, holds just the position which Crönert assigns to Zeno—expresses himself on this point in his essay "Against the Geometers":

(A) Thus as regards the principles of geometry the outcome [of the preceding argument which started at 18] is that they are unfounded;

(B) and these having been refuted, no other geometrical proposition [i.e. no theorem] can stand" (*Adv. math.* 3.92).

Neither the (A) nor the (B) part of this pronouncement has any counterpart in Proclus' account of Zeno's view. The opening clause (lines 11–12), "having already conceded the principles of geometry," would demolish Crönert's whole thesis all by itself, if taken at face value.[16] But since it could be argued—with what justification it is unnecessary to consider—that it only means to say that Zeno's concession was made *argumenti causa,* let us merely note that, even so, the difference from (A) would be material since, at the very least, Proclus does *not* tell us that Zeno rejected the principles. The difference from (B) in the rest of Proclus' sentence (12–14) is no less decisive: Zeno is not represented as claiming that the theorems of Euclid are indemonstrable *simpliciter* (as they would be, if they were baseless), but only [153] that they cannot be demonstrated "unless they [the geometers] are granted some further proposition not previously included among the principles." As Proclus represents Zeno's complaint here, it could be met in full by simply *adding* some further propositions to Euclid's postulate-set, without any suggestion that this addition, if made, would falsify the postulate-set as a whole or in part.

Ζήνων ἐκεῖνος, . . . ὅτι κἂν ταῖς ἀρχαῖς τις ἐπιτρέψῃ τῶν γεωμετρῶν, οὐκ ἂν συσταίη τὰ ἐφεξῆς, μὴ συγχωρηθέντος αὐτοῖς ὅτι δύο εὐθειῶν τὰ αὐτὰ τμήματα οὐκ ἔστιν. Here the wording is somewhat more favorable to Crönert's interpretation (though this is no excuse for his curiously garbled citation, which conflates the first three clauses from the second passage in Proclus, 214.19–21, with the last clause of the first passage, 199.13–14, inexplicably substituting *touto* in the third clause for *ta ephexēs* of the text). But neither does this text support the claim that Zeno thought the Euclidean principles *false:* all it says is that the theorem (Euclid I.1) would not stand unless an *additional* principle were conceded: and this does not take us one inch beyond position [II], i.e., that Euclid's postulate-set does not provide *sufficient* premises for the deduction of his theorems.

16 It was so read by Apelt ⟨above, n. 7⟩, 255: "Zeno erkennt die Principien *(archai)* und das Beweisverfahren der Mathematik an. Er tadelt aber an Euklid die Unvollständigkeit seiner Prämissen."

This programmatic sketch of Zeno's position at 199.11ff. is borne out to the letter in the subsequent discussion of Zeno's allegations against Euclid at 214.15ff. The criticism of Euclid I.1, as Proclus reports it, does not cast the slightest aspersion on the truth of a single principle in Euclid. Its only point is that the proof would not be valid, unless (to repeat the phrasing of 199.13) "we are granted some further proposition not previously included among the principles." This "further proposition" is that no two (distinct) straight lines have a common segment. To add this to Euclid's postulate-set would be only to improve it in respect of explicitness.[17] If Euclid's critic is to be judged by this recommendation and its twin (that the same stipulation for circles should be added to the principles), the worst that we could say about him is that he is a severe and fussy, but certainly not an unfriendly, critic of the Euclidean systematization of geometry. He is, if anything, overanxious to perfect it.

How is it then, it may be asked, that Proclus should introduce Zeno's objection to Euclid I.1 by saying that those who make it "think they are refuting the whole of geometry" (214.16–17)? Although Crönert does not bring it up, this is the strongest item of evidence for his thesis in the whole of Proclus. Nonetheless it is susceptible of an entirely different construction: Convinced of the correctness of his indictment of this first proposition in Euclid, Zeno would feel that, if the requisite addition to the postulate-set were not made, this proposition would be invalidated, and *a fortiori* all its logical pendants and any number of others whose proof (in Zeno's view) presupposes directly the no-common-segments principle for lines and circles. A criticism which, if not met, would have such far-reaching consequences *could* be represented as "refuting the whole of geometry." Should this suggestion strike the reader as a partisan construction of Proclus' sentence, let him ask himself what else it could possibly mean *in this context*. I italicize the last three words, for otherwise that sentence might mean anything, including all that Crönert thinks it means, with mathematical [154] atomism thrown in for good measure.[18] Fortunately we know the precise move to which it refers: a criticism which, in the critic's view, could be met by adding the no-common-segments postulate to the Euclidean postulate-set.

Another criticism of Euclid reported by Proclus (322.4ff.)[19] which Crönert thinks was Zeno's is the one directed against Euclid's proof of I.20: that the sum of any two sides of a triangle is greater than the third. If the author of this criticism was Zeno, why should Proclus refer to him only as "Epicureans"?

---

[17] I have remarked on this point in Section I of "Minimal Parts in Epicurean Atomism," n. 12 above.

[18] As I mentioned above, Crönert himself does not ascribe mathematical atomism to Zeno. Believing the argument in Proclus 277.35ff. to be Zeno's, Crönert takes the proposition that a line does not consist of indivisibles to be firm Zenonian doctrine.

[19] Discussed briefly in Section I of "Minimal Parts in Epicurean Atomism" ⟨above, n. 12⟩.

Crönert does not explain.[20] But suppose we gave him his conjecture. It would still do nothing to advance his thesis. For the critic's only complaint is that Euclid gives a proof for a proposition that needs no proof. How could this evidence a conviction that Euclid's principles are false? The critics, clearly, are implying that this proposition (or a logically equivalent one) should be upgraded, raised to the status of a principle. The simplest means of doing this would be to substitute "shortest distance between two points"[21] for the received definition of a straight line (a quaint and almost totally useless piece of machinery). This would be a marked improvement of the Euclidean postulate-set. If Zeno made this criticism, we would have to reckon him, as before, a constructive critic.

A last criticism reported by Proclus (277.35–278.12) which Crönert also ascribes to Zeno is directed against Euclid's proof of I.10, "to bisect a given finite straight line." Here too the ascription to Zeno, having only the most tenuous evidence to support it,[22] is not worth quarreling [155] over for our present purpose; for even if it were right, it would give no support to Crönert's

---

[20] All he says on this matter is, "Auf Zenon muss ferner der Kampf zurückgehen, den nach [Proclus] 322, 4 die gegen den 13. Lehrsatz . . . geführt haben (vg. *Schol. in Eucl* 5.156 Heib.)" (109). But the scholion to which he refers is worthless as evidence for the ascription to Zeno: there is no more of a mention or allusion to Zeno there than in Proclus. Nor does the scholion add anything else of value to what we learn from Proclus; it is only a rehash of the latter.

[21] Which Proclus (110.10–12) takes to have been Archimedes' definition of a straight line. As Heath points out (⟨above, n. 7⟩, 166), in *On the Sphere and Cylinder* Archimedes lists this as "an assumption" (*lambanomenon*). But it could certainly be made into a definition, and a vastly better one than the one in Euclid.

[22] *Sc.,* that here too a proof in Euclid is faulted on the allegation that it presupposes an unacknowledged principle. But was Zeno the only one who made this kind of criticism of Euclid? For all we know to the contrary, there may have been scores of others who did the same. Crönert takes no account of known antecedents of the argument in Proclus 278.3–9: e.g., Eudemus fr. 100 (Wehrli) (= Simplicius [citing Alexander], *Phys.* 930.35–931.6); Ps.-Arist., *De lineis insec.* 970a29–34. For other references see Luria (⟨above, n. 7⟩, 167n. 152), who seems to take it for granted that the source is Eudemus. This could be true, even though the Eudemus fragment does not come from Eudemus' *History of Geometry* but from his *Physics* (see F. Wehrli's comments on this book in his *Eudemos von Rhodos* [Basel, 1955], 87ff.). We can be fairly confident that Proclus would be familiar with this argument, if not from Eudemus, then from some other source(s), and that it occurred to him that it could be used as the basis of a criticism of Euclid's proof of I.10. But it is just as possible that he was borrowing from someone else who had already used it for just this purpose: Eudemus himself may have used it to find fault with some earlier axiomatization of geometry which had failed to list infinite divisibility among its *archai* (for his own recognition of it as such, cf. Simplicius, *Phys.* 55.22–24). This is, of course, only to pit speculations against Crönert's own that Zeno had been Proclus' immediate source. Whichever of these surmises be the right one, my overall argument against Crönert would be unaffected. Accordingly I have been content in the text above to ascribe the argument in Proclus 277.25–278.12 noncommittally to an unspecified "critic." Note that if the source was Zeno, this would give us no more reason for thinking Zeno a destructive critic of geometry than for casting Eudemus in such a role.

thesis. For here, as in the criticisms of I.1 and I.20, we get again a purely methodological stricture: The critic takes no issue with the truth of I.10 itself or with any of the principles from which Euclid purports to deduce it. His only objection is to the *proof*, alleging that this presupposes a principle not listed in (or entailed by) Euclid's postulate-set, *sc.*, the infinite divisibility of (continuous) magnitudes. To make good his objection, he asks you to consider the consequences of the hypothesis, *H*, that *lines consist of indivisibles* (as he assumes they would, if magnitudes were not infinitely divisible): Take a line consisting of an odd number of indivisibles. To bisect this you would have to cut at the midpoint, since to cut either to the right or to the left would yield unequal segments. But to cut at the midpoint would be to divide an indivisible. Hence:

[1] *H* conjoined to Euclid I.10 entails absurdity (Proclus 278.3–9); hence:

[2] lines [and, by parity of reasoning, all continuous magnitudes] are infinitely divisible (9–10); hence:

[3] the infinite divisibility of magnitudes must be acknowledged[23] as a principle of geometry (10–12). [156]

Here [1] is the gist of the argument that the demonstration of Euclid I.10 presupposes the infinite divisibility of lines; [3] represents the conclusion the critic draws from [1] and [2], this being his *only* objection to Euclid. There is not a word here to imply, or suggest, that the critic himself rejects infinite divisibility or that he thinks it incompatible with one or more propositions in the Euclidean postulate-set. That his only plea is that this principle should be added to the Euclidean principles is also clear from Proclus' rejoinder (278.12–279.4): to defeat the critic, Proclus (following Geminus) thinks it sufficient to argue that the principle presupposed by the geometers is not, as the critic claims, that of *infinite* divisibility, but only of *divisibility: infinite* divisibility, Proclus insists, is demonstrable (being entailed by the proof of incommensurability), hence not a principle. Regardless of who is right in this controversy, it should be clear that this whole text—the critic's argument and Proclus' retort—gives absolutely no ground for thinking the critic an enemy of the Euclidean system. His wish for it is evidently the same as that of Zeno in his criticism of Euclid I.10—to augment it by a principle which would complete the set of premises required to validate all of its proofs.

Now it so happens that Sextus in *Adv. math.* 3.110–11 lays out a criticism of Euclid I.10 which is partly the same as the one we have just seen in Proclus

---

[23] I take this to be the *point* of the conclusion that this "has been admitted" (*hōmologēsthai*) and "is" (*einai*) a geometrical principle: since nothing of the kind appears in the Euclidean postulate-set, to argue that it is already admitted by one who runs through Euclid's proof for 1.10 is to urge that admission should be made, not surreptitiously, but openly, by giving it the status of a formal principle.

and partly differs in ways which are of the highest consequence for Crönert's argument, but which have evidently escaped Crönert's notice.[24] What is the same here is what I marked [I] in the analysis of the argument (in Proclus 278) in the preceding paragraph: here too, it is argued, and for the same reasons as in Proclus, that the conjunction of *H* (lines consist of indivisibles) with Euclid I.10 (every line is bisectable) entails absurdity. But there is a vast difference: We find nothing here to correspond to the critic's conclusion in Proclus' text which I marked as [3] above. Sextus does not put out the argument at [I] to win a place for infinite divisibility among the principles of geometry but for an entirely different purpose: [157] to convince us that lines cannot be bisected, i.e., that Euclid I.10 is false.[25] And this reveals a radically different attitude to the Euclidean system: it puts Sextus in the position of a substantive critic, a hostile one, who builds on the assumption that *H* is true: if he did not assume that lines consist of indivisibles (the one in his example consists of 9), his refutation of Euclid I.10 would come to nothing. And if he does think *H* true, he must think the Euclidean system rotten down to its foundations, beginning with its definitions of point, line, and so on.[26] If Crönert could give us reasons to think that *this* critic is Zeno, he would prove his case to the hilt. But where

---

[24] The only difference he sees between the two texts is intimated in the following sentence: "Bei Sextus nun kehrt die Begründung fur die Behauptung, dass die Linie nicht aus unteilbaren Punkten bestehen könne, in etwas ausführlicher Darstellung wieder (Procl. 278, 3–9 = Sextus 110–11), während die ebenfalls zenonische Aufstellung der anderen *archē* nur bei Proklos erscheint" (109). As I shall show directly, so far from offering a "Begründung" for the proposition that lines do not consist of indivisibles, Sextus at 110–11 presupposes the very contrary: This blunder skews Crönert's comprehension of the import of the position set forth in the Sextus text and therefore vitiates the conclusions Crönert draws from what he takes to be its relation to its counterpart in Proclus.

[25] What Sextus says he will prove at 110–11 is clearly stated in the opening sentence of 110: καὶ μὴν οὐδὲ ἡ ἀπὸ ταύτης [τῆς ἐπὶ τοῦ ἄβακος] κατὰ μετάβασιν νοουμένη [γραμμὴ δίχα τμηθήσεται]. Having proved to his satisfaction at 109 that a geometrical line cannot be bisected by bisecting a sensible line (the one "on the board"), he goes on to prove at 110 that neither can it be done by bisecting the line "conceived by transference" from the one on the board, i.e., the purely abstract line: in either case, Sextus argues, the bisection of the geometrical line is impossible.

[26] Which is, of course, only to be expected from Sextus' announced position: cf. the citation from 92 in the text above and also, e.g., his statement at 18 of what he proposes to show in this essay: "Passing on, let us show in the next place that the principles of their art are in fact false and incredible. . . . [These principles] refuted, the rest [the theorems] will be refuted with them. . . . When the principles are indicted, the particular demonstrations [of the theorems] cannot come off. . . ." If *P* stands for the conjunction of Euclid's principles and *T* for any of his theorems, Sextus denies that (*a*) *P* is true and also that (*b*) *T* is true, while the critic in Proclus 277.35ff. and Zeno in Proclus 214.15ff. denies only (*c*) that *P entails T* in the case of Euclid I.10 and I.1, respectively. Crönert does not even consider (let alone refute) the possibility that the critic of Euclid I.10 in Proclus and Zeno, with whom Crönert identifies that critic, might have denied (*c*) but *neither* (*a*) *nor* (*b*). The difference between a purely *methodological* criticism of Euclid [denial of (*c*)] and a *substantive* one [denial of (*a*) and/or (*b*)] is never mooted by Crönert.

is he going to find such reasons? All Crönert can get out of Sextus is the fact that a dozen paragraphs earlier (at 98) a criticism of a definition of a straight line had been cited from "the Epicureans." But what is this worth for the present purpose? How can the fact that Sextus borrowed something from "Epicureans" at 98 be taken to imply that he has borrowed from an Epicurean source (and that this source is Zeno) the objection to Euclid I.10 in a later section of the book?[27]

I cannot believe that it would have [158] even occurred to Crönert to build an argument on such an uncertain base if he had not labored under the misapprehension that the criticism of Euclid I.10 in Sextus is *the same criticism* as that in Proclus and, therefore, felt that he could count on his assumption that the latter expresses Zeno's views to support his claim that the one in Sextus ⟨expresses it⟩ also. Once that misapprehension is dispelled, it becomes evident that, even if we knew that the criticism of Euclid I.10 in Proclus represented Zeno's *ipsissima verba,* we would still have no reason to think that the criticism of the same proposition in Sextus is also Zeno's. Quite the contrary: the critic of Euclid I.10 in Proclus argues that the assumption that lines consist of indivisibles leads to absurdity in order to win acceptance for an infinite divisibility postulate which would validate Euclid I.10: while the critic in Sextus, who *rejects* infinite divisibility, uses the same argument to *in*validate Euclid I.10. Once this diametrical opposition of the views of the two critics is understood, Crönert's case for their identity falls apart. Nothing is then left to connect Sextus, whom we know to have controverted the whole of Euclidean geometry, with Zeno, whom we know only to have been a methodological critic of some of its proofs.

---

[27] *Adv. math.* 3 falls into the following sections: (1) objections to the geometers' postulational method (1–17); (2) first set of objections to their principles (18–91); (3) second set of objections to their principles (94–107); (4) objections to their theorems (108–16). How can the fact that an Epicurean source is utilized for one item in section (3) establish a presumption for the use of the same source for some item of disputed provenance in section (4)?

BIBLIOGRAPHY

THE WORKS OF GREGORY VLASTOS

Note: Starred items (e.g., "1955*") are included in the present collection.

1929. "Whitehead, Critic of Abstractions (Being the Story of a Philosopher Who Started with Science and Ended with Metaphysics)." *The Monist* 39:170–203.

1930. "The Problem of Incompatibility in the Philosophy of Organism." *The Monist* 40 (October):535–51.

1931. Review of Henry Nelson Wieman, *The Issues of Life. Christian Century* 48:17.

1932. Review of Wilhelm Pauck, *Karl Barth: Prophet of a New Christianity? Christian Century* 49:19–20.

1933a. Review of Joseph Needham, *The Great Amphibium. Journal of Religion* 13:100–101.

1933b. Review of Stewart Means, *Faith, An Historical Study. Christian Century* 50:984.

1934. *The Religious Way*. New York: Women's Press.

1935a. What is Love? *Christendom* 1:117–31.

1935b. Review of Reinhold Niebuhr, *An Interpretation of Christian Ethics. Christendom* 1:390–94.

1936a. (Coeditor with R.B.Y. Scott.) *Towards the Christian Revolution*. Chicago: Willett, Clark.

1936b. "The Ethical Foundation." In *Towards the Christian Revolution*, 51–74.

1937a. "Jesus' Conflict With the Pharisees." *Christendom* 2:86–100.

1937b. "Organic Categories in Whitehead." *JP* 34:253–63. Reprinted in G. L. Kline, ed., *Whitehead: Essays in His Philosophy*. (Englewood Cliffs, N.J.: Prentice-Hall, 1963), pp. 158–67.

1937c. Review of John MacMurray, *The Structure of Religious Experience. Christendom* 2:293–96.

1938. "Fighting For the Future of Spain." *Christian Century* 55:1156–58.

1939a. "Barth Rethinks Barthianism." *The Christian Century* 56:1065–66.

1939b. *Christian Faith and Democracy*. New York: American Press.

1939c.* "The Disorderly Motion in the *Timaeus*." *CQ* 33:71–83. Revised in Allen, pp. 379–99.

1941a. Review of Reinhold Niebuhr, *On Human Nature: The Nature and Destiny of Man*, Vol. I. *The Christian Century* 58:1202–4.

1941b. "Slavery in Plato's Thought." *PR* 50:289–304. Reprinted with "Postscript (1959)" in M. I. Finley, ed., *Slavery in Classical Antiquity* (Cambridge: Heffer, 1960), pp. 133–49. Reprinted in *PS*, pp. 147–63.

1942a. "The Religious Foundations of Democracy: Fraternity and Liberty; Fraternity and Equality." *Journal of Religion* 22:1–19, 137–55.

1942b. Review of A. D. Winspear, *The Genesis of Plato's Thought. PR* 51 (1942): 421–23.

1945.* "Ethics and Physics in Democritus I." *PR* 54: 578–92. Reprinted in Furley and Allen II, pp. 381–89.

1946a.* "Ethics and Physics in Democritus II." *PR* 55:53–64. Reprinted in Furley and Allen II, pp. 390–408.

1946b.* "On the Pre-History in Diodorus." *AJP* 67:51–59.

1946c.* "Parmenides' Theory of Knowledge." *TAPA* 77(66–77).

1946d.* "Solonian Justice." *CP* 41:65–83.

1947a.* "Equality and Justice in Early Greek Cosmologies." *CP* 42:156–78. Reprinted in Furley and Allen I, pp. 56–91. Also reprinted in part in James Collin, ed., *Readings in Ancient and Medieval Philosophy,* The College Readings Series, 6 (Westminster, Md.: The Newman Press, 1963), pp. 16–30.

1947b. *"Plato's Theory of Man."* *PR* 56:184–93. Review Article on John Wild, *Plato's Theory of Man* (Cambridge, Mass.: Harvard University Press, 1946).

1949. "Religion and Medicine in the Cult of Asclepius." *The Review of Religion* 13: 269–90. Review article on Emma J. Edelstein and Ludwig Edelstein, *Asclepius* (Baltimore: The Johns Hopkins Press, 1945).

1950a.* "The Physical Theory of Anaxagoras." *PR* 59:31–57. Reprinted with revisions in Furley and Allen II, pp. 381–408. Also reprinted in A.P.D. Mourelatos, ed., *The Pre-Socratics: A Collection of Critical Essays* (Garden City N.Y.: Doubleday & Co., 1974), pp. 459–88.

1950b. Review of Felix M. Cleve, *The Philosophy of Anaxagoras, PR* 59:124–26.

1952a. "The Constitution of the Five Thousand." *AJP* 73:189–98. Greek political history.

1952b. "Religion and Democracy." In *Liberal Learning and Religion,* A. Wilder, ed. New York: Harper, pp. 267–95.

1952c.* "Theology and Philosophy in Early Greek Thought." *PQ* 2:97–123. Reprinted in Furley and Allen I, pp. 92–129.

1953a.* *"Isonomia."* *AJP* 74:337–66. Followed by sequel, *"Isonomia Politike,"* (1964).

1953b. "Of Sovereignty in Church and State." *PR* 62:561–76. Review article on Jacques Maritain, *Man and the State* (Chicago: University of Chicago Press, 1951).

1953c.* Review of J. E. Raven, *Pythagoreans and Eleatics. Gnomon* 25:29–35. Reprinted in Furley and Allen II, pp. 166–76.

1953d. Review of Jean Zafiropoulo, *L'Ecole éléate. Gnomon* 25:166–69.

1954a.* "The Third Man Argument in the *Parmenides."* *PR* 63:319–49. Reprinted in Allen, pp. 231–61, with Addendum (1963).

1954b. Rejoinder to "The Question of Civil Autonomy" by M. Whitcomb Hess. *PR* 63:424–27.

1955a.* "Addenda to the Third Man: A Reply to Professor Sellars." *PR* 64:438–48.

1955b. Review of G. S. Kirk, *Heraclitus: The Cosmic Fragments. AJP* 76:310–13.

1955c.* "On Heraclitus." *AJP* 76:337–68. Reprinted in part in Furley and Allen I, pp. 414–29.

1955d.* Review of F. M. Cornford, *Principium Sapientiae. Gnomon* 27:65–76. Reprinted in Furley and Allen I, pp. 42–55.

1956a. (Editor) *Plato's Protagoras.* New York: Liberal Arts Press. Introduction, pp. vii–lvi.

1956b.* "Postscript to the Third Man: A Reply to Mr. Geach." *PR* 65:83–94. Reprinted in Allen, pp. 279–91.

1956c. Review of Giorgio del Vecchio, *Justice*. *University of Pennsylvania Law Review* 105:267–95.

1957a. "Justice." *Revue internationale de philosophie* 11:324–43.

1957b.* "The Paradox of Socrates." *Queen's Quarterly* 64:496–516. Spanish Translation in *Revista de Occidenta* (Madrid), 11 (1964), pp. 129–57. Reprinted in Vlastos, ed., *The Philosophy of Socrates* (1971a), pp. 1–21.

1957c. "Socratic Knowledge and Platonic 'Pessimism.'" *PR* 66:226–38. Review Article on John Gould, *The Development of Plato's Ethics*. Reprinted in *PS*, pp. 204–17.

1959a. Review of G. S. Kirk and J. E. Raven, *The Presocratic Philosophers*. *PR* 68:531–35.

1959b.* Review of Hermann Fränkel, *Wege und Formen frühgriechischen Denkens*. *Gnomon* 31:193–204. Reprinted in excerpts in Furley and Allen II ("A Note on Zeno B1," pp. 177–83; "One World or Many in Anaxagoras?" pp. 354–60).

1960. "Some Contributions of Religion to Social Life." In *The Student Seeks an Answer*, J. Clarke, ed. Waterville: Colby College Press, pp. 11–33.

1961a. "Uses of Excellence." *Forum* 3:38–46.

1961b. "Zeno." In *Philosophical Classics*, W. Kaufmann, ed. Englewood Cliffs, N.J.: Prentice-Hall, pp. 27–45. Repudiated in later articles on Zeno.

1962a. "Justice and Equality." In *Social Justice*, R. Brandt, ed. Englewood Cliffs, N.J.: Prentice-Hall, pp. 31–72. Reprinted in part in Joel Feinberg, ed., *Moral Concepts* (London: Oxford U. Press, 1970), pp. 141–52; in part in A. I. Melden, ed., *Human Rights* (Belmont, Cal.: Wadsworth, 1970), pp. 76–95; and in full in Jeremy Waldron, ed., *Theories of Rights* (Oxford: Oxford University Press, 1984), pp. 41–76.

1962b. Review of C. Ramnoux, *Héraclite, ou l'homme entre les choses et les mots*. *PR* 71:538–42.

1963a.* "Note on the Unmoved Mover." *PQ* 13:246–47.

1963b. Review of H. J. Krämer, "*Arete* bei Platon und Aristoteles." *Gnomon* 35:641–55. Reprinted in *PS* under the title "On Plato's Oral Doctrine," pp. 379–98.

1964. *Isonomia Politike*. In J. Mau and E. G. Schmidt, eds., *Isonomia: Studien zur Gleichheitsvorstellung im griechischen Denken*. Berlin: Berlin Academy, pp. 1–35. Sequel to "*Isonomia*" (1953a). Reprinted in *PS*, pp. 164–203.

1965a.* *Anamnesis* in the *Meno*. *Dialogue* 4:143–67. Reprinted as "The Theory of Recollection in the *Meno*" in the Bobbs Merrill Reprint Series in Philosophy, #215.

1965b.* "Creation in the *Timaeus:* Is It a Fiction?" In *Studies in Plato's Metaphysics*, R. E. Allen, ed. London: Routledge & Kegan Paul, pp. 401–19.

1965c. Degrees of Reality in Plato. In *New Essays in Plato and Aristotle*, R. Bambrough, ed. London: Routledge & Kegan Paul, pp. 1–19. Reprinted in *PS*, pp. 58–77.

1965d.* "Minimal Parts in Epicurean Atomism." *ISIS* 56:121–47.

1966a. "A Metaphysical Paradox." *Proceedings of the American Philosophical Association* 39:5–19. Presidential address to Eastern Division, American Philosophical Association, 1965. Reprinted in *PS*, pp. 43–57.

1966b.* "A Note on Zeno's Arrow." *Phronesis* 11:3–18. Reprinted in Furley and Allen II, pp. 184–99. Translated into Greek in *Deucalion* 11 = Vlastos (1974a).

1966c. Review of Alvin Gouldner, *Enter Plato. American Sociological Review* 31:548–49.

1966d. Review of I. M. Crombie, *An Examination of Plato's Philosophical Doctrines,* vol. II. *PR* 75:526–30. Reprinted in *PS,* pp. 374–78, under the title "Plato on Knowledge and Reality."

1966e.* "Zeno of Sidon as a Critic of Euclid." In L. Wallach, ed., *The Classical Tradition: Literary and Historical Studies in Honor of Harry Caplan.* Ithaca, N.Y.: Cornell University Press, pp. 148–59.

1966f.* "Zeno's Race Course: With an Appendix on the Achilles." *JHP* 4:95–108. Reprinted in Furley and Allen II, pp. 201–20.

1967a. "Plato's Supposed Theory of Irregular Atomic Figures." *Isis* 57:204–9. Reprinted in *PS,* pp. 366–73.

1967b.* "Was Polus Refuted?" *AJP* 88:454–60.

1967c.* "Zeno of Elea." *The Encyclopedia of Philosophy.* Ed. Paul Edwards. New York: Macmillan, 8:369–79.

1968a. "The Argument in the Republic That Justice Pays." *Journal of Philosophy* 65:665–74. Used in "Justice and Happiness in the *Republic*" (Vlastos 1971e).

1968b. "Does Slavery Exist in the *Republic?*" *CP* 63:291–95. Reprinted in *PS,* pp. 140–46, under the title "Does Slavery Exist in Plato's *Republic?*"

1969a. "Justice and Psychic Harmony in the *Republic.*" *Journal of Philosophy* 66:505–21. Used in "Justice and Happiness in the *Republic*" (Vlastos 1971e).

1969b. "Plato's 'Third Man' Argument (*Parm.* 132A1–B2): Text and Logic." *PQ* 19:289–301. Reprinted with revisions in *PS,* pp. 342–65.

1969c. "Pre-Socratic Philosophy." In *Encyclopedia Americana,* vol. 22. New York: Americana Corporation.

1969d. "Reasons and Causes in the *Phaedo.*" *PR* 78:291–325. Reprinted in *Plato* I (Vlastos 1971b), pp. 132–66, and in *PS,* pp. 76–110.

1969e. "Self-Predication in Plato's Later Period." *PR* 78:74–78. Reprinted in *PS,* pp. 335–41.

1969f.* "Socrates on *Acrasia.*" *Phoenix* 23:71–88.

1971a. (Editor) *The Philosophy of Socrates: A Collection of Critical Essays.* Garden City, N.Y.: Doubleday & Co.

1971b. (Editor) *Plato: A Collection of Critical Essays I: Metaphysics and Epistemology.* Garden City, N.Y.: Doubleday & Co.

1971c. (Editor) *Plato: A Collection of Critical Essays II: Ethics, Politics, and Philosophy of Art and Religion.* Garden City, N.Y.: Doubleday & Co.

1971d.* "A Zenonian Argument Against Plurality." In John P. Anton and George L. Kustas, eds., *Essays in Ancient Greek Philosophy.* Albany, N.Y.: State University of New York Press, pp. 119–44.

1971e. "Justice and Happiness in the *Republic.*" In *Plato II* (Vlastos, 1971c), pp. 66–95. Garden City, N.Y.: Doubleday and Co. Reprinted in *PS,* pp. 111–39.

1972. "The Unity of Virtues in the *Protagoras.*" *RM* 25:415–58. Reprinted in *PS,* pp. 221–69.

1973. *Platonic Studies.* Princeton N.J.: Princeton University Press. Second printing, with corrections, 1981. Essays in this collection that were not previously published:

1. "The Individual as an Object of Love in Plato"; 11. "An Ambiguity in the *Sophist*"; 12. "The 'Two Level' Paradoxes in Aristotle"; 19. "What Did Socrates Understand by his 'What Is F?' Question?" 20. "Socrates on 'The Parts of Virtue.'" Essays 18–20 are new in the second printing.

1974a. Σημείωση γιὰ τὸ βέλος τοῦ Ζήνωνα. *Deucalion* 11:310–18. Greek translation of "A Note on Zeno's Arrow" (1966b).

1974b. "A Note on 'Pauline Predications' in Plato." *Phronesis* 19:95–101. Reprinted with corrections and deletions in *PS*, pp. 270–322.

1974c.* "Socrates on Political Obedience and Disobedience." *Yale Review* 63:517–34.

1975a. *Plato's Universe.* Seattle, Wash.: University of Washington Press. Text of the Jessie and John Danz Lectures at the University of Washington, 1972.

1975b. Review of W.K.C. Guthrie, *A History of Greek Philosophy,* Vol. IV. *TLS* (3,848) (12 Dec.):1474–75.

1975c.* "Plato's Testimony Concerning Zeno of Elea." *JHS* 95:136–62.

1975d. "What is Required of Us?" *University: A Princeton Quarterly* 65:2–5.

1977.* "The Theory of Social Justice in the *Polis* in Plato's *Republic.*" In Helen North, ed., *Interpretations of Plato: A Swarthmore Symposium.* Leiden: E. J. Brill, pp. 1–40. *Mnemosyne* Suppl. vol. 50.

1978a. Review of Harold Cherniss, *Collected Papers.* *AJP* 99:537–43.

1978b.* Review of T. Irwin, *Plato's Moral Theory. TLS* (3,961) (Feb. 24):230–31.

1978c.* "Rights of Persons in Plato's Conception of the Foundations of Justice." In H. Tristram Englehardt and Daniel Callahan, eds., *Morals, Science and Society,* The Hastings Center, Hastings-on-Hudson, N.Y., pp. 172–201.

1979. "On 'The Socrates Story'" *Political Theory* 7:533–36. Discussion of I. F. Stone article in Magazine section, *New York Times,* April 8, 1979, p. 22.

1980a. Review of Ellen Meiksins Wood and Neal Wood, *Class Ideology and Ancient Political Theory. Phoenix* 34:347–52.

1980b.* "The Role of Observation in Plato's Conception of Astronomy." In John P. Anton, ed., *Science and the Sciences in Antiquity,* Delmar, N.Y.: Caravan Books, pp. 1–31.

1980c. "Graduate Education in the Humanities: Reflections and Proposals." In William K. Frankena, ed., *The Philosophy and Future of Graduate Education.* Ann Arbor: University of Michigan Press, pp. 64–81.

1981a. "Socrates' Contribution to the Greek Sense of Justice." *Archaiognosia* 1:301–24. "Drastically revised" in "Socrates' Rejection of Retaliation" in *SIMP* (Vlastos, 1991), pp. 179–99.

1981b.* "On a Proposed Redefinition of 'Self-Predication' in Plato." *Phronesis* 26:76–78

1983a. "The Historical Socrates and Athenian Democracy." *Political Theory* 11:495–516. Reprinted in *SS* (Vlastos, 1994), pp. 87–108. Reprinted in R. Sharples, ed., *Modern Thinkers and Ancient Thinkers* (London: University College London Press, 1993), pp. 66–89.

1983b.* Review of E. N. Platis, *Socrates' Accusers. AJP* 104:201–6. Review of Ἐ. Ν. Πλατής, Οἱ κατήγοροι τοῦ Σωκράτη. Φιλολόγικη μελέτη (Athens, 1980).

1983c. "The Socratic Elenchus." *Oxford Studies in Ancient Philosophy* 1:27–58 and 71–74. Reprinted in *SS* (Vlastos, 1994), pp. 1–37.

1984a. "Happiness and Virtue in Socrates' Moral Theory." *Proceedings of the Cam-*

bridge Philological Society N.S. 30:181–213. Reprinted in *Topoi* 4 (1985):3–22. Reprinted with revisions in *SIMP* (Vlastos, 1991), pp. 200–32.

1984b. Review of Richard Kraut, *Socrates and the State*. *TLS* (4,247) (Aug. 24):931–32.

1985. Socrates' Disavowal of Knowledge. *PQ* 35:1–31. Reprinted in *SS* (Vlastos, 1994), pp. 39–66.

1987a. "'Separation' in Plato." *Oxford Studies in Ancient Philosophy* 5:187–96. Reprinted with corrections in *SIMP* (Vlastos 1991), pp. 256–64, as Additional Note 2.5.

1987b. "Socratic Irony." *CQ* 37:79–96. Reprinted in *SIMP* (Vlastos, 1991), pp. 21–44.

1988a. "Elenchus and Mathematics: A Turning Point in Plato's Philosophical Development." *AJP* 109:362–96. Reprinted as "Elenchus and Mathematics" in *SIMP* (Vlastos 1991), pp. 107–31. Reprinted in Hugh H. Benson, ed. *Essays on the Philosophy of Socrates* (New York: Oxford University Press, 1992), pp. 137–61.

1988b. "Socrates." *Proceedings of the British Academy* 74:89–111. British Academy Master-Mind Lecture. Superseded by chs. 2–3 of *SIMP* (Vlastos, 1991), pp. 45–106.

1989a.* "Was Plato a Feminist?" *TLS* (4,485) (Mar. 17):276, 288–89.

1989b.* "Review of T. C. Brickhouse and N. D. Smith, *Socrates on Trial*. *TLS* (4,524) (Dec. 15):1393.

1989c. "Socratic Piety." *Proceedings of the Boston Area Colloquium on Ancient Philosophy* 5.213–38. Reprinted in *SIMP* (Vlastos, 1991), pp. 157–78.

1990. "Is the 'Socratic Fallacy' Socratic?" *Ancient Philosophy* 10:1–16. Reprinted in *SS* (Vlastos, 1994), pp. 67–86.

1991. *Socrates, Ironist and Moral Philosopher*. Cambridge: Cambridge University Press and Ithaca, N.Y.: Cornell University Press.

1994. *Socratic Studies*, ed. Myles Burnyeat. Cambridge: Cambridge University Press.

INDEX LOCORUM

GENERAL INDEX

RITTER LIBRARY
BALDWIN-WALLACE COLLEGE